Licensing Law Guide

Licensing Law Guide

Third edition

Jeremy Phillips BA

Solicitor; partner, Osborne Clarke

Members of the LexisNexis Group worldwide

United Kingdom	LexisNexis Butterworths Tolley, a Division of Reed Elsevier (UK) Ltd, Halsbury House, 35 Chancery Lane, LONDON, WC2A 1EL, and 4 Hill Street, EDINBURGH EH2 3JZ
Argentina	LexisNexis Argentina, BUENOS AIRES
Australia	LexisNexis Butterworths, CHATSWOOD, New South Wales
Austria	LexisNexis Verlag ARD Orac GmbH & Co KG, VIENNA
Canada	LexisNexis Butterworths, MARKHAM, Ontario
Chile	LexisNexis Chile Ltda, SANTIAGO DE CHILE
Czech Republic	Nakladatelství Orac sro, PRAGUE
France	Editions du Juris-Classeur SA, PARIS
Hong Kong	LexisNexis Butterworths, HONG KONG
Hungary	HVG-Orac, BUDAPEST
India	LexisNexis Butterworths, NEW DELHI
Ireland	Butterworths (Ireland) Ltd, DUBLIN
Italy	Giuffrè Editore, MILAN
Malaysia	Malayan Law Journal Sdn Bhd, KUALA LUMPUR
New Zealand	LexisNexis Butterworths, WELLINGTON
Poland	Wydawnictwo Prawnicze LexisNexis, WARSAW
Singapore	LexisNexis Butterworths, SINGAPORE
South Africa	Butterworths SA, DURBAN
Switzerland	Stämpfli Verlag AG, BERNE
USA	LexisNexis, DAYTON, Ohio

A CIP Catalogue record for this book is available from the British Library.

First edition 1995
Second edition 1998

ISBN 0 406 95226 4

Printed by Bell & Bain Ltd, Glasgow

Visit Butterworths LexisNexis *direct* at www.butterworths.com

To Mary and our children—
Laura, Toby, Joseph, Rachel and Adam

FOREWORD

It is generally agreed that liquor licensing in England and Wales is outdated, unduly complex and inaccessible. As one commentator recently put it: 'reading the Licensing Acts is like being drawn into some ancient, dark, cobweb-strewn labyrinth controlling access to a dangerous beast'. Beyond the complexities of the legislation itself, there has grown up a huge volume of practice and procedure. Much of this is unintelligible to the uninitiated and of such bewildering banality that even the most experienced practitioner has difficulty committing it all to memory.

This book comes to the rescue. For the experienced it is a quick and accessible reference work and for those new to licensing it provides an invaluable guide.

Licensing Law Guide sets out clearly the relevant legal provisions and then goes on to outline the practice, procedure and case law that have built up around them. The reader is taken through the practical steps that are required in order to undertake the various licensing applications, both administratively and before licensing committees/courts. Common mistakes are highlighted and strategies offered that are designed to facilitate smooth and untroubled applications. The reader is reminded that thorough preparation and research are vital and then very helpfully directed to the issues that commonly need to be addressed.

Over the years I have recommended the volume to a number of lawyers making an initial or one-off foray into licensing law, or to those in the early stages of a licensing practice. Without exception they have reported back most favourably on the assistance derived from the book. In some cases they have told me that its clear exposition and practical approach helped them to turn hidden panic into apparent professionalism!

Liquor licensing generates more than its fair share of technical points and there are many traps for the unwary. *Licensing Law Guide* identifies many of these issues and demonstrates how best to avoid them. It also offers solutions for problematic situations and provides alternative options should things go wrong.

The strength of the volume lies in the skill and vast experience of its author. This enables Jeremy Phillips to lay out the law in clear and accurate terms and generously to impart to the reader knowledge gleaned and lessons learned from his many years as a leading licensing practitioner.

When *Licensing Law Guide* first appeared in 1995 it was well-received and enjoyed considerable success as an affordable, accessible and trustworthy guide to liquor licensing. The second edition, published in 1998, built upon this success and the book became firmly established as the most practical, helpful and straightforward volume available on liquor licensing—the perfect companion to *Paterson's Licensing Acts*. This, the third edition, continues in that tradition. It provides a much-appreciated service to all of those involved in liquor licensing.

Professor Roy Light
Faculty of Law, UWE, Bristol

PREFACE TO THE THIRD EDITION

In this third edition of the *Guide* I have endeavoured to draw the reader's attention to those cases of significance which have occurred in this field since 1998.

As far as legislation is concerned, I have touched upon the Disability Discrimination Act 1995, as well as the deregulatory measures in the area of Sunday dancing and licensing. The provisions of the Criminal Justice and Police Act 2001 in relation to closure orders and under-age drinking have been considered in the main body of the work and have also been inserted into the text of the statute, the principal sections of which appear in the Appendices. With the help of my European and continental colleagues at Freshfields Bruckaus Deringer (Vienna), CMS Lexcelis (Brussels), Olsens (Jersey), Dragsted & Helmer Nielson (Denmark), Dittmar & Indrenius (Helsinki), Cabinet D'Avocats Soulier & Associés (Lyon), Wessing Berenberg-Gossler Zimmermann Lange (Munchen), Simcocks (Isle of Man), Gianni, Origoni, Grippo & Partners (Roma), Bonn Schmitt Steichen Avocats (Luxembourg), CMS Derks, Star, Busmann (Utrecht), L'Estrange & Brett (Belfast), Hill Brown Licensing (Glasgow), Cuatrecasas Abodagos (Barcelona), Setterwalls Advokatbyra (Stockholm) Chapter 9 has been substantially revised, whilst my good friend Dale Collins here at Osborne Clarke has kindly undertaken the lion's share of the research required for the wholly new Chapter 11 entitled 'Licensing and the Human Rights Act 1998', which I hope readers will find increasingly useful.

I am conscious as I write that others are at the same time taking on the Herculean task of drafting an entirely new Alcohol and Entertainments Bill, parts of which could become law as early as mid-2003, although it is likely that the majority will not come into force until the following year. It would not be overstating the position to say that this legislation, if approved by Parliament, would be the most significant single development in licensing law in England and Wales since a system of licences was first established 450 years ago. Whilst some will be uncertain as to the benefits to be derived from such a change, it is undoubtedly the case that the present legislation is manifestly far from perfect. Undoubtedly all those in the field, whether interested as a magistrate, local government officer, justices' clerk, police officer, operator of licensed premises, solicitor or barrister, will wish to contribute to the forthcoming lively national debate.

In the meantime, until the new law comes into force—and for a period thereafter—I hope that this work will continue to be a reasonably accessible guide to the much-amended Licensing Act 1964.

As ever, the two areas for which it is my indisputable privilege to claim full responsibility are those of 'errors and omissions'. Despite the valiant and much appreciated efforts of Butterworths Tolley staff and my assistant Debra Stone, to remove such imperfections, any that stubbornly remain are all my own.

Jeremy Phillips
Osborne Clarke
2 July 2002

EXTRACT FROM THE PREFACE TO THE FIRST EDITION

In writing this book my guiding principle has been that the book should be of practical benefit to the majority of those having some involvement with the licensing system. Inevitably this has meant that there has been a continual requirement to compromise. Those who practice in the law might well, on occasion, have appreciated a more academic exposition on the development of a particular concept as it has taken shape and substance through a series of decisions or statutory provisions. There will be other instances where the business man or licensee, for example, might have hoped for a little less detail as they pursue their tantalisingly simple objective: to manage an efficient, profitable business within the terms of the law. To each of these circumstances I have applied a simple test: is the issue one which arises in practice with reasonable regularity? Applying this test I have, rightly or wrongly, excised all references, for example, to canteen licences, theatres, new towns, vineyards, airports and licences in suspension. To readers who find that my pruning has in certain cases been too forgiving or in others too severe, I apologise.

Jeremy Phillips
22 September 1995

CONTENTS

Index

TABLE OF STATUTES

TABLE OF STATUTORY INSTRUMENTS

TABLE OF CASES

R

S

T

V

W

Y

PART I
JUSTICES' LICENCES

CHAPTER 1

THE FRAMEWORK

1.01   What is a justices' licence? Why is it needed? Who grants it—and under what authority? How are the proceedings conducted and what are the options available to the body presiding? These are just some of the basic questions that are addressed in this opening chapter, which is intended as a general introduction to the (unnecessarily) mysterious subject of liquor licensing law.

1.02   An understanding of the licensing laws of England and Wales begins perhaps with the appreciation that it is generally a criminal offence[1] to sell or expose for sale[2] by retail[3] intoxicating liquor,[4] unless the seller is either the holder of a justices' licence[5] or has the authority of such a person to effect that transaction. Most individual consumer purchases will qualify as retail sales, being in quantities of less than two cases (or 20 litres) for beer or cider, or one case (or 9 litres) for spirits or wine.[6] Supply of liquor without charge (eg at a wedding or private party) does not require the authority of a licence. However, retailers with cunning plans to promote sales of other products with the offer of a 'free' gift of a can of beer or a bottle of wine should be aware that the courts have always been very ready to find such transactions to be in the nature of a 'sale'.[7] Around this need for a justices' licence has developed a comprehensive system which regulates their issue, transfer and renewal, as well as the terms upon which such licences may operate.

[1]   Licensing Act 1964, s 160(1).
[2]   Transactions in members' clubs (ie those in which all profits accrue to the benefit of the members) are not deemed *sales* because the members are paying for property in which they have a legal interest. However, such supplies are caught by s 39, which requires members' clubs to be registered: see chapter 8.
[3]   For definition see below.
[4]   Strength more than 0.5 per cent. For full definition see s 201(1) (as amended by Licensing (Low Alcohol Drinks) Act 1990, s 1).
[5]   Or an occasional licence or permission: see chapter 10.
[6]   Alcoholic Liquor Duties Act 1979, s 4.
[7]   See eg *Horgan v Driscoll* (1908) 42 ILT 238, *Graff v Evans* (1882) 8 QBD 373 and Licensing Act 1964, s 196(1).

THE STATUTES

1.03   The principal statute is the Licensing Act 1964. The main provisions of this Act (as amended by subsequent legislation, including the Deregulation and Contracting Out Act 1994 and the Criminal Justice and Police Act 2001) are reproduced in Part II of this work. Frequent reference will be made throughout this book to 'the Act' (as it will be described from now on). In general the reader will find it helpful to consider this commentary in the light of the legislation itself.

THE LICENSING JUSTICES

1.04   The responsibility for issuing and controlling the subsequent operation of justices' licences rests with a committee appointed by magistrates for a particular petty sessional division. The boundaries of a petty sessional division generally equate to those of the relevant local authority, be it a city, district or borough council. The licensing justices so appointed convene as a committee (as opposed to a court), meeting at what are known as transfer sessions, generally every four to six weeks. By law the committee is obliged to meet in the first 14 days of February each year (traditionally known as the Brewster Sessions) thereafter holding at least four transfer sessions during the course of the year.

1.05   A minimum of three licensing justices must sit upon the committee when it is dealing with applications under the Act. Certain committees have historically sat with considerably larger numbers. However, in a guide to good practice first published in 1994 by the Justices' Clerks' Society and recently updated annually it was recommended that committees should 'normally sit three members at a time, never more than five'. It should be noted that in law the person sitting as the chairman of the licensing justices has no casting vote. Accordingly, it is undesirable to have an even number of licensing justices sitting to determine an application because of the risk of there being an equality of votes.

1.06   The Act contains provisions[1] disqualifying certain individuals from being appointed as licensing justices generally, or from determining applications for premises in which they have a particular interest. Further, where there is a real likelihood of bias on the part of a member of the committee because of some general association with either the applicant or the premises concerned, then the person concerned should not take part in that case. Any decision made in proceedings in which such a person had a part would be liable to be quashed by the High Court on the grounds of bias and breach of Article 6 of the European Convention on Human

Rights, now enshrined in the Human Rights Act 1998. In practice, such allegations rarely arise. Where they do consideration should be given to the notes to the Licensing Act 1964, s 193 in *Paterson's Licensing Acts*, the only work of reference on this subject, which provides a range of helpful decisions on the issue.

[1] Section 193.

1.07 It is most important to understand that licensing committees are entitled in law to regulate their own proceedings. Most committees these days publish a statement of their policies and also guidelines for the non-statutory procedures which are generally adopted. Whilst the contents of the policy vary widely from committee to committee, the following matters are frequently covered:

(a) periods of notice for application;

(b) procedure at the hearing;

(c) proof of service of notices;

(d) notice of objection to be given;

(e) requirements in relation to plans;

(f) guidelines for the exercise of discretion;

(g) criteria for suitability of applicant(s);

(h) standards for premises.

The above is necessarily a brief summary of the matters that may be included within any particular policy document.

1.08 There are great disparities between divisions, with some publishing no such policies and others having documents which run to a hundred or more pages. Where such policies are published, justices are nonetheless obliged 'to consider fully the facts of the application before them in order to decide whether the general policy is to be applied to that particular case'.[1] Wherever possible, individuals appearing before licensing committees should clearly endeavour, as a matter of expedience, to comply with any published policy. Failure to do so is probably the most common reason for the adjournment of applications. The application of such policies to different categories of proceedings will be considered throughout this work.

[1] *R v Torquay Licensing Justices, ex p Brockman* [1951] 2 KB 784.

1.09 Because a licensing committee does not sit as a court of law it is not bound by the strict rules of evidence and will frequently agree to entertain hearsay evidence and unproved documents. Further, many committees will permit individuals other than qualified solicitors or barristers to appear before them to act as advocates in support of applications or objections. Licensed property brokers, for example, quite frequently present applications for the transfer of justices' licences. Again, an inquiry of the clerk to the relevant committee or his licensing assistants, who can be contacted at the local magistrates' courts, should readily ascertain the position concerning rights of audience.

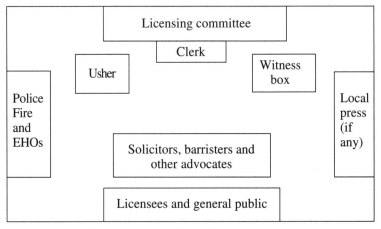

Typical layout of licensing proceedings

DIFFERENT TYPES OF LICENCE

1.10   The principal types of licence may be summarised as follows:

(1) *On-licence* (authorises sales both on and off the licensed premises). Types of liquor:[1]

    (a) intoxicating liquor of all descriptions (a *full* on-licence);

    (b) beer, cider and wine only;

    (c) beer and cider only;

    (d) cider only;

    (e) wine only.

(2) *Off-licence*

    (a) intoxicating liquor of all descriptions;

    (b) beer, cider and wine.

As at 30 June 2001 there were some 110,256 on-licensed premises and 44,696 off-licensed premises in England and Wales.[2] An analysis of these licences appears at para **1.27**.

[1] See s 1(3)(a).
[2] Home Office Statistical Bulletin, published 14 March 2002.

1.11 When granting a justices' licence, a licensing committee cannot specify that it shall authorise the sale of combinations of liquor other than those specified in the Act. This applies both to on-licences[1] and off-licences.[2] There remains uncertainty concerning 'no *draught* beer' conditions, following a decision of the Inner London Crown Court (unreported), whilst it is considered that unqualified conditions of 'no off-sales', which are commonplace, may well fall foul of the same rule. In *R (on the application of Ashton) v Bolton Combined Court*[3] the Administrative Court held that the imposition of a condition providing 'The licence holder shall not apply for a special hours certificate or an extended hours order' was not a proper or lawful exercise of the justices' discretion and that accordingly the condition should be quashed. Consequently, practitioners need to exercise some care to avoid devising conditions which might be said to go against the general scheme of licences set out in the Act.

[1] *R v Crown Court at Inner London, ex p Sitki* (1993) 157 JP 523, where a full on-licence was granted subject to a condition prohibiting the sale of beer. The High Court held the entire licence was invalid.
[2] *R v Leicester City Licensing Justices, ex p Bisson* [1968] 2 All ER 351.
[3] [2001] All ER (D) 26 (Sept), (2002) 47 LR 25.

1.12 A full on-licence will authorise all of the sales which may be made under each of the licences listed above. Not only may justices grant one of the four lesser forms of on-licence, but they may also attach conditions to such licences. Potentially there are an infinite number of such sub-categories of on-licence. Why do they exist? The answer is that by curtailing the 'parent' licence in this way licensing committees can, if they wish, confer no greater authority to sell alcohol than is actually required by the local population, or is sensible having regard to the structure of the building, the character of the locality or any other factors that they may consider to be of relevance. Further, the conditions attached may require, for example, the introduction of some special procedure for controlling the premises. The meaning of any conditions imposed needs to be readily apparent.[1]

[1] *R v Hammersmith and Fulham London Borough Council, ex p Earls Court Ltd* (1993) Times, 15 July, where a general condition requiring the organisers in all advertisements to encourage visitors to use public transport was declared unreasonable because its precise meaning was sufficiently obscure as to render it incapable of enforcement.

CONDITIONS SPECIFIED BY STATUTE

1.13

(1) *On-licence*

    (a)   on-licence with conditions;[1]
    (b)   proprietary club licence;[2]
    (c)   seasonal licences;[3]
    (d)   six-day and early-closing licence;[4]
    (e)   off-sales department;[5]
    (f)   restaurant licence;[6]
    (g)   residential licence;[7]
    (h)   restaurant and residential licence.[8]

(2) *Off-licence* None, save as may be effected by undertakings or assurances (see below).

[1]   Section 4(1).
[2]   Section 55.
[3]   Section 64.
[4]   Section 65.
[5]   Section 86.
[6]   Section 94.
[7]   Section 94.
[8]   Section 94.

1.14   In the case of on-licences the licensing justices can (unless it is a licence for wine only) attach such conditions as they think proper in the interests of the public.[1] In practice this is an extremely important provision, the implications of which are considered in detail in the next chapter. *Old beerhouse licences* (pre-1 May 1869) and *old on-licences* (pre-15 August 1904) enjoy special protection upon proceedings for transfer, renewal or revocation (ie cancellation). Again, this is considered in detail elsewhere in this book. *Seasonal licences* are those subject to a condition that sales may not take place (other than to residents) under the licence during specified periods of the year. *Six-day* and *early-closing licences* are granted subject to conditions that there shall be no permitted hours (ie hours during which alcohol may be sold) on a Sunday, and that permitted hours shall end one hour earlier than general licensing hours respectively. In general terms sales of liquor may take place only during permitted hours, although there are exceptions (eg residents), which are set out more fully in chapter 7.

[1]   Section 4(1).

1.15   Where on-licensed premises have an off-sales department which is not connected internally with the bar or other drinking areas, the licensee may require the licensing justices to insert a condition in the licence specifying that the hours for that area will be those appropriate to an off-licence. Application may be made at any transfer sessions. Such conditions, previously common, are now rarely sought or exercised as the old public house 'offies' have long been superseded by increasingly specialist and substantial wine merchants and, of course, the ubiquitous superstore.

1.16 A *restaurant licence* is one which is granted principally subject to a condition that intoxicating liquor may only be sold as an ancillary to a table meal. It can be granted only for premises which habitually provide a customary main meal at midday and/or in the evening. A *residential licence* permits supplies in premises providing board and lodging (breakfast and a main meal, ie not bed and breakfast only) only to residents or their guests, provided that only the resident may pay for the drink. A *restaurant and residential licence* combines these facilities. The conditions attaching to each type of licence are set out in Part IV of the Act.

1.17 In general the only way to vary conditions is to apply for a new licence, offering the existing licence for surrender when the new one is granted.[1] Exceptions to this rule may be found in certain cases relating to seasonal, six-day and early-closing licences, off-sales departments in on-licensed premises and restaurant licences.

[1]   *Drury v Scunthorpe Licensing Justices* (1992) 157 JP 401.

Undertakings

1.18 The Act does not entitle licensing justices to attach conditions to an off-licence. Since it is often as much in the interest of the applicant as the licensing committee that the latter should be able to limit or regulate in some way the operation of such a licence (which they might otherwise not be prepared to grant) a practice has developed over the years of licensing committees being offered and accepting undertakings or assurances from applicants for off-licences. Whilst the subsequent breach of such assurances will not of itself give rise to any criminal offence it may well provide a ground upon which the licensing justices could properly refuse to renew the licence, or entertain an application for its revocation.[1] Accordingly, such assurances should not be given lightly, nor should they be overlooked upon the acquisition of premises with the benefit of a justices' off-licence.

[1]   See *R v Windsor Licensing Justices, ex p Hodes* [1983] 2 All ER 551: such indirect sanctions could be imposed in an appropriate case. The case is also authority for the important proposition that new or further undertakings or assurances may not be

exacted upon renewal unless there has been a material change in circumstances (other than the justices' policy).

1.19   In the case of old on-licences, the giving of undertakings has statutory recognition.[1] Breach of such an undertaking can provide a ground upon which justices may refuse to transfer or renew the licence. Strangely, even though the justices may ask for an undertaking to be given, they may not *insist* if the licensee is unwilling, unless it can reasonably be said that no fit and proper person would decline to comply with that request.[2]

[1]   Section 12(5).
[2]   See eg *R v Dodds, ex p Roberts, Birkenhead Licensing Justices* [1905] 2 KB 40.

Duration of licences

1.20   Following the Licensing Act 1988, justices' licences have had effect until 4 April 1989, or any third anniversary of that date. Although committees are obliged, as indicated above, to hold a general annual licensing meeting (or Brewster Sessions) in the first 14 days of February each year, the renewal of licences therefore only takes place every third year (ie 1992, 1995, 1998, 2001, 2004 etc).[1]

[1]   Any licence granted within the last three months of a licensing period (ie after 4 January) will have effect until the end of the following licensing period. This is an important provision, the practical effect of which will be explained in chapter 3.

1.21   Further, it should be noted that a provisional grant of a justices' licence does not create a 'valid' licence. Until that licence has been declared final, therefore, it will not require renewal, although 'outline' provisional grants[1] must be affirmed within one year, failing which they lapse. In addition, some committees require the applicant to give an assurance that a final order will be sought within a defined period. See chapter 2 for a further discussion on the point.

[1]   Section 6(5)(g).

1.22   A justices' licence which has been granted notwithstanding an objection raised at the hearing will not come into effect until a period of 21 days has elapsed or, if an appeal is lodged within that period, until the grant has been confirmed upon appeal or the appeal withdrawn. It is important that this fact should be reflected in any contract to purchase, or agreement to lease, premises, failing which the purchaser could in an extreme case find himself or herself owning a property which subsequently proves to be unlicensed if an appeal against a grant succeeds.

1.23   If a justices' licence is revoked by order of the licensing committee that order for revocation will not take effect until 21 days have elapsed or, if an appeal is lodged within that period, until such time as the committee's decision has been confirmed by the Crown Court or the appeal withdrawn. This is dealt with more fully in chapter 6.

REGISTER OF LICENCES

1.24   The chief executive to the licensing justices is required by law to maintain a register containing the following details in respect of each presently and previously licensed property:

(1) details of justices' licences granted;

(2) name of premises;

(3) name of licensee;

(4) name of owner/mortgagee in possession;

(5) name of any other person (at that person's request) having a prior or superior interest to the occupier;

(6) all licensing offences committed by the licensee;

(7) offences committed by the licensee concerning the adulteration of drink;

(8) any forfeiture of licence;

(9) any disqualification of premises;

(10) any conviction for bribery or permitting bribery in reference to any election, such behaviour taking place upon his licensed premises, under the Representation of the People Act 1983.

1.25   The only persons entitled to inspect the register are:

(1) any payer of council tax to the relevant local authority;

(2) any owner of licensed premises within the licensing division;

(3) any licensee within the licensing division;

(4) a police constable;

(5) an officer of Customs and Excise.

1.26   It is frequently the case that an original justices' licence is mislaid. In that event the court is entitled to issue a certified copy for the requisite fee.[1]

---

[1]   Currently £10.

1.27   With the conclusion of this first chapter it is hoped that the reader will have gained a clearer idea of the general licensing system. The remainder of the book is devoted to a more detailed analysis of its practical implications.

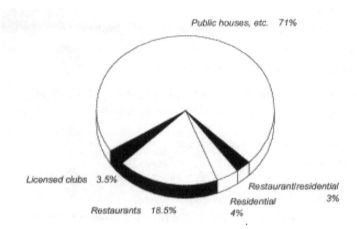

On-licensed premises, England and Wales, 30 June 2001

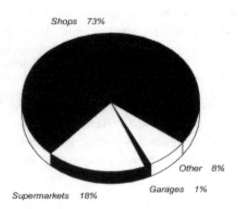

Off-licensed premises, England and Wales, 30 June 2001

CHAPTER 2

THE APPLICATION AND OBJECTIONS

2.01 Figures published by the Home Office in 1995 show that over a 12-month period in 2000/2001 some 5,012 applications were submitted in England and Wales for the grant of new justices' on-licences, of which 587 were refused (see para **2.02**). As might be imagined, the prospect of success for an application will improve significantly if the case is prepared and presented in a careful and efficient manner. Whilst this is, perhaps, a statement of the obvious, it reflects the fact that if an applicant is not prepared (or perhaps able) to present his proposal in a professional manner, then many licensing committees will draw the inference that any resulting business is likely to suffer from the same poor standards.

PRELIMINARY STEPS

2.02 As soon as a decision has been made to apply for a justices' licence it is prudent to contact the clerk's office at the local magistrates' court to establish:

(1) whether they have jurisdiction for that specific address or site;

(2) if the committee has published a policy document (if so, ask for a copy to be sent);

(3) the dates of the next two transfer sessions.

Armed with this information, it is then possible to establish a suitable timetable for the application, making appropriate allowance for the time that will be needed for, for example, planning permission to be obtained, detailed plans to be prepared and an interest secured in the property.

Table 3   New licences and registrations applied for and granted, 1976-2001

England and Wales

Year to 30 June	On-licensed premises								Off-licensed premises		Total On- and off-licensed premises		Registered clubs (Number)	
	Public houses, etc		Residential and Restaurant		Licensed clubs		Total							
	Applied for	Granted	Applied for	Granted	Applied for	Granted	Applied for	Granted	Applied for	Granted	Applied for	Granted	Applied for	Granted
1976	1,297	1,163	1,597	1,544	269	149	3,163	2,856	2,429	2,221	5,592	5,177	844	838
1977	1,389	1,218	1,860	1,803	234	209	3,483	3,230	2,866	2,559	6,349	5,789	866	851
1978	1,403	1,213	2,034	1,868	225	210	3,662	3,391	2,747	2,437	6,409	5,828	858	848
1979	1,318	1,178	2,137	2,052	236	206	3,690	3,436	2,832	2,443	6,522	5,879	761	747
1980	1,436	1,226	2,285	2,168	225	205	3,946	3,599	2,910	2,384	6,856	5,983	729	725
1983	1,606	1,493	2,139	1,992	316	282	4,261	3,767	3,394	2,624	7,666	6,391	694	683
1986	2,201	1,826	2,351	2,274	369	340	4,921	4,440	3,407	2,607	8,328	7,047	537	510
1989	2,354	1,937	2,493	2,341	264	238	5,111	4,516	2,707	2,139	7,818	6,655	373	368
1992	2,188	1,878	1,679	1,568	172	157	4,039	3,603	2,136	1,712	6,175	5,315	444	433
1995	2,371	2,128	1,469	1,403	206	198	4,046	3,729	2,078	1,823	6,124	5,552	684	639
1998	3,261	2,785	1,557	1,485	163	169	4,981	4,429	2,053	1,689	7,034	6,118	707	539
2001	3,522	3,072	1,320	1,211	152	142	5,012	4,425	2,381	2,057	7,363	6,482	1,126	1,045

PLANNING PERMISSION

2.03   Before proceeding with any licensing application, consideration needs to be given as to whether planning permission is required for the intended use. If planning permission is required for the construction of the premises or a change of use which falls within another 'use class', then many licensing committees will insist that such planning permission (and even, on occasion, building regulations approval) be obtained before the licensing application proceeds. Indeed, the grant of such a planning permission may well operate to the benefit of the applicant since it will serve to indicate that the local authority for its part finds no grounds upon which to object to the application in terms of its suitability for the area, the potential impact upon the amenity of neighbours, the extent to which it can be properly serviced, etc. Each of these matters is dealt with elsewhere in this chapter.

NOTICES

2.04   Many an experienced licensing practitioner will still feel a slight tremor of apprehension when the clerk to the licensing justices checks the accuracy of the statutory notices in open court prior to the hearing of the application. The delay, not to say the additional costs, occasioned by an adjournment at this stage can be both professionally and financially embarrassing. However, if some care is taken when the notices are prepared there should be no reason for any lack of confidence while they are being scrutinised.

2.05   Schedule 2 to the Act sets out the statutory requirements. Additionally, there are certain items of information which it is both customary and expedient to include. Precedents appear in Part II of this work. The following guidance may be helpful.

Addressees

2.06   It is customary for the names of those authorities to which the notice has been sent to appear at the head of the licensing notice. The names and addresses will also be set out in a certificate of service or some other document proving that the notices were indeed delivered by hand or sent by post within the statutory period. The following should be noted.

Chief executive to the licensing justices

2.07   The address of the appropriate office will appear in *Shaw's Magistrates' Court Guide*, or alternatively can be obtained following a telephone call to directory enquiries. (Note that the office dealing with such correspondence may not always be the same location as that where the applications are heard.)

Chief officer of police

2.08   Technically, this means that in central London the application must be served upon the Commissioner of Police for the City of London or the Metropolitan Police district, or in any other police area the Chief Constable.[1] In practice, however, notices tend to be served upon the officer having operational responsibility for the particular division or sub-division in which the premises are situated, or even the police officer or civilian to whom responsibility for dealing with licensing matters has been delegated. Generally the clerk's office will be pleased to assist with the relevant details, although independent confirmation should be sought from the police station concerned.

[1]   Section 201(4).

Local authority

2.09   The Act requires that notices are directed to 'the proper officer' of the local authority concerned. Again, a rather more specific requirement for the notice to be served on, perhaps, the chief executive, the chief environmental health officer, the chief planning officer or the building control officer of the local authority concerned (or, in some cases, each of the above) may be forthcoming from the clerk's office. The 'local authority' may be either a city, borough or district council.

Parish/town/community council

2.10   The proper officer of the local council, which may be designated either a parish or town council or, in Wales, a community council, is likely to be a private citizen. As such, the names and addresses of these officers frequently change and the most certain method of establishing their identity is to speak to the planning department of the relevant local authority, with which they are likely to have regular dealings.

Fire authority

2.11 Again, technically, the service of the notice upon the relevant county council ought to suffice, since that council will carry out the statutory function of the fire authority. In practice, however, the clerk's office will generally be able to provide, either over the telephone or within the policy document, the address of the local fire brigade having responsibility for the area in which the premises are situated. In Greater London the notices are generally served upon the London Fire and Emergency Planning Authority (LFEPA). From 1 June 1992 building control inspectors were given additional responsibility for fire precautions. To minimise the risk of licensing applications being adjourned while the fire officer circulates papers to the building control inspector, in certain areas it is advisable to serve both with plans of the premises, informing each that this has been done. (It would be unwise to assume that the notice already required to be served upon the 'proper officer' of the local authority will, in fact, be considered by the building inspector, the planning officer or, indeed, any person other than the recipient!) It is not wholly unknown for a fire officer and a building inspector to differ on the degree of fire protection required and consultation with both at an early stage can prevent unpleasant surprises later on. Circular 13/92 issued by the Department of the Environment details the relevant statutory instruments setting out their respective responsibilities.

Registered owner/licensee

2.12 If the application is for a removal (ie relocation) of a licence to alternative premises, it is necessary to serve notice on the registered owner, whose details may be ascertained from the register maintained at court. Service must also be effected upon the existing licensee, unless it is the licensee himself who is applying for the removal.

General

2.13 It is critical that the notice is served upon the correct individuals and authorities. Wherever possible any information from the clerk's office should be double-checked with the proposed recipient of the notice. The underlying principle to recognise is that it is the responsibility of the applicant or his legal advisers to comply with the statute. The excuse that the person responsible for dispatching the notices was misinformed is (quite properly) unlikely to be accepted.

Applicant

2.14   The application for the new licence may be made in the name of the person intending to manage the premises or, in the case of large companies, by the person responsible for identifying the site or having operational responsibility for the region. Prior to making a final decision on this point reference should be made to the committee's policy document (if any), as in some areas the licensing justices insist upon the applicant being the person who will be responsible for the day-to-day management of the premises. In other areas committees will not, for example, grant licences to area managers having more than a specified number of licences (eg 12) even if an undertaking is given at the hearing that the licence will be transferred prior to opening into the name of the manager designate.

2.15   The notice must identify the name and address of the applicant and his occupation during the preceding six months. On a practical note, it is prudent to identify only the business address within the notice, for security reasons. The police should, of course, be supplied with the applicant's home address.

Date and location of hearing

2.16   As indicated above, the hearing may well take place at a different location from that to which the notices are sent. Strangely, the only statutory requirement is for the chief executive to the licensing justices to advertise the time and place for such hearings in a local newspaper, after these details have been agreed at the beginning of each year. However, it is the invariable practice that notices should contain the details of the intended hearing. Where this information is inaccurate and could be said to be misleading it is almost inevitable that the licensing committee will wish to adjourn the application to enable the correct details to be inserted and the notices re-served and/or displayed and/or advertised, as the committee may direct.[1] Where an application has been adjourned for some other reason (eg insufficient time for the hearing) then, unless the committee so directs, it is not necessary to dispatch, advertise or display new notices bearing the date of the adjourned hearing, since it is assumed that all interested parties will have attended before the committee on the original occasion.

[1]   Schedule 2, para 7.

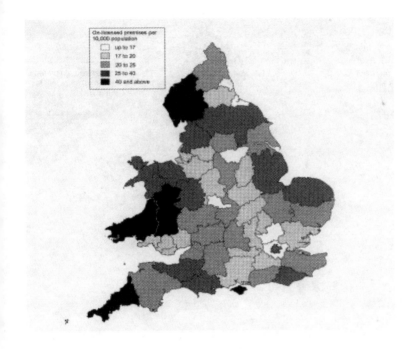

Map 1: On-licences per 10,000 population by county, England and Wales, 2001

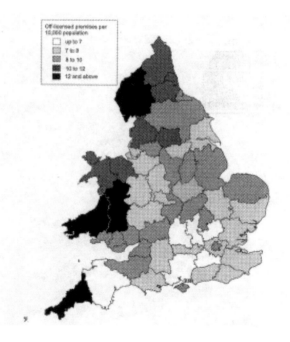

Map 2: Off-licences per 10,000 population by county, England and Wales, 2001

Type of grant

Provisional licences

2.17   The notice may indicate that the application is either for the grant or the provisional grant of a justices' licence. It is always possible to downgrade from a full application to a provisional one at the hearing itself, but the converse cannot be achieved without new notices. In the case of premises which are already structurally complete and require only to be fitted out as an off-licence, it is sensible to apply for the full licence since the justices have a discretion to grant the licence in this form, so avoiding the necessity of a final order.[1] A Part IV licence may be granted as a provisional licence although it is thought by some operators to be less necessary, given the justices' reduced entitlement to refuse such applications (see Part IV Licences).

[1]   *R v Spelthorne Licensing Justices, ex p Bance* [1961] Brewing Tr Rev 418.

Special and ordinary removals

2.18 Alternatively, the notice might specify that the applicant seeks a special or ordinary removal. It is frankly difficult to see the merit of such an approach since licensing committees have exactly the same discretion to grant or refuse the removal of a justices' licence as they have in relation to a new application. Further, in relation to the removal, there are a number of additional hurdles to overcome.

2.19 First (as indicated above), it is necessary to give notice of the application to the registered owner of the premises, as well as the holder of the licence (unless he is also the applicant). For an on-licence the burden of proof lies on the applicant to show that neither of these persons objects to the relocation of the licence. For an off-licence only the consent of the licensee must be produced. In either case, therefore, this absolute requirement can mean that the outcome of the application is entirely dependent upon the consent of a manager/licensee, who might well not be retained after the closure of the existing unit. Second, the justices have a discretion to entertain objections from third parties.[1] Having decided a third party has the *right* to object to a removal, Mr Justice Kay sitting in the Crown Court in Mold took the view that the wording of s 5(5) left the committee with a discretion to refuse to grant the removal.[2]

[1] *Patel v Wright* (1987) 152 JP 210.
[2] *R v Crown Court at Mold, ex p Lewis* (16 July 1996, unreported) considering dicta in *Patel v Wright*.

2.20 Each of these difficulties relating to removals can be overcome if the application is listed simply as being one for the grant of a new justices' licence, with an indication in the notice that the licence presently attaching to the existing premises will be offered for surrender prior to the exercise of any new licence. The House of Lords long ago recognised this alternative route and it is suggested that it is difficult now to justify the use of the statutory procedure for ordinary removals.[1] In the unusual situation where premises have an old on-licence and are obliged to relocate for certain reasons there may be some benefit in taking advantage of the procedure for special removals.[2]

[1] *Laceby v E Lacon & Co* [1899] AC 222.
[2] Section 15.

Descriptions of liquor

2.21 Select one of the five recognised categories for on-licences, or one of the two categories for off-licences. The Act requires that this information appears in the notice of application. It perhaps goes without saying that the more restricted the licence sought in respect of either the categories of liquor to be sold or the conditions volunteered, the more likely it is that the application will ultimately prove successful. Of course, a balance has to be struck between the desire to succeed and the commercial practicality of operating under such restrictions. It would be imprudent for an applicant to assume that having secured a limited licence he will be able to upgrade the licence or release himself from all or part of its restrictions in future years. At that later date the justices may well take the view that there has been no change in circumstance sufficient in their view to justify any relaxation of conditions or extension in the types of liquor to be sold.

Name and location of premises

2.22   Again, these details must be stated with as much accuracy as possible, although there are a number of helpful authorities which tend to suggest that there is some margin for error.[1] Other cases where licensing justices were held entitled to take the view that no one had been misled include references to an 'off' rather than an 'on' beer licence[2] and a reference to premises situate somewhere in a market place, which comprised 17 different houses.[3]

---

[1]   Chitty LJ expressed the view that licensing notices should not be 'scrutinised as closely as the old forms of pleading' (*R v Lyon, ex p Skinner* (1898) 14 TLR 357, CA).
[2]   *Ex p Clayton* (1899) 63 JP 788, DC.
[3]   *R v Penkridge Division of Staffordshire Justices* (1892) 56 JP 87.

Ownership

2.23   Whilst there is no statutory duty to state the identity of the owner of the premises in the notice of application itself, this information will be required by the clerk's office if the licence is granted,[1] and so it may be helpful to provide the information in the first instance. Further, some policy documents *insist* upon it.

---

[1]   Section 32(1).

Conditions

2.24   If the applicant is entirely content that any licence granted should be subject to standard conditions (eg restaurant and/or residential) or individual conditions of his own devising (see precedents in Part II), then there is no disadvantage in setting these out in the notice of application. As indicated above, volunteering to accept a conditional licence will undoubtedly enhance the application's prospect of success. Advertising such an intention in the notice of application may discourage certain individuals who might otherwise raise an objection. If, on the other hand, the applicant is uncertain as to the conditions that the police, for example, might wish to see attached to the licence, or wants to establish whether the licensing committee will insist upon imposing *any* such conditions, then clearly the notice should not contain any reference to conditions.

Signature of applicant

2.25 The Act requires that the notice be signed by the applicant or his authorised agent.

Service of notice

2.26 The following time limits must be strictly adhered to.

Delivery

2.27 Notices must arrive with the authorities indicated above not less than 21 days before the date of the appropriate transfer sessions. As a rule of thumb, if a hearing is on, say, a Thursday, the notice needs to be received by the appropriate parties on the Wednesday three weeks earlier; if on a Monday, arrangements should be made for delivery by the appropriate Saturday at the latest. Although there is no legal requirement to serve personally delivered notices within business hours, it is prudent to do so as it can otherwise be difficult to establish safe receipt. Notices served by post are deemed to be delivered at the time when this would normally occur in the ordinary course of post.[1] However, if there is evidence that the notices actually arrived after the deemed day the later date will be taken as the date of service for the purposes of the Act.

[1] Interpretation Act 1978, s 7.

2.28 In practice there does not seem to be any difficulty with serving licensing notices by facsimile or, with some courts, by e-mail, although care should be taken to ensure that the notice is actually received by the addressee in a legible form and by the due date.

Advertisement

2.29 Notice of the application must appear in a newspaper circulating in a place where the premises to be licensed are situated, not more than 28 days or less than 14 days before the hearing. Particular care needs to be taken if it does not prove possible, for some reason, to dispatch notices until shortly before the statutory deadline for service (ie 21 days), since in certain rural areas that will leave insufficient time to meet the deadline for delivery of advertising copy to a weekly newspaper. For that reason the date of the proposed advertisement should be planned shortly after one has ascertained the most convenient date for the hearing. The notice may be a foreshortened version of the notice served by post, omitting the heading bearing details of the recipients and commencing, therefore, with 'To whom it may concern'. It has been known for licensing committees to require re-advertisement where too small a print size has been used.

2.30   Care needs to be taken to ensure that the advertisement appears in a newspaper which is acceptable to the licensing justices. In certain cases there can be difficulty in establishing that it does indeed circulate in the appropriate area, although note that the newspaper need *not* be an exclusively local one.[1] Many committees do not look favourably on free newspapers. As ever, it is sensible to review the policy document (if any) to see whether any preference is indicated. The newspaper publishers should be asked to supply complete copies of the relevant edition as many courts require the whole paper to be lodged, with the relevant advertisement outlined in red.

[1]   *R v Westminster Betting Licensing Committee, ex p Peabody Donation Fund (Governors)* [1963] 2 QB 750.

Display

2.31   The notice of application needs to be displayed on or near the premises to be licensed (or, in the case of an application for a provisional grant, on or near the proposed site of those premises) for a period of seven days in a place where it can conveniently be seen *and* read by the public. This display must take place not more than 28 days prior to the hearing, and one or two committees express a preference (it can be no more) for the display to take place between the 14th and 21st days. It is (or, on reflection, perhaps it is not) surprising how many applications fail at this point. To begin with, the applicant must heed the fact that the intention of the Act is that members of the public *should* be able to see and read the notice! Accordingly, he should not be surprised if licensing justices disallow a display which is not at head-height, is too far removed from a public footpath, or is concealed at times by a shutter or open door or even (as occurred in one case) by articles placed within an overloaded builder's skip. In the case of premises yet to be constructed it is frequently necessary to exercise a considerable degree of ingenuity and perseverance if one wishes to guarantee the display of a notice on a boarding, post or tree for the seven-day period. Unfortunately (unlike provisions within the Gaming Act 1968, for example), it is *not* sufficient for the applicant merely to use reasonable endeavours to keep the notice so displayed. It is an absolute requirement and any failure to comply will inevitably lead to the adjournment of the case.

Failure to comply with notice provisions

2.32   If, despite the utmost care having been exercised, a mistake does occur in connection with certain of these matters it may be possible to salvage the situation. The 'slip rule' afforded by para 7 of Sch 2 provides as follows:

> 'Where the applicant for the grant of a justices' licence has, through inadvertence or misadventure, failed to comply with the requirements of . . . [paras 1 to 6 of Sch 2] . . ., the licensing justices may, upon such terms as they think fit, postpone consideration of his application; and if on the postponed consideration they are satisfied that any terms so imposed have been complied with, they may deal with the application as if the applicant had complied with those requirements.'

2.33   Although most clerks tend to take the view that it is implicit in the provision that the purpose of any such adjournment must be to ensure that the application, when heard, complies fully with the statutory requirements of Sch 2 as outlined above, it can properly be argued that there is certainly no absolute *legal* requirement to this effect. Instead, the justices should adopt a commonsense approach, with a view to ensuring that any potential prejudice to those who might, for example, be affected by the application, is avoided. If, for example, owing to late delivery only 19 days' notice of the application has been given to the district council, the committee may—instead of insisting upon an adjournment of the application to another hearing at least two days thereafter—adjourn it to later in the session, by which time the council may have confirmed by facsimile that it offers no objection.

Plans

2.34   The *statutory* requirements in relation to plans are relatively limited; the Act provides that one copy of a plan of the premises should be deposited with the notice of application if the application is for the grant or ordinary removal of an on-licence, or the provisional grant or ordinary removal of an off-licence. In practice, however, both the policies of most licensing committees and common sense dictate the need for far greater attention to be paid to the preparation and presentation of plans, which often form the central feature of a licensing application.

The principal considerations in relation to plans are as follows.

Preparation

2.35   This should be put in hand at the earliest opportunity since it is generally the production of plans which is most likely to cause a delay in the submission of an application. The notices themselves can be prepared relatively speedily. Reference should be made to the committee's policy document (if any). The provisions of any such policy will, of course, be paramount and will override the guidelines set out below where any conflict arises.

Scale

2.36   The scales most commonly adopted are 1:100 (alternatively 1 inch to 8 feet) or 1:50 (1 inch to 4 feet). Obviously much will depend upon the size of the premises. The aim should be to produce a plan which is capable of showing individual features (eg doorways, seating areas) in some detail, but not so large that it cannot conveniently be handled by magistrates sitting in the confines of a courtroom. On occasion it may be helpful to produce additional plans drawn to a different scale from the main plan so that a feature of particular importance (eg a kitchen area) can be shown in greater detail.

Quality

2.37   Plans should be drawn to a reasonably professional standard. Unless the applicant is particularly gifted or has the appropriate training it is unlikely that a home-drawn plan will do justice to the application or compare favourably with those generally considered by the licensing committee. Many policy documents insist that the plans bear the date of their preparation and the name of the architect or draughtsman responsible.

Detail

2.38   Plans should contain as much information as possible, whilst excluding that which is likely to be superfluous to the application. For that reason plans prepared in connection with an application for building regulations, for example, which may contain details of drainage, electrical systems, structural beams etc are likely to prove confusing to many members of a licensing committee. The information that will be useful includes: all points of access (showing the direction and swing of each door), the bar counter, seating areas (showing fixed and moveable tables and chairs), toilet accommodation, kitchens, liquor storage areas and the locations of any closed-circuit television cameras or security mirrors, if proposed. The nature of each room should be clearly described. Even though the plans are to scale, some committees require the dimensions and areas of each room to be set out on the plan. Another requirement is often to show the name or type of adjoining premises on the same plan, together with adjacent street names.

2.39 If the committee has published a form of colour code, then obviously it should be strictly adhered to. An example of a colour code favoured historically might be:

(a) areas in which intoxicating liquor may be purchased or consumed— pink;

(b) toilet accommodation—green;

(c) bar counters—brown;

(d) food preparation and staff areas—yellow;

(e) liquor storage—blue.

Again, if there is no published policy one can create further categories if, in a particular application, for example, it is necessary to show the extent of an area set aside exclusively for restaurant use or dancing.

2.40 Since the widespread adoption of the Good Practice Guide it is now usual for committees to require only that the areas to which the public have access (eg the public side of the bars, lobbies, passageways and sometimes external drinking areas), together with the cellars and the kitchens, should be outlined in red as designating the areas to be licensed. As practices still vary widely from court to court it is prudent to check with the clerk's office in each case. Of course, as indicated in the preceding chapter, an on-licence authorises both on- and off-sales and it is into the latter category that any drinks taken outside that red line will fall. This is the basis upon which the majority of public house gardens operate, with off-sales being consumed outside the licensed premises. As mentioned above in some cases, however, the garden will be included within the licensed area, either because the licensee wishes to sell liquor from an outside bar (ie an on-sale), or because when considering the initial application the committee wished to exercise a greater degree of control over the use of such potential drinking areas, ensuring that they are, for example, governed by the provisions concerning permitted hours. If the perimeter of the building is not outlined in red, or there are simply no plans in existence, it is arguable that the extent of the licensed premises may be ascertained only by reference to the description of the premises on the face of the licence. Unless that description specifically restricts the area to which it relates, the licence may be said to extend to the curtilage of the property itself.[1]

[1]   See *R v Weston-super-Mare Licensing Justices, ex p Powell* [1939] 1 KB 700.

2.41   Particular considerations apply to off-licences, according to their type. In the absence of any guidelines published by the committee it is appropriate, again, to outline in red the entire premises, be they a supermarket, grocery, convenience store or specialist off-licence. This is now the course recommended by the Good Practice Guide. The particular areas or units used for the display of intoxicating liquor may be shaded in pink, for example.

2.42   In some cases committees will insist upon an arrangement whereby only the wines and spirits shelves and any counters or checkouts through which the intoxicating liquor is to be sold should be outlined in red. That area is then defined as the 'licensed premises', with the consequence that any alteration in the location of the intoxicating liquor will necessitate an application for a new licence. This subject is dealt with more fully in chapter 4. In the case of a specialist off-licence all the shelving will be so identified. Certain committees will even insist that any proposed floor or window displays (even if the latter are not intended for sale) are shown and coloured on the plan.

'Outline' provisional grant

2.43   If the applicant is not in a position to prepare detailed plans of the premises, he can seek what may be termed an 'outline' provisional grant under s 6(5) of the Act. In this case the requirement is to lodge (a) a site plan, and (b) a description of the premises, to include the proposed size and character of the outlet.

With such applications justices will be obliged to assume that the premises will be fit and convenient for their intended purpose.

2.44   As noted earlier, a provisional licence does not require renewal and will continue indefinitely unless the licensing justices have made it a condition that a final order should be sought within a specified period. Within 12 months of any grant, the holder of an *outline* provisional licence must, however, apply for it to be affirmed,[1] failing which the licence will become void. If an appeal is lodged against the original grant time does not begin to run until the appeal is disposed of. Conditions can only be imposed at the time of the original grant and not at the affirmation stage.

[1]   Section 6(5)(b).

Location

2.45 It is always helpful if any layout plan is also endorsed with, or accompanied by, a plan identifying the location of the premises in relation to adjoining streets and properties. Again, many committees will insist upon the production of such a plan, generally drawn to a scale of 1:500.

Numbers

2.46 Sufficient copies of the plan(s) need to be prepared for service upon each of the statutory authorities, while leaving an appropriate number for circulation among the licensing committee and witnesses at the hearing. Distribution might be as follows:

(a)   chief executive to the justices—four copies;

(b)   police—one copy;

(c)   local authority—one copy;

(d)   fire brigade—two copies (one being returned to the applicant with the brigade's comments);

(e)   building inspector (advisable)—two copies (one for comments);

(f)   town/parish/community council—one copy;

(g)   applicant—one copy;

(h)   advocate—one copy;

(i)   any objector—one copy for the hearing;

(j)   spare—two copies.

RADIUS MAPS

2.47 As will be explained subsequently, it is occasionally still necessary on an application for a new licence to satisfy the licensing committee that there is a need or demand for the grant of a new licence in that particular area. Nowadays, following the recommendation of the Good Practice Guide, most committees explicitly disclaim any interest in such matters.

2.48 In the rare cases where 'need' remains an issue then to assist them in their deliberations some licensing committees require the applicant to produce at the hearing a radius map identifying the nature and locations of other licensed premises within a certain distance from the applicant's premises. Such committees may require such plans to be lodged, say, ten days prior to the hearing. Since it can take some time for the plans to be obtained from the local agent for the ordnance survey or other suppliers, it is, again, prudent to ensure that the preparation of the radius map is undertaken at the earliest opportunity. Regard should, of course, be paid to any policy document published by the committee. If a policy document is silent on the point (but makes it clear that demand may be an issue) the most commonly used plan is one showing premises within a quarter of a mile of the applicant's premises. Where the premises are situated in a less densely populated area, or where potential competitors are few and far between, a radius of half a mile or more might be appropriate. Where the matter is left to the discretion of the applicant, he should consider what in practical terms is likely to be the actual catchment area for his particular business. If it is to be argued that the nature of the operation is such that customers will travel distances of three or four miles and that there is no comparable outlet within that geographical area, why not produce an additional map to demonstrate the point?

2.49   On the quarter- or half-mile map it will be necessary, as indicated, to identify the applicant's site and the other licensed premises. Some committees will insist that the map shows all licensed premises, even including the so-called Part IV licences (ie restaurant and/or residential licences). Why they do this is not entirely clear since, in dealing with the grant of Part IV licences, the committee's discretion is limited to certain practical matters and does not extend, for example, to issues such as need or demand. However, it could be argued by those committees that they are still entitled to take into account the general availability of alcohol in a particular area when deciding whether or not to create additional outlets, of whatever category. In any event, unless the committee so specifies, it is recommended upon an application for the grant of a new on-licence that the radius plan should not include Part IV licences, registered clubs or off-licences. The remaining premises might, in the absence of a policy document, be identified as follows:

(a)   full on-licences—red;

(b)   conditional on-licences—blue;

(c)   beer, wine and cider (and other limited categories)—green;

(d)   closed premises—purple;

(e)   applicant's premises—black.

2.50   In the case of off-licences, the following coding might be adopted:

(a)   full on-licences—red;

(b) supermarkets/grocers—green;

(c) specialist off-licences—blue;

(d) closed premises—purple;

(e) applicant's premises—black.

2.51 It is arguable that there should be no need to include public houses when making application for an off-licence since the available evidence suggests that only minimal off-sales take place through such outlets. However, since the on-licence does, of course, technically authorise all off-sales it may be prudent to ensure their inclusion on the map.

2.52 Radius maps should either be endorsed with the name of each licensed premises or be accompanied by a numbered schedule with names and addresses. On a general note, radius maps should again be prepared to a reasonable standard. There are a number of surveyors' practices specialising in this work. Their details can usually be obtained from any busy licensing court or solicitor regularly acting in this area of work. Nothing is less helpful to an application than the failure (however inadvertent) to show the locations of potential competitors upon the map produced to the licensing committee.

2.53 In preparing the radius map either the applicant or any licensing surveyor instructed will wish to inspect the register of licences maintained by the chief executive to the justices. Technically this register may be inspected only by a local ratepayer, the owner of licensed premises or a licensee within the division.[1] However, requests made by individuals who do not technically qualify under any of these categories are rarely refused.

[1] Section 34(1).

2.54 A radius or street map may be useful to illustrate not only need, but also a range of other issues including the availability of public transport, locations of objectors or supporters, parking, and the possible impact upon local amenity.

OTHER EVIDENCE

2.55 At this stage consideration should be given to the commissioning of other evidence to be produced at the hearing, which might include:

(1) *Photographs* These can be used to illustrate the present state of the premises, particular features of the area or potential competitors.

(2) *Menus* Since food is increasingly an essential feature of most on-licensed premises it is always helpful to be in a position to produce

sufficient copies of a menu showing the quality and variety of the food to be offered.

(3) *Product list* The strength of certain cases lies in the particular products which are to be, perhaps uniquely, available through the applicant's premises. In applications for specialist off-licences, in particular, it is commonplace for much of the case to be concerned with comparisons of the range, quality and price of the wines to be offered. Lists should therefore be produced of the applicant's own range and those offered by any competitors.

(4) *Petitions* Although these are often viewed with some scepticism by licensing committees, there is no doubt that the production of a weighty petition by local people, the preparation of which has been properly controlled and supervised, can be to an applicant's advantage. If the petition is not to prove counterproductive great care should be taken in the manner of its circulation. Local objectors are likely to be well aware if it has been commissioned in anything other than a straightforward and honest fashion. If the applicant intends to produce the petition as evidence that a particular section of the community (eg residents in one street, taxi drivers, etc) wants a facility, that is a legitimate tactic. On the other hand, if the petition is to be presented as expressing views which are typical of the applicant's existing customers, then clearly it would be improper for the applicant either to make the signing process selective, to pressure particular customers or to circulate the document away from the premises. Frivolous names or comments should also be discouraged since they tend to give the impression that insufficient respect is being paid to the (quasi-judicial) proceedings. Many committees now insist that where a petition is produced the party calling that evidence also calls at least three of the signatories as witnesses as to the manner in which it was taken.

(5) *Market research* This is always an expensive process since it is generally felt that upwards of 200 interviews need to be conducted to give a statistically representative sample. If consideration is being given to the production of market research to establish opinions in the locality it is recommended that the services of an expert be retained, both to advise upon the drafting of the questionnaire (which itself requires very careful consideration) and to give evidence if required on the significance of the results.

(6) *Licensing surveyor* If the applicant has significant experience in the trade, or is very knowledgeable about the area and the potential competition, he may be the best person to speak on the issue of demand. Where, however, the most professional presentation is required major operators generally instruct the licensing surveyor

responsible for the preparation of the radius maps also to prepare a proof of evidence in readiness for a court appearance. The benefit of calling such experts is that they have great experience of appearing in court proceedings. They are also very familiar with the different market sectors and will be able to draw comparisons between the balance of outlets to be found in the particular location and those that might obtain in other similar communities (see the figures at para **2.16**). It also means that the applicant can concentrate on dealing with practical and operational matters, leaving the expert to deal with the more intangible issue of 'need' or, more commonly these days, the potential impact upon the local community. The Local Government Act 2000 includes a requirement on a local authority to prepare a community strategy to promote or improve economic social and environmental well-being. This exercise is likely to impact on the licensing regime.

(7) *Demographic profiles* Certain organisations specialise in producing a population analysis of a chosen area, breaking down that population by reference to such matters as income, occupation, age, size of family, drinking habits, etc. It goes without saying that such an analysis can prove extremely useful in the right case, although it can also prove counterproductive if not fully understood by the witness producing the document!

PRIOR TO THE HEARING

Dealings with the court

2.56 Once notices have been served the next two or three weeks should be actively used for communicating with the authorities involved. The clerk's office should be contacted to see whether there are any outstanding requirements under any published policy documents. Such requirements might include the lodging of Fitness of Applicant and Suitability of Premises forms as well as (more rarely these days) contracts of employment, resolutions of the applicant's employer authorising the application to proceed, the lodging of certified copies of any contract for the acquisition of the premises, or agreement for lease and so on. Any such requests for information and/or documentation need to be strictly complied with since many committees are now automatically adjourning applications where the paperwork is not in order a specified number of days (typically seven or ten) prior to the hearing. The clerk's office should also be asked whether the committee is likely to visit the premises and, if so, whether it will require the attendance of the applicant or whether his authorised representative will suffice. Nearer the hearing an indication may be given if objections have been notified, or if the application is likely to be adjourned in any event owing to the number of matters on the court list for that day.

Consideration of the applicant

2.57   Similar discussions need to take place with the police officer responsible for considering the application. He may wish to know a great deal more about the intended operation before deciding whether or not the police should formally object, or make informal 'representations'. If the applicant has *any* previous convictions (other than for minor motoring offences) it would be as well for these to be disclosed at the earliest possible opportunity, even though they may technically be regarded as 'spent' under the Rehabilitation of Offenders Act 1974. Under s 7(3) of that Act, licensing justices are entitled to exercise their discretion and have regard to such matters if they consider it to be necessary in the interests of justice. Such a determination should not be arrived at lightly, since the High Court will quash any subsequent refusal to grant or transfer if the convictions are so old and/or minor that no reasonable bench of licensing justices would consider them to be relevant. Further, the committee would be well advised to exercise considerable care in the procedure which it adopts when determining whether the convictions should even be considered.[1]

[1]   See *Adamson v Waveney District Council* [1997] 2 All ER 898, QBD and the notes thereto in the Preface to *Paterson's Licensing Acts* (106th edn). See also 'Convictions' at para **3.09**.

2.58   Conversely, even if a prospective licensee has been *acquitted* of a criminal offence, licensing justices are still entitled to have regard to the circumstances which led to him being charged, when deciding whether he is in fact a fit and proper person to hold the licence. The reasoning behind this decision[1] is that whereas to secure a conviction the criminal court is required to be satisfied beyond all reasonable doubt, the licensing committee need apply only the civil standard of proof, namely the balance of probabilities.

[1]   *R v Crown Court at Maidstone, ex p Olson* (1992) 136 Sol Jo LB 174.

2.59   From the police point of view, honest disclosure of all convictions at the initial interview is likely to present the applicant in a far more favourable light than will concealment.

2.60 Note that at the hearing the applicant may well be asked whether or not he is a 'disqualified person'. This is a reference to the provisions of s 9 of the Act, which specifies as disqualified: sheriff's officers or bailiffs, persons convicted of forging or knowingly making use of a forged justices' licence or those who have permitted premises (of which they were the licensee) to be used as a brothel. Unsurprisingly, one rarely finds that s 9 presents any difficulties!

Suitability of the premises

2.61 It is to be hoped that the building inspector and/or fire officer will have been consulted at an early stage, preferably before plans have been produced. Ideally their recommendations will then have been fully incorporated into those plans. If not, the general practice is for the fire officer to return one copy of the plans duly indorsed with various hieroglyphics and accompanied by an explanatory key and schedule of recommendations. This should be considered carefully by the applicant and his advisers since, on occasions, compliance with those recom-mendations can prove extremely expensive—if, for example, additional fire separation is required between floors. In other cases, particularly those relating to applications for public entertainment licences (which are dealt with elsewhere in this book), there may be some discussion as to the limit that should be set upon the occupancy of the premises. Often such figures can be increased if the applicant is prepared to create additional fire exits or widen existing ones. In general, however, no difficulties are presented by the fire officer's requirements so far as the hearing is concerned if a simple undertaking is given at the hearing confirming that there will be compliance prior to the opening of the premises.

PREPARATION OF THE CASE

2.62 If the applicant is being represented it will be helpful if his adviser is familiar with the premises (if they already exist), as well as with the locality in which they are situated. This does not necessarily mean that the applicant needs to be represented by a local solicitor or barrister, since there are a number of specialists who operate on a national basis. Whether it will be worthwhile using such a person will depend upon factors such as the complexity, difficulty or importance of the case. Very often large companies find it easier in any event to retain a limited number of specialist advocates, who thereby acquire an intimate understanding of their business, rather than explain matters afresh to a local solicitor on each occasion.

2.63   Whoever represents the applicant (or if he represents himself) the golden rule is that *every* application should be fully considered and prepared before it is presented to the licensing committee. Not only should this be done as a matter of courtesy but, just as with the plans, the extent to which an applicant has troubled to prepare his case may well be taken as an indication of his likely attitude to the business if the licence should be granted. Factors to be considered during the preparatory meetings include those discussed in the following subsections.

Applicant

2.64   What is the applicant's background? If not from the licensed trade, to what extent has his previous experience prepared him for this business? Has he attended any training courses? In the case of new licensees, committees are increasingly asking that applicants should attend a recognised course resulting in the issue of a National Licensee Certificate prior to the hearing. Inquiries should be made of the clerk to the licensing justices as to whether any such mandatory requirement for training new licensees exists in the particular division concerned. Does the applicant have any recognised qualifications? If there are convictions, to what extent may these be said to reflect upon his character? Are there others involved in the proposed business who might make up (or, conversely, add to) these deficiencies?

2.65   The Act provides that licensing justices may grant a licence only to a person whom they consider to be 'fit and proper' to hold such a licence.[1] Since consideration of this provision most commonly arises in relation to applications to transfer a justices' licence, the various criteria which committees may apply are more fully set out in chapter 3 relating to such applications. However, it is worth noting at this point that justices are entitled to go beyond the mere character or experience of the applicant and consider whether his status[2] or intentions[3] might render him unsuitable. Committees may even properly consider the terms of any contract under which the applicant is employed to manage the premises, or the provisions of any lease or tenancy agreement, but have no power to attempt to regulate the terms upon which he is to conduct his business unless they can properly come to the conclusion that the terms upon which he intends to operate are such that the *only* legitimate inference from consideration of these terms is that the applicant cannot carry on his business without infringing the law.[4]

---

[1]   Section 3(1).
[2]   *Nicholson & Sons Ltd v Upton, Maidenhead Justices, ex p R* [1923] BTRLR 38.
[3]   *R v London Borough of Haringey, ex p Sandhu and Sandhu* (1987) 151 JP 696.
[4]   See *R v Hyde Justices* [1912] 1 KB 645.

Company

2.66   If the application is being submitted in respect of an existing company, what is the reputation and profile of that company within its industry sector? Has it received any awards or accolades? If so, can these be made available? What makes it *special?*

Premises

2.67   The Act provides that licensing justices shall not grant a new justices' on-licence for premises unless those premises are, in their opinion, structurally adapted for the class of licence required.[1] Certain premises are automatically disqualified, namely:

(1)   garage premises which are used *primarily* for the retailing of petrol or derv or for the sale or maintenance of motor vehicles[2] (it is for local justices to ascertain the 'primary use' of premises, according to the criteria that they consider to be most appropriate).[3] Such applications have become increasingly common in recent years as consumer trends have led to forecourt shops substantially expanding their share of the retail market, with many having substantial convenience stores or even supermarkets in operation. Note that the disqualification applies only to premises which are used primarily etc. It is possible to apply for a provisional licence for a site if the justices can be satisfied that upon completion they 'would have granted' a full licence (per s 6(1)). The principal difficulty is the evidential one of forecasting the balance of trade with sufficient accuracy.

(2)   premises that are primarily motorway service areas;[4]

(3)   those where two licensees have severally forfeited their licences in respect of the premises within a two-year period;[5]

(4)   (in certain cases, for Part IV licences only), where a disqualification order has been made by a court dealing with specific offences.[6]

[1]   Section 4(2).
[2]   Section 9(4A) and (4B).
[3]   *Green v Inner London Licensing Justices* (1994) Licensing Review, October, QBD. In this case the High Court did not comment adversely upon a suggestion that criteria relevant to establishing primary use *might* include a comparison of 'disqualified' net turnover with remaining sales, or a consideration of the purposes for which customers visited a site.
[4]   Section 9(3) and (4).
[5]   Section 9(2).
[6]   Section 100.

2.68   Are there any practical matters arising out of the layout plans? Consideration should be given to control at the point of entry, where appropriate (as in the case of some late-night venues). Within the premises all parts should be capable of effective supervision. If, as in so many areas, there is a known problem with controlled substances, the local drugs officer should be consulted for his comments. Particular attention should be paid to concealed seating areas within the premises, as well as to the lobbies and toilet accommodation. Are the premises secure and will they be properly alarmed? What makes them particularly appropriate for the intended use in terms of their character, size and location? Conversely, is it likely to be to the public detriment if they remain closed, or are put to an alternative use? To what extent are other sites likely to become available?

Authorities

2.69   Are all of the authorities content with the plans? Have planning permission and building regulations approval been granted? If this is not a specific requirement of the licensing committee, will the absence of planning permission, for example, adversely affect the ability to meet any objections that might be raised? What will be the applicant's investment in the building?

Interest in the premises

2.70   The Act does *not* require an applicant for the grant of a justices' licence to have a legal, or equitable, interest in the premises concerned. The phrase in s 6(1) 'a person interested in any premises' should be construed in the broadest sense. Nonetheless, the policy of many licensing justices is to require the applicant to deposit, in advance of the hearing, documents showing the nature of his *intended* interest in the property, even if that has not reached the stage of a legally binding contract. In fact, it may well be in the interests of the applicant to enter into such a contract prior to the hearing of the application, since otherwise there remains the risk that the vendor may decide to market his newly licensed property elsewhere. Of course, it would be prudent for any such contract or agreement for lease to be conditional upon the grant of the application, subject to licence conditions (if any) which are acceptable to the applicant. Provision should also be made to cover the possibility, albeit somewhat remote, that an unsuccessful objector will appeal against the grant and subsequently succeed on that appeal.

Operation

2.71   Each aspect of the operation needs to be considered in careful detail. During what hours will the premises operate? How will the business vary during each trading period? What staffing arrangements will there be? How will the staff be selected and trained? What supervision will be exercised by the employer?

Requirement for a licence

2.72   This is the most nebulous and potentially difficult area to deal with. Even though the applicant may have complied fully with all procedural requirements and be in a position to satisfy the committee that he is a fit and proper person and the premises are perfectly adapted for the intended use, why *should* the committee exercise its discretion to grant the application?[1] What practical benefit will the outlet bring, other than (presumably) some financial advantage to the licensee? It is this question which presents the greatest challenge to the advocate. In most cases the applicant genuinely does believe that there will be some benefit to the public; if he did not believe that then it would, one assumes, be difficult to justify the time and effort required of any new commercial venture. The advocate needs to achieve the best possible understanding of that potential market, if necessary probing the strengths and weaknesses of the business plan. At this stage, of course, he will also need to look at the facilities offered by the competition, as well as the objections that might be voiced by the police, local residents or other traders.

[1]   Until now it had been thought that a committee might not adopt a restrictive policy concerning the grant of licences relying simply upon national concerns as to alcoholism etc, in support of its insistence upon proof of 'need' or 'demand', without at the same time examining the relevance of those considerations to local conditions. The purpose of the policy had to be established and evidence adduced to demonstrate that the grant of the licence would be in conflict with that purpose, if a policy on 'need' was to be relied upon as a ground for refusal (*R v Crown Court at Sheffield, ex p Mead* (1992) Licensing Review (January), QBD). However, in *R v Crown Court at Sheffield, ex p Consterdine* (1998) Licensing Review (July), QBD Turner J suggested that in such cases the onus was upon the applicant to establish why the justices should depart from their published policy.

THE HEARING

2.73   Upon arrival at the court the applicant and his representative should report to the court usher, usually identified by the black gown he or she will be wearing. The ushers may have some control over the order in which cases are called and should accordingly be treated with due respect—although perhaps not so much as was recently accorded by one well known licensing commentator who was moved to ask for his client to be brought in by ' the *learnéd* usher'! Often it is necessary to fill in a slip of paper identifying the name of the advocate, description of the premises, nature of the application and the estimated length of hearing. Most courts tend to deal with such matters as occasional permissions and transfers first, leaving the more involved applications till later in the day.

2.74   Some clerks helpfully attempt to minimise waiting time by allotting a time when applications will be heard. This approach is now recommended in the Good Practice Guide. Where it is known that cases will be contested, prior adjournments are encouraged. Anyone who has ever calculated the aggregate cost to business represented by each hour wasted by perhaps dozens of lawyers and their clients will readily appreciate the value of such a system. All waiting time may not be entirely wasted, however, since by listening to the earlier cases the advocate and his client will often gain a better impression of the particular concerns of the committee sitting on that day.

2.75   When the case is called the advocate should stand and, if necessary, introduce himself to the committee. The clerk will call for any objectors formally to express their interest. The guidelines now published by most courts will set out the order of proceedings. However, it is customary then for the applicant's advocate to outline briefly the principal features of the applicant's case and to prove the service of the notices and advertisement of the application, if this has not already been dealt with in correspondence with the clerk's office. The applicant then takes the form of oath appropriate to his religion or beliefs. To avoid embarrassment it is prudent to raise this prior to the hearing so that the relevant card and/ or book can be produced by the usher. A word of warning: most courts take the greatest exception to persons who continue their conversations during the taking of the oath. The applicant's advocate should stand both during his opening speech and while the applicant is giving his evidence. Having taken the oath the applicant should remain standing, taking particular care to address his answers to the committee, rather than to the person who is taking him through his evidence. As a matter of courtesy he should also avoid putting his hands in his pockets, since such behaviour often causes needless offence to those before whom he appears.

2.76   The applicant's evidence will begin with confirmation of his full name, address and occupation. So as to dispose of the formalities he might then be asked to deal with the display of the notice of application on the premises.

2.77   The applicant will be expected to be familiar with the principal requirements of the Act, with particular reference to the laws concerning children on licensed premises, those to whom liquor may not be served and the rules concerning permitted hours.

2.78 Thereafter, he may be taken through the various aspects of the application outlined above. With the permission of the committee leading questions may be asked in respect of those matters which are unlikely to be in any way contentious. Other than that, the questions put to the applicant should be neutral in form and not designed to prompt a particular (helpful) response. Care should be taken to avoid repetition, or the introduction of matters which are likely to be considered wholly irrelevant.

2.79 The experienced advocate will be entirely comfortable in this environment. The greatest danger is that he may be inclined rather to disregard the potential gulf between the experience of the applicant and that of the licensing committee. The former may be enormously enthusiastic and knowledgeable about his chosen trade, but he may have little or no experience of appearing in a courtroom environment. His reaction may be either to suppress the enthusiasm (which it is so very necessary to communicate to the committee) or, alternatively, to make light of the process—an attitude which is unlikely to operate to his benefit. The licensing committee, on the other hand, will know a great deal about court procedure and the technical operation of the licensing laws (although they are, of course, lay magistrates and ultimately rely upon their clerk to provide legal advice on any contentious issues). However, because of the technical and repetitive nature of the majority of the applications that are presented to them on a regular basis, not all the licensing justices will, in fact, have an intimate understanding of the commercial realities of every type of licensed business (there are certain exceptions which are well known to those in the trade). The great challenge to the advocate is to bridge that gap, acting where necessary as a translator and ensuring that each party fully appreciates the viewpoint of the other. If he is successful the applicant will be better able to address the legitimate concerns felt by the magistrates on issues of law and order while they, for their part, may be infected by the enthusiasm and commitment which the applicant brings to this new venture. That at least is the theory!

2.80 Once the applicant has given his evidence-in-chief, any objector is entitled to cross-examine. There are few constraints upon such questions, which may well be designed to challenge the evidence previously given by the applicant. If the objector intends to call evidence which directly conflicts with that given by the applicant, this should be put to the latter during his evidence, to give him an opportunity to comment. The advocate is entitled to re-examine, confining himself to points raised during cross-examination. Following this the committee may or may not wish to put its own questions to the applicant.

2.81   This process is repeated in respect of each of the witnesses called to give evidence on behalf of the applicant. The most telling evidence in support of an application is generally that provided by members of the public who have been prepared to make the effort to come to court to tell the licensing committee of the need in their particular area, among people of a certain age or background, for the proposed premises. Although cross-examination may reveal that these witnesses are presently patronising existing outlets (without evident dissatisfaction), or may perhaps be insufficiently aware of the availability of those facilities, it is nonetheless difficult for the objector or his representative to challenge effectively the evidence of an intending user.

Once all such witnesses have given their evidence the applicant's case is concluded.

2.82   If the application is contested the objectors may then call evidence, in which case the same procedure will be adopted, with the applicant's advocate being entitled to cross-examine each of the witnesses. Alternatively, the objector may indicate that he does not intend to call any evidence, perhaps because he does not wish the motives of those instructing him to be examined in any great detail under cross-examination. Alternatively, he may hold a legitimate belief that the objector's case is such that he may confine himself entirely to matters of comment.

2.83   When both sides have concluded their evidence there will be an opportunity for any of the authorities (eg police, fire, local authority) to make representations to the licensing committee. It is suggested that if an objection has not been notified at the outset, then as the status of objector has an important legal significance in matters such as costs and appeals (see below), these representations should not be in the form of objections to the grant.

2.84   It is then the opportunity of the parties to sum up the case. Generally, the objector goes first, followed by the applicant or his advocate. Note that some committees will allow the applicant only one speech; the position should be established with the clerk at the outset. If a second address is allowed there is little point at this stage in simply repeating the arguments that have previously been presented. What the advocates should seek to achieve is to put the application or the objection in some sort of context, so as to assist the licensing committee when considering whether or not to exercise its discretion in all the circumstances. If a point of law arises during the summing up on behalf of the applicant, then the objector or his representative is entitled to deal with that point. The precise procedure adopted is a matter for the particular committee and as indicated above is usually covered in the published guidelines.

2.85 The licensing committee will then generally retire to consider the evidence. If it requires assistance on a point of law it may ask the clerk to accompany it to the retiring room.

THE DECISION

2.86 Upon returning to the court the committee will announce its decision. Historically there was no requirement to give reasons for that decision,[1] although it is now the invariable policy of most committees to give such reasons at the hearing itself, in the light of Article 6 of the European Convention on Human Rights, now enshrined in the Human Rights Act 1998, which requires that in every case determining 'civil rights and obligations ... judgement shall be pronounced publicly'. Further, the Licensing Act 1964 specifically requires written reasons to be given where, for example, an application for the grant of a Part IV (restaurant and/or residential) licence is refused.

[1] For the position in the Crown Court on appeal, see para **2.116**.

2.87 If an application for a new justices' on-licence has been refused, it is worth considering immediately whether to invite the licensing committee to grant instead an application for a restaurant and/or residential licence under the rarely exercised power afforded by s 99 of the Act. Where the original application was refused because the applicant was not regarded as a fit and proper person it is unlikely that the magistrates would take any different view in respect of a Part IV licence, although it is conceivable that one could be regarded as unsuitable to run a public house but sufficiently experienced to operate, for example, a restaurant. If, on the other hand, the full on-licence was refused on the ground of need it is entirely appropriate that the committee should instead be invited to issue the alternative licence. In deciding whether to apply under s 99, the question for the operator then to decide is whether the limitations of a restaurant and/or residential licence would be of any practical benefit to him. It is unclear whether the grant of a licence under s 99(1) will prevent the applicant from appealing against the original refusal. In the author's view such an appeal may still proceed since s 99(1) makes reference to the applicant having also duly made an alternative application. The entitlement to appeal under s 21(1) includes the right to appeal against a 'decision . . . refusing to grant a new justices' licence'. It remains the case that the original application was refused, albeit a subsequent alternative application has been granted. If an appeal against the original refusal succeeded, presumably the Crown Court would be prepared to accept the surrender of the alternative Part IV licence.

PART IV LICENCES

2.88   As indicated elsewhere, a Part IV licence is one which is granted as a restaurant licence or residential licence or residential and restaurant licence. Such licences are described in more detail in chapter 1. The conditions which the Act provides must be attached to each such licence are set out in detail in Part II.

2.89   In relation to Part IV licences the justices do not have the same wide discretion that they enjoy in relation to other on-licences. The grounds upon which such applications may be refused are strictly defined in s 98 and include the following.

(1)   The applicant is not a fit and proper person.

(2)   The premises do not accord with the relevant statutory definition. These are:

(a)   *Restaurant licence* premises adapted and intended to be used for providing the customary main meal at midday and/or evening, with intoxicating liquor being sold to individuals only as an ancillary to a table meal consumed by them on the premises.

(b)   *Residential licence* premises used habitually for providing board and lodging for a consideration, the meals provided including breakfast and at least one other customary main meal. The licence is to provide that intoxicating liquor may be sold or supplied only to residents—or guests whom they are entertaining at their own expense—for consumption on the premises, or off with a meal supplied at the premises (eg a packed lunch).

(c)   *Restaurant and residential licence* one where the premises comply with each of the requirements (a) and (b) above and sales accord with either.

(3)   The premises are not suitable and convenient for use under one of the Part IV licences, because of their character and condition, the nature and extent of the proposed use and (where it applies) the requirement for the operator of a residential licence or a restaurant and residential licence (unless dispensation is given) to provide adequate sitting accommodation in a 'dry' room, or (excluding residential licences) the supply of alcohol as ancillary to a table meal.

(4)   In the case of either a restaurant licence or a restaurant and residential licence that customers are not habitually served with the kinds of (table) meals to which intoxicating liquor might be ancillary.

(5)   There is evidence of specific breaches occurring within the preceding 12 months[1] or because intoxicating liquor is to be supplied by way of self-service (if the justices consider this to be undesirable).

(6)   In general a large proportion of the persons frequenting the premises are under 18 and unaccompanied.[2]

(7)   The police, fire or local authorities have been denied access to the premises.

[1]   Section 48(1)(c).
[2]   Section 98(3)(a) and (b).

2.90   Despite this comprehensive list, it remains the case that a properly presented application for a Part IV licence made on behalf of a suitable applicant in respect of suitable premises ought not to fail. To demonstrate this point, for the three years between 1998 and 2001 (the last period for which statistics are available) fewer than one in every 10 applications heard were unsuccessful, nonetheless double the rate for 1992 to 1995. One can only speculate as to why this is—could it be that courts are now requiring a higher specification for premises, or are more applicants perhaps failing to satisfy them as to their fitness and propriety?

OBJECTING TO LICENCES

2.91   A prospective objector to a licensing application needs to undertake the preparation of his case with the same degree of thoroughness as the applicant, if that objection is to have a reasonable prospect of success.

2.92   The right of any person to object to an application for the grant of a new justices' licence is well-known. At the earliest opportunity an objector should address the relevant issues, which may include the following.

Policy of licensing committee

2.93   What does the committee's policy document (if any) say upon the matter in issue? Most committees, for example, now specifically discount the traditional criterion of 'need', arguing that market forces should regulate the numbers of licences. A few, however, still require a prospective applicant to prove that there is an element of unsatisfied demand for an additional licence in the area.

Planning permission

2.94   Is planning permission required and, if so, has it been granted for the proposed use? If it is still outstanding, most committees will be reluctant to hear an application, even if it is for a provisional grant. In an excellent commentary upon the matters generally appearing in policy documents the former editor of *Paterson's Licensing Acts*, the late J N Martin OBE, expressed his disapproval of this practice, which is, unfortunately, still widespread. Most committees do however recognise now that they should not thereafter venture into areas which are properly the province of the planning authority.

Restrictive covenants

2.95   Inquiries may reveal the existence of a covenant affecting the land. Again, some committees will be reluctant to proceed with an application for a licence until the applicant is in a position to satisfy them that any such licence could lawfully be exercised without further permission or consent. The majority now subscribe to the contrary view, which is that justices should confine the exercise of their discretion to matters more generally regarded as being within their remit, as opposed to arrangements of a private nature between two parties. If the applicant does trade in breach of a covenant it will be for the beneficiary of that covenant to seek to enforce it in the civil courts, where questions as to its nature and extent may well arise.

Parking

2.96   What are the facilities in the area and would the grant of a licence exacerbate any perceived problem, beyond that which would be created by any other occupant within the same 'use class'?

Existing outlets

2.97   Provided the justices' published policies do not wholly discount such factors, consideration should be given to the extent to which existing outlets are meeting public demand in terms of trading hours, quality of service, range of products, etc. Few licensing committees make a practice of paying formal visits to each of the premises within their division and so this knowledge should not be assumed. Note that the committee is not entitled to consider as a factor the extent to which the grant of *this* application may be said to 'open the floodgates' for other similar premises in future. This is a common error.[1]

[1]   See eg *Meade v Brighton Corpn* (1968) 67 LGR 289, DC.

Development of area

2.98   Again, detailed information as to past or anticipated movements in residential/commercial population figures for the locality can be helpful.

Licensing register

2.99   A careful analysis of the register can reveal trends in the issue/ lapse of certain types of licences that had not previously been appreciated.

2.100   In addition to the above, the objector might reasonably regard it as his role, where appropriate, to challenge evidence and assertions advanced by or on behalf of the applicant, to the extent that these are not already being examined critically by the committee or the authorities. In adopting this stance he may in fact be able to assist the justices considerably by virtue of his relevant experience in trading in the locality.

COSTS

2.101   The effect of s 193B of the Act is that the licensing justices *cannot* award costs in respect of an application for a new licence where the premises are, as yet, unlicensed. If, however, the application for a new licence is made so as to vary a condition attaching to an existing licence, which is to be offered for surrender,[1] it will be possible to apply for an order that any unsuccessful objector pay the applicant's costs, or the applicant those of a successful objector.

[1]   *Drury v Scunthorpe Licensing Justices* (1992) 157 JP 401.

2.102   In *Bradford Metropolitan District Council v Booth*[1] the appeal court said that the justices were wrong to rely on the principle that costs follow the event. A magistrates' court has discretion to make such orders as to costs as it thinks just and reasonable both as to the amount of costs to be paid but also as to which party should pay them.

1   (2001) 164 JP 485, DC.

2.103   The police appear to be in a special position in that the Divisional Court has held that, even if unsuccessful in their objection, costs should not be awarded against them if, in the exercise of their public duty to maintain law and order, they were properly representing a reasonable concern that the grant of a licence could give rise to specific abuses of the licensing laws, or perhaps make drunkenness and disorder more likely.[1] Similarly in *Chief Constable of Derbyshire v Goodman and Newton*[2] the Divisional Court concluded that a costs order should not be made against a party discharging a statutory duty unless there was some good reason for doing so. Had the Chief Constable not acted in good faith or if he had run a case without, that might have been a good reason for ignoring the general approach. This approach was followed in *R v Crown Court at Merthyr Tydfil, ex p Chief Constable of Dyfed Powys* and *Chief Constable of the West Midlands Police v Coventry Crown Court and Tubman*[3] where an order for costs made in the Crown Court against the applicant was quashed, as the judge found that the police who had behaved entirely properly at all stages of the proceedings.

[1]   *R v Totnes Licensing Justices, ex p Chief Constable of Devon and Cornwall* (1992) 156 JP 587.
[2]   [2001] LLR 127, DCS.
[3]   [2001] LLR 133, [2001] LLR 144.

2.104   On 11 March 2002 the Court of Appeal held that there was no power to award costs under s 193B against a person who was opposed to the grant of a licence application if the opposition was withdrawn prior to the substantive hearing of the application.[1]

[1]   *R (on the application of Luminar Leisure) v Licensing Justice for the Petty Sessional Division Of North West Essex* [2002] EWCA Civ 414, (2001) 47 LR 23.

AFTER THE HEARING

2.105   If the application has been granted there may be more to do than simply pay the court fee and open up for business! If the case was contested then, as indicated in chapter 1, the licence will not become effective until 21 days have elapsed.[1] If an appeal is brought within that period the licence will not become effective until the appeal has been withdrawn, or determined in the applicant's favour. After the expiry of that period the licence will come 'into force' (subject to any necessity for final order etc) *even if* an unsuccessful objector should subsequently gain leave from the Crown Court to appeal out of time. In such a case the respondent would however be at risk if he or she proceeded with any development of the premises, since there would remain the possibility that the Crown Court might over turn the original decision.

¹ Section 27(2).

2.106 If the application was not contested, or no appeal is brought against any grant, plans may be made for the next stage. Where the application was for existing premises and has been expressed as a full grant, there may be little more to do prior to opening than to ensure that any undertakings given to the licensing committee are complied with and that the licensee's name is displayed in the approved form.¹ If, as will more often be the case, a provisional licence has been granted it will be necessary to consider how and when to apply for a final order.

¹ Section 183 and precedents in Part II.

FINAL ORDERS

2.107 As noted elsewhere, a provisional licence does not require renewal and will continue indefinitely unless the licensing justices have made it a condition that a final order should be sought within a specified period.

2.108 Within 12 months of any grant, the holder of an outline provisional licence, however, must apply for it to be affirmed,¹ failing which the licence will become void. If an appeal is lodged against the original grant time does not begin to run until the appeal is disposed of.

¹ Section 6(5)(b).

2.109 The licensing committee will be obliged to affirm any outline provisional grant if satisfied that the premises, when completed in accordance with the plans deposited, will be fit and convenient for their purpose. Conditions may not be added to a licence at the affirmation stage.

2.110 The Act does not fix a notice period in respect of an application for a final order. Generally, licensing committees require notice to be given at least 14 or even 21 days in advance of the transfer sessions. As usual, the policy document should be checked for any indication on this point. When giving notice of the intended application to the licensing justices it is prudent also to serve the police and the fire authority. Some committees require service upon each of the authorities served with notice of the original application.

2.111 If the proposed layout of the premises has been modified in any way then the alterations should be approved, ideally before the work commences.[1] Frequently that is not possible, as where the alteration is the consequence of some unforeseen difficulty arising during the course of the construction. In that event, the licensee may be obliged to invite the licensing committee to consent to the modified plans at the same time as it is asked to *declare the provisional grant final*.

[1]   The application is made under s 6(3). The Act does not specify the notice required. Most committees, however, now ask for at least 21 days' prior notice of such application, with plans being served on each of the statutory authorities. The justices have a discretion to agree to the modification if the premises, as altered, will still be 'fit and convenient for their purpose'.

2.112   It is important to understand that licensing justices are *obliged*[1] to declare a provisional grant final on being satisfied:

(1)   that the premises have been completed in accordance with the plans deposited, or in accordance with those plans with any modifications approved under s 6(3); and

(2)   that the holder of the provisional licence is not disqualified by the Act (or any other Act) from holding, and is in all other respects a fit and proper person to hold, a justices' licence.

[1]   Section 6(4).

2.113   It should be noted that different committees will place their own interpretation upon the words 'have been completed'. Does this merely refer to structural works, or does it extend to fixtures and fittings? In the absence of any indication to the contrary it is only prudent to assume that the premises should, in all respects, be ready to open for trading. Further, difficulties can arise where the premises have not been completed by the date of the committee's pre-hearing inspection, but *are* made ready during the intervening period. Of course, if the committee is satisfied on the evidence that the premises have, indeed, been completed, it ought to grant the final order, but in practice the committee will often wish to re-inspect. In that event the following options arise:

(1)   The application for final order can be adjourned to the next transfer sessions. Since these may not take place before one or two months have elapsed, it may not prove an attractive option for the businessman who is seeking to open at the earliest possible opportunity so as to secure a return upon his investment.

(2)   The committee declares the provisional grant final, but directs that it be held in the court office pending a final inspection by such persons (eg fire officer, environmental health officer etc) as the committee may direct. This is an unofficial, but practical, way of resolving the difficulty.

(3) Apply for a single justice's direction.[1] If it is anticipated that this type of application will be required it is prudent to advise the clerk to the justices of the applicant's intention when listing the application for final order. The Act provides that licensing justices *may* delegate the power to grant a final order to a single licensing justice if they are satisfied that:

(a) the premises are likely to be completed before the next licensing sessions; and

(b) the holder of the provisional licence is a fit and proper person.

In practical terms, the applicant will need to satisfy the committee, either by producing appropriate documents or by oral evidence, that the premises will indeed be completed before the due date. That having been done he will then need to persuade the committee to exercise its discretion to appoint a single justice. As regards the latter, factors relevant to the decision might include the extent of the likely delay if the application is refused, and the measure of the probable financial loss.[2]

Note that a significant disadvantage of this procedure (as with the power of clerks to grant licence transfers as an administrative act) is that single justices are not at the same time conferred with authority to grant s 34 permits for fruit machines, s 68 certificates, final orders on provisional special hours certificates or children's certificates. Consequently, although premises may become in this way authorised to sell intoxicating liquor they will not be able through this means to take advantage of those ancillary permits and certificates which may be crucial to the success of the venture.

(4) As an alternative to the above, the committee may be prepared to adjourn the case to a special interim sessions, for the consideration of this and any other application that might not have been dealt with at the transfer sessions owing to procedural defects or lack of time.

[1] Section 6(4A).
[2] *R v City of London Licensing Justices, ex p Mecca Leisure* (1988) 153 JP 193.

CONSIDERATIONS FOLLOWING APPLICATION FOR NEW LICENCES

2.114 There are three principal avenues of appeal open to anyone aggrieved by the decision of licensing justices to grant or refuse to grant a new on- or off-licence, or to impose conditions upon the former: reapplication, or an appeal to the Crown Court or to the High Court. The choice of which to follow will depend upon a multiplicity of factors, including:

(a)   potential improvements to evidence (by applicants or objectors);

(b)   mistakes as to law;

(c)   anticipated delay;

(d)   costs.

Each of these factors will now be considered, where appropriate, in relation to the three options.

Reapplication

2.115   Before proceeding automatically to appeal, consideration should be given to the merits of submitting a further application. Other than in the case of special removals[1] there is no statutory restriction on the submission of 'repeat' applications. In *R v City of London Licensing Justices, ex p Davys of London Wine Merchants Ltd*[2] the High Court held that licensing justices erred in law in refusing to hear a renewed application for the grant of an on-licence (following their earlier refusal to grant) and in requiring a change of circumstances to be shown by the applicant. Accordingly, if there are grounds for believing that the justices may have arrived at a different conclusion if certain aspects of the application had been modified, it could be worthwhile to submit a renewed application. This course of action will almost certainly be both quicker and cheaper than any appeal—which will, of course, remain an option if the move is unsuccessful.

[1]   Section 15(6).
[2]   (1985) 149 JP 555.

Crown Court

2.116   An appeal to the Crown Court against a refusal to grant is commenced by the appellant serving notice of appeal within 21 days[1] upon the following persons:

(1)   the chief executive to the licensing justices (justices are respondents);[2]

(2)   any person who opposed the grant (objector(s) is/are respondent(s)).[3]

If the appeal is brought by an objector who is aggrieved by a decision to *grant*, the notice is served upon the applicant (who is technically the only respondent) as well as the chief executive to the licensing justices.

[1]   The court has a discretion to give leave to appeal out of time.

2   Section 22(1).
3   Section 22(3).

2.117 The notice of appeal must be in writing and set out the grounds for the appeal.[1] Upon receipt of the notice of appeal the chief executive to the licensing justices is obliged to transmit the notice to the appropriate officer of the Crown Court. Usually the notice is accompanied by copies of the papers lodged with the application.

1   See Crown Court Rules 1982, Sch 3, Part III.

2.118 The time taken for licensing appeals to come before the Crown Court varies considerably across the country. One particular difficulty which presented itself historically to Crown Court listing officers was that the court hearing the appeal needed to comprise a judge sitting with four licensing justices, two of whom came from the petty sessional division against which the appeal was brought, as required by the Crown Court Rules 1982, r 3(2). In *R (on the application of the Chief Constable of Lancashire) v Crown Court at Preston*[1] it was argued by the appellant that such a court so constituted could not be seen to provide a fair hearing by an impartial and independent tribunal, as required by Article 6(1) of the European Convention on Human Rights. Upholding the decision of the Crown Court judge the Administrative Court applied the 'blue pencil test' to the provision so that the words 'and two (but not more than two) of whom are justices for the petty sessions area in which the premises are situated' were severed from r 3(2). The Act also provides that a justice shall not act in the hearing of an appeal from any decision in which he took part.[2] Further, the High Court has indicated that justices who have been involved in the recent past in applications concerning the premises should not become involved if a reasonable and fair-minded observer would conclude in all the circumstances that a just hearing of the appeal would not be possible.[3] Typically, any such appeal might take between two and four months to come before the Crown Court, although in all cases inquiries should be made of the listing office to ascertain any current delays. If it does appear that there will be undue delay in convening the Crown Court for the hearing of the appeal the judge may direct that the hearing should take place with only two justices. Indeed, if the parties appearing at the hearing of the appeal agree, the judge may even sit without one or both of those two remaining justices.

1   [2001] EWHC Admin 928, (2002) 48 LR 17.
2   Section 22(7).
3   *R v Crown Court Bristol, ex p Cooper* [1990] 2 All ER 193, CA.

2.119 Once the hearing has commenced, the withdrawal or absence of one or more of the justices will not cause the proceedings to be discontinued.

2.120   If the appellant abandons the appeal prior to the Crown Court hearing, the respondent (the party who originally opposed the grant and is named in the notice of appeal) is entitled to make application to the magistrates' court for an order in respect of any costs that he might have incurred in preparing to resist the appeal.[1]

[1]   Magistrates' Court Act 1980, s 109(1).

2.121   The appeal in the Crown Court is by way of a full rehearing, there being no obligation upon the Crown Court to have regard to the evidence before the justices, or the reason for their decision. The appellant may raise all issues of fact and law in his attempt to persuade the Crown Court to reverse the licensing committee's decision.

2.122   Appeals against the *grant* of a justices' licence are relatively unusual, since it is generally thought unlikely that the Crown Court will be minded to interfere if local licensing justices have taken the view that there *is* a requirement in the area for the proposed outlet. Such an appeal is most likely to be brought if the aggrieved objector can argue that the committee was misled as to some material fact. As indicated earlier, the effect of an objection against the grant of a licence is to delay the operation of that licence until such time as the appeal has been withdrawn or determined in the respondent's (ie proposed licensee's) favour.

2.123   If the decision is confirmed (ie no licence is granted) the Crown Court may order the appellant to pay the costs of any objector who appears and *must* order him to indemnify the justices against any costs that they have incurred as a consequence of the appeal. If the appeal against the refusal of a justices' licence is allowed, an order for costs may be made against any person who also appeared in the Crown Court to oppose the appeal.

2.124   Note that the appellant will not be ordered by the Crown Court to pay costs if he abandons the appeal in accordance with the terms of r 11 of the Crown Court Rules 1982, giving notice to the chief executive to the licensing justices, the appropriate officer of the Crown Court and any other party to the appeal, not later than the third day before the date fixed for the hearing of the appeal.

2.125   An appeal to the Crown Court will be appropriate if the appellant feels that he has a good case on matters of both law and fact, which is not likely to be significantly diminished when the matter comes to be reheard. The procedure is relatively quick and if the applicant has a good case on the merits there ought to be a reasonable prospect of success.

High Court

2.126   Given that the Crown Court has jurisdiction to deal with matters of both law and fact, why consider an application to the Divisional Court (part of the High Court), which will deal only with matters of law? The principal justification for selecting this route must be that the appellant or his advisers take the view that the licensing committee has made an error of law which (perhaps in the absence of any clear authority on the point in question) is likely to be repeated in the Crown Court. Further, the view may be taken that, on the facts as they found them, the licensing justices effectively had no alternative but to grant or refuse the application, as the case may be. If the High Court shares that opinion then it is probable that the court will direct the justices to determine the application accordingly. On the other hand, were the unsuccessful applicant to pursue his remedy in the Crown Court, he might find that his case appears less convincing *on its merits* at the rehearing, perhaps because the objectors have taken the opportunity to improve their own position. Further, the Crown Court might simply exercise its discretion and refuse to reverse the justices' decision.

2.127   It is not within the scope of this essentially practical guide to deal with the intricacies of the statutory and prerogative powers available to the High Court. They may, however, be summarised briefly under (a) case stated, and (b) judicial review.

Case stated

2.128   Under this procedure any party to proceedings before a magistrates' court can require the justices to state a case for the consideration of the High Court.[1] The procedure is initiated by the applicant writing to the chief executive to the licensing justices within 21 days of the decision complained about, identifying the questions of law on which the opinion of the High Court is sought. The Magistrates' Court Rules 1981 set out a strict timetable for, first, the justices to respond with a draft case (after the applicant has provided a recognisance, if so required). Thereafter, time is allowed for each party to review the position. At the end of this procedure, the chief executive to the justices sends the applicant the case, duly signed by the justices, for lodgment with the High Court.

[1]   Magistrates' Court Act 1980, s 111.

2.129   Unless a direction for an expedited hearing is made, it is likely that the hearing will not take place for many months. Again, inquiries should be made at an early stage with the High Court.

2.130   The hearing in the High Court will confine itself to the facts as stated by the justices. Generally, the appellant will be represented by counsel. The justices may also be represented. If not, then the High Court may appoint an *amicus curiae* to argue matters of law from an independent position. The court may reverse, confirm or amend the justices' decision, or simply express its opinion upon the stated case. It may *not* direct the justices to rehear the application.

2.131   Note that the Crown Court cannot be asked to state a case for the consideration of the High Court, even though its decision may be challenged by way of judicial review, in appropriate circumstances.

Judicial review

2.132   Judicial review is one of the High Court's prerogative powers now governed by the CPR 1998, Pt 54 . The remedy can be used against an inferior court, tribunal or other body (including licensing justices and the Crown Court) where that body has made an error of law, is in breach of the rules of natural justice, has taken into account some legally irrelevant material or failed to take into account some legally relevant material, or has otherwise come to a decision or acted in such a way that no reasonable body of that sort could or should have reached or done (this last is sometimes called '*Wednesbury*' unreasonableness, after the decision in *Associated Provincial Picture Houses v Wednesbury Corpn*).[1] If the High Court finds that licensing justices or the Crown Court have dealt with a hearing in a manner which may broadly be described as contrary to natural justice, for whatever reason, it may, in its discretion, exercise its power to grant one of the following orders:

(1)   a quashing order (formerly *certiorari*), which quashes an order of the inferior court made in breach of the rules of natural justice, or a decision which is self-evidently wrong in law or which the inferior body had no power to make;

(2)   a mandatory order (formerly *mandamus*), which directs justices to comply with their statutory duty and is appropriate where, for example, licensing justices are disinclined to comply with their duty to determine an application as provided by statute;

(3)   a prohibitory order (formerly *prohibition*), which will, as its name suggests, prohibit justices from proceeding in a certain manner. The remedy is available during the course of proceedings where there is evidence that the justices are likely to act in excess of their powers.

---

[1]   [1948] 1 KB 223.

2.133 Before proceeding with any application for judicial review the applicant must, within three months of the decision complained of, apply to the High Court for leave. If leave is granted the case proceeds by way of notice of motion. The licensing justices may appear or, alternatively, respond by way of affidavit.

2.134 If the High Court takes the view that the justices ought to have been asked to state a case, or considers that in all the circumstances it would be inappropriate to grant judicial review, it may exercise its discretion to refuse the application for relief.[1]

---

[1]   See *R v Birmingham City Council, ex p McKenna* (1991) 156 LG Rev 486 and RSC 1981, Ord 53.

CHAPTER 3

INTERIM AUTHORITIES, TRANSFER OF LICENCES ETC, AND RENEWALS

TRANSFERS

3.01 Since the managers of licensed premises (and particularly of public houses in the wake of the Report of the Monopolies and Mergers Commission[1] and the Beer Orders[2]) relocate with relative frequency, by far the greatest number of applications coming before most licensing committees relate to the transfer of justices' licences.

[1] 'The Supply of Beer: a report on the supply of beer for retail sale in the United Kingdom' (Cm 651).
[2] Supply of Beer (Tied Estates) Order 1989, SI 1989/2390 and Supply of Beer (Loan Ties, Licensed Premises and Wholesale Prices) Order 1989, SI 1989/2258.

3.02 A transfer is required when the sale of alcohol at premises ceases to take place under the authority of the person whose name appears on the justices' licence. Any person who sells alcohol without that authority will be guilty of the offence of selling or exposing for sale by retail intoxicating liquor without holding a justices' licence authorising the sale of that liquor.[1] Every other occupier of the premises who is proved to have been a party, or consented, to any such sale will also be guilty of an offence.[2] The maximum penalty for a first offence is six months' imprisonment and/or a fine not exceeding level 4.[3] A second conviction for the same offence may lead to the guilty party being disqualified from holding a justices' licence for a period of up to five years; a third or subsequent conviction could give rise to a lifetime ban.

[1] Section 160(1)(a).
[2] Section 160(2).
[3] A maximum of £2,500 at the time of going to press.

3.03 For reasons which are self-evident, it is therefore important to ensure at all times that a person selling intoxicating liquor is duly authorised to effect that sale, either as, or on behalf of, the licensee.

3.04 Anyone who has sat in court listening to transfer applications will know that they are not infrequently adjourned or refused for one or more of the following reasons:

(a) failure to prove service of notices;

(b) non-compliance with the committee's policy document (eg furnishing references—see below);

(c) insufficient experience of applicant;

(d) ignorance of licensing laws—usually failure to gain a National Licensees Certificate;

(e) previous convictions.

Of course, there will always be instances where the application ought properly to be dismissed. However, in the majority of the cases outlined above, appropriate preparation and advice tendered before the hearing would have given the application a reasonable prospect of success.

Nature of transfer

3.05 The first matter to be understood is that a transfer of a justices' licence is, like a renewal or a removal, technically the grant of a new licence.[1] The significance of this fact becomes apparent when it is appreciated that the humble transfer has always been thought capable at a stroke of negating a previous order revoking a licence (where an appeal against revocation has kept that licence alive), or of acting in certain circumstances as an invaluable alternative to a renewal. However, some doubt has been cast upon this belief by a recent decision of the Administrative Court[2] when it was held that, in the particular (and somewhat involved) circumstances of the case a renewal which replaced a licence which was subject to potential revocation, created a licence which was subject to the same potential revocation. It is very possible that the courts could hold at some stage in the future that the same principle should apply to transfers as well.[3]

---

[1] Section 3(2).
[2] *Ryan, Hulme and Henricksen v Rees* [2001] EWHC Admin 482, [2001] All ER (D) 181 (Jan), Latham LJ.
[3] Section 26(1)(c).

The applicant

3.06 It is not the case that *any* person can simply apply for the transfer of a justices' licence. Section 8 of the Act is quite specific as to who may apply. Its principal provisions are set out below in the order that they most commonly arise. As ever, the reader should refer to the Act (reproduced in Part II of this book) if there is any doubt in respect of a particular case. Transfers may be granted to the new tenant or occupier of the licensed premises in the following cases.

(1) The purchaser, lessee or new occupier of premises—where the licensee or his representatives have vacated or are about to vacate the premises.[1] Note that by ceasing to carry on the business the licensee is deemed to have given up occupation for the purposes of this provision.[2] A provisional licence may also be transferred by this means.[3] The arrangement applies both to situations where the licensee has voluntarily vacated the premises and also to those instances where he has been compelled to do so.[4]

(2) Following the death of the licensee (his personal representatives may also apply).

(3) Where the licensee becomes incapable of carrying out the business (his assignees may also apply).

(4) Where the licensee has been adjudged bankrupt, entered into a voluntary arrangement or is subject to a deed of arrangement (the trustee of the estate or the supervisor of the voluntary arrangement may also apply).

(5) Where the *occupier* of the premises (ie not necessarily the licensee) has deliberately failed to apply for the renewal of the licence prior to vacating.

(6) Where the owner of the premises or his nominee has been granted a protection order under s 10(3) (ie where the licence has been forfeited or the licensee disqualified), in which case the holder of the protection order may apply for the transfer not later than the second licensing sessions after the date of the making of the order.[5]

---

[1] Section 8(1)(d).
[2] Section 8(2).
[3] Section 8(3).
[4] *R v Portsmouth Licensing Justices, ex p Walker and Harmes* (1993) Licensing Review (January), QBD.
[5] Section 8(1)(f).

Qualities of applicant

3.07   As previously indicated, the licensing committee is empowered to transfer a licence only to persons whom it regards as fit and proper.[1] The committee may not, for example, grant a licence to an unfit person, for the purposes of a subsequent transfer to another more fit, merely because it is convenient to do so.[2] Neither should it grant a full licence to an individual who neither has nor intends to have any involvement in the premises, but is merely acting as a 'front' for an unsuitable company or person.[3] The following guidelines emerge from both the law and practice as applied to transfers.

[1]   Section 3(1).
[2]   *R v Woodhouse (Leeds Justices)* [1906] 2 KB 501 at 531, per Fletcher Moulton LJ.
[3]   See *R v Crown Court at Preston, ex p Cooper* (22 November 1989, unreported).

Disqualification

3.08   If the applicant is legally disqualified from holding a licence there is little that can be done. The categories of persons so disqualified under s 9 were considered in the preceding chapter. Persons may also be disqualified as a consequence of offences committed under other provisions of the Act (eg s 160—see para **3.02** or, in respect of Part IV licences only, s 100). In practice, it is extremely unusual to come across a licensee who has been so disqualified.

Convictions

3.09   Unfortunately, it is *not* unusual for a licensee to fall into this category. Indeed, it is frequently (and perhaps with some justification) argued that, in certain very difficult locations, only those who understand and are able to deal with their more robust customers will, in reality, be able to manage a public house in such an area, without fear or favour and according to the law. Of course, there are a potentially an almost infinite number of combinations of applicants, convictions, areas, licensing committees and so forth. It is truly a case of taking each application on its merits, but the following general rules emerge.

(1)   *Disclosure* An applicant is far more likely to receive sympathetic treatment by the police if he honestly and openly discloses his previous convictions before they are revealed by a search of the Criminal Records Office database. Neither will his solicitor or barrister thank him if such matters are revealed only at the doors of the court!

(2) *'Spent' convictions* Although the Rehabilitation of Offenders Act 1974 does apply, s 7(3) of that Act entitles licensing justices to exercise their discretion and have regard to spent convictions where they consider that it would be in the interests of justice for them so to do.[1] Of course, it will be difficult for the committee to determine the issue until it has seen details of those convictions,[2] and at that stage the applicant's advocate may feel that more will be gained by a full and frank explanation than by an attempt to invite the justices to disregard those convictions. If, however, justices unreasonably decide to admit particular spent convictions and then refuse a transfer, that decision is likely to be quashed by the High Court following judicial review.

(3) *Nature of convictions* As with all matters, attitudes vary from division to division. Some committees will invariably refuse transfer applications submitted by those with a previous conviction for a drink/driving offence, while others will almost always grant similar applications provided that the period of disqualification has ended. Much, of course, will depend upon the nature of the representations that the police make in relation to the offence. Where it is known that the police will object on the grounds of the applicant's previous convictions, which may be for relatively minor recent offences, or a string of substantial matters followed by a period of good conduct, the case should be prepared with particular care. The advocate should consider the circumstances of those offences, the applicant's subsequent good behaviour, his career prospects, family circumstances and the likely consequences of the present application being granted or refused. Wherever possible, independent witnesses should be called as to the applicant's general good character and his ability properly to carry out the functions of a licensee. If such persons will not or cannot attend court the committee may be persuaded to entertain written references, particularly if these have been made available to the police for verification some days in advance of the hearing.

---

[1]   See para **2.57**ff for further discussion on this point.
[2]   See *Adamson v Waveney District Council* [1997] 2 All ER 898, QBD in which the Divisional Court gave detailed guidelines to courts and advocates dealing with the disclosure of spent convictions.

Bankruptcy

3.10   This does not automatically disqualify a person from retaining or being granted a justices' licence. The circumstances of the bankruptcy may, however, be taken to reflect upon his fitness. The adjudication may also be considered to have some bearing upon his ability to conduct the business in the future.

Age

3.11   Again, there is no specific provision in the Act as to the minimum (or maximum) permitted age of a licensee, although it is clear that a licence may not in practice be granted to persons under 18 in respect of either an off-licence or off-sales department,[1] or an on-licence with a bar.[2] The policies of some committees suggest that a person under 21 is unlikely to be regarded as suitable. Otherwise, youth is technically no obstacle; indeed it is sometimes argued that the younger licensee is better able to judge the ages of those who might attempt to purchase intoxicating liquor while still minors.

[1]   Section 171A.
[2]   Section 170.

Status

3.12   Because of the very difficulties indicated above following the sudden departure or dismissal of a sole licensee, many breweries or other multiple operators of on- and off-licence premises make a practice of arranging for the majority of the licences attaching to their premises to be held in the joint names of the manager and the person to whom he answers on operational matters. In certain areas this will not be possible, as some committees insist that there be only one licensee in respect of each premises. Others, however, positively favour a second licensee since they view it as ensuring that a more senior person within the owning company will be concerned to see that the licensing laws are properly observed. Other committees take the view that such arrangements should be condoned only as long as the number of licences held by the senior person does not exceed a certain figure (typically eight to fifteen).

3.13   If the business operates during extended hours and for more than five days a week, certain committees will insist that a second, third, fourth or even fifth licensee should be added so as to ensure that there is always a licensee on the premises when intoxicating liquor is being sold. While that may be a matter for the committee's discretion, it is suggested that the inflexible application of such a policy can quite unnecessarily increase the financial burden upon small businesses, for which it is not viable to employ persons of assistant manager status. Certainly the law does not require a licensee to be present on the premises at all times that intoxicating liquor is being sold, as long as he has properly authorised some person to carry out that function on his behalf. This view has been supported by a decision of the High Court which, in the instant case, reversed decisions of the justices and the Crown Court requiring particular licences to be held by multiple licensees.[1] It is, of course, in the licensee's interest to ensure that the person delegated is fully aware of his duties and responsibilities under the law, since it is likely that the former will suffer a conviction if a breach occurs and, in certain circumstances, he is unable to prove that he exercised all due diligence to avoid the commission of the offence (see chapter 6).

[1]   *R (on the application of Thompsett) v Croydon Crown Court* [2000] All ER (D) 1245, (2001) 46 LR 32, QBD.

3.14   In practice, although one can invite the committee to deal with each application on its merits (as indeed it is bound to do by law), in the majority of cases the committee's policy is likely to be implemented. It is obviously essential that individuals owning or operating licensed premises, or contemplating a transfer application, should be fully aware of the relevant licensing committee's policies in relation to the number and status of licensees. The recommendation of the Good Practice Guide is that the number of persons to appear on a licence should be primarily a matter for the operator and that committees should not specify such matters in advance of a hearing.

Experience and training

3.15   This has rapidly become *the* major issue for many justices. For many years certain committees have encouraged or insisted upon new licensees, or licensees new to their division, attending brewery or other recognised training courses. After a pilot scheme run in Coventry, the Lord Chancellor's Department extended the scheme to cover 12 nominated divisions around the country. Now the majority of new licensees are required to obtain a so-called National Licensee Certificate before applying for the transfer of a justices' licence. Accordingly it behoves the intending applicant to ascertain at an early stage whether the committee concerned has any particular policy concerning attendance at training courses. Owners of independent off-licences or grocers may not have access to a suitable training course. In that event an acceptable alternative may be evidence that the applicant has seen a training video produced by the Portman Group (2d Wimpole Street, London W1M 7AA, telephone: 0207 499 1010).

Fitness of applicant

3.16   This form has no bearing upon the physical health of the applicant(s), but rather his or her suitability to hold a justices' licence. It is invariably now required by the justices.The form appears in the Precedents section at the end of this work.

References

3.17   Certain committees require two or three references to be either lodged with the police substantially in advance of the hearing of the transfer application or, alternatively, produced in court. Again, inquiries should be made of the clerk's office as to any such requirement.

Contracts of employment

3.18   Few committees require these to be produced. If so it will be mentioned in the court's Practice Directions distibuted following receipt of the transfer notice.

Company resolutions

3.19   Evidence is sometimes required that the employer of the applicant has authorised him to make the application.

Limited companies

3.20   Technically, a company may be regarded as a fit and proper 'person', although such findings are almost unheard of in the context of justices' licences.

Deed of appointment of receiver

3.21   If applicable, and not already submitted at the hearing of any protection order application, the original deed (or a certified copy) should be lodged with the clerk's office.

Timing of transfer

3.22   Caution is needed if there has already been a transfer of the licence within the preceding year, since the Act entitles licensing justices to regulate the minimum period that should, in ordinary circumstances, elapse between transfer applications.[1] Where such regulations have been made (specifying, typically, that an application should not be made within six months of an earlier one), the information should appear in the committee's policy document. In an appropriate case the rule may be dispensed with—where, for example, the application arises owing to the wholly unforeseen illness or incapacity of the existing licensee. Procedures in relation to such policies vary, with some committees requiring an applicant who seeks a dispensation to submit a letter in advance of the hearing (or even, sometimes, before the application is lodged) setting out the grounds on which such a concession is sought. Other committees make it clear that where the application arises following the premature departure of a management company it is the *owner* of the premises who should be asked to explain why the rule should not apply.

1   Section 8(4).

3.23   Generally, a transfer will take effect when the application is granted. However, it should be noted that justices do have the power to specify that the transfer is not to come into effect until a given date.[1]

1   Section 26(2).

3.24   Somewhat strangely, a licence may be 'transferred' even though it has ceased to exist at the date of the hearing. This unusual provision applies in relation to applications made following: the illness or other infirmity of the licensee,[1] the occupier's deliberate failure to apply for renewal prior to departure,[2] or where the owner or his nominee seeks to follow up a protection order granted as a consequence of the forfeiture of the licence or the disqualification of the licensee.[3] The second of these can prove particularly useful when a departing licensee seeks to make mischief upon his departure at renewal time.

1   Section 8(1)(b).
2   Section 8(1)(e).
3   Section 8(1)(f).

Notices

3.25   A form of notice is set out in Part II of this book. The notice needs to be served not less than 21 days prior to the relevant transfer sessions (ie if the hearing is on a Wednesday, notice must be received by the Tuesday three weeks earlier).[1] Service should be effected upon each of the following:

(a)   chief executive to the licensing justices;

(b)   chief officer of police;

(c)   proper local authority;

(d)   town/parish/community council (if any);

(e)   existing licensee(s).

For a detailed commentary upon the identification of the relevant authorities, see chapter 2.

¹   See chapter 2 for further information on service of documents.

3.26   Often it is not possible to locate the whereabouts of the existing licensee, in which case it is suggested that the notice should be served at his last known address. Generally this will be acceptable to the committee.

3.27   The transfer notice is *not* required to be served upon the fire authority, nor need it be displayed on the premises or advertised in the local press.

3.28   Notices should be dispatched in good time to ensure that they are received not less than 21 days before the hearing. Although, under the Interpretation Act 1978, notices sent by ordinary first class post will be deemed to have been received on the second day after posting, where it is proved that they were *actually* received after that date and 'out of time', Sch 2 to the Act, which sets out the procedure in such cases, will not have been complied with. Reference should then be made to para 7 of that Schedule, which entitles the justices to specify the terms upon which the non-compliance might be remedied. See para **2.32** for further comment upon this point.

3.29   Whatever the additional requirements of the committee, as set out above, the following documents should, wherever possible, be lodged in advance of the hearing:

(a)   certificate of service;

(b)   statutory fee (£30.00 at the time of going to press);

(c)   consent of the existing licensee(s).

3.30   If the consent of the existing licensee has not been forthcoming, its absence should never be fatal since there will often be circumstances in which the existing licensee is incapable of or unwilling to consent to the transfer of the licence into the name of a successor. This difficulty is considered in further detail at paras **3.48** and **3.79**.

3.31   Note that where the premises have the benefit of amusement machines for gaming (or 'AWPs' or 'fruit machines'), the application should be made at the same time for a permit in the name(s) of the proposed licencee(s), since any existing permit will cease to have effect upon the transfer of the justices' licence.¹

¹   Gaming Act 1968, Sch 9, para 20(1)(a).

Preparation

3.32 Where the transfer application is being submitted on behalf of an experienced licensee it is fair to say that a great deal of preparation for the hearing itself should not be required. In cases, however, where the applicant has not previously held a justices' licence or, perhaps, has not had much experience in licensed premises, it is suggested that it is the duty of that person's solicitor to ensure that the applicant is made fully aware not only of the requirements of the law in relation to the particular type of licence that he will be holding, but also the general format of the court hearing.

3.33 The detailed requirements of the law in relation to every aspect of the proposed business are, again, too numerous and lengthy to set out in this brief chapter. (The intending licensee might be well advised to invest in one of the available guides to the conduct of licensed premises.) In any event, the advocate should take it upon himself to ensure that the applicant is able to answer the following questions, which are those most frequently raised during the course of transfer applications.

(1) Is the applicant a 'disqualified person'? (The applicant should be referred to the provisions of s 9 and asked to confirm that none of them applies to him.)

(2) Is the applicant aware of the categories of persons to whom intoxicating liquor may *not* be sold? Principally, these comprise:

  (a) Persons under 18—if either the licensee or his staff are in any doubt whatsoever, proper identification should be sought, in the form of a document bearing the applicant's date of birth, photograph and signature. The 'Prove-It' scheme run by the Portman Group was set up to cater for young persons who might not otherwise conveniently have access to such identification. If, for whatever reason, doubt still remains in the minds of the licensee or his employees, the sale should be refused without hesitation.[1]

  (b) Drunken persons—it is an offence to sell intoxicating liquor to a drunken person and also for the licensee to permit drunkenness or any violent, quarrelsome or riotous conduct on licensed premises.[2]

  (c) Police constables on duty—the offence is committed when a licensee permits any constable while on duty to remain on the licensed premises (except for the purpose of the execution of his duty) or to purchase or receive any liquor *or* refreshment, save where authorised by his senior officer.

(3)   What are the 'permitted hours'?

   (a)   *off-licences*

      Monday to Saturday: 8.00 am to 11.00 pm

      Good Friday (only): 8.00 am to 10.30 pm

      Christmas Day: 12 noon to 3.00 pm; 7.00 pm to 10.30 pm

      Sunday: 10.00 am to 10.30 pm.[3]

   (b)   *on-licences*

      Monday to Saturday: 11.00 am (or, at the justices' discretion, any time after 10.00 am) to 11.00 pm

      Good Friday and Sunday: 12 noon to 10.30 pm.[3]

      Christmas Day: 12 noon to 3 pm; 7.00 pm to 10.30 pm.

Note that the commencement time for on-licences on weekdays may be brought forward from 11.00 am to a time not earlier than 10.00 am if the licensing justices have so directed at their Brewster Sessions (in February of the particular year).

The prospective licensee will be expected to know that some 20 minutes' 'drinking-up time' may be allowed after the end of permitted hours, save where the liquor was supplied for consumption as an ancillary to a meal, in which case the period is extended to 30 minutes.[4]

Where the premises have the benefit of additional hours under a s 68 (supper hours) certificate, s 70 (extended hours) order or a s 77 (special hours) certificate, the licensee will be expected to know both the revised ending time and the special rules applicable to each of these provisions, which are dealt with elsewhere in this book.

(4)   Conditional on-licence—if the existing licence is subject to conditions, undertakings (eg old on-licence—see below) or assurances, the applicant will be expected to be familiar with these, particularly since the committee may ask him to repeat any undertakings or assurances.

[1]   Breach of this provision is an offence under s 169.
[2]   Section 172(2) and (3).
[3]   Extended by the Licensing (Sunday Hours) Act 1995 which came into force on 6 August 1995. Note that 'large' shops may still not trade on Christmas Day when it falls on a Sunday, or on Easter Day, under the Sunday Trading Act 1994.
[4]   Section 63(1)(b).

Hearing of the application

3.34   Increasingly transfers are dealt with in the absence of the applicant[1] so long as all the paperwork is in order and there is no objection to the application. As usual, regard should be had to the committee's policy document.

¹   Schedule 2, para 8.

3.35 Further, the clerk to the licensing justices *may* now grant a transfer (or an interim authority—see para **3.97**) on behalf of the justices and outside the licensing sessions if the applicant is *either* an existing licensee *or* has held a licence within the preceding three years. It should be understood that this is a discretionary power; the clerk may refer the matter to the justices if he considers there are circumstances which make it desirable.¹

¹   Section 193AA, introduced by the Deregulation (Licence Transfers) Order 1998, SI 1998/114.

3.36 Note that the clerk will not technically have power to grant a s 34 permit for fruit machines and so if the justices' licence is transferred in advance of such a permit then any gaming permit currently in force will cease to have effect until a new permit can be granted at the next licensing sessions.¹

¹   See Gaming Act 1968, Sch 9, para 1(a) and para 20(1)(a).

3.37 Most licensing committees commence their sittings at 10.00 or 10.30 am, although there are a few that sit earlier and some that do not start until 2.00 pm. Since transfers and occasional permissions are generally taken first on the list, applicants should ensure that they arrive at court early on the day. Usually they will be required to advise the usher of their presence. He may be able to confirm whether anyone else connected with the application has already arrived.

3.38 Having dealt with any final details concerning the application, the parties will wait in the courtroom or hall for their case to be called. This interval may also help to prepare the nervous or inexperienced applicant for what is to follow.

3.39 When the case is called the applicant or his advocate may briefly explain the circumstances in which the application comes to be made, if these are in any way unusual. If not, it may be expedient simply to deal immediately with the evidence. Most committees require applicants to take an oath according to their religious persuasions or beliefs; some do not. If the case is first on the list, inquiries can be made beforehand of the clerk to the justices.

3.40 The applicant will first state his full name, address and occupation and then, typically, deal with the following matters:

(1)   his experience: if experienced in licensed trade, this will cover the nature of his interest in the premises or employee status, number of years' experience, details of premises recently managed and licences held, confirmation that he is fully aware of the duties of a licensee (especially as regards young persons), and (particularly if a joint licensee) the extent of his attendance at the premises; if not experienced in licensed trade, he should state the nature of his interest in the premises or employee status, deal (briefly) with his previous business experience, give details of any previous bar work (often part time) and of training received and/or to be undertaken, confirm his awareness of the law relating to persons to whom liquor may not be sold and to the permitted hours, and (particularly if a joint licensee) show the extent of his attendance at the premises;

(2)   the date of any protection order granted and confirmation that no difficulties have been encountered during the intervening period;

(3)   establish that he is not a disqualified person.

3.41   The applicant might then be asked questions by objectors (if any) as well as by the police and the fire or local authority, even when they are not objecting. The police may wish to ask the applicant about some detail of his previous experience, or whether he appreciates the nature of the business he is taking over or of the area he is moving into. Any previous convictions may be shown to the applicant for his verification and then handed to the committee.[1] Very occasionally either the fire officer and the representative from the local authority (most likely the environmental health officer) may wish to ask the applicant some questions about the present state of the premises and his intentions in that context. Although the licensing committee has a wide discretion in relation to transfers, it has been held that, in connection with such applications, objections relating to the state of premises may be entertained only to the extent that the applicant's intentions in that regard indicate whether he might be a fit and proper person to hold a licence.[2]

[1]   See the note to *Adamson v Waveney District Council* in chapter 2 concerning 'spent' convictions.

[2]   *R v London Borough of Haringey, ex p Sandhu and Sandhu* (1987) 151 JP 696.

3.42   The applicant's advocate may then re-examine upon any of the points raised, if clarification is required. Finally, the licensing committee may wish to put questions to the applicant upon any of these points or, indeed, any other matter that it feels might have a bearing upon his suitability.

3.43   At this stage the advocate should confirm that the chief executive to the justices has already received (as is recommended) a certificate establishing the proper service of notices by post, together with the written consent of the existing licensee(s). Alternatively, the existing licensee(s) can be asked to make himself/themselves known to the committee and formally indicate that he/they have no objections to the present application. The case will then be determined. Four matters should, however, be noted.

Joint names

3.44 If a justices' licence is held in joint names, the transfer application should be submitted in the names of both the new and the continuing licensees. For example, the licence is held at present in the names of Smith, the area manager, and Jones the manager, who is to be replaced by the new manager, Brown. The transfer application should be submitted in the names of Brown and Smith.

Fruit machines

3.45 Where the transfer application relates to on-licensed premises likely to contain fruit machines, inquiries should be made as to whether or not the company responsible for installing those machines will lodge the necessary notices for the grant of a new permit under the Gaming Act 1968, s 34. If not, the necessary notices in Part II should be prepared by the applicant or his representatives and lodged, together with the appropriate fee. Care should also be taken to ask the clerk to the licensing justices *not* to grant the transfer of the justices' licence by way of delegated powers as there will not be the same authority to deal with the s 34 permit, so giving rise to the temporary cessation of the latter (see para **3.34**ff).

3.46 If it is intended to increase the number of machines, inquiries should be made of the clerk's office to establish whether the committee is likely to require additional evidence to be tendered at the hearing in relation to the suitability of the proposed location of, or even the need for, those additional machines. With certain committees this is quite an important issue, particularly where more than two machines are involved. In such cases consideration may be given to the overall size of the premises, the usage of the existing machines, the extent to which any players or queues block doors or passageways and the disturbance caused to individuals frequenting the licensed premises. If the *grant* of the new permit (note that it is not, technically, a transfer) is (as is usually the case) entirely non-contentious the committee should merely be reminded immediately after the transfer application that a new permit is sought.

3.47   Note that machines which pay out the maximum prize (currently £25 from 1 January 2002) in cash, should be located in the bar area of public house, where children under 14 may not generally be admitted.[1]

[1]   Gaming Act 1968, s 34(5A) and Sch 9, para 10A, inserted by the Deregulation (Gaming Machines and Betting Office Facilities) Order 1996, SI 1996/1359.

Objection by existing licensee

3.48   It is occasionally the case that the existing licensee does not leave the premises of his own volition. He may try to give vent to his grievance by withholding his consent, or even objecting, to the transfer. In that event the committee will doubtless be advised by its clerk that it can entertain the objection only to the extent that, again, it may be said to have some bearing upon whether the applicant himself is a fit and proper person. If, as is more usually the case, the outgoing licensee is merely arguing that he has been treated unfairly by his employers, the committee should decline to take such matters into consideration. In *R v Melksham Justices, ex p Collins*[1] (which is frequently quoted in this context) licensing justices refused to grant a protection order to the managing director of a company owning licensed premises. They did so in order not to prejudice an application to an industrial tribunal by the former manager, who was claiming unfair dismissal. The High Court held that they had misdirected themselves: their sole concern ought to have been whether the applicant was a fit and proper person to be the subject of a protection order, not whether some other person might *also* be so regarded if successful in his claim to another tribunal.

[1]   (1978) Times, 7 April.

Old licences

3.49   These are dealt with in greater detail in the section below on renewals. Note, however, that where justices refuse the transfer of an old on-licence (broadly, one in existence before 15 August 1904) or an old beerhouse licence (an on-licence for the sale of beer or cider continuously in operation in one form or another since 1 May 1869), they will be required to state the grounds for their refusal in writing.[1] The special rules applicable to such licences are of little practical consequence, however, since the transfer of either category of licence may be refused on the ground most generally cited in relation to such refusals, namely that the applicant is not a fit and proper person.

[1]   Section 12(6) and (7).

Appeals

3.50 Any person aggrieved by the refusal of the licensing justices to transfer a licence may appeal to the Crown Court against that decision.[1] Note that the right to appeal extends beyond merely the applicant to any other person (often the owner of the premises) who is directly affected by the decision. If the owner also wishes to appeal in the name of the applicant, reference should be made to the precise terms of any lease or tenancy agreement granted to him to ascertain whether the agreement authorises him to proceed even if the licensee decides not to appeal. As owner it is often prudent to appeal following a refusal in any event, even if the licensee *does* appeal, to guard against the possibility that the licensee might subsequently withdraw his appeal. It should be noted that an objector has no right to appeal against the *grant* of a transfer. If the committee decides to agree to the transfer of a licence to one or more co-applicants, but not to all, it is submitted that those whose application has, effectively, been refused have the right to appeal to the Crown Court since to find otherwise would be to deprive those individuals of an important judicial remedy. There is, however, no clear authority on the point. If the proposed appellant's grievance relates merely to some point of law, or to the manner in which the committee was constituted or conducted itself, then in certain circumstances a more appropriate remedy might be to apply to the justices to state a case for the benefit of the High Court or, alternatively, to apply to that court for a judicial review of the justices' finding. (See chapter 2 for details of the matters that might fall to be considered when deciding which course to adopt.)

[1]   Section 21(1)(b).

PROSPECTIVE LICENSEES

3.51 The approval of a person as a prospective licensee entitles that person, in certain circumstances thereafter, to exercise the rights (and undertake the obligations) of the holder of a justices' licence. This provision,[1] introduced in 1998 was presumably intended to assist the operators of licensed premises in overcoming the difficulties presented by licensing committees which insist upon justices' licences granted by them being held in the name of sole licensees only. Consequently, where that individual leaves without due warning, or is dismissed, the authority to sell intoxicating liquor at the premises will generally determine forthwith.[2]

[1]   The Deregulation (Licence Transfers) Order 1998, SI 1998/114.

² But see *DPP v Rogers* (1991) 155 JP 891 in which it was held that a relief manager might lawfully carry on the business pending an appeal against the dismissal by a licensee.

The applicant

3.52   The only criteria set out in the Act, as amended[1] is that the applicant must be both a 'fit and proper person' and someone who is not disqualified from holding a justices' licence. Each of these matters have been considered in detail in the preceding provisions concerning the transfer of licences. It is important to note that *at this stage* it is not necessary for the intending prospective licensee to have any particular interest in the premises, or establish the present or likely future intentions of the existing licensee, as he would have been obliged to do under s 8(1), in the case of a transfer.

3.53   It is suggested that applications for approval of an individual as a prospective licensee of premises can only be made in respect of a full, as opposed to a provisional, licence. Section 8A(1) provides that application can be made for 'licensed premises', which by s 200(1) is defined as premises for which a justices' licence is 'in force'.

3.54   The new provisions do not oblige licensing justices to approve prospective licensees where they are satisfied as to the suitability of the applicant; they are merely conferred with a discretion so to do. The only specific direction given to the justices in the amended Act in relation to that decision requires them to refuse an application if they form the view that:

'. . . there is a likelihood that, if he became a licensee of the premises under subsection (2) of this section, he would be prevented by other commitments from properly discharging his functions as such a licensee.'

3.55   When nominating an applicant, consideration needs to be given to the other commitments that person may have *at the time he exercises his authority as a prospective licensee.*

3.56   It has already been noted that the applicant cannot be a disqualified person. In relation to other matters, the comments set out above concerning applications to transfer a justices' licence (ie convictions, bankruptcy, age, status, experience and training, references, contracts, company resolutions etc) would apply equally to applicants for approval as a prospective licensee. Differences will arise principally as a consequence of the fact that the approval may come into force on some indeterminate date in the future and further, it would appear, will operate for at least as long as the licence itself subsists.

[1] See s 8A.

Notices

3.57 A suggested form of notice is as set out in Part II. A little strangely, perhaps, the requirements for publication are precisely those which apply to an application for a new justices' licence, rather than a mere transfer. Consequently, in relation to the notice of application the applicant is required to:

(a) serve the following authorities:

    (i)   chief executive to licensing justices

    (ii) chief officer of police

    (iii) proper local authority

    (iv) town/parish/community council (if any)

    (v) fire authority.

    Note that (unlike a transfer) he is not required to give notice to the existing licensee or (as with a removal), the registered owner. Although this is technically not an application for a 'new licence' he is also required to serve the fire authority.

(b) Display a copy of the notice of application on the premises for a period of least seven days, no more than 28 days before the licensing sessions.

(c) Advertise the notice of application in a local newspaper no more than 28 and no less than 14 days before the licensing sessions.

The reader should refer to paras **2.26–2.33** for a detailed consideration of the statutory requirements concerning the giving of notices.

3.58 The notice must indicate the name and address of the applicant and his occupation during the preceding six months. As with transfers, renewals and new applications, the notice should be signed by the applicant or his authorised agent.

3.59 The chief executive to the jurisdiction is required to record the giving of the notice in his licensing list which will remain open for inspection. The usual rules will enable technical defects to be remedied upon application (see para **2.32**). It is not clear from the amended Act whether committees may deal with such applications in the absence of the applicant but, given the effect of any approval, it would seem to be almost inconceivable that the applicant's attendance would not be required.

3.60 Generally, it would be helpful to lodge these documents in advance of any hearing:

(a)   certificate of service;

(b)   statutory fee (currently £30);

(c)   statutory advertisement;

(d)   evidence of display (alternatively, this may be proved orally at the hearing).

Preparation and hearing

3.61   Save as to the procedural differences outlined above, the steps to be taken will follow largely along the lines of those suggested for a transfer application above. The principal difference, as previously suggested, is that the authority exercised by the prospective licensee does not begin until that person has so elected (see para **3.55**). Further, since the prospective licensee does not actually *hold* the justices' licence but merely elects that the laws relating to the sale of alcohol and the conduct of licensed premises shall apply *as if the licence were transferred to him*, it would seem that once the authority comes into force, it will operate for at least as long as the licence itself—and possibly longer. It has been suggested by some clerks that a prospective licensee approval will cease to have effect upon each transfer of the relevant justices' licence. The authority for such a suggestion is presumably the interaction of s 8A(4) and s 3, which provides that each transfer is a new grant. If it were subsequently held to be the case, the effect of such a position would be to negate almost entirely the effect of the provision.

3.62   It should be noted however that the Deregulation Committee of the House of Commons also took the view that such approvals required re-grant upon each transfer or renewal of the parent licence.[1] Since this Order came into effect very little use has been made of the provisions. In any case it is reasonable to suppose that some committees will be concerned as to the longevity of these approvals. Prior to any grant, they may therefore wish to hear in some detail as to the applicant's intended career path. Since this will, naturally, offer no certainty as to the future, it is also reasonably likely that in consideration of their exercising their discretion favourably, some committees will seek assurances from applicants that they will not elect to exercise any approval beyond a specified period of time, or if there has been a material change in their circumstances. Depending upon the view of the committee, a 'material change' might include factors such as promotion, responsibility for a specified number of additional premises, the grant of additional approvals as prospective licensee, determination of employment, a change in the ownership of the premises or the cessation of the licence by surrender, revocation or non-renewal. Obviously such matters are mere conjecture at this stage but it does seem likely that such practices will arise, particularly given that the principal value of prospective licensee approvals will arise within those Petty Sessional Divisions where committees have traditionally been reluctant to permit joint licensees or, perhaps, to allow transfers to take place with too great a frequency.

[1]   Thirteenth Report of the Deregulation Committee of the House of Commons, Session 1996–97, para 14.

3.63   If the application is granted, a memorandum of approval shall be endorsed on the licence itself, although the prospective licensee will not necessarily have carriage of the original licence, which may remain in possession of the existing licensee. Further, one assumes that clerks will wish to enter a note of the approval in the register of licences even though it is not, strictly speaking, one of those matters set out in s 30(1).

Appeals

3.64   Given the importance of the provision, which is certainly of no less status than a transfer, it is perhaps a little strange that Parliament has not thought fit to make provision for any right of appeal. Any challenge, therefore, may only be by way of application to the High Court on a point of law.

Coming into force

3.65   The approval of an individual as a prospective licensee will be of no effect until that person so elects. That election is by way of written notice to both the chief executive to the licensing justices and the chief officer of police. A suggested form of notice appears in Part II of this work. Any such notice will have effect immediately after that notice has been duly given. From that point the prospective licensee will both have authority to sell intoxicating liquor of the categories authorised by the existing justices' licence in force for the premises, subject to any conditions attaching to that licence and be entitled to receive those notices to be served upon the licensee as well as bear the usual liabilities of the licensee (see chapter 6). Note, however, that an election may *not* be given by a prospective licensee at any time; it can only be given in one of those circumstances which would entitle an individual to apply for a transfer of the justices' licence set out at para **3.06**. Broadly, these include the death, incapacity, bankruptcy or departure or intended departure of the licensee, as well as his intentional failure to renew the licence, or the grant of a protection order following a forfeiture of the licence or disqualification of the licensee. For the sake of clarity and good order it would be prudent for the prospective licensee when notifying his election to specify within that notice the particular ground upon which he intends to rely. Since the issue would not in the normal course of events fall to be considered by any authority it would seem that the only remedy available to the police if they wished to challenge such an election, would be to bring proceedings for the sale of intoxicating liquor without a licence. In defending those proceedings it would be for the prospective licensee to establish that a valid election had been made, so rendering such sales lawful.

3.66   To summarise, this procedure is undoubtedly well-intentioned and designed to afford retailers an additional measure of security in circumstances where a licensee leaves for whatever reason on short notice. This could be of benefit in relation to substantial premises where even a very brief interruption in sales of intoxicating liquor could give rise to a significant loss.

PROTECTION ORDERS

3.67   A protection order is an authority to sell intoxicating liquor on premises which is additional to the authority already held by the licensee of those premises. Such an order should be sought when the existing licensee has ceased to be involved with the premises, or to manage or authorise liquor sales. Its sole advantage over a transfer is that it can be obtained with relative speed. It should be understood that a protection order is *not* a temporary transfer since it in no way diminishes the authority of the existing licensee to sell intoxicating liquor at the premises if he should, for some reason, return or remain.

3.68   The second matter to be borne in mind is that protection orders are granted by justices sitting as an ordinary bench of magistrates, not as a licensing committee. Two principal consequences flow from this: first, applications can be made on any day that the magistrates' court is sitting and the time is available; and, second, that any decision made by the magistrates should not be taken as binding upon the (entirely separate and independent) licensing committee. Many a potential licensee has paid dearly for his failure to appreciate this latter point.

3.69   The situation commonly arises where a sole licensee has been suspended by his employers on disciplinary grounds. Is it incumbent upon the employers in those circumstances to seek an immediate protection order? *DPP v Rogers*[1] suggests not. In that case the manager was suspended from all duties pending the hearing of his appeal against dismissal. In the interim period the public house was operated by relief managers, on whose behalf no application for a protection order was submitted. It was held by the High Court that there was an implied delegation of the licensee's authority, just as there is when the licensee is ill or on holiday. Note, however, that the policy documents of certain committees require the court to be notified and/or applications for protection orders to be made where the licensee is absent from the premises for more than a specified period of time (say, 14 days).

[1] (1991) 155 JP 891.

Deemed grant

3.70 In certain circumstances the law provides that a protection order is deemed to have been granted. Briefly, there will be a deemed grant to the following persons in the event of the licensee:

(a) dying—to his personal representatives;

(b) being adjudicated bankrupt—to the trustee of his estate;

(c) having a voluntary arrangement approved[1]—to the supervisor of the arrangement;

(d) executing a deed of arrangement[2]—to the trustee appointed for the benefit of the creditors.

In each of these cases the protection order will be deemed to have come into effect upon the date of the relevant event.[3]

[1] Under Pt VIII of the Insolvency Act 1986.
[2] Under the Deeds of Arrangement Act 1914.
[3] Section 10(5).

3.71 Applications for protection orders may be heard by a stipendiary magistrate or by two or more lay magistrates (a licensing committee is not quorate unless three justices are present).

Applicants for protection orders

3.72 The categories of persons who, and the situations in which they, may apply for a protection order are the same as those for transfers[1] (see para **3.06**ff). In addition, the Act provides that the owner or his nominee will be entitled to seek a protection order in a range of circumstances where the licensee himself has become technically disqualified from holding a licence or that licence has been forfeited as a consequence of orders made under other provisions of the Act. In these highly unusual circumstances reference should be made to the list of those provisions set out in s 10(3).

¹ Section 10(1).

Notices

3.73   Notices in the form set out in Part II of this work need to be served upon both the chief executive to the licensing justices and the police. In general, at least seven days' notice of the intended application is required. Many courts specify days of the week for such applications. It should be emphasised, however, that the justices are under a duty, if so required by the applicant, to consider whether any short notice that has been given to the police is reasonable in all the circumstances of the case.[1] It is suggested that they cannot simply refuse to list the application, since to adopt that attitude would be to fail to exercise their discretion as required by the Act. Having said that, it will be incumbent upon the applicant to establish that, for whatever reason, the notices could not have been dispatched at an earlier time. It is fair to say that many magistrates' courts and police licensing officers are proving increasingly resistant to 'short notice' protection order applications owing to a feeling on their part that many are not the result of a genuine emergency but, rather, are due to inefficiency or delay on the part of the applicant or his advisers.

3.74   A protection order, like a transfer, may be granted before the actual change in ownership or right to occupy arises.

3.75   Although not required by statute, it is customary also to serve a copy of the notice of application upon the existing licensee(s). As a matter of courtesy, if nothing else, that person should be advised of the intention by another to seek authority to sell intoxicating liquor at premises for which he remains the licensee.

3.76   No action is required to be taken in relation to any permit under s 34 of the Gaming Act that may attach.

¹ Section 11(3).

The hearing

3.77   Since applications for a protection order are not, of course, entertained as part of any licensing sessions, it is likely that they will be taken with applications for extensions (see chapter 7) before the general criminal list. The questions to be put to the applicant will be broadly the same as those in relation to transfers (see para **3.33**ff), with the additional need to establish the applicant's intention to transfer. It is imperative that both the applicant and his legal advisers understand that a protection order can be granted only to a person 'who proposes to apply for the transfer of a justices' licence for any premises'.[1] If, *at the time of the hearing*, the applicant does not have such an intention, the application for a protection order *must* be refused. This provision frequently presents applicants and their advisers with a real dilemma since it is not always easy to identify at short notice a person who will be suitable or agreeable to remain at the premises in the long term. However, that is the law and there is little that those organising the protection order can do but find an applicant who does so intend or consider the option of an *interim authority* (see para **3.86**).

[1]   Section 10(1) and *R v Birmingham Magistrates' Court, ex p Bass Mitchells & Butlers Ltd* (1988) 152 JP 563.

3.78   The fact that the protection order is to be followed by a transfer can sometimes be turned to an applicant's advantage. If that person is slightly lacking in experience, the time elapsing between the protection order and the transfer can be used as, in effect, a probationary period. Of course, as indicated above, the magistrates must be satisfied that the applicant is a person to whom the licensing justices could grant a transfer of the licence. However, in such cases it is not uncommon for the police (or even the magistrates, who may also sit on the licensing committee) to indicate that they will reserve their position as to the transfer, or that they would prefer the transfer application to be deferred to the second sessions immediately following the protection order rather than to the first. In the meantime, note that, in relation to the observance of the licensing laws, the holder of a protection order is in the same position as if he were licensee of the premises.[1]

[1]   Section 10(2).

3.79   It is suggested that some committees attach undue weight to the attitude of the existing licensee. As has already been noted, the Act does not even require the applicant to serve a copy of the notice of application upon the existing licensee, let alone satisfy the magistrates that he consents to the application.[1] If there is clear evidence that, although he has not formally consented, it is apparent that the existing licensee does not object, or would not be in any position to object,[2] for example, because he has been dismissed, the application should nonetheless proceed.

[1]   Cf the position on removal of a justices' licence, above.
[2]   Per *R v Melksham Justices, ex p Collins* (1978) Times, 7 April.

3.80   Bear in mind that the magistrates may not necessarily be members of the licensing committee and therefore may not have as complete an understanding of the technicalities of the licensing laws—albeit that they will, of course, have the benefit of their clerk's advice.

Duration

3.81   A protection order will remain in force until the conclusion of the second licensing sessions following the date of its grant. Its operation will automatically extend beyond that date if a transfer properly listed at those sessions is adjourned for subsequent determination.

3.82   The order will cease to have effect if a further protection order, transfer or removal is granted in respect of the premises. Where a further protection order is sought, the justices must be satisfied that:

(1)   the holder of the existing protection order consents to it being superseded; *or*

(2)   that he no longer proposes to apply for a transfer of the licence; *or*

(3)   that he is no longer qualified to apply for the transfer; *or*

(4)   that he is unable to carry on the business.

3.83   It follows that notice of such applications should be served upon the holder of any subsisting protection order, as well as on the court, police and existing licensee(s).

Costs

3.84   Magistrates cannot make orders for costs in relation to protection orders.

Appeals

3.85   Other than appeals to the High Court on points of law, there is no right of appeal against a decision of magistrates granting or refusing to grant a protection order. The only recourse for an aggrieved applicant or objector is to wait until the transfer application, which, if refused, entitles the applicant to appeal to the Crown Court.

INTERIM AUTHORITIES

3.86   For the reasons given above it is not always possible to identify an individual with a sufficiently long term interest in the licensed premises as to justify the grant of a protection order. Consequently, taking advantage of legislation designed to facilitate deregulation, in 1997 the government introduced a new measure designed for use in such circumstances, the interim authority.[1]

[1] Sections 9A and 9B of the Licensing Act 1964 inserted by the Deregulation (Licence Transfers) Order 1998, SI 1998/114, art 3 introduced under the Deregulation and Contracting Out Act 1994, s 1.

3.87 In certain circumstances an interim authority is deemed to come into effect immediately the appropriate notices have been given, thereupon authorising the applicant to exercise the authority of the licensee from that moment. It will seen, therefore, that in certain circumstances it is capable of proving an extremely valuable remedy for the short term.

Deemed grant

3.88 Once again, circumstances in which a transfer *could be* granted trigger an entitlement to make an application for an interim authority. Those circumstances, which appear in s 8(1) of the Act are set out at some length in the commentary above on transfers, prospective licensees and protection orders and so will not be repeated at length here. Suffice to say, those circumstances include; the death, incapacity, bankruptcy, departure or intended departure of the licensee or his representatives, or the failure of a departing occupier to apply for renewal of the licence, or the grant of a protection order to the new owner or his representative following a forfeiture of the licence or disqualification of the licensee.

3.89 In making an application for an interim authority, it will be for the applicant to decide which of these circumstances apply to his situation and that decision might conveniently be reflected in the Notice of Application (see Part II). Critically, if the application for an interim authority is made within seven days of the relevant event (eg departure of the licensee) then an interim authority is *deemed to have been granted from the date of the application.* If the licensee left *more than seven days* before the date of the application then there will be *no deemed grant.* Although it is not entirely clear from the statutory instrument, it would be reasonable to conclude that the application must be received by the chief executive to the licensing justices and the chief officer of police within seven days of the relevant date and, further, that it comes into effect from the moment of receipt. The reason for this interpretation, is that s 9A(2) refers to application being made 'by notice in writing to' those authorities. Further, as a matter of practical expedience it would seem unlikely that the courts will wish to find that individuals can assume to themselves the authority of a licensee without any third party being made aware of that development. Enforcement of the penal provisions in the legislation would also become difficult if it were held that such notices had effect prior to receipt. The reliance upon the date of the application may be compared with similar provisions in relation to the applications for the grant of registration certificates, where the application itself is made by lodging the necessary papers with the chief executive to the justices.

3.90   Once an interim authority has come into force as a consequence of such a deemed grant, then it will continue in operation for a period of 14 days, beginning with the date of the application.

Effect of interim authority

3.91   The 'holder' of an interim authority is placed in the same position as if he were the holder of the justices licence, save in relation to renewals, transfers or protection orders. Consequently, it would seem he can: object to a removal of the licence,[1] be required to carry out structural alterations,[2] insist upon notice of revocation[3], be liable for various offences as to sales to young persons etc (see chapter 7), apply for s 68 certificates,[4] s 70 orders,[5] apply for 'extensions'[6], bring into effect a special hours certificate,[7] be liable for failure to post notices,[8] apply for a children's certificate[9] and call upon the police for assistance in respect of drunkards.[10] It would seem too that, technically each holder of an interim authority is required to display his name above the door pursuant to s 183—surely an unintended consequence of the broad powers and liabilities conferred by s 9A(5).

[1]   Section 5(5)(a) and (b).
[2]   Section 19(4).
[3]   Section 20A(3).
[4]   Section 69(1).
[5]   Section 71(1).
[6]   Section 14(1)(a) and (4)(a).
[7]   Section 76(1)(b).
[8]   Section 89.
[9]   Section 168A(1).
[10]   Section 174(1).

Cessation of deemed grant

3.92   Any grant deemed to have been made in the circumstances outlined above, shall cease to have effect if, within that same 14-day period, the chief officer of police (or any police officer given due authority by him) serves a notice in writing objecting to the grant of an interim authority.

That notice of objection must be served on both the applicant and the licensing justices.

3.93 There is no requirement in the amended Act for the police to give grounds for their intended objection. The notice takes effect automatically. It is to be hoped that forces will not as a matter of course serve notices merely because their inquiries have yet to be completed, but will instead give formal notice only where circumstances which give cause for concern exist. To do otherwise would be to defeat the apparent intention of the legislation.

Applicants for interim authorities

3.94 The persons who may apply for interim authorities are those who may similarly apply for status as a prospective licensee, namely 'fit and proper persons' who are not disqualified from holding a justices' licence. It is most important to note in this respect they can be distinguished from applicants for transfer and/or protection orders, each of whom must have at the time of the application an intention to become the licensee of the premises either at the time of the hearing (generally, in the case of a transfer) or upon some future date. This, as has previously been observed, is a highly restrictive and inconvenient measure for the trade, which the interim authority was designed to overcome.

Notices

3.95 A suitable notice is suggested in Part II of this book. The Act requires copies to be served upon both the chief executive to the licensing justices and chief officer of police. It is suggested that the same notice that gives rise to the deemed grant under s 9B(1) also serves as the application for the actual grant under s 9A(2), although it should be made clear to the court that a hearing or other determination is required. The Act does not specify any period of time that must elapse between the giving of the notice and the hearing of the application: the application might therefore be heard on the same or the following day, although courts may generally wish to allow the police to have sufficient time to complete their inquiries and serve notice of objection, which, as indicated above, will determine a deemed grant. Although such applications are to be determined by licensing justices, rather than ordinary magistrates, the Act specifically provides that a single justice may determine applications, otherwise than at licensing sessions. Further, on that occasion, the single justice is empowered to examine the applicant on oath if there is a hearing.

3.96   The question has arisen whether the power of a single justice to grant an interim authority is an administrative act. Although the position is not entirely clear, it would seem to be so. The clerk can clearly grant the authority otherwise than at transfer sessions (per s 193AA(3)). There is the same provision for single justices in s 9B(3)(b), which notably is absent from the provisions concerning single justices and final orders (see chapter 2). Nonetheless many justices continue to grant final orders 'on site' and there is little doubt that they have power to grant interim authorities otherwise than in open court.

3.97   The clerk to the licensing justices (note—not, it would seem, clerks to the justices generally) now has power to grant transfers where the applicant for a licence either holds a justices' licence or, alternatively, has held such a licence during three years preceding the date of the application. There is like power in relation to the grant of an interim authority. However, as with transfer applications, the clerk may decline to exercise that power if he 'considers that there are circumstances which make it desirable for the matter to be considered by the justices'. The Act makes it clear that the clerk can determine such applications at any time.

3.98   The practical effect of these important provisions, is to enable an applicant to secure an authority to trade for a 14-day period, merely by serving a notice upon the court and the police. The application itself, if made by an existing (or recent) licensee, may then be granted by the clerk without any hearing. In practical terms this could ensure, for an experienced licensee, continuity of trading with a minimum of bureaucracy.

3.99   Documents to be lodged in advance of any hearing will include:

(1) certificate of service;

(2) cheque—£10.00 (at the current time payable, it is submitted, on the actual grant only).

3.100   In addition, just as it has become customary for the justices to require evidence that the existing licensee would have no objection for the granting of the application, it would seem reasonable to assume that most courts will impose a similar requirement in relation to the interim authority.

3.101   No interim authority may be granted for premises where such an authority is already in force.[1] Once such an authority has been granted it cannot be determined except by effluxion of time unless, as it may be entitled to do, the court accepts a surrender. Where a 'relevant event' has occurred at the licensed premises such as might give rise to the power to transfer a justices' licence,[2] then justices may not grant more than two interim authorities in reliance upon that particular event.

[1] Section 9A(6)(a).
[2] Once again see s 8(1) which sets out such circumstances which include the death, incapacity, bankruptcy, departure or intended departure of the licensee, as well as the occupier's failure to apply for renewal of the grant of a protection order to the owner or his representative following the forfeiture of the licence or the disqualification of the licensee.

3.102 Whereas the provisions relating to protection orders specifically require justices to endorse the licence with a memorandum of the order, there is no such requirement in relation to an interim authority. Possibly it is intended to reduce the paperwork arising on such applications. Despite there being no specific provision in s 30, one assumes that the courts (most of which now print off a computer data base) will maintain a central record of such grants.

Duration

3.103 As indicated above the *deemed* grant of an interim authority (which must be applied for within seven days of the departure, death etc of the existing licensee) will remain in force for a period of 14 days from the date that the application is made. If the police serve notice of objection then the deemed grant (but not an *actual* grant—see s 9B(2)) ceases immediately.

3.104 Any interim authority which is subsequently *actually* granted, either by the clerk, a single justice or the licensing committee, will operate for a period of 28 days 'beginning with such date as may be specified in it', most appropriately the date of any hearing (or determination by the clerk), or from such date as appears on the face of the authority. If an application for the transfer of a justices' licence is made by any persons within the 28-day period mentioned above, then the interim authority will continue in force until the application is disposed of, which could be some months hence. Arguably this can be done following a *deemed grant*, whch may nonetheless be a *grant* within the meaning of s 9A(4), so meaning that no actual determination of the interim authority is ever required. Although the provision is not entirely clear, it would seem that the mere lodging of the transfer notices will be sufficient to extend the operation of the authority. Unlike the provisions relating to protection orders which limit their authority to just two sessions (subject to adjournments), there is no such arrangement concerning interim authorities.

3.105   It should be noted that the very procedures intended to assist pub operators and retailers in overcoming the difficulties posed by the protection order can operate so as to defeat this objective. An efficient court can grant an interim authority administratively within a matter of days of receipt (there is no *obligation* to allow the police 14 days within which to object). A transfer then lodged within 28 days to extend the life of the interim authority may, even if it is intended by the applicant to be listed for some weeks or months hence, be granted again within a matter of days by the clerk to licensing justices exercising his administrative authority. Consequently, the operator intending to buy some time by putting forward a temporary manager may find that person very quickly becomes the new licensee, in turn leading to potential difficulties concerning s 8(4) and suggestions of 'revolving door' licensees (see para **3.22**).

3.106   Note that whilst *justices* may not grant more than two interim authorities, this would not seem to preclude repeated applications giving rise only to successive *deemed* grants (see s 9A(6)(b)).

Costs

3.107   Unlike protection orders, justices may make orders for costs in relation to contested applications for interim authorities, either for payment to the applicant by any person opposing the application, or by the applicant to any such person.[1]

[1]   See s 193B.

Appeals

3.108   There is no right of appeal against a refusal to grant an interim authority other than an application to the High Court on a point of law. As with an unsuccessful application for a protection order, the only remedy to the aggrieved applicant is to pursue a transfer application which, if refused, does carry with it an entitlement to appeal to the Crown Court.

RENEWALS

3.109   Applications should be submitted for the renewal of every justices' licence at the relevant annual general licensing meeting to be held in the first fortnight of February 2004 and every three years thereafter, except where that licence has been granted, removed or transferred after 4 January in the renewal year. Where licences are not so renewed (or granted by way of a new licence, removal or transfer) they will expire on 5 April.

Notices

3.110   The Act does not set down any procedure for giving notices of application to renew a justices' licence. Practice varies across the country, but most chief executives dispatch to licensees a reminder, accompanied by a pro forma application to renew, between mid-October and the end of December immediately preceding the Brewster Sessions in the renewal year. It should be emphasised, however, that there is no obligation to remind licensees to renew their justices' licences. If no such reminder has been received it is for the licensee to write to the chief executive to the licensing justices seeking the renewal of the licence, preferably not later than the end of December. The letter should be accompanied by a cheque made payable to the 'Chief Executive to the Licensing Justices' for the appropriate fee (currently £30.00). It should also set out the name of the owner of, or person entitled to receive a market rent for, the premises. The letter should also invite the court to acknowledge safe receipt.

3.111   Any person intending to oppose an application for renewal needs to serve a written notice, containing the grounds of the objection, upon both the applicant and the chief executive to the licensing justices not less than seven days before the Brewster Sessions. The committee has no jurisdiction to entertain an objection unless the notice has been so served.

3.112   The application for renewal must be submitted by the licensee.[1] It should not, for example, be submitted by the holder of a protection order or the owner of the premises unless he is also the licensee or authorised under the terms of a lease or tenancy agreement to apply in the name of the licensee. If such a procedure is adopted the committee may require an explanation of why the licensee has failed personally to apply.

[1]   Section 3(3)(a).

Hearing of application

3.113   A power conferred by the Licensing Act 1988[1] gives the clerk to the licensing justices authority to renew licences provided that the following conditions are fulfilled:

(1)   an application to renew at the general annual licensing meeting has been submitted; and

(2)   the application is not opposed; and

(3)   the justices have not directed to the contrary; and

(4)   the application is not made in conjunction with another application relating to the licence; and

(5)   the licensing register in respect of the premises in question has not been indorsed with details of any conviction, forfeiture or disqualification of premises[2] relating either to the applicant or the premises for which the licence renewal is sought.

[1]   Section 193A(2).
[2]   Section 31.

3.114   Most licensing committees will deal with validly submitted applications to renew in the absence of the licensee. Indeed, the Act provides that applicants *shall not* be required to attend unless objection is made to the renewal.[1] Where the applicant *is* required to attend court to give evidence the Act provides that such evidence shall be given on oath.[2]

[1]   Schedule 2, para 8.
[2]   Section 7(4).

3.115   Where the renewal of a licence is opposed the procedure adopted will be similar to that followed upon an application for the grant of a new licence, with an opening address, evidence-in-chief, cross-examination, re-examination and summing up. Invariably the objector or objectors will commence the process, so that the applicant for the renewal (which would otherwise have been a formality) may know the case he has to meet.[1]

[1]   See eg *Sharpe v Wakefield* [1891] AC 173.

3.116   The licensing committee has a wide discretion in relation to the renewal of a justices' licence. In general it is unlikely that renewal will be refused unless the licensee has to some extent been at fault in the management of the premises. The police frequently serve notices of objection to renewal where houses have remained closed for a significant period of time. However, except in so far as it is required by any condition upon the licence, no duty is imposed upon a licensee to keep licensed premises open during permitted hours.[1] Further, it has been held that justices are entitled to renew a licence notwithstanding that the applicant intends to close the premises.[2] In such cases it is incumbent upon the committee, it is suggested, to consider whether the closure of the house is in fact due to a genuine absence of need in the locality or rather (as may frequently be the case in the wake of the MMC Report and the Beer

Orders), the manifestation of an upheaval in the market, which may be resolved when normal conditions are restored.

1   Section 90.
2   *Leeds Corpn v Ryder* [1907] AC 420.

3.117 The licensing committee cannot decline to renew a justices' licence simply because it has changed its policy as to the way in which licensed premises must be conducted. In *R v Windsor Licensing Justices, ex p Hodes*[1] licensing justices authorised their clerk to object to the renewal of the licence on the ground that the committee had decided that all supermarkets should thenceforth sell intoxicating liquor from a separate off-sales department, rather than by way of self-service within the general food area. The licensee declined to give such undertaking to do this and the renewal was refused. That decision was upheld in the High Court. In the Court of Appeal, however, Waller LJ said that in order to justify an objection to the renewal of an off-licence there must be some change of circumstances, either in the manner in which the off-licence was being operated, or because the way it was being operated caused some particular trouble outside the premises. Since there was no evidence before the justices that the premises had, in fact, caused any difficulty, the licence would be renewed.

1   [1983] 2 All ER 551, CA.

3.118 It is a common misconception among licensees that their licence is at risk only if it can be shown that any noise or disturbance in the area has been generated by persons within, or leaving, the premises. In fact, the justices may have grounds for refusal to renew if there is evidence of public disorder in the neighbourhood of the premises generally.[1]

1   See *Lidster v Owen* [1983] 1 All ER 1012; *Sharpe v Wakefield* [1891] AC 173.

3.119 An objection may be raised by any person, including the justices themselves.[1] It is most important that the applicant for renewal should have advance notice of the particular objections raised. Any matters not covered by the notice of objection should not be entertained by the committee.

1   *R v Howard, Farnham Licensing Justices* [1902] 2 KB 363.

Part IV licences

3.120 Note that an application for the renewal or transfer of a Part IV licence may be refused only upon grounds for which the justices would be entitled to refuse the grant of the licence.[1]

1   Section 98.

Old on-licences

3.121   Ordinarily, the fact that a licensee holds a licence granted before 15 August 1904 will be of absolutely no significance, save that he should be aware that it imposes an *obligation* (not applicable to on-licences granted subsequently) to supply suitable refreshment, other than intoxicating liquor, at a reasonable price.[1] The precise status of his on-licence may well become of greater significance, however, should objection be made to its renewal.

[1]   Section 12(4)(b).

3.122   As previously indicated, an old on-licence is one which in general has been continuously in force since 15 August 1904; an old beerhouse licence is one which can be shown to have been in force on 1 May 1869, authorising the sale of beer or cider, and maintained continuously since that date without removal.

3.123   Whereas licensing justices have a wide discretion to refuse the renewal of 'ordinary' justices' licences, the grounds upon which they may do so in the case of the old licences described above are restricted to the following:

(1)   *Old beerhouse licence*:
  (a)   failure to produce satisfactory evidence of good character— the extent to which this bears a different meaning from the requirement for all applicants to be fit and proper persons is a somewhat moot point, perhaps deserving of investigation in an appropriate case;
  (b)   the premises, or adjoining premises owned or occupied by the licensee, are of a disorderly character or frequented by persons of bad character;
  (c)   the licensee has previously forfeited a licence or been disqualified from holding a licence on the grounds of misconduct.

(2)   *Old on-licence*:
  (a)   the applicant is not a fit and proper person;
  (b)   the premises have been ill-conducted—this will include persistent and unreasonable refusal to supply suitable alternative refreshment (see above) or failure to fulfil any reasonable undertaking previously given to the justices;[1]
  (c)   the premises are structurally deficient or unsuitable—care should be taken to distinguish between structural defects and the mere want of decorative repair or proper cleansing.[2]

¹   Section 12(4)(b).
²   Section 12(4)(b).

3.124   Upon the renewal of an old on-licence, licensing justices may ask the applicant to give an undertaking. In that event the Act¹ requires them to adjourn the hearing of the application and cause notice of the desired undertaking to be served on the registered owner of the premises, giving him an opportunity of being heard. However, strangely perhaps, the committee has no power to insist that the licensee give the undertaking as a condition of renewal. This is the case even where such an undertaking has previously been given upon transfer, or upon renewal without notice to the owners.²

¹   Section 12(5).
²   *R v Dodds, ex p Roberts, Birkenhead Licensing Justices* [1905] 2 KB 40; *R v Crewe Licensing Justices, ex p Bricker* (1914) 79 JP 26 and *R v Finsbury Justices* [1912] Brewing Tr Rev 266.

3.125   If the renewal of an old on-licence is refused the licensing committee must provide the applicant with written grounds of refusal.¹

¹   Section 12(6).

3.126   At the request of the licensee, licensing justices may upon renewal of any justices' on-licence impose conditions such as to make the licence a seasonal, six-day or early-closing licence.¹ Similarly, a condition under s 86 permitting the operation of an off-sales department may be applied upon renewal. Part IV conditions may also be attached at this time.

¹   Sections 64 and 65. Provisions apply to 'old' and 'ordinary' on-licences.

Late renewals

3.127   Where the opportunity to renew a licence at the Brewster Sessions has been missed, the applicant will wish to know as a matter of urgency what can be done to overcome this difficulty. The position is as described below.

Renewal before expiry on 5 April

3.128   Application to renew can be made at a transfer session taking place before 5 April if the applicant can satisfy the committee that he had reasonable cause for not applying at the Brewster Sessions. It is unlikely that mere forgetfulness will be sufficient. Notice of the intended application must be served at least 21 days prior to the application upon the chief executive to the licensing justices, the police, local authority and parish council/meeting or community council (if any). There is no requirement to display such notice on the premises or to advertise.

Grant, transfer or removal after 4 January and before 5 April

3.129   If a licence has been granted by way of a new grant, transfer or removal after 4 January but before 5 April 1998 or any third anniversary thereof (ie 2004 etc) that licence will have effect until the end of the licensing period, which will be 5 April three years thereafter.[1] Accordingly, if the renewal that should have taken place at the Brewster Sessions in the first fortnight of February in the relevant year has been missed, there is always a possibility that one may be able to list an application to transfer the justices' licence if a licensing sessions has been arranged to take place before 5 April. The opportunity could be taken, for example, to add the licensee's spouse or some other appropriate individual to the licence. Obviously there will still be a requirement to satisfy the committee that the applicants are fit and proper persons. Indeed, although the application will have the effect of a renewal, it is suggested that the licensing committee is obliged to entertain it as though it were a transfer. The *Sandhu* case[2] perhaps illustrates this best, emphasising that the committee may consider only the suitability of the applicant for a transfer and may not take extraneous matters into account.

[1]   Section 26(1) and (5).
[2]   *R v London Borough of Haringey, ex p Sandhu and Sandhu* (1987) 151 JP 696.

3.130   Note, however, that s 12(7) provides that the transfer of an old on-licence may be refused upon precisely the same grounds that its renewal might be refused, with the added proviso that an old beerhouse licence might be refused on the ground that the applicant is not a fit and proper person.

3.131   It has been argued by some that technically a notice of election given by a prospective licence pursuant to s 8A(2) has the effect of a 'grant' under s 3(3), so operating as a 'renewal' under s 26(1). Although the issue has yet to be tested by the higher courts it is submitted that this view is incorrect; sub-s (2) provides only that the enactments concerning the sale of liquor and licensed premises shall apply *as if* the licence were transferred. It is clear that *de facto* and *de jure* a transfer has *not* taken place and so reliance cannot be placed upon a literal interpretation of s 26.

Temporary continuation of authority to sell after 5 April

3.132   If the justices' licence has lapsed following failure to renew and the only solution is to apply for a new licence at the next transfer sessions, then it is possible to obtain authority for sales of intoxicating liquor pending the hearing of that application. One way is by making application for an occasional licence,[1] which, it has been held, may be used to maintain sales in an on-licence,[2] an off-licence[3] and clubs with registration certificates.[4] Alternatively, application may be made for a protection order, which confers the same authority as the justices' licence in force, or last in force, provided it is to be followed by a 'transfer' of the 'expired' licence (see below).

1   Section 180.
2   *R v Bow Street Stipendiary Magistrate, ex p Metropolitan Police Comr* [1983] 2 All ER 915.
3   *R v Brighton Borough Justices, ex p Jarvis* [1954] 1 All ER 197, although in that case (which was some years before *Bow Street*) the High Court disapproved of the practice.
4   *R v Woolwich Justices, ex p Arnold* [1987] Crim LR 572.

Transfer after 'expiry' on 5 April

3.133 Even though the justices' licence may have expired on 5 April it may, nonetheless, be possible to apply for the 'transfer' of that licence where the application is made:

(a)   following the illness or incapacity of the licensee;[1]

(b)   where the former occupier of the premises, prior to his departure, deliberately failed to apply for the renewal;[2]

(c)   where a protection order has been granted to the owner or his nominee following the forfeiture of the licence or the disqualification of the licensee.[3]

1   Section 8(1)(b); see *R v Birmingham Justices, ex p Walker* (1981) Times, 20 February.
2   Section 8(1)(e).
3   Note s 8(1)(f) and s 10(3).

Application for a new licence after 5 April—deemed renewal

3.134 If a transfer is not possible by any of the means described above an application by the (former) licensee, heard not later than the next general annual licensing meeting (ie within 12 months of the Brewster Sessions), seeking a similar licence will be treated as an application for renewal. It is submitted that the notices that are to be served are those that would be appropriate to a new application, including advertisement and display (although some clerks, it should be said, interpret the law as requiring mere notification to the statutory authorities). To avail himself of this provision it will, however, be necessary for the applicant to satisfy the licensing committee that he had reasonable cause for his failure.

Again, it is suggested that mere forgetfulness, without some other mitigating circumstances, will probably not be considered to amount to 'reasonable cause'.

3.135   Where the justices are satisfied as to the reasons for the failure to apply for renewal it is unlikely that they will require the applicant to give any evidence over and above that which he might be asked to give upon an ordinary application for renewal (if any). If, on the other hand, the committee are not so satisfied, in theory the applicant may be required to meet all of the usual criteria in relation to the grant of a new licence, including dealing with the premises, business operation, requirement in the area etc. In practice, it would be prudent for the applicant to speak to the clerk to the licensing justices in advance of the hearing to ascertain what evidence is likely to be needed in either event.

ORDER FOR ALTERATIONS

3.136   Upon an application for renewal of a justices' on-licence (by way of either the standard procedure or a transfer as outlined above[1]) licensing justices have the power to insist that the licensee first deposit with them a plan of the premises and then, within a specified time, carry out such structural alterations to that part of the premises where intoxicating liquor is sold or consumed as they think reasonably necessary to secure the proper conduct of the business. (This provision can prove extremely useful if it is sought to secure retrospective consent for alterations, upon renewal of the licence.[2])

[1]   Section 19(6).
[2]   See commentary in next chapter.

3.137   The committee cannot make more than one such order within a five-year period. Notice of any such order must be served upon the registered owner[1] of the premises. The licensee or any person aggrieved (most probably the owner) may appeal against the order.[2]

[1]   Section 32.
[2]   Section 21(1)(d).

3.138   Failure to comply with such an order amounts to a criminal offence, together with a further offence for every day on which the default continues after the expiration of the time fixed by the order.[1] A level 1 fine may be imposed (currently a maximum of £200, as from 1 October 1992).

[1]   Section 19(4).

Appeals

3.139 A person aggrieved has a right of appeal against a refusal (but not a grant) of a renewal of a justices' licence.

3.140 When notice of appeal has been given against a decision by licensing justices to refuse to renew a licence then either the justices or the Crown Court may, upon such conditions as they think fit, order that the licence shall continue in force beyond 5 April. Unless such application is made the licence will automatically cease to have effect upon the due date.

LICENSED PREMISES—OTHER RENEWALS

3.141 Each year a substantial amount of time and effort is invested by licensees in dealing with the consequences of their failure to renew various other licences and certificates attaching to their premises. The most common failures relate to the following:

(1) *Section 34 permit* (fruit machines)—the Gaming Act 1968[1] requires that these permits should be for a minimum three years' duration. An application for renewal must be submitted at least one month before the expiry date. An appropriate note should be made at the end of the diary to carry the renewal date forward to the next year.

(2) *Part III registration certificate*[2] (jackpot machines)—valid for five years from the date of registration. Application for renewal to be made not more than three months and not less than six weeks prior to expiry.

(3) *Public entertainment licence*—granted under the Local Government (Miscellaneous Provisions) Act 1982, such licences will generally operate for a period of one year, but may well be granted for a shorter period such as three or six months. The renewal of the licence will usually not be granted on less than 28 days' notice,[3] but the licence will not expire provided the application for renewal or transfer has been submitted before the expiry date.

[1] Schedule 9, para 18.
[2] Gaming Act 1968.
[3] Schedule 1, para 6(1).

3.142 It is critical that the renewal of a public entertainment licence should not be overlooked since the expiry of that licence will give rise *automatically* to the lapse of any special hours certificate[1] (see chapter

7), which is so often the mainstay of the profitability of many licensed premises.

¹　Section 81(1).

CHAPTER 4

THE PREMISES

CONTROL BY COMMITTEE

4.01   The failure by a licensee to appreciate that he will, in certain circumstances, need the authority of the licensing committee to alter his own premises can have catastrophic consequences. Alterations to licensed premises should be carried out only after careful consideration has been given to both the provisions of statute and local policy.

JUSTICES' ON-LICENCES

Requirement to change

4.02   The tone is set by s 19, which, as observed in the previous chapter, entitles licensing justices upon renewal to direct that such structural alterations shall be made in the part of the premises where intoxicating liquor is sold or consumed as they think reasonably necessary to secure the proper conduct of the business.

4.03   The qualification that such an order can be made only once in every five years[1] may be of little comfort to the licensee who has unexpectedly been required to spend several thousand pounds to remedy some supposed defect in the layout of the premises. Note that the test applied is not an objective one but essentially a matter for the opinion of the licensing justices, who are entitled to give such direction as they think reasonably necessary. Even though there is no reasonableness test (ie as they reasonably think necessary etc) the justices may clearly not act capriciously, in the *Wednesbury* sense (see para **2.132**).

---

[1]   Or, in practice, generally six years since renewals are every third year.

4.04   Licensees should not forget that the Disability Discrimination Act will come into full effect in 2004, by which time licensed premises will have to make 'reasonable adjustments' to provide disabled people with the same quality of service and access as other customers. Steps which might be considered include installing wheelchair access, introducing an element of table service and and perhaps nominating certain staff for sign language where required.

4.05   The provision does not apply to off-licences, and the licensing justices are not entitled to interfere in the layout of such premises upon renewal without proper cause.[1]

[1]   See commentary upon *R v Windsor Licensing Justices, ex p Hodes* [1983] 2 All ER 551, CA, at para **3.117**.

Consent to alterations

4.06   Experience shows that the only safe rule for the licensee is to assume that every alteration to on-licensed premises requires the justices' prior consent unless he has been advised, or can satisfy himself, to the contrary. Misinterpretation of the rule could lead to the destruction of the works, the forfeiture of the licence and the finding that the individual cannot be regarded as a fit and proper person.

4.07   It will be seen from the consequences outlined above that the utmost care needs to be taken in relation to the construction of this important provision, which is therefore worth setting out verbatim:

'Section 20 Consent required for certain alterations to on-licensed premises

(1) No alteration shall be made to premises for which a justices' on-licence is in force if the alteration—

(a) gives increased facilities for drinking in a public or common part of the premises; or

(b) conceals from observation a public or common part of the premises used for drinking; or

(c) affects the communication between the public part of the premises where intoxicating liquor is sold and the remainder of the premises or any street or other public way;

unless the licensing justices have consented to the alteration or the alteration is required by order of some lawful authority.'

4.08   The most important factors arising from this important provision may be summarised in the following way.

(1)   '*Alteration*'—the most common misconception is that s 20 relates only to structural alterations. It does not. Thus alterations which involve the installation or removal of a non-structural partition or

divider between two bars could require the committee's consent. If the licensee or his advisers are in any doubt as to the position an application for consent should be submitted; it can always been withdrawn if the clerk to the justices subsequently advises that in his view it is not necessary.

(2) *'Premises'*—this term extends not only to the premises as they are but also to the premises as they might be once altered. Accordingly it is not possible, before consent has been obtained, to alter adjoining premises with a view to connecting the two following the hearing of the application.[1] If it can be argued that the extension takes the premises beyond the ambit of the original licence, or so alters the identity of the building as to create a new entity, then consideration should be given to lodging also (or instead) an application for the grant of a new justices' licence.[2] Some committees apply the rule of thumb that any alteration which extends the premises by more than 50 per cent of the existing floor area is likely to require a new licence. In cases where there is any doubt the only prudent course of action is to speak to the clerk to the licensing justices to see what view his committee is likely to adopt.

(3) *'Increased facilities'*—note that this does not necessarily mean an increase in the drinking area; an extension of the bar might lead to a reduction in the area but an increase in the facilities for drinking.

(4) *'Public or common part'*—accordingly, staff areas do not qualify.

(5) *'Affects the communication'*—alterations to doorways opening into the drinking area are caught by this provision. Note also that it is an offence to make, use or allow to be made or used any internal communication doorway between licensed premises and any other unlicensed premises to which the public have access.[3]

(6) *'Have consented'*—this means that consent *must be given prior* to the alterations being commenced. If this is not done then invariably the only solution will be to make application for the grant of a new licence,[4] which, if granted, would be followed by the surrender of the existing licence. It has been suggested by some commentators that such a procedure is no longer possible because of the limited circumstances in which a licence may be surrendered following *Drury*.[5] However, it is suggested that a surrender in such circumstances is analogous to one offered in return for the grant of a new licence with varied conditions, and so unlikely to be declared unlawful by a higher court. As indicated above, there is an argument that a committee may (if it is so inclined) be able to grant retrospective consent upon the renewal of the licence by exercising its power under s 19 to require structural alterations.

(7) '*Order of some lawful authority*'—it should not be forgotten that the justices' consent is *not* required if the alterations are indeed being carried out as a result of the order of (usually) the fire authority or the local authority.

[1]   *R v Wyre Licensing Justices, ex p Frederick Wilkinson* (1991) 155 JP 312.

[2]   *R v Weston-super-Mare Licensing Justices, ex p Powell* [1939] 1 KB 700; *R v Isle of Wight Justices* [1931] BTRLR 124 and *R v Axbridge Justices, ex p Ashdown* [1954] Brewing Tr Rev 408.

[3]   Section 184(1).

[4]   *R v Crown Court at Croydon, ex p Bromley Licensing Justices* (1988) 152 JP 245.

[5]   *Drury v Scunthorpe Licensing Justices* (1992) 157 JP 401. See para **1.17** for a reference to the surrender of a licence when seeking to vary conditions.

Notices

4.09   The Act is silent as to the manner in which an application for consent to alterations should be submitted. In practice most committees require at least 14 (and frequently 21) days' notice of intention to apply, usually given in the form of a simple letter. Some committees provide pro-forma documents for the making of the application.

4.10   If there is no policy document giving guidance on the point it is suggested that four plans should be submitted (scale 1:100 or 1:50) showing the premises both as they exist and as they are intended to be, with the alterations identified in red. Additional copies should be prepared and distributed (D) (or retained (R)) as follows:

chief executive to the licensing justices	(D)	4	(as explained above)
fire officer	(D)	2	
building inspector	(D)	2	
local authority	(D)	1	
police	(D)	1	
witness	(R)	2	
file	(R)	2	
TOTAL		14	

4.11   It should be emphasised that the only statutory provision is that the licensing justices *may* require plans to be deposited with their chief executive at such time as they may determine. However, many committees do require such plans to be served upon both the police and the fire authority. Because of the overlapping roles of the fire officer and the building inspector in relation to matters of fire safety, it is sensible to consult both at the same time. Further, some committees will require the involvement of the local authority (particularly the environmental health officer), which is not unreasonable given that it is consulted as part of any new application. As ever, reference should be made to the policy document.

Hearing of application

4.12   Applications for consent to alterations are frequently called on in the transfer sessions after transfers but before the grant of new justices' licences. Such applications are often dealt with by the licensee himself, or by the surveyor responsible for the project.

4.13   Justices are not automatically entitled to consider on an application for consent to alterations how, for example, the conditions attaching to a music and dancing licence or a special hours certificate might be affected.[1] Neither may committees refuse consent to alterations on grounds of heritage or aesthetics.[2] They do nonetheless retain a wide discretion (eg maintaining public bars;[3] closing outside means of access).[4]

[1]   *R v Crown Court at Sheffield, ex p Mecca Leisure Ltd* (1983) 148 JP 225.
[2]   *R v Crown Court at Chelmsford, ex p Larkin* [1990] COD 447.
[3]   *R v Steyning Justices, ex p Charrington & Co Ltd* [1976] Brewing Rev 254.
[4]   *R v Watford Licensing Justices, ex p Trust Houses Ltd* [1929] 1 KB 313.

Failure to apply

4.14   Apart from giving rise to the cost and uncertainty of an application for a new licence, failure to apply exposes the perpetrator to the following risks:

(1)   within six months, the lodging of a complaint, usually by the police, seeking the forfeiture of the licence or a direction that the premises be restored to their original condition;[1]

(2)   if the works have been undertaken prior to or upon the new proprietor moving in (as is not uncommon while the new occupier is making his mark), the refusal of his subsequent transfer application;

(3)   an application for revocation of the licence on the grounds that the licensee is not a fit and proper person, or that the premises are unsuitable;

(4)   the non-renewal of the licence on the same grounds.

[1]   Section 20(3).

Appeals

4.15   There are rights of appeal to the Crown Court in each of the above eventualities, as well as where the licensing justices refuse to grant consent under s 20.[1]

[1]   Sections 20(5) and 21(1).

JUSTICES' OFF-LICENCES

4.16   As enacted, the Licensing Act 1964 gives licensing committees very few powers in relation to the structure of premises having the benefit of justices' off-licences. In practice, however, many committees have so arranged matters that the most minor alteration to such premises can endanger the licence if prior consent is not sought.

4.17   As we have seen, the Act obliges an applicant for a justices' off-licence to deposit plans of the premises to be licensed only if the application is for a provisional grant. Invariably, however, committees will require all applications for the full or provisional grant of an off-licence to be accompanied by plans. Having so considered and approved those arrangements many apparently feel that it would be illogical if they did not continue to exercise some control over the internal layout of the premises. A supermarket or multiple off-licence chain routinely inviting licensing committees to comment upon plans setting out proposals to alter premises will generally receive one of three responses.

(1)   *No control*—the committee takes the view that the premises have been licensed and since s 20 (consent to alterations) does not apply to off-licences, the licensee may do as he pleases. Since the publication of the Good Practice Guide this is increasingly the response.

(2)   *Informal approval*—the committee appreciates the courtesy of the approach and the plans will be put before the chairman of the committee at the earliest possible opportunity. If he or she is content with the arrangements the appropriate indication will be given; if not, the applicant may be required to make an informal appearance before the committee at the next transfer sessions to explain further his proposals.

(3)   *New licence*—the existing licence attaches strictly to those shelf units and counters outlined in red on the deposited plan, in accordance with the policy document. Any revision will require a new licence.

Speak to the clerk!

CHAPTER 5

CHILDREN'S CERTIFICATES

5.01 The general rule embodied in s 168(1) is that until a child has achieved the age of 14, he will not be allowed in the bar of licensed premises during permitted hours. Under the Deregulation and Contracting Out Act 1994 the government introduced a system enabling licensing committees to certify those bars which they consider provide a suitable environment for accompanied children. The effect of this provision is to permit children during specified periods within permitted hours to be present in a bar in which a certificate is in force and operation, provided they are in the company of a person who is 18 or over.

5.02 The purpose of this chapter is twofold: to analyse the options which previously existed to overcome the general prohibition and, to the extent that these may not have always provided a solution, to consider the strengths and weaknesses of these subsequent provisions.

5.03 Since this chapter will be concerned exclusively with the rules concerning the presence in a licensed bar of persons who are *under 14* (as opposed to the provisions concerning the sale and supply of intoxicating liquor, which variously affect those under 16 and those under 18 years of age), all references to *children* in this chapter refer to those aged 13 or under.

OTHER OPTIONS

5.04 Since the prohibition on children in uncertificated premises applies only to *bars* in *licensed premises* during *permitted hours*, it follows that, in the four situations described below, children will be allowed to enter and remain in premises where alcohol is being sold or consumed.

Outside the bar

5.05 There is no hard and fast rule that readily establishes whether or not any particular place should be regarded as a bar. The first test to apply is that provided by the definition in the Act, which states that it includes any place exclusively or mainly used for the sale and consumption of intoxicating liquor.[1] If the designated area is used predominantly for drinking, it is likely to fall within the definition. However, by using the word 'includes', the Act contemplates that there may be other areas not used primarily for drinking which could still be considered to be a bar. In *Carter v Bradbeer*[2] the House of Lords considered the definition in some detail and concluded that:

> 'with no physical demarcation line it would be difficult to regard one ill-defined area of the floor space of a room as not being a "bar" and to regard the remaining parts in the room as being a "bar"' [per Lord Morris of Borth-y-Gest].

> 'That usual meaning is in my opinion, a bar counter over which drinks are sold and, on occasions, a room' [per Viscount Dilhorne].

> '[In finding that the area in question was a bar,] I am not prepared to say that the result would be the same in the case, eg of a genuine ballroom containing a bar counter, either as regards the room itself, the bar counter or any area adjacent to the bar counter' [per Lord Kilbrandon].

> 'I respectfully share the dislike expressed by Lord Widgery CJ of their [ie Torbay Justices] "notionally dividing each room into a dancing area which was not a bar and a remaining area which was a bar"' [per Lord Edmund-Davies].

> 'the majority of your Lordships . . . are of the opinion that every bar counter is necessarily a bar for the purposes of section 76(5)[3] of the Licensing Act 1964, and the minority, of whom I am one, . . . are not prepared to express so categorical a view' [per Lord Diplock].

[1]   Section 201(1).
[2]   [1975] 2 All ER 571; affd [1975] 3 All ER 158, HL.
[3]   Since repealed.

5.06 It emerges from these judgments that in most licensed premises not only the bar counter but also the remainder of a room used *exclusively or mainly* for the sale or consumption of intoxicating liquor *will* be regarded as a bar. Where, however, the room as a whole has some other primary purpose (eg a ballroom) even the bar counter itself may not so qualify. It is submitted that such an interpretation is in fact entirely consistent with the purpose of the section, which expressly excludes a bar situate 'in any railway refreshment-rooms or any premises constructed, fitted and intended to be used bona fide for any purpose to which the holding of a justices' licence is merely ancillary'. Licensed restaurants are the most obvious example of premises where the licence is ancillary to the principal use.

5.07   Thus it is certainly arguable that the prohibition does *not* apply to, for example, licensed sports centres, cricket clubs or other buildings (eg offices) which have not been constructed for the primary purpose of being used as licensed premises. It should be said that such a view may not readily be accepted in certain areas by either the police or the licensing committee and so, if the licensee wishes to avoid unnecessary conflict and the risk of prosecution, some consultation should take place.

5.08   Other decisions have a bearing on the interpretation of 'a bar':

'The bar of a public house is as we know, strictly speaking the counter over which liquor is served, and it has come to be extended to the space in front of it where people stand.'[1]

A beerhouse kitchen, also fitted out as a drinking room, has been found to be a bar.[2] Conversely, gardens have been held in the particular circumstances of a case to be a place where children might lawfully sit with adults at tables where alcoholic liquor is being served. In another case a billiard room was similarly found to be a place where children might be present.[3] Clearly, each case needs to be considered independently upon its merits.

[1]   *Donaghue v McIntyre* 1911 SC (J) 61.
[2]   *Pilkinton v Ross* [1914] 3 KB 321.
[3]   For a commentary on these cases see 'Children's Rooms in Improved Public Houses' XCIX JP Jo 655.

In unlicensed premises

5.09   There is no general prohibition upon children within the bar of premises having the benefit of a club registration certificate (ie registered premises) save as may be found in the rules of the club itself. See chapter 8 for further details.

Sole means of access or resides on premises

5.10   The Act specifically excludes circumstances where a child is in a bar solely for the purpose of passage from one area to another, to or from which there is no other convenient means of access or egress,[1] or if he is the licensee's child or resides (but does not work) on the premises.[2]

[1]   Section 168(4)(c).
[2]   Section 168(4)(a) and (b).

Set apart for table meals

5.11   Notwithstanding that an area is generally a bar, it will not so qualify at any time *when it is usual* for it to be (and is) set apart for the service of table meals *and* intoxicating liquor is sold only to persons as an ancillary to their meals.[1] The effect of this provision is that on Sundays, for example, one may designate a bar as a restaurant area, operating it (substantially) according to restaurant conditions. During that time it will be permissible for children to be present.

[1]   Section 171.

5.12   From the above three paragraphs it will be seen that it has always been possible in recent years to allocate for the use of children a room which is clearly *not* a bar by reason of its layout, location or usage. Such arrangements have, however, frequently proved unsatisfactory from the point of view of the licensee (who may not be able adequately to supervise the area), the adult or teenage customer (who may find the atmosphere sterile and tedious) and the licensing justices (who might be aware of these practical shortcomings and be willing to permit a more mature arrangement, if they are able also to regulate it by way of conditions). This is the justification for the children's certificate.

CHILDREN'S CERTIFICATES

5.13   One of the conclusions of the much respected Erroll Committee Report, published in 1972, was that 'the licensing justices should be able to issue a certificate, on application by a personal licensee, to the effect that the premises are licensed and that the public interest and convenience does not require the exclusion of children under 14 years of age from part or parts of the premises'.

5.14   The report went on to state:

'The licensing justices should have absolute discretion in deciding whether to grant a certificate, and they should be able to attach conditions to it governing the conduct of the premises. Justices should be able to suspend or revoke the certificate on complaint, and a personal licensee should be able to extinguish it himself after giving appropriate notice to the clerk to the justices. The justices would be required to have regard to the suitability of the premises for children under 14, and there would be a right of appeal against their decisions.'

5.15   The somewhat belated enactment of this recommendation, almost without qualification, is testimony to the committee's success in achieving its stated goal of anticipating the likely development of leisure patterns and consumer needs over the subsequent 20 years.The provision finally came into force in England and Wales on 3 January 1995.

Procedure

Notices

5.16   The full terms of the provisions, which are introduced by way of amendment to the Licensing Act 1964, are set out in Part II of this book.

5.17   Prior to the application, the Act[1] requires that notice of the intended application, stating the location of the premises and signed by the applicant or his authorised agent, be served at least 21 days before the relevant transfer sessions upon the chief executive to the justices and the chief officer of police. In addition, some committees require service upon each of the statutory authorities.

[1]   Schedule 12A, paras 1 and 2.

5.18   It would be prudent to check the committee's policy document, since some justices require that the notice should clearly indicate the parts of the premises to which the application relates, as well as the days and hours for which the certificate is sought. Occasionally courts require that the fee (presently £16.00) be paid in advance.

5.19   The application need not be made by an *existing* licensee—it can be submitted at the same time as application is made for the grant of a new justices' licence.[1] However, since the Act (as amended) requires the committee to be satisfied that 'the area to which the application relates *constitutes*' a suitable environment, it would appear that the premises must be ready for trading, as with a special hours certificate (see below).

[1]   Section 168A(7) and Sch 12A, para 5(4)(b).

5.20   If the police wish to oppose the application, then at least seven days before the transfer sessions they must serve written notice specifying, in general terms, the grounds of their opposition. It is suggested that the wording of the Schedule excludes the possibility of any party other than the police having an entitlement to oppose such an application. However, that would not preclude the police calling such other persons as witnesses, or relying upon their arguments in making out the police's own objection.

An example of a notice of application is set out in Part II of this work.

Plans

5.21   The amended Act provides only that licensing justices *may* decline to entertain an application until a plan has been lodged in cases where the premises include a bar which is not included in the area to which the application relates. Presumably the thinking behind this provision is that in such circumstances committees may wish to have regard to the extent to which children might be affected by the activities taking place in the uncertificated bar. It is implicit, perhaps, that where it is sought to certificate the *whole* of the premises justices are obliged to entertain an application, even though it may not be accompanied by a plan. However, since, as will be seen, the scheme of the provisions is that the committee have the widest discretion in the matter, little purpose will be served in failing to supply such plans if the committee indicates in its policy document that plans would assist it in arriving at its decision. Applicants who wish to give themselves the best prospects of success would be well advised, in the author's view, to have available suitable plans. (See chapter 2 for the preparation of plans generally.) Again, upon these plans reference could be made to the features indicated below.

Criteria to be applied

5.22   Committees will *not* be entitled to grant a certificate unless they are satisfied:[1]

'(a) that the area to which the application relates constitutes an environment in which it is suitable for persons under 14 to be present, and

(b) that meals and beverages other than intoxicating liquor will be available for sale for consumption in that area.'

The view has been expressed by the High Court that a substantial sandwich accompanied by beetroot and pickles might be a table meal.[2] In another case it was found that, although borderline, sandwiches and sausages on sticks were a meal.[3]

[1]   Section 168A(2).
[2]   *Timmis v Millman* [1965] Brewing Tr Rev 23.
[3]   *Solomon v Green* (1955) 119 JP 289.

5.23   Note that food must be available throughout the period in which the certificate is to be operational. Accordingly, some provision should be made, for example, for the afternoon period when an establishment's kitchens may be closed.

5.24   What is a suitable environment? There is likely to be a wide divergence of views. To satisfy themselves most committees will wish to visit the premises. Even once a committee is satisfied that such an environment exists, there is no *obligation* to grant the application, merely a discretion so to do. Persuading committees to exercise that discretion may not always be entirely straightforward, particularly since some divisions have in the past expressed forceful views against the provision of family rooms in, for example, city centre public houses. Of course, now that they are empowered to control that provision by way of conditions there may be a different attitude, but nonetheless the task of reasoned persuasion should not be undertaken lightly, or without appropriate preparation.

Possible issues

Existing clientele

5.25   What is the character of the house? What is its reputation in the locality? To what extent will the existing clientele be displaced if the premises are increasingly frequented by families? Have any views been expressed by those existing customers?

Location of premises

5.26   Is the house essentially providing a convenience service (eg street-corner) or is it a so-called destination venue to which people will travel from some distance away? There will be arguments to be advanced in favour of each style of outlet.

Play areas

5.27   Is there a garden? Does it have facilities for children (eg swings, climbing frames, etc)? Are these safe? Are the grounds secure and free from other unreasonable hazards? Do the neighbours have any views upon such a transition?

Premises

5.28   Do the premises contain separate areas for families/adults only? Set out below are some of the issues that may be addressed in respect of the premises.

(1)   Do they have toilets which children can conveniently gain access to and use?[1] Some licensees have already successfully persuaded

committees that they should not be required, for example, to provide low-level urinals as these facilities are not available in the home and younger boys often accompany their mothers in any event.

(2) Do they have smoke-free areas/air conditioning? This has proved to be the most contentious area, as responsible licensees have shown themselves reluctant to agree to conditions which may be almost impossible to abide by, or prohibitively expensive. One solution is, of course, for the licensee to undertake, or accept a condition requiring him, to display notices inviting customers not to smoke in the certificated area. Such a condition is of course substantially less onerous than one specifying that there shall be no smoking in that area.

(3) Do they have facilities for infant children?

(4) Do they have loud music?

(5) Do they have fruit machines in all areas? Again, the common requirement that such machines be excluded from certificated areas has already proved extremely contentious, it not being an offence for young persons to be in the presence of (or even play) such machines, which often represent an essential source of revenue to the licensee.

[1] It should, of course be remembered that s 168(4)(c) already provides that a child may be present in a bar solely for the purpose of passing to some other part of the premises to which there is no other convenient means of access.

Food

5.29 Is there a children's menu, or are children's portions provided at a reasonable price? It is, of course, a requirement in any event that meals and beverages other than intoxicating liquor be available throughout the period the certificate is operational.

Drink

5.30 Is there a full range of soft drinks at reasonable prices?

Seating

5.31 Are highchairs and/or raised seats available?

Supervision

5.32 What is the level of supervision in the designated area?

Character of other houses in locality

5.33 To what extent can it be said that this facility is already available within a reasonable travelling distance?

5.34 Whilst certain committees might be inclined to consider some of the matters in particular cases, the Home Office has suggested that they should not take too prescriptive or dogmatic an approach. Children will experience all sorts of environments, both within and away from the home. On the continent controls upon their presence in such premises are the exception, but the perception may be that those children are no better or worse behaved than their English counterparts. The controlled introduction of children into the sociable environment of the family public house *under the guidance of an adult*, is perhaps to be preferred to a rapid introduction at 18 or thereabouts to an atmosphere which, probably, has little in common with that person's previous experiences.

Hearing of the application

5.35 As for the notices of application, in general it is likely that both the court and the police will confirm at the hearing that they received the notices in good time. However, the applicant should be prepared to prove service if necessary (see form in Part II).

5.36 The applicant will then need to satisfy the committee as to whether the 'condition precedent' for the grant of a certificate has been satisfied, namely that meals and beverages other than intoxicating liquor will be available for sale for consumption in that area. That will be a question of fact, established by the production of menus and drinks lists as well as, possibly, details of the ability of the kitchen and staff to provide the appropriate level of service.

5.37 Thereafter, the applicant should address directly the issue of a suitable environment. Where committees do not make a practice of visiting licensed premises prior to a hearing, the attitude of the police in relation to this somewhat nebulous test may well substantially influence the minds of the justices. If the police confirm that in their view the environment is suitable, it may be necessary to call very little additional evidence. If they are neutral the applicant will need to identify those features which he relies upon to satisfy the committee on the point. If the police are opposed to the application then, of course, the applicant will already have been made aware of the grounds of that opposition and can address each in turn. In addition to dealing with the matters of oral evidence outlined above, the applicant might seek to produce the following:

(a) plans;

(b) menus;

(c) drinks lists;

(d) photographs;

(e) petition;

(f) existing and potential customers.

5.38   Once the applicant has given his evidence it will, of course, be open to the police to cross-examine if they are objecting. Even if they are not, it is likely that both they and any of the other statutory authorities may be invited by the committee to put any queries to the applicant in relation to the matters such as fire safety, food hygiene, etc. The applicant's advocate will then have an opportunity to re-examine, after which the committee may well put its own questions.

5.39   If the application is opposed by the police they may call evidence which will, again, be subject to cross-examination by the applicant and his representative. It is suggested that the police should confine themselves to the grounds set out in the notice of opposition served.[1]

[1]   Schedule 12A, para 2(2).

5.40   At the conclusion of the case it is anticipated that both objectors and applicants (in that order) will be given an opportunity to sum up their case. The committee may then retire before announcing its decision.

Conditions

5.41   The Act provides that all children's certificates will be subject to a condition that meals and beverages other than intoxicating liquor are available for sale for consumption in the area to which the certificate relates at all times when the certificate is operational.

5.42   In addition, licensing justices have an unfettered discretion to impose such other conditions as they think fit including (in particular) conditions restricting the hours and/or days upon which the certificate is operational.[1] Conditions which might be attached include:

(1) *Hours* Subject to any provision to the contrary, a children's certificate will be operational at any time up to 9.00 pm. That time may be extended,[2] either generally or for particular days or periods, but an extension may be granted only if sought by the applicant

(although not necessarily in the terms sought).[3] Some committees have already granted certificates to 11.00 pm in the belief that families will wish to make their own decision and an earlier 'clearing out' time might be difficult in practice for the licensee. The provisions also introduce the new concept of 'eating-up time', whereby the child and any person accompanying him is entitled to an additional 30 minutes in which to consume a meal purchased for either child or adult before the terminal hour.

(2) *Child safety* It would not be unreasonable to expect premises seeking to cater for children to meet the same safety standards as might reasonably be found in their homes (eg guarded plug sockets, covered electric fires, etc).

(3) *Children's menu* Given that the intention of Parliament appears to be to ensure that an environment will be provided that will be conducive to the comfort of the whole family, it may not be thought unreasonable to ask licensees to provide a range of foods in appropriate portions for children.

[1] Schedule 12A, para 4(2) and (3).
[2] Schedule 12A, para 5(2).
[3] Schedule 12A, para 5(2) and (3).

5.43 Whilst there must be a temptation on the part of the licensing committee to devise ever more complex conditions designed to meet every conceivable need of the family, one might, perhaps, ask whether such an approach is entirely appropriate. The imposition of onerous conditions, with which it will be unduly expensive to comply, has proved already a substantial disincentive to licensees to apply for or retain such certificates. Therefore, whilst it might be considered to be in the interests of families to have these facilities in the particular house which is the subject of the application, it might not be so regarded if the imposition of such conditions leads indirectly to that family being excluded from a significant number of other houses which have consequently chosen not to apply! In some areas in Scotland it is said that fewer than 1 per cent of houses have chosen to apply, possibly for this reason. At the end of the day commercial forces will regulate the position: if families do not like what they find they will not return.

5.44 In the matter of conditions, it was clearly not the intention of the government when introducing these provisions that they should give rise to an unnecessary degree of further regulation. In a letter to all clerks, committee chairmen and chief officers of police, the Home Office said:[1]

'While licensing justices are free to impose these conditions as they see fit, they may wish to note that during Parliamentary debate on Children's Certificates the Parliamentary Under-Secretary of State for Corporate Affairs stated that the Government's intention was that there will be the least possible alteration to the normal operation of the bars concerned. He went on to say that in drawing up proposals for a system of Children's Certificates the Government have tried to put in place a regime containing adequate safeguards to ensure that accompanied children under 14 will not be allowed into premises that are unsuitable, but that does not impose unnecessarily expensive and time-consuming burdens on the police and courts who will have to administer it, or the licensees.'

1   Home Office Circular No 57/1994.

5.45   A variation of the conditions attaching to a certificate may be achieved by way of a surrender of the existing certificate and an application for the grant of a new one. The only exception to this rule is where an extension to the 9.00 pm terminal hour is sought, in which case there is no statutory provision as to the period of notice required. Check the policy document.

The decision

5.46   Following the hearing of the application the licensing committee may:

(1)   grant the certificate subject only to the standard condition as to meals and beverages;

(2)   grant subject to additional conditions;

(3)   refuse the application.

Where an application is refused the justices are obliged to specify their reasons in writing.[1]

1   Schedule 12A, para 3.

Public notice

5.47   Where a certificate has been granted the licensee is obliged to post in a conspicuous place in the area to which the certificate relates a notice which both states that a certificate is in force in relation to that area and explains the effect of the certificate and any conditions attaching to it. For an appropriate notice see Part II.

5.48   Failure to display such a notice (the only offence specifically created by these new provisions) is punishable by a level 1 fine.[1] A due diligence defence is available.

1   Present maximum £200.

Appeals

5.49 An applicant who is aggrieved by a decision of the licensing justices either refusing the grant of a certificate or imposing conditions upon such a grant, or declining subsequently to extend hours may within 21 days of it appeal to the Crown Court against that decision. The chief officer of police has no right to appeal against a grant. In the Crown Court the licensing justices are entitled to be indemnified as to any costs that they are unable to recover from an unsuccessful appellant.[1]

[1] Schedule 12A, para 11.

5.50 The judgment of the Crown Court will be final. There may, of course, be a judicial review of the Crown Court's procedure or decision (see chapter 2).

Duration and revocation

5.51 Once granted a children's certificate will remain in force until revoked. It will not require transfer or renewal. Either the licensing justices or the police may apply for the revocation of the certificate. The committee has a discretion to revoke if it is satisfied either:

(1) that the area to which the certificate relates does *not* constitute an environment in which it is suitable for persons under 14 to be present; or

(2) that there has been a serious or persistent failure to comply with one or more conditions attached to the certificate.

5.52 Note that if at any time the provisions of s 168(3A) (eg accompanying person is not 18 or over, or the certificate is not operational at that particular time) are not complied with, the offence of permitting children to be within the bar during permitted hours will have been committed, subject to the existing defences.

5.53 As previously mentioned Parliament has provided for 30 minutes' 'eating-up time', so that food purchased before the terminal hour on the certificate may be consumed within the bar during the 30 minutes following that terminal hour.

5.54 The enforcement of these provisions may not be straightforward. Questions may well arise as to how the courts should construe 'in the company of a person who is 18 or over'. How continuous does the accompaniment need to be? What is an acceptable ratio of adults to children, etc? How is it to be decided whether a child is consuming a meal during the 30 minutes eating-up period? If meals or beverages cease to be available a breach will have been committed, which may perhaps begin to form the basis of an application for revocation of the certificate. Failure to comply with other conditions imposed upon a certificate may have similar consequences.

5.55   Whether the application is launched by the licensing justices or the police, the applicant for revocation is required to give at least 21 days' notice to the licensee of the intention to apply at the relevant transfer sessions. The police also need to notify the chief executive to the licensing justices. The notice of application for revocation must be in writing, setting out in general terms the grounds for the proposed revocation. If the certificate is revoked the licensee has a right of appeal to the Crown Court.

5.56   Alternatively, the licensee may himself upon 14 days' written notice to the chief executive to the licensing justices and the chief officer of police secure the revocation of the certificate at the end of that period. This provision addresses a defect which is inherent in the similar system operating in Scotland. As a consequence, the holder of the certificate can now effectively procure its surrender if, for example, he finds that compliance with the conditions exposes him to unreasonable expense.

5.57   A certificate will automatically be treated as revoked if the area to which is relates ceases to form part of licensed premises.[1]

[1]   Schedule 12A, para 8.

Costs

5.58   Save where the application accompanies one for the grant of a new justices' licence the committee will be entitled to award costs, subject to the comments made in chapter 2.[1]

[1]   Section 193B.

CONCLUSION

5.59   Since the origins of this provision can be traced so clearly back to the careful and measured deliberations of the Erroll Committee, it seems appropriate to conclude this chapter with the views of that much respected body upon the criteria that should be applied both to the grant of a certificate and to the imposition of conditions.

5.60   As to the grant, the Erroll Committee suggested the following factors might be taken into account:

'the type of clientele, the provision of seats and tables, any record of misconduct or disorder, the availability of food and drink other than intoxicating liquor, toilet arrangements and the numbers of people likely to use the premises at any one time.'

5.61 And the committee concluded with the following plea:

'we would hope however, if our proposals are implemented, that licensing justices would not frustrate our general intentions by adopting too restrictive a policy towards applications for certificates. We would hope in particular, that applications would be considered on their merits, and not in the light of any prior policy decision that the presence of children in bars is undesirable in any circumstances—a view with which we strongly disagree.'

CHAPTER 6

OFFENCES AND REVOCATIONS

6.01 The holder of a protection order,[1] interim authority or a justices' licence faces a bewildering range of rules and regulations, with which few licensees, lawyers or police officers would claim to be entirely familiar. Fortunately, however, such offences are relatively rare and it is not the intention of this work to compete with other excellent texts, such as *Paterson's Licensing Acts*, which already provide the comprehensive analysis that is appropriate when defending criminal proceedings. To assist the licensee in avoiding such an eventuality the author has selected for the first part of this chapter, four of the more common hazards that are likely to present themselves, together with an analysis of the concept of 'due diligence'. The chapter concludes with a consideration of the revocation proceedings that might follow such a course of conduct.

[1] Under s 10(2).

SALES TO PERSONS UNDER 18

6.02 As with so many provisions of the Licensing Act 1964 (which consolidated the provisions of a number of earlier Acts) the law relating to children and licensed premises is somewhat convoluted and difficult to follow in the first instance. The chart at para **6.03** sets out the basic position.

6.03 Probably the concern most frequently expressed by licensing committees at transfer sessions relates to the purchase of intoxicating liquor, from public houses and off-licences, by persons under 18.[1] Of course, the majority of licensees take great pains to prevent this happening and, where there is a doubt, insist upon age being verified in a number of ways, the most well-known of which is the production of a 'Prove It' card, pioneered by the Portman Group. Equally, the courts have recognised that they have a part to play, publishing in March 1998 their *Good Practice Guide on Under Age Drinking*, which calls for a partnership between the courts, public, licensees, local authorities and the Portman Group.[2] Nonetheless, whether innocently or knowingly, sales to minors will inevitably occur. The purpose of this section of the book is to examine in some detail the offence, possible defences and means which might be adopted in the first place to avoid such difficulties.

[1]   Note that the Confiscation of Alcohol (Young Persons) Act 1997 gives the police the power in certain circumstances to confiscate alcohol from young persons or those associating with them. See also Home Office Circular No 38/97 and DCMS Circular No 02/2001.

[2]   Copies of the Guide are available from the Justices Clerks' Society, The Magistrates' Court, 107 Dale Street, Liverpool L2 2JQ.

The offence

6.04   Historically the principal offence in licensed premises was the sale by the licensee *or his servant*, of intoxicating liquor to a person under 18, or the licensee knowingly allowing any person to do so. Following the Licensing (Young Persons) Act 2000 which came into force on 23 January 2001 *any person* is guilty of an offence if he sells intoxicating liquor to a person under 18 in licensed premises.

6.05 From the coming into force of s 30 of the Criminal Justice and Police Act 2001 in December of the same year it has been necessary for the vendor to demonstrate that he believed that the purchaser was not under 18; *and either* that he had taken all reasonable steps to establish the person's age *or that* nobody could reasonably have suspected from his appearance that the person was under 18. For the purposes of this section a person shall be treated as having taken all reasonable steps if he requests evidence of his age, unless it is shown that the evidence was such that no reasonable person would have been convinced by it. Where charged by reason of the act or default of some other person, the due diligence defence will continue to apply. The Act also authorises test purchases by minors acting under the direction of police constables or weights and measures inspectors.

6.06 The Licensing (Young Persons) Act 2000 also created for the first time in England and Wales the specific offence of the proxy purchase of intoxicating liquor in licensed premises. Here a person is guilty of an offence if he buys or attempts to buy intoxicating liquor on behalf of a minor. It is also now an offence to buy or attempt to buy for consumption in a bar. In such circumstances it is a defence to prove that the purchaser had no reason to suspect that the person for whom the liquor was purchased was under 18. For a prosecution to succeed, therefore, the prosecuting authority will need to establish:

The law relating to children, licensed premises and intoxicating liquor

	In a 'bar'	Other than a 'bar'
	Section 201(1): 'Bar ... includes any place exclusively or mainly used for the sale and consumption of intoxicating liquor'.	(Eg restaurant area, some functions rooms, family rooms, beer gardens, bar converted to restaurant by a t?1, etc)
Under 5	No alcohol in any place save for medical reasons (see Children and Young Persons Act 1933, s 5).	
Under 14*	Excluded during permitted hours unless licensee's child/resident/merely passing through (s 168), or relevant area has the benefit of a children's certificate and the child is accompanied by a person aged 18 or over.	Permitted at any time to be present. May consume alcoholic drinks (if purchased by an adult).
16 and over*	Offence to purchase or consume intoxicating liquor (s 169).	Permitted to purchase beer, porter, cider or perry with a meal in a restaurant area (s 169(4)).
18 and over	May purchase and consume intoxicating liquor	

[Note that the above restrictions will apply in registered clubs only if the rules so specify.]

(1) *Sale*—Because, of course, intoxicating liquor in a members' club is supplied to members, rather than sold, it follows that an offence will not be committed if a person under 18 is supplied with intoxicating liquor in premises operating under a club registration certificate (see chapter 8). The prosecution may not always have evidence that money changed hands. This will not be fatal, however, since evidence that *a transaction in the nature of a sale* took place will be sufficient evidence of such a sale,[1] unless that presumption can be rebutted by actual evidence to the contrary called by the licensee.

(2) *In licensed premises*—The offence can be committed as a result of a sale in premises having the benefit of either a justices' on-licence or a justices' off-licence. Sales under the authority of an occasional licence are also covered.[2]

(3) *Intoxicating liquor*—Since the Licensing (Low Alcohol Drinks) Act 1990 came into force on 1 January 1994 this definition includes products of a strength in excess of 0.5 per cent at the time of the sale or other conduct in question. Note, however, that a person aged 16 may purchase beer, porter, cider or perry for consumption *with a meal* in a part of the premises usually set apart for the service of meals. The Act requires that such an area must *not* be a bar. It will in any event not generally fall within the definition of a bar if it is so set apart.[3]

(4) *Person under 18*—It is prudent in these cases for the prosecution to serve a s 9 statement by the minor's parent or guardian, exhibiting a birth certificate, to establish the person's age. Evidence from the minor alone on this point is, of course, technically hearsay.

[1]   Section 196(1).
[2]   Section 200(1).
[3]   Section 169D(c).

6.07   Remember to check also that the prosecution has complied with all procedural requirements as to the laying of the information, time limits (generally six months from the date of the alleged offence), jurisdiction, duplicity (disclosure of more than one offence in a single charge) and form. Any interviews by police officers which might reasonably lead to the witness incriminating himself should be carried out under caution, with the opportunity being given to check and sign the interview notes.

Defences

6.08   The nature of the defence available to the vendor depends upon whether *he* made the sale to the minor, or whether he is prosecuted as licensee by reason of a sale by another.

Charged as vendor

6.09 As will be seen from the provisions above, it is no longer necessary for the prosecution to establish that the sale was made knowingly as regards the purchaser's age. In other words, to secure a conviction the prosecution does not need to prove that the licensee either had actual knowledge or wilfully closed his eyes to an obvious source of knowledge.[1] All the prosecution has to establish is that, in fact, the purchaser was of that age and that such a sale took place in licensed premises. The vendor then has to prove either:

(a) that he had taken all reasonable steps to establish the person's age; *or*

(b) nobody could reasonably have suspected from his appearance that the person was under 18.

[1] See eg *Goodwin v Baldwin* (1974) 138 JP Jo 225.

6.10 Where the vendor is charged by reason of his own act (ie he effected the sale) it is more likely that he will seek to rely upon the second line of defence, namely that nobody could reasonably have suspected from his appearance that the person was under 18. Typically, reference will be made to the young person's height, appearance, clothing and general demeanour on the day in question. Remember that this may be very different from his or her appearance in court on the day of the hearing. It is always prudent in such cases for the defence to ask those prosecuting the case to ensure that the minor attends court in attire (and make-up, if a girl) similar to that worn on the day of the alleged incident. If the person who made the sale maintains that the purchaser could reasonably be taken by any person to be 18 or over then he should invite the magistrates to make their own assessment. Of course, it is particularly difficult for the magistrates to undertake this exercise with any degree of objectivity since, unlike the vendor at the time, they *know* beyond any doubt that the purchaser was under age and may, in fact, be only 15 or 16 years old. They are therefore being asked to find that they too would have made an incorrect judgment, notwithstanding the evidence they now have before them. Since the onus is upon the defendant to establish his defence, he must prove his case on the balance of probabilities.

6.11 It is conceivable that a vendor will, in the alternative, seek to rely upon the defence afforded by (a) above. This might arise where he concedes that he *did* have reason to suspect that the person was under 18. Accordingly he may then have asked for proof of age which, on being supplied, satisfied him sufficiently to complete the sale. It is said that in certain areas forged identity cards are quite freely available to young persons. Of course, if that is the case it will equally be said that local licensees should be aware of this fact and consequently be ever more vigilant. Remember for the purposes of this section a person shall be treated as having taken all reasonable steps if he requests evidence of his age, unless it is shown that the evidence was such that no reasonable person would have been convinced by it. Ultimately of course, it will be for the justices to decide whether the defendant has satisfied them that he had taken all reasonable steps to establish the person's age having regard to all the circumstances.

Charged as licensee (not vendor) only

6.12   A prosecution may well be brought against the licensee even though he did not effect the actual sale in question since, as has been mentioned, it is also an offence for the licensee knowingly to allow any person to sell intoxicating liquor to a person under 18. Further, the licensee may be prosecuted even if he was absent from the premises. In such a case it will be contended by the prosecution that he had delegated his responsibilities under the licence to an employee who did himself knowingly (which will include recklessly) allow the sale.[1] In either event, he is entitled to rely upon the defence afforded by s 169A(3), namely that, again, he exercised all due diligence to avoid the commission of the offence. In this case, however, the evidence that he will seek to call is unlikely to relate to the actual sale itself but, rather, will be based upon the instruction, warnings, training etc given to members of his staff. Since this is a matter of the utmost concern to many licensees, both those who are multiple licence holders (eg area managers) and those who simply control large numbers of staff in one premises, it is worth considering in some detail the matters which should be considered if the defence is to be made out.

[1]   *Howker v Robinson* [1973] QB 178.

All due diligence

6.13   Establishing a defence based on 'due diligence' often involves the same degree of diligence by the lawyer as is required in the person he or she is trying to defend.

6.14   In common with food safety, trade descriptions, and other consumer-orientated legislation, the Licensing Act 1964 enables company representatives to avoid conviction for certain offences if they can establish that they have exercised 'all due diligence' to avoid the commission of that offence. Although the reference to due diligence suggests that an element of reasonableness should enter the proceedings, in practice rather more stringent tests tend to be applied by the courts. As a consequence, a modus operandi that may have seemed entirely reasonable within the context of one's daily business can suddenly be made to seem hopelessly inadequate with the benefit of hindsight. If consideration is being given to running this statutory defence, the lawyer must therefore undertake the most searching and impartial appraisal of all the facts.

6.15 He will also need to take on the roles of the businessman, exhibiting a full understanding of the company's affairs; the politician, persuading people to part with the necessary information; the analyst, collating these items and identifying those of importance; and, finally, the salesman, offering up the results in an attractive and intelligible manner.

The law

6.16 Where the issue of due diligence arises it is for the magistrates to decide as a question of fact. This might seem self-evident, but in *Hammett (RC) Ltd v Crabb*[1] it was necessary for the High Court to consider upon a case stated whether, among other things, the justices had been right in law in holding that the defendants had failed to prove that they had exercised due diligence. The court held that the question was meaningless because there was no legal definition of due diligence for the purpose of the statute. In seeking to establish that the facts support the contention that all due diligence has been exercised, the onus of proof is quite clearly upon the defendant.

[1] (1931) 145 LT 638.

6.17 However, whilst the prosecution needs to prove its case 'beyond all reasonable doubt', applying the higher test appropriate to criminal cases, the defendant has merely to satisfy the civil test, ie 'on the balance of probabilities'. Where the offence requires mens rea, but there is no *actual* knowledge of the relevant breach, can the defendant be convicted on the basis of imputed knowledge, or recklessness, if at the same time he is found to have exercised due diligence? In *Buxton v Chief Constable of Northumbria*[1] it was held that, prima facie, such findings would be inconsistent. If due diligence was made out that would afford a complete defence.

[1] (1983) 148 JP 9.

6.18 Although the question of whether or not all due diligence has been exercised will be decided on the facts of each case, it is possible to obtain some guidance from various authorities as to the degree of care likely to be required by the courts. Many of these cases have arisen under the Trade Descriptions Act 1968, but the principles arising have general application.

6.19   In *Sherratt v Geralds, the American Jewellers*[1] a 'waterproof' watch was sold by the defendants. It was found to fill with water after being in a bowl for one hour. The defendants relied upon the reputation of their supplier. The court would have none of this, suggesting that the elementary precaution of dipping the watch in a bowl of water would have established the inaccuracy of the supplier's claim!

[1]   (1970) 68 LGR 256.

6.20   In *Taylor v Lawrence Fraser (Bristol) Ltd*[1] the company tried to avoid liability under the Toys (Safety) Regulations 1974 for selling toys painted with an inappropriate substance by stating that the trading standards officers had previously been invited to take samples for analysis. The defence failed; the responsibility for ensuring compliance with the law rested with the company. This is an important principle; it is not at all uncommon for defendants (particularly in licensing prosecutions) to argue that the regulatory or enforcing authority had knowledge of a certain practice and made no complaint. Not only is it *not* possible to shift responsibility to the enforcing authority, it is also very difficult to transfer such responsibility to a third party by way of a blanket delegation without further inquiry. The courts will generally require evidence of some positive act by the party having primary responsibility.[2]

[1]   [1978] Crim LR 43, DC.
[2]   *Rotherham Metropolitan Borough Council v Raysun (UK) Ltd* (1988) 153 JP 37.

6.21   Perhaps the care with which magistrates now investigate these cases is shown most clearly in the decision in *Knowsley Metropolitan Borough Council v Harry Cowan,*[1] arising under the Weights and Measures Act 1985. The facts were briefly as follows: Mr Cowan was the owner of a butcher's business, trading from ten separate shops. At one of these shops a manager had taken on a young man as an assistant. While a relief manager was on duty, the assistant overcharged representatives from the Trading Standards Office on a number of test purchases.

[1]   (1991) 156 JP 45.

6.22   Superficially, it appeared that the owner of the shops had a good defence: he had employed an experienced manager to run the shop, he had delegated to his managers generally the administration of the shops, and staff selection and training. The shop manager agreed with these facts and conceded that it was his fault the assistant had not been trained adequately. The magistrates accepted that the owner had exercised all due diligence and dismissed the case. On appeal, the Divisional Court held that they had been entirely wrong and remitted the case with a direction to convict. In particular, their Lordships drew attention to the following weaknesses in the company's arrangements:

(1) Mr Cowan was aware of the problems arising from a particular type of price tag, but did not see that those tags were replaced;

(2) he failed to offer guidance to managers on the interviewing or selection of staff;

(3) although managers were liable to train any staff recruited, no formal training programme was prescribed;

(4) he failed to supervise the managers in the exercise of these functions.

6.23 It follows from these cases that the courts will be prepared to embark upon a critical examination of the systems and practices operating within the business concerned. As the present tendency for businesses to be judged according to quality programmes and accreditation schemes continues to gather pace it would seem likely that the courts will require ever higher degrees of performance before being satisfied that due diligence has been established. In terms of licensed premises such a move would be consistent with the increasing tendency of licensing justices to require new licensees to undergo a period of formal training.

The business

6.24 If the case is being prepared by the company's regular lawyer, it is likely that he will already have a good understanding of the allocation of responsibilities and systems in operation. The newly-instructed lawyer may require some direction. In either event, the best starting point is the offence itself, from which the chain of causation can be traced back. With luck it will stop short of the defendant!

6.25 If we take a fairly typical case arising under the Licensing Act 1964, that of a licensee by his servant selling intoxicating liquor to a person under 18, the aspects of the company's business requiring consideration for a defence of due diligence upon the prosecution of a multiple licensee might include:

(a) management structure: the allocation and delegation of responsibilities;

(b) staff rota/wage records: to establish that adequate staff were on duty;

(c) staff cost analysis: demonstrating levels are appropriate;

(d) personnel records: to show experience and training of relevant staff;

(e)   operations manual: containing advice to company employees on the law and setting out any prescribed systems in necessary detail;

(f)   minutes of meetings: confirming that these matters were discussed on a regular basis;

(g)   notices: the nature and location of advisory and statutory notices;

(h)   defendant's diary: giving details of any relevant supervisory visits;

(i)   statements: taken from all staff to ascertain any possible failings in the system;

(j)   police records: for evidence of previous similar incidents.

These are, of course, just examples of a few of those items requiring consideration in a typical case. The lawyer must carry out a thorough and painstaking review of the management of the business in an effort to ensure that there has been no avoidable mistake that can reasonably be laid at the door of the defendant.

6.26   It is, of course, extremely common in such cases for there to be allegations and counter-allegations of blame passing between the defendant's employees. These are all grist to the prosecution's mill! If the possibility of such disputes cannot be ruled out, particularly between employees operating at different levels within the company, separate representation should be arranged. The advocate must not be constrained in his conduct of the case by a conflict of interest which may not become apparent until the second or third day of a trial.

The politics

6.27   Identifying the information required is usually less than half the battle. Extracting it from the relevant departments or individuals can involve a great deal of the politician's art—and plain dogged persistence. Items may have been misplaced, destroyed or, quite simply, withheld for fear of the apportionment of blame. Witnesses may be reluctant to come forward for the same reason. Although there will be occasions when it is subsequently proved to have been a waste of time, it is generally worth investigating any potential offences at the earliest possible opportunity.

The analysis

6.28   Next comes the hard work! The information which has been collated needs to be sorted into three main categories:

(1)   that which is of direct assistance in establishing the statutory defence;

(2)   that which *might* be of assistance in rebutting a challenge to the

defence by the prosecution, or a co-defendant ploughing his or her own furrow; and

(3) that which can be discarded (invariably the largest pile: unfortunately, it is not possible to avoid generating it as the true significance of many documents will be apparent only after the investigation).

Although the task may involve considering countless files and manuals the greatest care should be taken to incorporate in the main bundle only those items which are relevant to the central issue. Allowing documents which are surplus to requirements will only serve to cloud the issue and delay proceedings.

The presentation

6.29 Whether the defence is presented in court by the lawyer responsible for preparing the case, or by a specialist solicitor or barrister, all efforts will have been wasted if the company's modus operandi cannot be conveyed to the magistrates. Although a lay bench, they may not have a full understanding of the business in question. In those circumstances the greatest difficulty is presented by the witness who is unable adequately to explain the reasons for particular procedures to someone outside his or her corporate culture. The best practice is to assume nothing whilst avoiding, of course, the tedious repetition which unfortunately remains the mark of so many advocates.

6.30 As will be evident, the establishment of the due diligence defence can be a time-consuming and expensive process. Before embarking on this course, therefore, the defendant company needs to weigh up the anticipated cost of the exercise, and prospects of success, against the fine and damage to its reputation which might arise from a guilty plea. In specific cases there may be other consequences, such as civil claims (always consider the question of insurance) or, for example, application for revocation of a justices' licence.

6.31 Whether it is worth running the statutory defence will depend upon the facts of each particular case. The temptation to avoid is adopting a middle course—that of pursuing the defence following inadequate preparation. Not only are you most likely to lose, but in so doing you will have both annoyed the magistrates and probably attracted a great deal of unwelcome publicity. In short, if it is to be successful the defence requires the same degree of diligence in its preparation as it does in the attitude it seeks to establish.

UNDER 14S IN BARS

6.32 As indicated in chapter 5 it is generally an offence for a licensee to allow persons under 14 to be in the bar on licensed premises during permitted hours. In future, of course, where premises hold a children's certificate the offence will not be committed if the young person is in the company of a person who is 18 or over and the certificate is operational at that time, or he is consuming a meal purchased within the permitted period and not more than 30 minutes has elapsed after the end of that period.

Ingredients of the offence

6.33 The prosecution will need to establish:

(1) *Licensee*—See above for the evidence that might be adduced to establish the identity of the licensee.

(2) *Person under 14*—Section 168(8) provides that a person will be deemed to be under 14 if that is the allegation and he appears to the court to have been under that age, unless the contrary is shown.

(3) *The bar*—See chapter 5 for a consideration of the various authorities on the definition of a bar. The onus will be upon the prosecution to establish this fact.

(4) *Licensed premises*—Note that the offence is not committed in a registered club, for example.

(5) *During the permitted hours*—Again, it will be for the prosecution to establish that the young person was present during the permitted hours *applicable to those premises.*

Defences

6.34 There is no offence if the person under 14:

(a) is the child of the licensee; or

(b) resides (but is not employed)[1] in the premises; or

(c) is merely passing through the bar to some other place to which there is no other convenient means of access;[2]

(d) is in the bar of any railway refreshment rooms or other premises constructed, fitted and intended to be used bona fide for any purpose to which the holding of a justices' licence is merely ancillary (see chapter 5 for a detailed consideration of this provision).

¹ Unless the person is aged 16 or over and the employment is part of an approved training scheme. See s 170A inserted by the Deregulation (Employment in Bars) Order 1997.
² Section 168(4).

6.35 Assuming that none of these exemptions applies, the licensee must establish either:

(a) that he exercised all due diligence to prevent the person under 14 from being admitted to the bar; *or*

(b) that the person under 14 had apparently attained that age.

6.36 If the licensee claims not to have seen the child he may seek to rely upon the first defence available, of all due diligence. This topic is considered in some detail above. In relation to the specific issue of persons under 14 preventive measures might include controlled entry to the premises where these are situate in, for example, a busy tourist resort or some other place where it is known that under 14s are quite likely to try to gain entry. It is not uncommon nowadays for licensed premises to have door control, at least on busy nights of the week. If this method is not adopted the licensee may seek to rely upon his own regular tours around the public house or, alternatively, those made by responsible members of staff when clearing ashtrays, glasses, etc. This is, of course, an extremely important part of the proper management of the modern public house since it can also assist in detecting at an early stage problems with the use of drugs. Additionally, not only will it detect under 14s who are not allowed in the bar but it will also assist in identifying under 18s on whose behalf drinks are being purchased by older friends. Note, however, the reference in the subsection to the licensee's duty to prevent under 14s from being *admitted* to the bar, rather than merely being present.

6.37 It may well be that the licensee concedes that he was fully aware of the young person's presence, but did nothing about it because he took him or her to be of the necessary age. It is not clear whether there is any particular significance in the reference to that person having 'apparently attained that age', as opposed to the wording of s 169, under which the licensee needs to prove that 'he had no reason to suspect' (in the context of that offence) that a person was under 18. It is conceivable, perhaps, that one might have reason to suspect persons of being under age because of, for example, their suspicious behaviour but that nonetheless no steps were taken because they had apparently attained the necessary age, having regard to their appearance. If that is right it would seem that the test in s 168 is marginally less onerous for the defendant. As previously, it is incumbent upon him to establish the defence on the balance of probabilities.

SELLING LIQUOR TO UNAUTHORISED PERSONS

6.38   As indicated in chapter 1 a full on-licence authorises sales of all types of intoxicating liquor to all persons who may lawfully purchase, for consumption both on and off the premises.[1] In practice, the authority conferred by many licences is strictly circumscribed, by reference to either the kinds of liquor that may be sold or the categories of persons who may make the purchase. This is an important control since it enables committees to issue more licences than they might otherwise be prepared to issue if each were able to cater for every member of the public. Each of the limited licences is designed to some extent to cater for a particular audience. Because of the importance of this arrangement Parliament has provided that a breach of conditions relating to the sale and supply of intoxicating liquor to unauthorised persons is therefore an offence, punishable upon conviction by the imposition of a substantial fine and/or imprisonment.[2] The only sanctions in respect of breaches of other types of conditions are an application to revoke, or objection to renewal, unless the condition is one restricting permitted hours, in which case an offence under s 59 (see below) may be committed.

[1]   Note that there is no obligation on the licensee to serve an individual with intoxicating liquor. Further, in addition to the entitlement of a licensee to expel violent or drunken customers under s 174(1), the courts have additional powers under the Licensed Premises (Exclusion of Certain Persons) Act 1980 and even the Protection from Harassment Act 1997.

[2]   Section 161(3).

Ingredients of the offence

6.39   It is necessary for the prosecution to establish:

(1)   *Holder of a justices' on-licence* See the earlier discussions.

(2)   *Sales or supplies* Again, see the earlier discussions.

(3)   *Intoxicating liquor* See the earlier discussions.

(4)   *To persons to whom he is not permitted by the condition of his licence to sell or supply* Evidence will need to be adduced as to the identities of the purchasers and the classifications into which they fall. Not infrequently the purchasers will be undercover police officers, who will clearly be able to give this information. Evidence of the conditions on the licence should be made available from the licensing register.[1]

(5)   *Knowingly* Two situations fall to be considered: sale by the licensee himself, and sale by someone with delegated authority.

[1]   Section 30(4).

Sale by the licensee himself

6.40 In this case it will be necessary for the prosecution to establish either that the licensee evidently knew that the purchaser was not a person to whom intoxicating liquor could be sold under the terms of his licence, or that the licensee recklessly disregarded whether he might be such a person. If there is clear evidence that the licensee actually knew that the purchaser was not, for example, a member of the club as required by the licence (perhaps because the police officers working undercover revealed at the time that they were not members), the prosecution will have no difficulty in establishing this fact. If there is no such direct evidence the prosecution must show that the licensee was reckless in this regard. This may be done by showing, in the example given, that there was no form of door control, membership card scheme, admission book or display of suitable advisory notices.

Sale by a person with delegated authority

6.41 Where, however, the sale or supply is not effected by the licensee himself, but by a manager or bar person working under his delegated authority, different considerations apply. In *Vane v Yiannopoullos*[1] the defendant had a restaurant licence which was subject to the usual condition that intoxicating liquor should be sold only to persons taking table meals. He had instructed his staff accordingly. However, when he was elsewhere in the building a waitress nonetheless served liquor to two customers who had not ordered a meal. The House of Lords held that the licensee was rightly acquitted because:

(a) the wording of the Act suggested that the licence holder himself should be proved to have had the necessary knowledge if he was to be convicted; and

(b) even if he could be liable because he had delegated his managerial functions to his servant, he would not be liable in this case because there was no evidence of sufficient delegation.

[1]   [1964] 2 All ER 820; affd [1964] 3 All ER 820, HL.

6.42 Two other cases illustrate how a licensee might be convicted in circumstances where there has been an effective delegation. In *R v Winson*[1] the defendant was the holder of a licence attaching to a discothèque. It was a term of that licence that intoxicating liquor should be sold only to persons who had been members of a club operating at the premises for at least 48 hours. Whilst the club was being run by a manager two undercover police officers were admitted to the premises and served with drinks, without the 48-hour waiting period having elapsed. It was held by the Court of Appeal (per Lord Parker CJ) that:

'A man cannot get out of the responsibilities and duties attached to a licence by absenting himself. The position of course is quite different if he remains in control. It would only be right that he should not be liable if a servant behind his back did something which contravened the terms of the licence. If, however, he wholly absents himself leaving somebody else in control, he cannot claim that what has happened has happened without his knowledge if the delegate had knowingly carried on in contravention of the licence.'[2]

[1]   [1968] 1 All ER 197.
[2]   [1968] 1 All ER 197 at 204.

6.43   To complete the picture, in *Howker v Robinson*[1] a barman sold beer to a 14-year-old boy. The evidence was that the licensee had delegated control of that particular bar to the barman, even though the licensee was elsewhere within the building. Both the barman *and* the licensee were convicted. The licensee's appeal failed because it was clear that he had delegated his authority for that bar, even though he remained on the premises.

[1]   [1973] QB 178.

6.44   In each of these cases it was contended that the person charged with selling the intoxicating liquor had done so knowingly. Even though they had no *actual* knowledge the issue was whether they could be liable under the principle of delegation. In *Buxton v Chief Constable of Northumbria*,[1] however, the High Court considered whether the licensee should be convicted of knowingly allowing the consumption of intoxicating liquor by a minor where he knew that some under 18s would inevitably succeed in purchasing liquor, simply because of the numbers of people attending. Applying a commonsense approach the court held that since the licensee was doing all that he reasonably could to enforce a system he could not be held to be closing his eyes to potential breaches, or acting so recklessly that it amounted to having knowledge, even though he knew that there would be some breaches of the law.

[1]   (1983) 148 JP 9, QBD.

6.45   In general terms a good test to apply is that suggested by Lord Diplock in *Tesco Supermarkets Ltd v Nattrass*,[1] namely that 'to exercise due diligence to prevent something being done is to take all reasonable steps to prevent it'.

¹ [1971] 2 All ER 127, HL: the case is also authority for the proposition that a limited company charged with an offence may properly seek to take advantage of the statutory defence (where available) that the matter arose due to the 'act or default of another person' even where that person is an employee of the company. In such cases it will be necessary to consider whether the employee is of a sufficiently junior status to be regarded as a servant or agent, or whether that person is sufficiently involved in the decision making process to be regarded as the embodiment of the company and therefore not 'another person'. However, see *Tesco Stores Ltd v Brent London Borough Council* [1993] 2 All ER 718, QBD.

SALES OUTSIDE PERMITTED HOURS

6.46 As well as laying great stress upon the categories of persons to whom intoxicating liquor may be served, the Act also gives prominence to the times when such persons may be served. This is evidenced by the comprehensive set of provisions concerning permitted hours and the means by which these may be extended upon a temporary or permanent basis.

Ingredients of offence

6.47 An offence will be committed either if intoxicating liquor is sold or supplied in licensed premises or registered clubs outside permitted hours or if it is consumed in or taken from such premises at such times.

Sold or supplied . . . outside permitted hours

6.48 The necessary ingredients of this offence are as follows.

(1) *Sale or supply*—reference has already been made to s 196(1), which raises the presumption that a sale has taken place even though there is no evidence that money passed. However, as has been pointed out previously, such evidence is subject to rebuttal by the defendant so that if, for example, it can be established that the intoxicating liquor was a bona fide gift, there will have been no *sale*.¹ If it seems likely that the defendant will be able to rebut the presumption of a sale, the prosecution might seek to establish the alternative charge of supplying. This will be the case in respect of a registered club where, as has previously been observed, intoxicating liquor is technically supplied to members rather than being sold. Note that there is no statutory presumption of a supply although this may be inferred from the circumstances in which the intoxicating liquor is provided.

(2) *Person ... by himself or by his servant or agent*—there is no requirement to establish that the sale has been effected by or on

behalf of the *licensee*, although it must be so for the sale to be lawful in respect of licensed premises.

(3) *In licensed premises or a registered club*—the terms of the Act make it clear that in the case of a registered club the premises referred to are those in respect of which the club is permanently registered so that premises used temporarily on a special occasion[2] will not be governed by the provisions concerning permitted hours. Equally, no offence will be committed if a sale takes place outside the periods specified in an occasional licence.[3]

(4) *Intoxicating liquor*—see the earlier discussion.

(5) *For consumption on or off the premises*—it is an offence to sell or supply outside permitted hours in relation to both an off-licence and an on-licence, whether or not for consumption on the premises.

[1]   *Petherick v Sargent* (1862) 26 JP 135.
[2]   Section 39(3).
[3]   Section 59(3) and *Southall v Haime* (1979) 143 JP 245.

Consumption in or taking from licensed premises/registered clubs outside permitted hours

6.49   To establish this offence the prosecution will need to prove:

(1) *Consumption in or taking from*—again, s 196 establishes the presumption that intoxicating liquor was being consumed where there is evidence that consumption of intoxicating liquor was *about to take place*. Further, liquor may not be consumed in or taken from licensed premises or registered clubs other than during permitted hours, or up to 20 minutes thereafter ('drinking-up time').[1] If it is taken from the premises during this latter period it *must* be in a sealed vessel. Additionally, it may be ordered *or* dispatched (but not both) by the vendor, beyond this time.

(2) *Intoxicating liquor*—again, see the earlier discussion.

[1]   Section 63(1)(a).

Defences

Occasional licences

6.50   Notwithstanding the definition of licensed premises in s 200(2), s 59(3) specifically provides (as mentioned above) that the provisions as to hours do not apply to occasional licences.

Drinking-up

6.51 Ordinarily, consumption within the 20 minutes following the expiry of the permitted hours is permitted.[1]

[1] Section 63(1)(a) and (b).

Consumption with meal

6.52 If a meal has been provided and the liquor was ancillary to that meal, the drinking-up time is extended to 30 minutes for that purpose.[1]

[1] Section 63(1)(b).

Residents/owners/managers, etc

6.53 The provisions as to hours will not apply to any person who purchases, receives or consumes intoxicating liquor in the same premises in which he then resides.[1]

[1] Section 63(2)(a).

6.54 An annex which is used in connection with the principal business and is under common management will also so qualify. Residents may similarly take intoxicating liquor *from* licensed premises.[1] Finally, they may also purchase liquor for such consumption by their private friends.[2]

[1] Section 63(3)(a).
[2] Section 63(3)(b).

6.55 For the purposes of these provisions the term 'resident' also applies to a person carrying on, or in charge of, the business on the premises.[1] An owner or manager may therefore legitimately entertain his (bona fide) friends, at his own expense, after hours. The onus of establishing such a relationship, should a prosecution arise, is upon the defendant.[2]

[1] Section 63(4).
[2] Note, however, that in the frequently cited case on this point, *Atkins v Agar* [1914] 1 KB 26, that onus of proof arose expressly under the Licensing (Consolidation) Act 1920 and in the absence of any similar provision in the current legislation it is possible to argue that it is for the prosecution to establish that the defence does *not* apply.

Ordering or dispatch of off-sales

6.56 Either ordering *or* dispatch may take place outside permitted hours if the liquor is to be consumed off the premises.[1]

¹   Section 63(2)(b). Note the distinction between the ordering of liquor *or* the dispatch of liquor outside permitted hours as opposed to a transaction where the liquor is both ordered *and* dispatched during such a period. The latter will contravene s 59 and amount to an offence. See *Mizen v Old Florida Ltd, Egan v Mizen* (1934) 50 TLR 349 and *Furby v Hoey* [1947] 1 All ER 236.

Sales to trade/registered clubs/canteen/mess

6.57   Such sales may take place at any time.¹

¹   Section 63(2)(c) and (d).

Employees

6.58   Employees may be supplied with intoxicating liquor provided that it is supplied at the expense of their employer (ie at no charge to employee) while the employee is still technically on duty.¹

¹   Section 63(3)(c).

CLOSURE ORDERS

6.59   The Criminal Justice and Police Act 2001 gave the police significant new powers to close licensed premises that cause disturbance or public order difficulties. Given the potential impact of these measures the government has agreed detailed guidelines with the Association of Chief Police Officers. These are critical to an understanding of the legislation and may readily be accessed via the DCMS website, where they appear as an addendum to DCMS Licensing Circular 01/2001. Despite some anxiety in the trade on account of the sweeping nature of the new powers, initial evidence suggests that they may be used sparingly. In the first six months of the measure only one case nationally has come to light. Of course this may change as the police become more familiar with their new weapon against public disorder.

6.60   The new powers are as follows: a police officer of the rank of inspector or above may make a closure order in relation to on-licensed premises if he reasonably believes that there is or is likely to be disorder on, or in the vicinity of and related to the premises and the closure of the premises is necessary in the interests of public safety. An alternative ground arises where a disturbance is being caused to the public by excessive noise emitted from the premises and the closure of the premises is necessary to prevent the disturbance. See the guidance for matters that such an officer should consider when preparing to issue such an order.

6.61   A closure order may require premises to close for up to 24 hours. It must describe the premises, the period for which they are to be closed and the grounds for making the order. The notice is also required to bear information as to the effects of the order and the provisions for appeal. The order comes into force as soon as notice of the order is given by a constable to the holder of the justices' licence for the premises; or a manager of the premises. The penalties for breach, without reasonable excuse, are a fine not exceeding £20,000 or to imprisonment for a term not exceeding three months or both.

6.62   As soon as possible after the coming into force of a closure order, the responsible senior officer must apply to the justices for them to consider the order and any extension of it. Notice must be given to the chief executive to the licensing justices indicating: that a closure order has come into force; the contents of the order and of any extension to the order; and the application to the justices.

6.63   The justices are the licensing justices for the licensing district in which the premises are situated. If no licensing justices are available within a reasonable time, justices of the peace acting for the petty sessions area in which the premises are situated may act. Additionally the powers may be exercised by a single justice and otherwise than at licensing sessions. Evidence given for the purpose of these proceedings shall be given on oath.

6.64   The justices shall 'as soon as reasonably practicable' consider whether to exercise their powers in relation to the order and any extension of it. They may either revoke the order, direct that the relevant licensed premises remain or be closed until the matter is dealt with at the next licensing sessions; or make such other order as they think fit in relation to the premises. If consideration is being given to closure then the justices must direct their minds to those criteria to be addressed in the first instance by the senior police officer when making the original order.

6.65   If, before the end of the period for which the premises are to be closed under a closure order or any extension of it, the police reasonably believe that justices will not have considered the order and any extension of it by the end of the closure period; and the original criteria remain, they may extend the closure period for a further period, not exceeding 24 hours.

6.66   At any time after a closure order has been made; but before the order has been considered by justices, the responsible senior police officer may cancel the order and any extension of it. He *must* do so if he does not reasonably believe that the criteria upon which the original order was made, continue to be satisfied. Where a closure order is cancelled the police shall ensure that notice of the cancellation is given to the licensee or manager of the premises.

6.67   Where a closure order has come into force licensing justices are required at the first licensing sessions taking place more than 14 days after the first hearing, to consider whether to revoke the justices' licence for the premises concerned; or to attach to it such conditions as they think fit. In either case licensing justices may only exercise their powers if, at least seven days before the commencement of the licensing sessions concerned, notice has been given to the licensee specifying in general terms the grounds on which it is proposed that the licence should be revoked; or (as the case may be) the conditions which are proposed to be attached to the licence and the reasons for them. As in other cases of revocation, any decision to revoke is exercisable on any ground on which licensing justices might refuse to renew a justices' licence or a justices' licence of that description. They may also make such other order as they think fit in relation to the closure order and any extension of it

6.68   Where licensing justices have decided to attach conditions to a licence under sub-s (2) of s 179E, the licensing justices may, on such terms as they think fit, suspend the operation of those conditions in whole or in part pending the determination of any appeal against the decision to attach them, or pending the consideration of the question of bringing such an appeal.

6.69   Where licensing justices have decided to revoke a justices' licence of this section, the revocation shall not have effect until the expiry of the time given for appealing against the decision; or if the decision is appealed against, until the appeal is disposed of. An exception to this rule arises where the premises have been closed to that date by virtue of an order by the justices, in which case, the premises shall remain closed (but the licence otherwise in force) until the expiry of the time given for appealing against the decision to revoke; or if the decision is appealed against, until the appeal is disposed of. Any person aggrieved may appeal against either the original justices' decision or that taken at the licensing sessions.

6.70   A person who, without reasonable excuse, permits premises to be open in contravention of such an order will be guilty of an offence and liable to a fine not exceeding £20,000 or to imprisonment for a term not exceeding three months or to both. There are also penalties for those failing to leave following a reasonable request. Certain of the offences specified may be committed by limited companies and their officers.

6.71 The measure protects individual officers and the chief of police from civil liability arising as a consequence of actions taken under these provisions, save where these can be demonstrated to have been taken in bad faith, or where such an entitlement would otherwise arise under the Human Rights Act 1998, s 6(1).

REVOCATIONS—JUSTICES' LICENCES AND SPECIAL HOURS CERTIFICATES

Introduction

6.72 Until 1 March 1989, justices' licences could not be terminated other than by forfeiture, surrender[1] or, more usually, non-renewal at the annual general licensing meeting (Brewster Sessions) taking place in the first fortnight of February. By the Licensing Act 1988 the duration of each justices' licence was extended from one year to three years, but at the same time machinery was introduced to enable any person to apply for the revocation of a justices' licence at *any* licensing sessions (other than sessions at which an application for renewal of the licence has been listed).[2] Conviction for any of the offences described in this chapter may, therefore, have far more drastic consequences than the mere imposition of a fine; in certain circumstances a conviction might found an application for the revocation of the licence itself.

[1] But see *Drury v Scunthorpe Licensing Justices* (1992) 157 JP 401, DC.
[2] Licensing Act 1964, s 20A(1) inserted by the Licensing Act 1988, s 12(1).

Revocation of justices' licences

6.73 Under the present licensing system the principal difficulty arising in relation to revocation lies in the fact that a single licence attaches to both the premises and the licensee. Accordingly, if the licence is revoked because the premises are in some way unsatisfactory the licensee might feel that the order is in some way a reflection upon his personal suitability; conversely (and far more commonly), if the licensee has been guilty of some misconduct the owner of the premises might be substantially prejudiced following the loss of the licence, through no fault of his own. There are a number of ways in which these difficulties can be minimised, but not always entirely averted.

Notice of application

6.74　Not less than 21 days before the relevant licensing sessions the person seeking the revocation of the licence (which may include the licensing committee) is required to serve notice in writing upon the licensee and the clerk to the licensing justices, setting out in general terms the grounds of the application. A specimen notice is reproduced in Part II.

Grounds of revocation

6.75　The Act provides that a justices' licence may be revoked upon any ground on which the licensing justices might refuse to renew a justices' licence *of that description.*

6.76　The grounds upon which justices' licences might not be renewed have been considered in chapter 3. In general terms, the committee has a wide discretion to refuse to renew the licence in cases where there has been any default on the part of the licensee, defect in the premises or evidence of any disturbance or annoyance in the neighbourhood, even if this last cannot be related directly to the management of the house.[1] In the cases of old beerhouse licences (pre-1 May 1869) and old on-licences (pre-15 August 1904),[2] limitations are placed on the grounds upon which licensing justices may refuse a transfer or renewal. Because of the reference in s 20A(2) to a 'justices' licence of that description', it is clear that such licences are similarly protected in relation to revocation proceedings. This may be highly significant where, for example, it is sought to revoke on the grounds of disrepair (which is not a ground upon which an old beerhouse licence may be revoked) or the closure of the premises for a period of time (a ground which cannot be used in respect of an old on-licence). See chapter 3 for details of the grounds upon which renewals and transfers of these licences may be refused.

[1]　*Lidster v Owen* [1983] 1 All ER 1012, which concerns the renewal of a music and dance licence.
[2]　Section 12.

6.77　Similarly, Part IV licences may not be revoked save upon one of the specified grounds set out in s 98 (see chapter 2).

6.78　Revocation proceedings will follow a similar form to opposed ·applications for renewal. Evidence must be given on oath.[1]

[1]　Section 20A(4).

Appeals

6.79 If the licence is revoked it will not cease to have effect until the expiry of the time for appealing against the decision (21 days) or, if an appeal is brought within that period, until the appeal is determined.

6.80 Any person aggrieved by a decision of the licensing justices to revoke the licence may bring the appeal. The licensee will, of course, so qualify. The expression will also, however, extend to the owner or mortgagee of the premises, who may decide either to serve a notice of appeal jointly with the licensee or to serve notice independently.[1] If the licensee decides to appeal himself there is no difficulty; if not, the owner or mortgagee must look to the lease or mortgage for authority to proceed in the name of lessee or mortgagee.

1   *Garrett v Middlesex Justices* (1884) 12 QBD 620; *Feist v Tower Justices* (1904) 68 JP 264.

6.81 The notice of appeal should set out the grounds upon which the appeal is brought. Both the licensing justices and the person upon whose application the licence was revoked should be named as respondents.

6.82 Pending the determination of the appeal, the licensing justices are obliged to hear and determine according to law any application properly lodged for the transfer of the justices' licence (which will have the effect of granting a new licence, see the reference in chapter 3 to a recent decision which casts some doubt upon this premise). Protection orders may also be granted.

6.83 If the revocation proceedings are brought by the police, they may seek to encourage the owners of the property, or those remaining in possession, to abandon any appeal (so allowing the licence to lapse) and pursue instead an application for a new justices' licence. In promoting such a course of action the view may be expressed that, since the licensing committee has seen fit to revoke the licence, it is somehow an abuse of the process to negate that order by listing an application for a mere transfer. Similar views have been expressed by some licensing committees in the past. Whilst the applicant may not agree with such views (which certainly do not reflect the legal position) he will have to weigh the merit of adopting a course of action with which the authorities have so clearly expressed their disapproval against the chances of succeeding with a new application. If a clear indication is given that neither the licensing committee nor the police have any intention to 'de-license' the premises on a permanent basis, the revocation being granted merely by reason of the conduct of the previous licensee, the applicant *may* decide that he can safely proceed with the submission of an application for a new licence, possibly even withdrawing or abandoning any appeal. That will give the licensing committee an opportunity to consider various aspects of the premises including their layout, style of operation, security of stock, etc, with a view to remedying any historical problems that have been evident. If there is no objection to that application (see chapter 2 for the delaying effect of such an objection) any appeal against revocation may be withdrawn immediately once the new licence has been granted.

6.84   If the authorities are unwilling to give any sort of indication concerning the licensing of the premises in the future (the justices could not, in any event, bind themselves in any way to limit their discretion), or if the appellant considers it likely that other objectors may appear to oppose an application for a new licence, the appellant may feel obliged to exhaust all available remedies.

6.85   The first of the options to be considered is, of course, the transfer of the licence. One of the difficulties the appellant may face is in finding persons who are willing to take on premises which are still subject to an order of revocation, albeit under appeal. Even if those persons are willing to proceed in the first instance, their attitude may change once they have been interviewed and apprised of the previous difficulties.

6.86   Any application for transfer of the licence should be determined according to the usual criteria (see chapter 3). If the transfer is refused an appeal may be brought against that decision, possibly to be heard consecutively with the appeal against revocation. If the appeal against revocation is allowed the licence will be reinstated. Alternatively, the appeal against the refused transfer could be granted and the revocation appeal withdrawn or dismissed. The Crown Court cannot revoke upon any ground not set out in the original notice of application for revocation, although it need not necessarily adopt the same ground as that cited by the licensing justices.[1] At the hearing of any applications for revocation, or appeals against such decisions, it should always be borne in mind that the licensee or the owner may need at some stage to apply to the licensing justices for the grant of a new licence. Accordingly, those seeking the revocation should always be asked to indicate to the committee their objective in bringing the proceedings. Although, in the early stages, their objection may be directed simply towards the licensee rather than the existence of the licensed premises themselves, it may subsequently be found that once the premises have closed the original applicants for the revocation change their strategy so as to ensure that this is a permanent arrangement. Whilst, it may be argued, they are perfectly at liberty to review their earlier position, it can equally be suggested on behalf of the licensee or the owner that the licensing committee might not have revoked the licence in the first place if it had thought that there would be any objection raised at a later date to the re-licensing of the premises themselves.

¹ *Ex p Gorman* [1894] AC 23.

Revocation of special hours certificates

6.87 It is anticipated that by far the most common reason that special hours certificates are revoked is that the public entertainments licence has been allowed to lapse through an inadvertent failure to renew.

6.88 As indicated in an earlier chapter, public entertainment licences are issued by local authorities for varying periods of up to one year. Renewals do not take place at any particular time of the year and so they are very easily overlooked. However, s 81(1) of the Act provides that the special hours certificate will automatically lapse as soon as the public entertainments licence ceases to be in force.

6.89 From 1 May 1998 the Public Entertainments Licences (Drugs Misuse) Act 1997 came into force, subject to guidelines issued by the government. Such guidelines are important, given the draconian powers given to local authorities to close down such premises where it is alleged by the police that so doing will 'significantly assist' in dealing with a drugs problem within the premises or 'any place nearby which is controlled by the licence holder'.

6.90 In addition, the chief officer of police may apply for the revocation of a special hours certificate upon any of the following grounds.

(1) The premises (or the relevant part of the premises) have not been used for the purpose of providing for persons resorting to the premises, music and dancing (or gaming, in the case of casinos) and substantial refreshment to which the sale of intoxicating liquor is ancillary. Under this provision the main thrust of the police evidence will be directed towards the *provision* of music and dancing (or gaming, in the case of casinos) and substantial refreshment, rather than the extent to which such facilities are *used* by the patrons. Evidence might be given as to the availability of a dance floor (or facilities for gaming), whether or not suitable music is played in the case of the former and, more commonly, whether there is available on the premises sufficient (or any) food for the persons visiting those premises.¹

(2)   There has been a sale, supply or consumption of intoxicating liquor at those premises outside permitted hours, for which a person has been convicted under s 59 of the Act.

(3)   That, on the whole, customers attending the premises during the hours[2] conferred by the special hours certificate, are there for the purpose of obtaining intoxicating liquor rather than to dance (or game) or take food (or, in the case of casino premises, for gaming and the obtaining of refreshments). The police evidence in this case would be directed towards the actual *usage* of the premises, so that observations may be made of the numbers of persons eating, dancing, gaming and drinking during any given period. Whilst it is not, of course, the case that *all* persons must either dance and/or eat substantial refreshments (there may legitimately be some who make use of neither facility), the two uses combined must constitute the primary use made of the premises, to which the sale and supply of intoxicating liquor are ancillary.

In the leading case of *Shipley*, the Court of Appeal upheld the view of the Divisional Court (and the earlier decision of *Marsden*) in finding that a special hours certificate does not confer additional, but rather *substitute*, hours for the sale of liquor. Consequently under this provision the music and dancing and/or the consumption of substantial refreshment must be the dominant use at all times the premises are open on days when the special hours certificate operates and not merely between 11 pm and the close of business.[3]

(4)   The revocation is expedient because of the occurrence of disorderly or indecent conduct in the premises.

[1]   Section 81(2)(a).
[2]   *R v Stafford Crown Court, ex p Shipley* [1998] 2 All ER 465, 162 JP 429, CA (1998) Licensing Review.
[3]   *R v Stafford Crown Court, ex p Shipley* [1998] 2 All ER 465, 162 JP 429, CA (1998) Licensing Review.

6.91   If the licensing committee is satisfied that any of the first three grounds is made out, it has a discretion to revoke the special hours certificate. In such circumstances they should not consider the evidence too narrowly, but should ascertain whether there has in general been a breach of the sub-paragraphs of s 81(2), having regard if necessary to the entitlement to brief interruptions according to s 83(2).[1] If, however, it is satisfied that the fourth ground is proved, the committee is *obliged* to revoke. Note, however, that in this case the committee is required to find that revocation is *expedient* before it may revoke upon this ground and so, in effect, it can be argued that the remedy is discretionary.

[1]   *Spence v Cooper* (1998) Licensing Review (January), DC.

6.92 In lodging an application for revocation of a special hours certificate, the police must give to the clerk to the licensing justices and the holder of the licence at least seven days' notice of intention to apply. The notice must be in writing specifying the grounds of the application.

6.93 When determining the application to revoke the justices may revoke, dismiss the application or impose limitations upon the certificate (see chapter 7).

Reinstatement

6.94 If a special hours certificate is revoked the order will have immediate effect; its coming into force will not be affected in any way by the service of a notice of appeal.

6.95 Conversely, following a decision by the licensing justices to revoke it, a licence will continue in force if an appeal is lodged in time (see chapter 2). Further, if the justices refuse to renew a justices' licence (so that it will expire on 5 April in the renewal year, or revoke it at such a time), either the licensing justices or the Crown Court may order that the licence should continue in force until the hearing of that appeal, even though that appeal might take place after 4 April. Conditions may be imposed.[1] If the appeal against revocation is subsequently allowed the Crown Court may further direct that the licence should continue in force until the date of the next transfer sessions.

[1] Section 21(4).

6.96 Any person aggrieved may appeal against a decision to revoke a special hours certificate. Thus, owners of licensed premises may jointly appeal with the licensee or proceed with their own separate appeal. If the licensee decides not to appeal regard must be paid to the terms of any contractual agreement between the owner and the licensee, entitling the former to appeal in the name of the latter.

6.97 Only the chief officer of police may appeal against a decision not to revoke a certificate or not to attach a limitation under s 81A(3). Further, a person may appeal against a decision not to attach a limitation (under s 81A(2)) upon the special hours certificate upon an application for revocation only if he has appeared before the licensing justices and made representations that the limitation should be attached.[1] There is no entitlement for the justices to be named as respondents in any such appeal, although they must be served with the notice of appeal, as must any objector.[2]

1   Section 81B(2).
2   See Crown Court Rules 1982, Part III, r 7.

6.98   If an appeal is successful the certificate may, of course, be reinstated. Alternatively, application may be made immediately thereafter for a new special hours certificate—although note that if the original certificate was revoked by reason of ground (2), above[1] (ie sale outside permitted hours), the application to reinstate may not be made within two months of the revocation, or any time up to 12 months, according to the direction given by the justices at the time the original certificate was revoked.

1   Section 81(2)(b).

6.99   In the meantime, if the certificate has been revoked owing to the inadvertent failure to renew the public entertainments licence consideration could be given to making application for an occasional licence (or a series of occasional licences) pending the hearing of the application for a new special hours certificate.

CHAPTER 7

HOURS

7.01 Part III of the Act, which concerns permitted hours, is founded upon the proposition that it is illegal to sell or supply in licensed premises, or registered clubs, or to consume in, or take from, such premises intoxicating liquor, except within permitted hours.[1] Breach of this provision is a criminal offence which can give rise to a level 3 fine.[2] The remainder of Part III sets out the general permitted hours which apply to most licensed premises and various provisions whereby these may be extended or curtailed upon a temporary or permanent basis. The chart at para **7.02** shows these diagrammatically.

[1] Section 59(1).
[2] Section 59(2): £1,000 at the time of going to press.

GENERAL PERMITTED HOURS

7.02 (1) *Justices' off-licences*
Monday to Saturday: 8.00 am to 11.00 pm
Good Friday (only): 8.00 am to 10.30 pm
Christmas Day: 12 noon to 3.00 pm; 7.00 pm to 10.30 pm
Sunday: 10.00 am to 10.30 pm.

(2) *Justices' on-licences*
Monday to Saturday: 11.00 am (or, at the justices' discretion, any time after 10.00 am) to 11.00 pm
Good Friday and Sunday: 12 noon to 10.30 pm
Christmas Day: 12 noon to 3.00 pm; 7.00 pm to 10.30 pm.

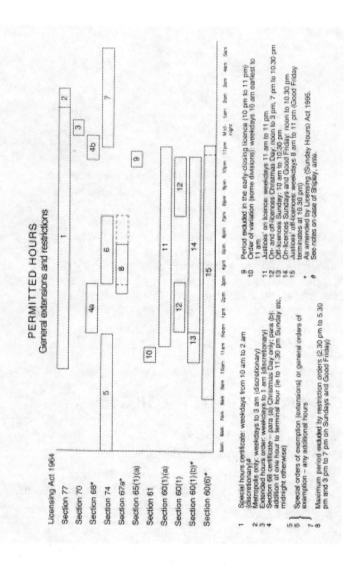

PERMITTED HOURS
General extensions and restrictions

Order of variation

7.03 Once a year at their annual general licensing meeting (held in the first fortnight of February) the licensing justices may direct that the opening hour should be brought forward from 11.00 in the morning to any time not earlier than 10.00 am. The variation need not be applied regularly throughout the year, but may make different provisions for certain weekdays or periods of the year.[1]

Every licensee or prospective licensee should ensure that he is familiar with any variations ordered by his local licensing committee.

[1]   Section 61.

RESTRICTED HOURS

7.04 Permitted hours in any individual premises may be restricted either by way of conditions on the licence or by an order of the licensing justices.

Conditions restricting hours

7.05 As described in chapter 1, a number of licences recognised in the Act exclude certain periods from the standard permitted hours.

Seasonal licences

7.06 During the hearing of any application for the grant of a justices' on-licence, or any time thereafter, justices may be invited to impose a condition specifying that there will be no permitted hours at certain times of the year. Such a licence is referred to as a seasonal licence.[1] The condition may be removed subsequently upon application.

[1]   Section 64.

Six-day licences

7.07 A similar procedure is available for the imposition of a condition that there will be no permitted hours in the premises on Sundays.

Early-closing licences

7.08 A condition may be imposed providing that permitted hours in the evening will end one hour earlier than the general licensing hours. Again, a procedure is available for removal of the condition.

7.09　As indicated earlier, in chapter 3, there is no obligation to open licensed premises during permitted hours. However there is always a risk that the failure to open for long periods or regular hours may lead to an application for the revocation of the licence, or opposition to its renewal, upon the ground that there is evidently insufficient public demand for such facilities.

Restriction orders

7.10　Any local person, head teacher or chief officer of police can apply to the licensing committee for a restriction order excluding any time between 2.30 and 5.30 pm on weekdays, or between 3.00 and 7.00 pm on Sunday and Good Friday, from the permitted hours of individual on-licensed premises, or part of such premises, or registered clubs.

7.11　Application is made by notice in writing, specifying in general terms the grounds of the application, sent to the chief executive to the licensing justices and the licensee not less than 21 days before the relevant transfer sessions.[1] The order may operate throughout the year, or apply to particular days or periods.

[1]　Schedule 8A.

7.12　The grounds upon which such an order may be granted are, broadly, that the premises are, during the hours specified, causing disturbance or annoyance to members of the public or persons represented by the applicant.

7.13　A restriction order will have effect only for the period specified at the time of its making and in any event for no more than one year. A procedure is laid down[1] for the making of applications to impose, vary or revoke an order. Such an application may not be made within six months of the date upon which any existing order came into force.

[1]　Schedule 8A.

7.14　Only the licensee has the right to appeal against the grant of or the terms of a restriction order.[1] If it is anticipated that the licensee may wish to bring an appeal, consideration should be given to the preparation of an appropriate notice *prior* to the hearing, since the restriction can take immediate effect, in which case only the service of a notice of appeal will suspend its operation.

[1]　Section 67B.

7.15 Where a restriction order is in force, the licensee is under a duty to display conspicuously a notice stating its effect.[1]

[1] Section 67D.

EXTENSION OF PERMITTED HOURS

7.16 In relation to any licensed premises the general permitted hours may be extended upon a temporary, semi-permanent or permanent basis.

Special orders of exemption (extensions)

7.17 Extensions, as they are most commonly known, are without a doubt the most frequent applications made in respect of licensed premises. Such orders are not granted by the licensing committee but by ordinary magistrates sitting within the petty sessional division.[1] Where granted for premises that have a licence for music and dancing, the order will automatically extend the latter also for that occasion.[2]

[1] In the City of London or Metropolitan Police District such applications are made to the Commissioner of Police.
[2] London Government Act 1963, Sch 12, para 11 and (outside London) Local Government (Miscellaneous Provisions) Act 1982, Sch 1, para 13.

7.18 There is no statutory requirement to serve a formal notice prior to the hearing although, in practice, it is customary to serve such notice upon both the chief executive to the licensing justices and the police some days beforehand, so that the police may have an opportunity to consider the matter. However, if the applicant is able to serve two copies of the application upon the chief executive to the justices at least one month before the date of the first event, the application may be heard in the absence of the applicant as long as the police do not serve written notice of objection within seven days of the chief executive posting to them a copy of the notice of application. Any such objection must be notified to the applicant.

7.19 Although, as has been indicated, there is no statutory provision in relation to the notice, it is customary for that document to contain the name and address of the applicant and of licensed premises operated by him, as well as the times, days and events in respect of which the extension is required.

7.20 In many areas it is also customary for the licensee to obtain, from the person on whose behalf the event is being organised, a letter confirming the request for facilities to be made available. That letter might also set out in a little more detail the nature of the event, any control over admission (eg ticket only) and the numbers attending.

7.21   Because of the numbers of applications coming before the courts there is, as one might anticipate, a wealth of Divisional Court authority upon what may, or may not, be considered a special occasion. Whilst the determination of that issue in any particular case will be for the magistrates to decide, the following decisions may offer some guidance.

Can be special occasions

7.22   Public holidays (Christmas Eve, New Year's Eve, etc)[1] are special occasions.

[1]   *Devine v Keeling* (1886) 50 JP 551.

7.23   Twenty-first, thirtieth, fortieth birthdays, etc, silver, ruby and golden anniversaries, weddings, retirement parties, etc are generally held by most magistrates to be special occasions. Eighteenth birthdays may also be so regarded, although many committees are reluctant to grant extensions for these because of the risk of under-age drinking (similar considerations—although for rather different reasons!—are often applied to christenings). Applications for fortieth and fiftieth birthdays are frequently considered not to be special, although again it must be emphasised that practice will vary from court to court. English football league matches may qualify in some areas[1]—although 46 extensions granted over two separate periods totalling 12 months were held to be an extreme (but just acceptable) interpretation of 'special occasions'.[2] In 2002 the Divisional Court held, departing form earlier decisions, that the football World Cup competition was capable of being a special occasion meriting the grant of extensions, notwithstanding the fact that the participation on the part of the customers of a public house was in the form of viewing the match on a large screen TV within the premises.[3] Friday nights and Saturdays preceding bank holidays have been deemed special occasions.[4]

[1]   *Browning v J W H Watson (Rochester) Ltd* [1953] 2 All ER 775.
[2]   *R v Llanidloes (Lower) Justices, ex p Thorogood* [1971] 3 All ER 932.
[3]   *Gough v Avon and Somerset Police Licensing Bureau* [2002] EWHC 658 (Admin), (2002) 49 LR 17.
[4]   *R v Woodstock Justices, ex p Holdsworth* (13 May 1977, unreported) and *R v Corwen Justices, ex p Edwards* [1980] 1 All ER 1035.

Not considered to be special occasions

7.24 (1) As a general principle, events organised primarily for the benefit of the licensee.[1]

(2) Christmas week shopping.[2]

(3) General repeated events: ordinary market days;[3] 'summertime';[4] railway company Sunday excursions;[5] weekly dances;[6] weekly shooting syndicate dinners over three months.

Note that a number of committees quite helpfully set out in their policy documents what events are and are not considered to be special in their division.

[1]   *Knole Park Golf Club v Chief Superintendent, Kent County Constabulary* [1979] 3 All ER 829—although in that case it was found that the events organised *were* special occasions since they related to special dinners, dances and competitions organised as part of the club's affairs.

[2]   *R v Cheltenham Justices, ex p Martin Bros (Wines and Spirits) Ltd* (1955) 120 JP 88.

[3]   *R v Butt, ex p Brooke* (1922) 38 TLR 537.

[4]   *R v Sussex Justices, ex p Bubb* [1933] 2 KB 707.

[5]   *R v Lancashire Justices, ex p Customs and Excise Comrs* (1934) 151 LT 376.

[6]   *Lemon v Sargent* [1971] 3 All ER 936n.

The hearing

7.25   As has been indicated above, the application may be heard in the absence of the applicant if notice is submitted at least one month before the event.

7.26   To avoid inconvenience to licensees, many courts will be prepared to grant block applications for extensions for a part of the year. Inquiries should be made of the local magistrates' court as to the practice that is followed in that division. Many courts will also be prepared to deal with applications for extensions in the absence of the licensee, even though less than one month's notice has been given.

7.27   The usual procedure is that the clerk will read out details of the extension sought. If there are any queries, either the clerk or the magistrates will direct these to the applicant. The principal concern may be as to the allegedly 'special' nature of the particular occasion. In addition, the magistrates may be interested in the numbers of persons attending, whether there have been any difficulties in the past, and so on. If the police are opposing the application they may at this stage make representations to the magistrates. The applicant may then respond and the justices will make their decision, which may be to allow the application in full, restrict it to fewer hours, or refuse it in its entirety.

7.28   Where they have accepted that there is a special occasion, but are concerned as to the noise or disturbance that might be caused, the magistrates should *not* refuse the application if they have no evidence before them upon which to make such an assessment but are merely acting upon their own supposition[1] or inflexibly applying a policy.[2] However, in another case the High Court upheld a magistrates' decision to refuse extensions for licensed premises at a football ground because of their general view that the absence of alcohol would inevitably reduce the incidence of violence and because they felt it inappropriate to grant such applications for extensions on Sundays.[3] The difference between the outcome in these two cases appears to arise from the fact that in the former the refusals were based upon narrow and specific concerns or consistent application, of a declared policy (without regard to the merits of an individual application), whereas in the latter it was founded upon the justices' general knowledge of football grounds and an aversion to extended Sunday opening.

[1]   *White, White & Gibbeson v South East Cornwall Justices* [1989] COD 402.
[2]   *R v Chester Justices, ex p Cecchini* (1996) 29 Licensing Review 19, QBD.
[3]   *R v Doncaster Justices, ex p Langfield* (1984) 149 JP 26.

7.29   Where substantial extensions of existing permitted hours are sought, for example for a wedding reception, magistrates often prefer to see a break of one or two hours before the second session begins.

7.30   The application may also be made by the holder of a protection order. Once granted for an event, the order may be operated by a subsequent licensee or protection order holder provided the event remains the same for that date.

Refusals

7.31   There is no right of appeal to the Crown Court against a refusal to grant an extension; application may be made, however, to the High Court on a case stated, or for judicial review. Magistrates have no power to award costs in these proceedings.

GENERAL ORDERS OF EXEMPTION

7.32   If magistrates are satisfied that a *considerable* number of persons attending a *public market or following a lawful trade or calling* in the *immediate neighbourhood* of a public house might be accommodated if they were to extend the permitted hours for that house, they may make a general order of exemption if they consider it *desirable* to do so. Examples of persons following a lawful trade or calling might be newspaper staff, railway workers, market porters, etc.

7.33   The general thread of the various authorities upon these provisions[1] is that the High Court will readily quash an over-generous order of the justices if it is found that they have not properly applied their minds to each of the matters italicised in the preceding paragraph.

[1]   Section 74(1).

7.34   A general order of exemption may be varied or revoked. If it is not expressed to expire upon a particular date it will continue in force without any need for renewal.

NEW YEARS'S EVE ETC

7.35   In 1999/2000 and 2001/2002 the government managed to secure deregulation orders which had the effect of extending permitted hours for licensed premises from 11 pm until 11 am the day following. Public Entertainment Licences were not affected and required individual applications to the relevant local authority for extensions. Further, for the Queen's Golden Jubilee, hours (other than in off licences, registered clubs and canteens) were extended by two hours, ie from 11 pm until 1 am the next day. At the time of going to press it appears likely that the experience of the New Year's Eves in 1999 and 2001 when hours were extended will be repeated in future years, save where New Year's Eve falls on a Sunday.

PERMANENT EXTENSIONS

7.36   There are three forms of 'permanent' extensions (ie those that will endure as long as the 'parent' licence subsists or until revocation, not requiring renewal themselves): the supper hour certificate, the extended hours order and the special hours certificate. These are capable of extending permitted hours to midnight, 1.00 am or 2.00 am (3.00 am in the metropolis) respectively. Each is dependent upon the provision of food, to a greater or lesser extent. These are dealt with in the next three sections of the chapter.

SUPPER HOUR/RESTAURANT CERTIFICATE (S 68 CERTIFICATE)

7.37   Applications for s 68 certificates are not generally contentious if the applicant is able to satisfy the licensing justices that the structure of the premises and their intended use accords with the criteria set out in the Act. Following the Deregulation (Restaurant Licensing Hours) Order 2002[1] from 2 April 2002 the holder of a restaurant licence or residential and restaurant licence granted under Part IV of the Act will automatically have the benefit of the additional hours conferred by both parts of s 68, without the need to make any such application.

[1]   SI 2002/493.

Additional hours

7.38   The s 68 certificate is capable of creating a permanent extension on Christmas Day to 'bridge' the break otherwise in force between 3.00 pm and 7.00 pm (para (a)) and to add a further hour at the end of the evening, extending permitted hours on Sundays, Christmas Day and Good Friday to 11.30 pm; on weekdays to 12.00 midnight (para (b)).[1]

[1]   Note that the 'afternoon break' on Sundays and Good Friday was removed by the Licensing (Sunday Hours) Act 1995, which came into force on 6 August 1995.

Notices

7.39   The procedure is governed by the Licensing Rules 1961. The Rules provide that at least seven days before the relevant transfer sessions the applicant must send a signed notice of the application, indicating the address of the subject premises, to the chief executive to the licensing justices and the chief officer of police.[1] It is also convenient for the notice to include details of the intended 'commencement date' of such certificate as may be granted. Since at least 14 days' notice of *commencement* needs to be given, it is prudent to serve the notice of application early to allow such a period to elapse before the sessions.

7.40   Although the Act does not so provide, many committees direct as a matter of policy that the notice should be accompanied by a plan delineating the area which is usually set apart for the service of persons taking table meals.

[1]   See para **2.08**.

Application

7.41 The Rules specifically provide that the justices shall deal with the case in accordance with the procedure ordinarily adopted for consideration of an application for the grant of a new justices' licence.[1] In order to secure a certificate the applicant must satisfy the justices that his premises meet the criteria set out in s 68(3) of the Act, namely:

'... that the premises are structurally adapted and bona fide used, or intended to be used, for the purpose of habitually providing, for the accommodation of persons frequenting the premises, substantial refreshment to which the sale and supply of intoxicating liquor is ancillary.'

[1]   Licensing Rules 1961, r 6.

7.42 In practice, the applicant will give evidence as to the following matters:

(1) *Part of the premises* If the service of table meals usually takes place in part only of the premises then, as indicated above, a plan should be produced defining that area.

(2) *Usually set apart*[1] This is frequently the issue which determines the outcome of applications for a s 68 certificate. To what extent can it be said that the delineated area is set apart—and is this usually the case?

   (a) *Usually* If the area is permanently set aside for restaurant use, of course no difficulty arises. Where the use of that part varies throughout the day or the week, it becomes a matter for the licensing committee to decide whether it considers that the area is indeed usually set apart. By way of example, in *Chief Constable of Greater Manchester v Flaherty*[2] an area within a public house was set aside for table meals between 11.00 am and 3.00 pm and from 5.30 pm until 8.30 pm on weekdays and between 12.00 noon and 7.00 pm on Sundays. It was held that in that particular case such an arrangement satisfied the criteria. Note also remarks in the case of *Shipley*, obiter Lord Justice Simon Brown in which he suggested that whilst the sale of liquor must be ancillary during the 'extra supper hour', 'there is no question of this having to be the position throughout the rest of the day'.[3] In practice this has often been the construction applied by many police licensing officers.

   (b) *Set apart* It is generally taken that these words refer not only to the physical demarcation, but also the usage of the area. Accordingly, justices generally expect to be able to identify upon the plan some distinguishing feature which will set apart the dining area from the remainder of the premises, whether it be a change in carpet, a step, a partial metal or timber screen or some such physical presence. The certificate may not be applied to an area which is usually used for casual drinking without meals, even if meals are available during those times.

(3) *Structurally adapted* Whether the premises are structurally adapted for providing substantial refreshment is, of course, a question of fact. If the issue is raised, consideration might be given to the adequacy of the kitchen arrangements, for example.

(4) *Bona fide used/intended to be used* There must be evidence of past or intended use of that part of the premises as a restaurant.

(5) *Habitually providing* The provision of substantial refreshment must be a regular feature of the business, rather than something that is available intermittently. Note also that the certificate is granted to provide a facility for persons taking *table meals*, which of course imposes an additional requirement to the provision of substantial refreshment.

(6) *Substantial refreshment* An uncomplicated test is whether the meal might ordinarily justify the use of a knife and fork. If not, then a *substantial* sandwich accompanied by some form of salad[4] or accompanied by sausages on sticks[5] has been held (in the particular circumstances of each case) to have been meals. The applicant should bring to court six copies of any menu that he has for the consideration of the licensing committee.

(7) *Table meals* The meal has to be taken by a person *seated* at a *table*— which may include a counter or some other structure which serves the purpose of a table, so long as it is not used for the service of refreshment to people not seated at a table[6] (this provision would exclude the main bar servery in most licensed premises, irrespective of the requirement for the area to be set apart, as indicated above).

(8) *Sale and supply of intoxicating liquor is ancillary* Again, this is a question of fact. If the foregoing criteria are satisfied it is generally assumed (rightly or wrongly) that the consumption of alcohol will be ancillary to the meals. If a closer analysis is required, whether a drink is truly ancillary to a table meal will depend upon a number of factors including the time that the refreshment is provided, the amount of drink served, the size of the meal, etc. In general terms, however, no difficulty will arise where an apéritif is served before the meal and a liqueur after it.

[1]   Section 68(2)(a).
[2]   (1988) 153 JP 242.

3   Per Lord Justice Simon Brown in *R v Stafford Crown Court, ex Shipley* (1998)
    Licensing Review, [1998] 2 All ER 465, 162 JP 429, CA.
4   See *Timmis v Millman* [1965] Brewing Tr Rev 23.
5   *Solomon v Green* (1955) 119 JP 289.
6   Section 201(1).

7.43   If the justices are satisfied that the premises are structurally adapted
and intended for the proposed use they are *obliged* to grant the application
and may not take into account other matters.[1]

1   *R v Spelthorne Licensing Justices, ex p Turpin* [1926] 2 KB 519; *R v Torquay
    Licensing Justices* [1933] BTRLR 61; *R v Lymington and New Forest Justices, ex p
    Armstrong* [1953] Brewing Tr Rev 501.

7.44   Where permitted hours are modified following the grant of a s 68
certificate, or by s 95(3) (which automatically applies both parts of s 68
to any premises with a restaurant licence or residential and restaurant
licence), an advisory notice must be displayed within the relevant area
stating the effect of the extension.

7.45   The licensee may disapply either para (a) or para (b) (or both) by
giving at least 14 days' notice to the chief officer of police, served not
later than 20 March in any year. Thereafter, either part of the section may
be resurrected, again on 14 days' notice.[1]

1   Section 69(1).

7.46   If any person (including, it seems, the licensing justices) ceases
to be satisfied that the premises qualify according to the provisions set
out above, they may cause written notice to be served upon the licensee.
The notice must be served at least seven days before a transfer session.
Thereafter, the procedure to be followed should accord, as far as possible,
with that of an opposed renewal.[1]

1   Licensing Rules 1961, r 4.

EXTENDED HOURS ORDER

7.47   Notwithstanding its complications, an extension under s 70 is
appropriate where the licensee seeks to provide intoxicating liquor until
1.00 am on weekdays or 12.30 am on a Sunday (into Monday), but is not
able to meet the requirements of the special hours certificate (see below)
as to the provision of a public entertainments licence or dancing on the
premises.

7.48   Extended hours orders are significantly less common than either
supper hour certificates or special hours certificates, due principally to

the requirements that they may be granted only where there is intended to be *live* entertainment (which is expensive) and that customers may consume intoxicating liquor only if it is ancillary to substantial refreshment (which may be rather too restrictive).

Notices

7.49   The notice required for an application for an extended hours order is the same as that which is necessary for an application for a new licence,[1] with the necessary modifications to the form of the notice itself (see form in Part II). It will be necessary therefore both to display a copy of the notice of application on the premises and advertise in the local press.

[1]   See chapter 2.

Application

7.50   Factors to consider in relation to the application include:

(1) *Justices' discretion*—Regardless of whether the applicant meets the other requirements of the Act, justices may refuse to make an order to 1.00 am in the morning or 12.30 am on a Sunday (into Monday), limit the order to earlier times on particular weekdays, periods of the year or different parts of the premises, or decline to make *any* order. This wide and varied discretion may be exercised 'if it appears to them reasonable to do so having regard to all the circumstances and in particular to the comfort and convenience of the occupiers and inmates of premises in the neighbourhood'. Special provisions apply in relation to Sundays, where justices are required to take into account the 'special nature of Sunday' and the guidance (165 JP 229) upon that subject issued by the Secretary of State. This touches matters such as the nature of the area and the position of those local residents who would gain no benefit from the premises, as against those who would use the facility.

(2) *Use/intended use*—Licensing justices are entitled to grant an order under s 70 only if they are satisfied that the premises are to be used during the additional hours for the same purposes as are required for the grant of a supper hour certificate (see above), ie habitually providing substantial refreshment, and for the provision of musical or other entertainment, the sale and supply of intoxicating liquor being ancillary to the refreshment and entertainment. The priorities of refreshment and entertainment will not matter, provided it can be said that the intoxicating liquor is ancillary to the two combined.

(3) *Musical or other entertainment*—The requirement in this regard is quite onerous. First, the entertainment must be by persons actually present and performing. This excludes cinematograph or video displays. Second, the Act specifically provides that the relevant area must be set aside for a substantial period preceding and also some time after the end of the general licensing hours on the relevant weekdays. Furthermore, such entertainment must be a regular feature on those days, to the extent that there may not be more than a two-week break in any 12 successive months.[1]

(4) *Time of sale and supply*—Unlike the supper hour certificate (where post-prandial drinks are permitted as long as they can be said to be ancillary to the meal) or the special hours certificate (where refreshment must merely be available), with an extended hours order intoxicating liquor must not be *supplied* after the entertainment and the substantial refreshment have ceased to be provided. Further, no sale or supply must take place to a person admitted to the premises either after midnight or less than half an hour before the entertainment ends. Note that even if the entertainment and refreshment cease to be available before the terminal hour, intoxicating liquor may still be *consumed* throughout that period and for half an hour after the entertainment ends.

(5) *Supper hour certificates*—Prior to the order coming into effect, it is necessary for there already to be a certificate under s 68 (ie a supper hour certificate) attaching to the premises; the effect of the extended hours order being to add to the hours already increased by the supper hour certificate.

[1] Section 70(1) and (4).

7.51 Upon the making of the order the applicant is under a duty within 14 days to serve notice of the making of the order upon the chief officer of police. Failure to do so constitutes an offence, punishable with a fine not exceeding level 1 on the standard scale.[1]

Notice of the effect of the order must also be displayed on the premises.[2]

[1] Currently £200.
[2] Section 89—see eg form re s 168A in Part II.

Appeals

7.52 There is no right of appeal to the Crown Court against the grant or refusal of such an order. The usual High Court remedies are available.[1]

[1] See chapter 2 on applications to the High Court.

Revocation

7.53   The chief officer of police may apply for the revocation of an order.[1]

[1]   Section 73(4).

SPECIAL HOURS CERTIFICATE (S 77)

7.54   Special hours certificates are greatly valued by licensees. However, with nearly one in seven applications[1] being refused, it is clear that such certificates are not lightly granted by licensing committees. Further, with their dependence upon a *current* public entertainments licence (save in the case of casino premises), the greatest care needs to be taken in both securing and maintaining a special hours certificate.

[1]   In 2001, locate through www.culture.gov.uk.

Additional hours

7.55   A special hours certificate is capable of conferring permitted hours at licensed premises *on weekdays* until 2.00 am or (3.00 am in specified parts of the metropolis) On a Sunday additional hours may be granted up to 12.30 am (into Monday).

7.56   A special hours certificate may be granted so as to operate only at particular times of the day or for particular days of the week and/or periods of the year. The certificate operates from the beginning of normal permitted hours unless justices have directed that permitted hours on a particular day or days commence from a specified time.[1] The committee should grant a certificate only for periods in respect of which it has been satisfied that music and dancing and food will be provided.[2]

[1]   Section 78A and see *Chief Constable of West Midlands Police v Marsden* (1995) 159 JP 405, QBD and *R v Stafford Crown Court, ex p Shipley* (1998) Licensing Review.
[2]   Section 80(1).

7.57   Prior to the cases of *Marsden* and *Shipley* many hundreds, if not thousands of public houses secured special hours certificates with a view to operating as traditional drinking establishments during the daytime and early evening, only changing to an entertainment-style venue with music and dancing being a significant feature from perhaps 9 pm or 10 pm. The Court of Appeal's decision in *Shipley* (leave to appeal to the House of

Lords was refused) makes it clear that where a certificate is in force music and dancing and food should be the principal element of the business at all times. In the aftermath of this important decision it is thought that many police forces will be reviewing the operation of such premises and where there is not compliance with the Act, making application for the revocation of the special hours certificate, or the imposition of a commencement time (before which there will be *no* authority to sell intoxicating liquor). Note that it is possible to have a supper hour certificate and a special hours certificate attaching simultaneously to different parts of the same premises, or even the same parts at different times.[1] This provision can be useful where there is, for example, a general requirement for an area to be put to a restaurant use, with perhaps buffet/dancing on Friday and Saturday nights.

---

[1] Section 82(1) and (2).

Public entertainments licence

7.58   Before proceeding with the hearing of an application for a special hours certificate, the applicant must be in a position to prove that a public entertainments licence is in force in respect of the premises, unless the premises are a casino. At the time of the application that licence need not be for the same terminal hour as is intended for the special hours certificate, although it is clearly expedient if they are complementary. Occasionally there is some dispute as to whether the public entertainments licence is, in fact, in force—if, for example, it is subject to a condition that it may not be exercised until the fire officer been carried out a further inspection (which has yet to be done).

Legislation in Greater London

7.59   Any premises in a London borough or the City of London to be used for public dancing or music[1] and any other public entertainment of the like kind requires a public[2] entertainments licence, granted under the London Government Act 1963, as amended by the London Local Authorities Act 2000.

---

[1]   See 'Copyright music licensing' at para **7.119**, which is an *additional* requirement.
[2]   Whether the event is truly *public* is a question of fact. Where the formation of a club is a 'transparent device designed to achieve the effect of circumventing the licensing requirements for this sort of entertainment', the entertainment is likely to be regarded as public and so requiring the appropriate licence: *Lunn v Colston-Hayter* (1991) 155 JP 384. See also *Gardner v Morris* (1961) 59 LGR 187 and *Panama (Piccadilly) Ltd v Newberry* [1962] 1 All ER 769.

7.60   Note that a public entertainments licence will *not* be required for the following activities in licensed premises:[1]

(a)   the use of a radio or television; or

(b)   recorded music and singing only; or

(c)   music and singing by one or two performers.

[1]   Section 182(1).

7.61   It is possible to have a combination of these events, so long as they do not take place simultaneously. Accordingly, karaoke *does* require the authority of a public entertainments licence as the entertainment is by way of both recorded sound and one (or more) performers.[1]

[1]   Recently confirmed in *Toye v Southwark London Borough* [2002] EWHC 292 (Admin), (2002) 49 LR 13.

7.62   Note also that the exemption does *not* apply to dancing on licensed premises. If a prosecution is brought under the appropriate legislation for public entertainments licences, the liability of the owner will depend upon the extent of his guilty knowledge in relation to *that particular occasion*. Where a licence is not obtained, perhaps because of the cost of compliance with local authority conditions or due to residents' objections, care should be exercised if the operator[1] is not to fall foul of the legislation. It should also be borne in mind that criminal proceedings may be brought against a wide range of persons directly *or* indirectly involved in the event or with the premises.[2]

[1]   See *Barking and Dagenham London Borough Council v Bass Taverns* (1993) Licensing Review (July), CA.
[2]   See *Chichester District Council v Silvester* [1992] Crim LR 886, QBD.

7.63   At least 21 days' notice of the application must be given to the relevant London borough, the Commissioner of Police and the London Fire and Emergency Planning Authority. It is also common for local authorities to require the advertisement and display of the notice of application. Inquiries should be made in each case of the relevant London borough. It is necessary to give 28 days' notice of intention to apply for renewal.[1]

[1]   London Government Act 1963, Sch 12, para 2.

7.64   Where a special order of exemption is granted for licensed premises then the music and dancing licence is automatically extended, in effect.[1]

[1]   London Government Act 1963, Sch 12, para 11.

Issues

7.65 The Act does not specify grounds upon which such applications might be refused. However, matters generally considered are the suitability of the applicant, the structure and layout of the premises (particularly with regard to fire safety and the containment of noise) and the likelihood of disturbance or annoyance being caused to persons residing or carrying on business in the area.[1]

[1] *Lidster v Owen* [1983] 1 All ER 1012, where it was held that the licensing authority is entitled to consider behaviour *outside* the premises upon renewal of a licence.

7.66 Although it will be seen that the issues upon an application for a public entertainments licence are not dissimilar to those commonly arising from the grant of a new justices' licence, greater attention will often be paid to the structure and layout of the premises because of the large numbers of persons frequently accommodated. In this regard note that invariably an occupancy figure is recommended by the fire officer and incorporated into the terms of the licence. It is not uncommon for objectors to found their objections upon the alleged consequences of intoxicating liquor being supplied because they see the public entertainments licence as the inevitable prelude to a special hours certificate. It is suggested, however, that this issue is more properly the province of the licensing justices when considering the application for a special hours certificate.

Conditions

7.67 Upon the grant of a public entertainments licence the local authority is entitled to impose general terms, conditions and restrictions by formulating their own regulations.[1] Although such regulations are frequently extremely lengthy and involved, it is most important that the holder of the licence consider each condition with great care.[2]

[1] London Government Act 1963, Sch 12, para 9.
[2] When granting a public entertainments licence, local authorities should not attach conditions which are imprecise or difficult for the licensee to observe (eg that all advertisements will encourage visitors to use public transport: *R v Hammersmith and Fulham London Borough Council, ex p Earls Court Ltd* (1993) Times, 15 July, DC).

Appeals

7.68 A right of appeal against a refusal to grant (or provisionally grant), renew, transfer or vary a public entertainments licence, or against an order revoking a licence, lies to the magistrates' court and thence to the Crown Court.[1]

¹   London Government Act 1963, Sch 12, para 19. Note also the provisions of the Public Entertainments Licences (Drug Misuse) Act 1997, which came into force on 1 May 1998, in relation to applications by the police to stem drug abuse.

Offences

7.69   Significant penalties[1] arise for those convicted of the offences of organising, managing, allowing or making available premises for an unlicensed entertainment. Offences are also committed if conditions attached to the licence are breached. The consequences[2] of such actions are not only that any person directly *or* indirectly involved is liable to be prosecuted, but also that the licence—and with it the special hours certificate—may be lost.

¹   Maximum fine of £20,000 and/or up to six months' imprisonment for an unlicensed entertainment or breach of a restriction upon occupancy.
²   See *Chichester District Council v Silvester* [1992] Crim LR 886 and *Westminster City Council v Mackay* (1997) 161 JP 690. The applicant for a transfer is not the licensee within the meaning of the 1963 Act.

Renewals

7.70   Licences will require renewal every 12 months, or within such lesser period as the council may determine.[1] Fees for each application are not fixed by statute, but instead may be for such amount as the council may fix.[2]

¹   London Government Act 1963, Sch 12, para 1(2).
²   London Government Act 1963, Sch 12, para 3.

Legislation outside Greater London

7.71   Until 1983 authority was vested in licensing justices to grant music, singing and dancing licences under the Public Health Acts Amendment Act 1890. Now, the Local Government (Miscellaneous Provisions) Act 1982 provides that local authorities are responsible for issuing licences for public entertainments taking place outside Greater London.

7.72   The 1982 Act provides that public dancing or music or other similar public entertainment shall not take place save in accordance with the terms of a licence granted by the relevant local authority.[1] Exceptions are made for religious worship and pleasure fairs. Open air entertainment may also be excluded unless the local authority has resolved to adopt paras 3 and 4 of Sch 1 to the 1982 Act, in which case conditions may be imposed for certain limited purposes.[2] A licence may not be granted for public dancing on a Sunday if payment is made for admission. If, however, the dancing takes place at a private event on a Sunday then of course no licence is required.

[1] See explanation at para **7.60** of limited exemption of licensed premises.
[2] Local Government (Miscellaneous Provisions) Act 1982, Sch 1, para 4(4).

7.73 Applicants for the grant, provisional grant, renewal or transfer of a public entertainments licence are required to give not less than 28 days' notice to the appropriate authority, the chief officer of police and the fire authority.[1] If there is an existing licence and the application is submitted prior to its expiry, that licence will be deemed to continue in force until the determination of the application, whether for transfer or renewal.

[1] For a detailed analysis of the position as to entertainment on a Sunday and the confusion created by statute and two decisions of the High Court, see the notes to Sunday Observance Act 1780, s 1, in *Paterson's Licensing Acts*.

7.74 The local authority has power to impose standard terms, conditions and restrictions.

[1] See para **1.12** concerning the enforceability of imprecise conditions.

7.75 Where the premises for which a public entertainments licence is in force also have the benefit of a justices' on-licence, then, where a special order of exemption (ie extension) is granted, the terminal hour on the public entertainments licence will automatically be so extended.[1]

[1] Local Government (Miscellaneous Provisions) Act 1982, Sch 1, para 3 and London Government Act 1963, Sch 12, para 11.

7.76 Serious penalties[1] may be imposed upon those who directly or indirectly[2] conduct public entertainments without the benefit of a licence, or allow or make available premises which they know, or have reason to suspect, will be used for public entertainment in the absence of such a licence. Further penalties may be imposed upon those involved in public entertainments which are conducted in breach of conditions of an existing licence.[3]

[1] Maximum fine of £20,000 and/or up to six months' imprisonment for an unlicensed entertainment or breach of a restriction upon occupancy.
[2] See *Chichester District Council v Silvester* [1992] Crim LR 886.
[3] See para **7.68**, fn 1 in relation to police applications concerning drug abuse.

7.77 There is a right of appeal against the refusal of an application to grant, renew or transfer an entertainments licence, and a refusal of the local authority to vary the conditions of that licence or a decision to revoke the licence. The appeal lies at first instance to the magistrates' court (within a period of 21 days) and thereafter to the Crown Court. If an appeal is lodged within the correct period, the existing licence is deemed to remain in force until such time as the appeal is determined.

7.78   Licences may be granted for a period of one year or less.

7.79   Notwithstanding the above, licences may be required for *private* entertainment where that entertainment is provided for private gain if the relevant local authority has adopted the Private Places of Entertainment (Licensing) Act 1967.

Special hours certificate—provisional applications

7.80   It is now possible to make application for a *provisional* special hours certificate, where premises have yet to be constructed or fitted out. The justices have to be satisfied that a justices' licence has been granted on a full or provisional basis and that the premises are either a casino or have the benefit of a music and dancing licence, even if this is subject to a condition that it remains ineffective until confirmed upon completion of the works.[1] They further have to be satisfied as to the intended provision of gaming or dancing facilities (as appropriate) and substantial refreshment, as set out in more detail below.

[1]   Section 77A(6). These provisions were inserted by the Deregulation (Special Hours Certificate) Order 1996, SI 1996/977.

7.81   In provisions which mirror those relating to provisional grants of justices' licences, procedures are specified for the modification of plans[1] after any provisional grant and a declaration of finality.[2]

[1]   Section 77A(2).
[2]   Section 77A(3).

Notices

7.82   The procedure for applying for a special hours certificate is governed by the Licensing (Special Hours Certificate) Rules 1982. It is necessary to:

(1)   serve notice in writing[1] upon the chief executive to the licensing justices and the chief officer of police (as well as the proper local authority if additional hours are sought for Sundays) at least 21 days before the relevant transfer sessions;

(2)   advertise in the local press no more than 28 days, or less than 14 days, before the hearing;

(3) not more than 28 days or less than 14 days before the hearing display a copy of the notice in a situation where it can conveniently be read by the public on or near the application premises for a period of seven days. The wording of this provision is ambiguous in that it can be construed to mean that the period of seven days should have been completed no less than 14 days before the hearing. Although this is a point taken principally by trade objectors seeking to restrict competition and is probably without merit, to avoid difficulties it is therefore recommended that the notice of application should be put up at least 21 days prior to any hearing.

[1] See form in Part II.

7.83 Any person who wishes to oppose the application must serve written notice upon the applicant and the chief executive to the licensing justices, setting out his general grounds of opposition, at least seven days prior to the transfer sessions. Since failure to comply with this provision means that the committee is unable to entertain the objection, some policy documents require that all applicants should advise intending objectors of this requirement in their notice of application. In *R v Inner London Crown Court, ex p Provis*[1] the police did not give evidence in an application to vary the terminal hour on a special hours certificate but made representations which were in reality objections. At the judicial review, the court gave guidance in relation to people who wish to make representations which are in effect objections.

1 (2000) 43 Licensing Review 21.

7.84 It is arguable that rule 7 of the 1982 Rules, which broadly provides for similar procedures to new licence applications, entitles applicants to take advantage of the 'slip rule' contained in Sch 2, para 7 to the Act, where there may be technical defects in the notices.[1]

[1] See Licensing (Special Hours Certificates) Rules 1982, SI 1982/1384 at para **A.140.**

Preparation

7.85 Prior to the hearing it is necessary to consider the following matters.

Public entertainments licence

7.86 Will such a licence be in force for the premises by the time of the hearing? If not, the application should be deferred until such licence is available. Are there any onerous or unusual conditions attached to the licence which might have a bearing upon the application?

Planning permission

7.87   Could it be argued that the intended use of the licensed premises takes it out of the existing use class (probably A3—food and drink) into another (probably D2—dance hall)? Inquiries should be made of the planning authority to ensure that there is no deemed change of use, or any condition attaching to the existing planning permission restricting the hours during which the premises may be operated. Given that the premises must be completed when the application is heard, some courts will also inquire as to building regulations approval.

Freehold/leasehold title

7.88   The deeds to the property should be checked to ensure that the intended use will not be in breach of any restrictive covenant or provision in a lease.

Justices' licence

7.89   Similarly, the justices' licence should be checked to ensure that there are no conditions attaching which would inhibit the proposed operation. In addition, if there is any indication from the published policy of the licensing justices, or evidence upon recent grants of a special hours certificates, that the committee likes to be in a position to impose conditions at the time of the grant, consideration should be given to lodging with the application for a special hours certificate an application for the grant of a new justices' on-licence. There is no provision in the Act for conditions to be attached to the special hours certificate itself.

Premises

7.90   Are the premises structurally adapted? Do they have adequate means of access/egress, kitchens, eating areas, dancing area, etc (see below). Unless there is a specific provision in the policy document, there is no requirement to serve plans of the premises with the notice of application. However, it would be prudent to ensure that plans are available for the entire committee, as well as for any witnesses and objectors, at the hearing itself. Have available at least eight copies. The plans should be coloured in accordance with any policy document or, if there are no such provisions, as indicated in chapter 2. The locations of dance floors, and eating areas particularly should be noted.

Music and dancing

7.91 Unless the premises are a casino (as to which, see below) it will be necessary to satisfy the licensing committee that the sale of alcohol will be ancillary to music and dancing *and* substantial refreshment. How easy it will be to satisfy this requirement will, of course, depend upon the nature of the premises. Where, however, there is likely to be any argument as to whether there are sufficient facilities available for music and dancing, consideration should be given to the size and location of the dance floor and even, on occasions, whether the type of music to be played would be conducive to dancing. In some of the larger cities, where nightclubs are likely to be a more significant factor in the social scene, it may be found that the licensing committee has published policies regarding the percentage of the total occupancy that should be capable of being accommodated upon the dance floor at any one time. A formula may also be suggested for the floor area that should be allocated in respect of each person dancing. Most committees will adopt a much more flexible approach, considering whether the facilities to be provided are appropriate having regard to the size of the premises and the general character of the anticipated clientele of the venue, in all the circumstances.

7.92 Further, s 83(2) specifically provides that references in the Act to dancing should be construed as references to providing facilities for dancing that are 'adequate having regard to the number of persons for whose reception in the premises or part of the premises in question provision is made'.

Casino premises

7.93 New provisions entitle the operation of casinos to secure a special hours certificate upon satisfying the justices that the premises will be used for the purpose of providing gaming facilities and substantial refreshments, to which the sale of liquor will be ancillary.

Substantial refreshment

7.94 The provision of substantial refreshment is a mandatory requirement of the Act[1] and is very often a matter of some concern to licensing justices, particularly in relation to existing special hours certificates. In many cases the police will suggest that patrons visit those premises primarily for the purpose of consuming intoxicating liquor. Whilst some may participate to a greater or lesser extent in dancing (or gaming), it is sometimes suggested that there is very little take-up of the food available. Whilst, of course, the priorities between the music and dancing (or gaming) and substantial refreshment do not matter provided the intoxicating liquor is ancillary to the two *combined*,[2] it is important to satisfy the justices at the time of the application that every effort will be made to encourage patrons both to dance (or game) and to eat. As regards the latter, consideration should be given during the preparatory stage to the adequacy of the kitchen in relation to the numbers likely to attend the venue, the accessibility of the food servery, the provision of any area dedicated to diners, the quality of the proposed menu and whether any part of the price of the food is included in any admission charge.

[1]   Section 77(b).
[2]   *Young v O'Connell* (1985) Times, 25 May.

Admission

7.95　Is there to be any charge for admission to the premises? Alternatively, is admission to be restricted to members of a club, or those attending bona fide private functions, for example? Examples of various conditions that might be attached to the new on-licence are set out in Part II. Will admission be permitted throughout the evening/early morning or will it be prohibited after, say, 11.00 pm so as to discourage those persons who merely wish to travel to the nightclub after leaving public houses?

Door control

7.96　Schemes for the registration or licensing of door staff have become increasingly popular in recent years. Such schemes generally operate on the basis that the holder of a public entertainments licence will be in breach of the conditions attaching to the licence issued by the local authority if he uses staff who have not been so approved. Registration generally takes place after the doorstaff have been vetted by the local police and attended a training course—generally designed to increase awareness of the licensing laws and the techniques that might be adopted to avoid confrontation with drunken or abusive members of the public. Are the numbers of door staff in the proposed venue adequate having regard to its size, layout, etc?

Parking

7.97 What percentage of the persons likely to use the premises will be driving, having regard to the drink/driving laws? Is there adequate parking in the area having regard to the number that will be sharing cars? Is there a convenient taxi rank or other form of public transport for those who will be travelling in this way?

Residents

7.98 To what extent is the area residential? If it is, are residents likely to be disturbed or annoyed by people going to and from the premises?

Public order

7.99 If a city centre venue, is there a history of public disorder? Where is it centred? Given that there is a need to provide such facilities for young persons, is this a good (or, even, the best) place for them?

Type of clientele

7.100 If the premises already exist in some form, what is their principal attraction? What is the nature of the existing clientele at the premises in terms of age profile, likely occupation, etc? Why are the premises likely to be popular in the future?

Competition

7.101 What are the main characteristics of the *existing* late night venues in the area? (Matters that might be considered include size, layout, clientele, atmosphere, safe and secure environment, prices for admission and drinks and food, etc.) Is the competition likely to object and, if so, what arguments will they advance?

Market research

7.102 Is it intended to instruct a market research organisation to carry out a street or door-to-door survey? Has the form of any questionnaire been agreed? Is the survey to be taken in the day or in the evening, when the individual who is more likely to use the venue will be present?

Petition

7.103   If it is an existing venue, is a petition being organised among the patrons? Will the taking of this petition be properly controlled and supervised, so as to avoid facetious remarks and fictitious names?

Witnesses

7.104   Will existing or proposed customers be prepared to come along and support the application? Are they familiar with the existing outlets and do they have adequate reasons for preferring the applicant's proposal? Which of the facilities will they be using: dancing, food, or intoxicating liquor?

Supervision

7.105   Within the premises will there be adequate supervision of all areas? Is closed-circuit television to be used inside/outside the premises?

Occupancy

7.106   What is the total permitted occupancy of the premises? How will the applicant ensure that this is not exceeded (most clubs use a system of counters, recording persons entering and leaving the premises and keeping a note of the difference)?

Licensing surveyors

7.107   Is it intended to call a licensing surveyor as an expert witness to deal with the issues of need, public order, conditions on existing licences, facilities within competitors' premises, etc? Are they producing maps to demonstrate these matters?

Sundays

7.108   Special provisions apply in relation to Sundays, where justices are required to take into account the 'special nature of Sunday' and the guidance (165 JP 229) upon that subject issued by the Secretary of State. This touches matters such as the nature of the area and the position of those local residents who would gain no benefit from the premises, as against those who would use the facility.

The application

7.109 The application will proceed in substantially the same manner as an application for the grant of a new justices' licence. It will be convenient to prove service, display and dispatch of the notices before the application proceeds.

7.110 Thereafter, the applicant should in any event give evidence as to the following matters:

(a) public entertainments licence—or that it is a casino;

(b) suitability of premises;

(c) intention to provide music and dancing—or gaming, if a casino;

(d) intention to provide substantial refreshment;

(e) requirement for a special hours certificate to authorise the sale of intoxicating liquor ancillary to the music and dancing—or gaming—and substantial refreshment.

7.111 If the application is not opposed it may well be that the committee will not require further evidence to be called. If, on the other hand, the application is opposed or the committee indicates that it needs to be satisfied generally as to the demand for the facility, the applicant should present his case fully, using such of the available evidence as is relevant to the matters in question.

7.112 As to the law concerning these applications, note that:

(1) Although the Act requires that there should be a public entertainments licence in force for the premises (save in the case of a casino), it is not, in fact, significant whether the functions to be held are public or private events.[1] Accordingly, a special hours certificate may be granted so as to enable a licensee regularly to cater for private parties, which might otherwise require successive applications for special orders of exemption.[2]

(2) The requirement is to *provide* music and dancing, or gaming, and substantial refreshment. There is no requirement at the time of the application to prove that all of the potential customers will use either or both of the facilities.[3]

(3) The Act requires that music and dancing, or gaming, and refreshment must be provided consistently at all times that the special hours certificate is capable of being used subject to any break for a period or periods not exceeding two weeks in any 12 successive months or on any special occasion or by reason of any emergency.[4]

[1] *Rowley v Stafford Licensing Justices* [1968] Brewing Tr Rev 78.

²   *Edwards v Crown Prosecution Service* (1991) 155 JP 746.
³   *Richards v Bloxham (Binks)* (1968) 66 LGR 739.
⁴   Section 83(2).

The decision

7.113   As previously indicated, the licensing committee is able to be entirely flexible in the issue of a special hours certificate, granting it for particular times of the day, days of the week or periods of the year, with different times being granted in respect of different days.[1] Where the court makes an order in relation to Sunday in spite of an objection from the local authority based upon the residential character of the area, the legislation requires reasons to be given.

1   Section 78A(2).

7.114   Costs may be awarded to or against an objector.

7.115   The licensee may also apply at any time to vary the limitations attaching to any special hours certificate that may have been granted.[1]

1   Section 81A(4).

7.116   There is a right of appeal to the Crown Court against a refusal to grant a full or provisional special hours certificate or a decision to attach *or not to attach* limitations as to its operation. Accordingly, an objector is not entitled to appeal against the grant of a special hours certificate although, if he appeared before the licensing justices as a formal objector or even as a person making representations, he is entitled to appeal against any decision not to attach limitations. Note that the Act does not provide that the licensing justices should be respondents in any appeal concerning special hours certificates.

Revocation

7.117   There are comprehensive provisions for the revocation of special hours certificates, which have been considered more fully in chapter 6.

EXCEPTIONS FROM PROHIBITION OF SALE OR CONSUMPTION OUTSIDE PERMITTED HOURS

7.118   These provisions are set out principally in s 63 of the Act.

(1)   *Drinking-up time* At the end of permitted hours 20 minutes is allowed

for the consumption of any liquor already supplied or, if in a sealed bottle or container, for taking that liquor from the premises. Thirty minutes' drinking-up time is allowed if the intoxicating liquor was supplied as an ancillary to a table meal.

(2) *Residents* are permitted to purchase and consume intoxicating liquor at any time in premises where they are residing. Those in charge of a business on the licensed premises are deemed to be residents for the purpose of this provision.[1] As noted elsewhere, a licensee is not obliged to sell intoxicating liquor merely because he is permitted to do so. It follows, therefore, that the proprietor of a hotel is not obliged to make this facility available to residents throughout the night, merely because he has that entitlement.

(3) *Orders or deliveries* may take place outside the permitted hours if the liquor is to be consumed off the premises.[2]

(4) *Traders and registered clubs* may purchase their requirements at any time.

(5) *Private friends* The licensee or any person residing on licensed premises is entitled *at his own expense* to entertain his private friends by supplying and permitting the consumption of intoxicating liquor on licensed premises outside permitted hours. Not only will a hotel resident be able to take advantage of this provision by supplying his friends, but also the owner or manager carrying on business on the premises. The burden of establishing that the persons so entertained are genuine friends and that the arrangement is not a mere sham will be on the host.[3]

(6) *Employees* A similar provision applies to the supply or consumption of intoxicating liquor to employees, provided that the liquor is supplied at the expense of their employer or the person conducting or owning the business.[4] This exception will apply only where at the time of the supply the employee is still employed there for the purposes of the business carried on by the holder of the licence.

[1] Section 63(4).
[2] See para **6.56** fn 1 concerning transactions which involve the ordering *and* delivery outside permitted hours.
[3] But see para **6.55** fn 2 for an argument to the contrary.
[4] Section 63(3)(c).

COPYRIGHT MUSIC LICENSING

7.119   Although the Act exempts the holders of justices' licences from the requirement to obtain public entertainments licences if they are providing music by way of records, tapes or compact discs only, they are still liable to account to the owner of the public performance and broadcasting rights in that music. In the majority of cases those rights have been vested in a company, Phonographic Performance Limited (PPL) of 1 Upper James Street, London W1F 9DE (tel: 0207 534 1000). Generally two different types of licence are issued: one where sound recordings are used solely for background music, the other for dances or discothèques. Fees are charged on a sliding scale and depend upon the hours of record use and the average attendances at the venue.

7.120   The entirely separate copyright of the music composers is vested in the Performing Right Society, 29/33 Berners Street, London W1P 4AA (tel: 0207 580 5544) which issues its own licences.

CHAPTER 8

CLUBS

8.01 Approximately one-fifth of all premises in which intoxicating liquor can be supplied for consumption on the premises operate by virtue of a club registration certificate issued under Part II of the Licensing Act 1964. Although a registered club may be virtually indistinguishable physically from its licensed counterpart, the rules governing its operation are in reality very different. For example, there is nothing in law preventing intoxicating liquor being supplied to children aged five years or more in the club's bar—which would constitute more than one serious offence in relation to licensed premises. Similarly, on special occasions the club may trade from other premises, beyond permitted hours if desired, without seeking any permission from the justices. A public house would, of course, need to apply for an occasional licence. These privileges put the club in a position far more akin in certain respects to that of the private individual than that of premises which have the benefit of a justices' licence. The reason for this may be, perhaps, that the legislature sees members' clubs as being, essentially, a collection of private individuals who have agreed jointly to provide an essentially non-profit-making social facility, rather than a business which has commercial interests entirely independent of those of its customers. Of course, there is a price to pay for these privileges and the members' club is subject to a plethora of carefully drafted rules designed to maintain its proper status.

THE APPLICATION

8.02 All matters concerning club registration certificates are governed by the magistrates' court having jurisdiction for the principal premises of the club. From the applicant's point of view this is beneficial since it means that the hearing of applications is not confined to designated transfer sessions, which may be relatively infrequent. Further, the separation of such business from the transfer sessions may make magistrates less inclined to fall into the error of applying the same criteria to registered clubs as they do to licensed premises; to do so is inappropriate because of both the entirely different character of the two operations and the many statutory provisions discouraging such an approach.

8.03   The Act provides that every application for the grant, renewal or, in certain cases, variation of a club registration certificate must contain certain information which is set out in Sch 5 to the Act. The form appearing in Part II of this book directs the applicant to the information that should be provided. Note that the club must already be established and have at least 25 members. The following additional points should be made:

(1) *Application*—Lodge an original and sufficient copies for the chief executive to be able to serve the police, fire authority and any local authority. Inquiries should be made of the clerk's office as to the precise numbers required.

(2) *Members of committee*—The application may either incorporate or have annexed a list of the names and addresses of the club's general management committee (GMC), the 'drinks purchasing' committee (if any) and the club's officers.

(3) *Rules of club*—These should be attached to the application and, whilst being bespoke for the particular club, should conform generally with the requirements of the Act and Sch 7, in particular (see below).

(4) *Signature*—The application (or amended application) should be signed by the chairman or the secretary of the club.

8.04   As indicated above, it is the responsibility of the chief executive to the justices to circulate copies of the application and supporting documentation to the various authorities. It is the club's duty, however, to give public notice of the application in the form appearing in Part II of this book or similar, either:

(a) displaying the notice on or near the premises, in a place where it can conveniently be read by the public, for the seven days beginning with the date of the application; or

(b) by advertisement on one at least of those days in a newspaper circulating in the place where the premises are situated. See the commentary in chapter 2 upon the choice of newspaper.

CLUB RULES

8.05   The rules constitute an agreement between those persons who found or join the club as to the manner in which they will regulate their financial and social affairs. Even if the starting point is a set of standard rules provided by a law stationer, these should be carefully considered by the founding members to ensure that they are appropriate in all respects to the way in which the members want the club's business to be conducted. As indicated above, however, the Act does specify criteria which should be applied to certain of the rules. Some of these requirements are mandatory; others are merely to be introduced into the rules at the discretion of the club and if they do not so appear it will be necessary to persuade the magistrates of the merits of the alternative provisions adopted.

8.06   The Act makes the following provision concerning club rules.

Club management

8.07   The rules must provide for the establishment of a GMC having responsibility for those affairs of the club which are not either assigned to the decision of members in a general meeting or otherwise specifically delegated to special committees.

Constitution of GMC

8.08   The Act requires that this must be an elective committee.[1] The provisions require:

(a)   that members must be elected by the club;

(b)   elections to be held annually;

(c)   all persons entitled to vote, who have been with the club for two or more years, to be capable of election;

(d)   equal rights of nomination (subject to restrictions upon re-election);

(e)   terms of office of between one and five years;

(f)   rules for retirement of elected members (if not all) each year;

(g)   general voting rules to apply (see below).

[1]   Schedule 7, para 4.

8.09   Where at least two-thirds of the members of the GMC are club members who have been elected in accordance with these rules, the Act provides that it will be duly treated as an elective committee, unless it has three or fewer members. Note that if any casual vacancy arises the person appointed to fill it will not be deemed to have been elected by the members of the club for the purposes of the two-thirds rule.

Membership

8.10 The club may have ordinary members and other categories of members, so long as this is not likely to result in the numbers of members in these categories being significant in proportion to the total membership. As regards ordinary members, the rules must provide that:

(a) they should be elected by an elective committee or club in general meeting;

(b) the name and address of an applicant must be prominently displayed, in a part of the club premises frequented by members, for two days prior to election.

8.11 Three further points should be noted. First, the elective committee dealing with the admission to membership may, in fact, be a sub-committee of an elective committee (see above). The sub-committee will be acceptable if its members are appointed by the committee and at least two-thirds of them (or, if three or fewer, all of them) have been formally elected to the principal committee in accordance with the rules outlined above and will cease to be members of the sub-committee when their appointment to the main committee determines.[1]

[1]   Schedule 7, para 4.

8.12 Second, at least two days *must* elapse between a person's application/nomination for membership and his or her actual admission to the privileges of membership. Where persons become members in some other way they may still not take advantage of that membership before two days have elapsed. This is an important provision and one of the matters which the club is required to confirm in its notice of application.[1]

[1]   See Sch 5, para 2 and s 41(1).

8.13 Third, voting rights may be modified. Notwithstanding the provisions in the Act for general equality of voting rights, the rules *may* provide that certain classes of members have either limited or no rights of voting in relation to the affairs of the club. In that event, the magistrates may be invited to give a direction under s 42(2) that the provision is:

'Part of a bona fide arrangement made in the interests of the club as a whole and of that class of members of facilitating the membership of persons who are precluded by distance or other circumstances from making full use of the privileges of membership and is not designed to secure for a minority of the members an unfair measure of control over the affairs of the club.'

General meetings

8.14   The rules must (subject to exceptions below) provide:

(1)   a general meeting must be held every year (not more than 15 months apart);

(2)   power to the GMC on reasonable notice to summon a general meeting;

(3)   that voting members are entitled to summon a general meeting at any time on reasonable notice. Rules may *not* require that this has to be done by more than 30 or more than one-fifth of the voting members;

(4)   that non-members may not vote at the general meeting;

(5)   that all members entitled to use the club premises must be entitled to vote (subject to the court's direction mentioned above);

(6)   that members must have *equal* voting rights—save that this provision may be modified in the following cases:

   (a)   on particular matters there may be an age qualification (not greater than 21) to vote;

   (b)   if the club is primarily a men's club, women may be excluded on certain matters;

   (c)   similarly, in what is primarily a women's club, men may be excluded on certain matters;

   (d)   in a club primarily for persons involved in HM Forces there may be exclusions covering particular matters or generally;

   (e)   if there are arrangements for family members/subscriptions, the rules may exclude the remainder of the family (ie other than the principal person joining) from voting on particular matters or generally.

Application of profit

8.15   The rules should provide that any money, property or profits arising from the club business should be applied for the benefit of the club as a whole, or for some charitable, benevolent or political purpose. Where there is any provision or arrangement to the contrary the magistrates are entitled to take that fact into account when considering whether the club is established and conducted in good faith as a club.[1]

---

[1]   Section 41(3)(b).

Assumed compliance

8.16   The court is entitled to make certain assumptions where the rules qualify in the following respects.

Qualification

8.17   Compliance with Sch 7 (management, general meetings, membership and elective committees).

Assumptions

8.18

(1)   The club is established and conducted in good faith as a club (unless rules contain an arrangement restricting the club's freedom of purchase of intoxicating liquor or direct that profits etc of the club may be applied other than to the club itself or to charitable, benevolent or political purposes) with not less than 25 members.

(2)   Intoxicating liquor is not supplied (or intended to be supplied) to members on the premises otherwise than by or on behalf of the club.

(3)   An elective committee or the club members will manage the club's purchase and supply of intoxicating liquor.

(4)   (Upon renewal only) No person has been receiving any private benefits for the purchase or supply of intoxicating liquor.

8.19   Note that s 41(4) provides that if the club's rules comply with Sch 7 then, in the absence of objection, the court should assume that the club is substantially qualified to receive a registration certificate. However, if the rules are in some different form it is still perfectly open to the magistrates to register the club; they merely need to consider such rules on the merits.

Qualification

8.20   Registered society under the Industrial and Provident Societies Act 1893 or the Friendly Societies Act 1896 (most working men's clubs).

Assumptions

8.21

(1)   The purchase, supply, etc of intoxicating liquor is managed by an elective committee (so long as the purchase is controlled by members or a members' committee).

(2)   There is conformity with Sch 7 (see above) if there has been *actual* compliance with rules concerning voting at general meetings and at elections or admissions to membership.

SALES TO PUBLIC

8.22 Under a club registration certificate a member may be *supplied* with intoxicating liquor.[1] It has been suggested that payment may be made *only* by the member (since a payment by a guest would not be a supply because the guest has no property in the liquor), although clearly the member can supply the guest with the drink.

[1] Section 39(1).

8.23 It is equally possible to take the alternative (and probably better) view that drinks may be sold to guests. Clearly, if rules making such provision have been accepted by the magistrates it is extremely unlikely that any prosecution would result from this practice.

8.24 The rules may provide that visiting teams, their officials and other specified clubs or categories of clubs can be temporary members (provided that their names are displayed on the club notice board two days beforehand, etc) as long as their attendance does not result in the exclusion of the existing club members from the facilities of the club.[1]

[1] *Coventry Football Club v Coventry Justices* (1973) 117 Sol Jo 855, DC.

8.25 In addition, the rules may provide for the club to admit persons other than members and their guests and for the *sale* to them of intoxicating liquor, for consumption on (but not off) the premises. Clearly, if such rules are too widely drawn any person would be able to obtain a drink at the premises, with the result that the supply of intoxicating liquor (in what had effectively become a public place) would not be subject to the stringent controls on licensed premises. In that event the magistrates would be entitled to find that the premises were not established and conducted in good faith as a club.[1] However, the court should not construe this provision so narrowly as to preclude or limit too strictly the club's facilities being made available to non-members where such provision does not, on the facts, mean that the club has ceased to be established and conducted in good faith, bearing in mind that the profits from such events will accrue to the benefit of the club members as a whole.

[1] Sections 49(2) and 41(2)(a).

8.26 In *The Little Ship Club* case[1] the court considered in some detail the issue of outside functions. Far from specifying that these should be limited to no more than 12 in any one year (as is often suggested), the following points emerge from the decision:

(1) the Little Ship Club rules actually provided for an unlimited number of functions associated with the club's activities (eg club parties), as well as up to 12 other events a year;

(2)   the figure of 12 events for non-club activities was one which happened to appear in the rules of this particular club. The court did not actually indicate that a higher figure would not have been accepted;

(3)   consideration must be given to the general operation and rules of the club in deciding whether it is, in reality, a sham.

¹   *City of London Police Comr v Little Ship Club Ltd* [1964] Brewing Tr Rev 702.

8.27   Since the ability to cater for non-members and private functions goes against the general rule that the club's facilities are provided for the use of members and their guests, the magistrates' court is entitled upon the issue or renewal of the registration certificate to attach such conditions restricting *sales* (ie other than to members or their guests) of intoxicating liquor on those premises as it thinks reasonable. Those conditions may further restrict or forbid the alteration of the rule concerning such sales. The magistrates' power in this respect is, however, limited to the extent that they may not prevent sales to members of another club, if:

(1)   the other club is registered in respect of premises in the locality which are temporarily closed; or

(2)   both clubs exist for learned, educational or political objects of a similar nature; or

(3)   both clubs exist primarily for and consist of members of HM Forces; or

(4)   both clubs are registered as working men's clubs.

8.28   Any such condition may be imposed, varied or revoked upon renewal, the application of the club or upon either the police or the local authority making a complaint in writing. Either the police or the local authority are entitled upon the hearing of the application for the issue or renewal of a registration certificate to make representations as to the conditions which ought to be attached to any such registration certificate, but only if they have previously given written notice of their intention so to do within 28 days of the application being lodged.¹

¹   Section 49(6).

8.29   Should the club rules be altered so as to extend the circumstances in which intoxicating liquor, or types of intoxicating liquor, may be sold beyond the provisions obtaining at the time of the issue or renewal of the registration certificate, the alteration will *not* be effective until the club secretary has given written notice to the police and the clerk to the local authority. The effect of this provision is that until notice has been given the person selling the liquor will be committing the offence of selling liquor without a licence.

MINERS' WELFARE INSTITUTES

8.30   There are special provisions for the registration of miners' welfare institutes.[1]

[1]   Section 56.

THE APPLICATION: FURTHER CONSIDERATIONS

Inspections

8.31   Before the first registration of the club, the police, fire and local authorities have rights, upon giving not less than 48 hours' notice, to inspect the premises at reasonable times within 14 days of the making of the application. The time for inspection may be extended by the court. Obstruction of the inspecting officer constitutes an offence.[1]

[1]   Section 45(2).

Objections

8.32   Within 28 days of the application being lodged with the court, the chief officer of police (or the officer designated by him) the local authority, the fire authority[1] or any person affected by reason of his occupation of or interest in other premises, may object to the application. Any such objection must:

(a)   be lodged with the chief executive to the justices;

(b)   be in writing (two copies);

(c)   specify the grounds of objection (unless it is suggested that the application is incomplete or inaccurate, in which case the ground may be stated as a matter of suspicion—with the reasons therefor);

(d)   particularise the matters giving rise to those grounds.[2]

[1]   Section 46(3)(b).
[2]   Schedule 6, para 11(1).

8.33   The following grounds (which are set out verbatim here, because of their importance) are recognised under the Act:[1]

'(a) that the application does not give the information required by this Part [ie Part II] of the Act, or that the information is incomplete or inaccurate, or the application is otherwise not in conformity with this Part of the Act;

(b) that the premises are not suitable and convenient for the purpose in view of their character and condition and of the size and nature of the club;

(c) that the club does not satisfy the conditions of sub-sections (1) and (2) of section 41 of the Act, or that the application must or ought to be refused under section 43 of this Act;

(d) that the club is conducted in a disorderly manner or for an unlawful purpose or that the rules of the club are habitually disregarded as respects the admission of persons to membership or to the privileges of membership or in any other material respect;

(e) that the club premises or any of them (including premises in respect of which a club is not registered or seeking registration) are habitually used for an unlawful purpose, or for indecent displays, or as a resort of criminals or prostitutes, or that in any such premises there is frequent drunkenness or there have within the preceding twelve months been illegal sales of intoxicating liquor, or persons not qualified to be supplied with intoxicating liquor there are habitually admitted for the purpose of obtaining it.'

¹   Section 44(1).

Hearing

8.34   The application may not be determined until 28 days have elapsed from the lodging of the application, or any amended application.¹

¹   *R v Willesden Justices, ex p Simpson* [1976] Brewing Review 393.

8.35   Although this will rarely be the case, the court is entitled to deal with an application by a club for the issue of a new registration certificate without hearing the club. Before an application is refused, however, the club must be given an opportunity to be heard.

8.36   Where the club appears before the magistrates it should either be represented by its chairman, secretary, member of GMC or other authorised officer of the club or it may be represented by a solicitor or counsel, supported by witnesses as necessary to deal with any matters of evidence.

8.37   The procedure at the hearing will be similar to that adopted by the court when hearing a complaint, in certain respects. Witnesses may be summonsed. At least two lay justices (but not more than seven) must sit.

8.38 Those appearing on behalf of the club might be asked to deal with the following matters:

(1) confirming the accuracy of the information given in the form of application;

(2) confirming that the rules are in conformity with Sch 7 (see above);

(3) confirming that there are no arrangements for any person to receive a private benefit in respect of either purchases of intoxicating liquor by the club or the supply of intoxicating liquor to members, guests or third parties;

(4) if there is a 'brewery tie' (ie an obligation to purchase a proportion of the stock from a nominated supplier), explaining how this arises and how it is necessary for the benefit of all the members;

(5) if any profits or assets of the club are to be applied other than for the benefit of the club or for charitable, benevolent or political purposes, explaining why this is necessary and does not reflect adversely upon the bona fide nature of the club;

(6) confirming that members will be provided with proper information as to the club's finances, for which proper arrangements and records will be maintained;

(7) establishing that the premises to be provided are appropriate for the club in question;

(8) addressing any specific objections that have been raised upon the grounds set out above, details of which will have been served prior to the hearing.

Decision

8.39 At the conclusion of the application the magistrates may either:

(1) grant a registration certificate, for a period of 12 months;[1]

(2) grant a registration certificate, subject to conditions restricting sales of intoxicating liquor on the club premises (and, if they think reasonable, forbidding/restricting the alteration of the rules of the club so as to prevent authority being given for sales not authorised at the time of the application to the court);[2] or

(3) refuse the application.

[1] Section 40(2).
[2] Section 49(3).

Refusal

8.40   An application may be refused on one of the following grounds.

(1)   One of the grounds of objection under s 44(1) (set out in full at para **8.33**) has been made out. Note that the court is *obliged* to refuse if the ground in sub-s (a) or (c) is made out. In the case of sub-s (b) (premises not suitable, etc), the application must also be refused 'unless the court thinks it reasonable not to, having regard to any steps taken or proposed to be taken to remove the ground of objection'.[1]

(2)   The premises have previously been disqualified, or are licensed premises, or include or form part of premises so disqualified or licensed premises. There are, in fact, a number of clubs which operate alongside licensed premises and the extent to which this practice is possible will depend upon the nature of the area covered by the justices' licence and whether each of the premises is capable of independent operation. The device has been used on occasions where the club seeks to use part of the building which it occupies to hold a significant number of commercial events, to an extent that might be thought by a court to threaten the bona fide nature of the club (but see *The Little Ship Club* case, above). In such cases clubs have retained registration certificates for their principal operation so as to ensure that they may continue, for example, to take advantage of privileges available to clubs such as the entitlement to allow members' young families into the bar. Where other club premises operate under the authority of a justices' licence, subject to appropriate conditions (see precedents at para **A.150**) the court is entitled to refuse the application for the registration certificate if, in such circumstances, it is of the opinion that the arrangement 'is likely to give occasion for abuse by reason of any difference in the permitted hours in the premises or otherwise'. This will, of course, be a matter of fact in each case (less common now that the special arrangements for clubs on Sundays have been repealed), but it is suggested that an entirely bona fide arrangement for the given purpose, which will benefit the members of a club as a whole, should not form the basis for a refusal under this provision.[2]

(3)   A person who is *likely* to take an active part in the management of the club, is not fit to be concerned in the management of a registered club, in view of his known character *as proved to the court*.[3]

---

[1]   Section 44.
[2]   Section 43(1) and (3).
[3]   Section 43(2).

8.41   Where the original application relates to two or more premises, the court may refuse the certificate in respect of some only of the club's premises.[1]

¹   Section 52(3).

8.42   Where magistrates refuse an application for the issue of a registration certificate they must state in writing the grounds of that refusal.

8.43   Unlike licensing committees, which have a broad discretion as regards the grant of justices' licences, magistrates may refuse an application for a club registration certificate only upon the grounds specified in the Act (see above). The significance of this difference can perhaps be seen most clearly in the figures for refusals in the last year for which records are available.[1] Less than 3 per cent of applications for registration were refused, compared with 14 per cent of applications for full on-licences.

¹   Home Office Statistical Bulletin ISSN 0143, 6384.

RENEWALS

8.44   The above provisions as to applications apply equally to renewals, subject to the following:

(1)   On a second or subsequent renewal the certificate may be granted for a period of up to ten years.

(2)   If the application for renewal is submitted at least 28 days before the certificate is due to expire the certificate will continue in force until the application is disposed of.[1]

(3)   If the rules conform with Sch 7, the magistrates must also assume that there are no arrangements for any persons to receive a private benefit in relation to either the purchase or supply of intoxicating liquor by the club.

(4)   The fire authority is also entitled as of right to inspect registered premises prior to renewal.[2]

(5)   On refusal to renew on the grounds in s 44(1)(c), (d) or (e) (see above), the court is entitled to order that the premises should not be occupied or used for the purposes of a registered club for a specified period.[3] On the first occasion such an order must not be for more than one year; thereafter the maximum period is five years.

(6)   If the club rules have changed, the application must particularise the changes since the date of the original grant or the last renewal.

(7) The application for renewal need *not* be publicly notified (by way of advertisement or display) unless it seeks a registration certificate in respect of different, additional or enlarged premises.[4]

¹   Unless the court makes a direction to the contrary under Sch 6, para 10—see s 40(5).
²   Section 46(1).
³   Section 47(1).
⁴   Schedule 6, para 5.

VARIATION

8.45 The Act defines club premises as being premises which are 'occupied by and habitually used for the purposes of a club'.[1] It further provides that a club is registered in respect of any premises if it holds for those premises a certificate. It is unclear from these provisions whether it is necessary to make application if the club seeks to occupy altered or enlarged premises. Whilst, in fact, such an application may not be required, it is prudent for a club to consider making one before carrying out the alterations, so as to avoid the risk of objections being raised when the certificate falls due for renewal.

¹   Section 39(6).

8.46 The rules set out above for the procedure relating to applications for new registration certificates apply equally to applications for variation, subject to the applicant providing details of:

(a) any variation sought in respect of club rules;[1]

(b) the alternative premises to be occupied by the club;[2]

(c) the additional or enlarged premises.[3]

Whilst an application for variation does *not* generally need advertisement or display, an application which would result in different, additional or enlarged premises *will* need to be advertised.[4]

¹   Section 49(5).
²   Section 52(1).
³   Section 52(2).
⁴   Section 52(2) and Sch 6, para 5.

CANCELLATION

8.47 The police or the local authority may lodge a complaint against the club for the cancellation of a registration certificate. The complaint must be made in writing to the magistrates' court and any summons issued as a result must be served on the chairman or secretary of the club, or the person who signed the last application for the issue or renewal of the certificate. In addition, the summons must be served upon such other persons as the justices issuing the summons may direct.[1]

[1]   See Sch 6, para 14, which provides that where undue difficulty or delay would arise in complying with these provisions, the court may order that service on the club be effected by serving the summons on a person named in the order, being a person who appears to the court to have, or to have had, an interest in the club, or to be or to have been an officer of the club.

8.48   An application for cancellation may be made on any ground upon which objection to a new grant might be made under the following provisions:[1]

(1)   non-compliance with qualifications for registration,[2] which include:

    (a)   provisions for two-day lapse prior to admission to membership;

    (b)   being established and conducted in good faith as a club;

    (c)   25 or more members;

    (d)   arrangements to ensure that the supply of intoxicating liquor to members is effected by or on behalf of the club;

    (e)   confirmation that an elective committee (or members) manages the purchase and supply of intoxicating liquor;

    (f)   no arrangements exist for private benefit concerning the sale or supply of intoxicating liquor by or on behalf of the club to members or guests;

(2)[3]   (a)   premises previously disqualified, or licensed;

    (b)   unfit person concerned in management;

    (c)   in preceding 12 months premises were licensed, prior to forfeiture or revocation;

    (d)   abuse likely to arise because of other licensed club premises;

(3)   'Club is conducted in disorderly manner or for an unlawful purpose, or that the rules of the club are habitually disregarded as respects the admission of persons to membership or to the privileges of membership or in any other material respect';[4]

(4)   illegal sales of intoxicating liquor have been made or persons who are not entitled to be supplied have been admitted or the premises have habitually been used for an unlawful purpose, etc (see above).[5]

As with renewals, upon the cancellation of a registration certificate the court can order that the premises be disqualified (at first instance) for a period of up to 12 months and thereafter for a period not exceeding five years.

[1]   Section 44(2) and 44(1)(c).
[2]   Section 41(1) and (2).
[3]   Sections 44(1)(c) and 43.
[4]   Section 44(1)(d).
[5]   Section 44(1)(e).

APPEALS

8.49   There is a right of appeal[1] to the Crown Court against the following decisions:

(a)   refusal to issue;

(b)   refusal to renew;

(c)   cancellation;

(d)   decision relating to conditions concerning sales;

(e)   disqualification of premises.

[1]   Section 50(1).

8.50   In the case of an appeal against refusal to renew, the court is entitled to order, upon such conditions as it thinks fit, that the certificate (as in force at the time of the application) shall continue pending the determination of the appeal, or pending the consideration of the question of bringing such an appeal.

8.51   The proper respondent to an appeal is any person who appeared before the magistrates' court to object to the application, or make representations. Even if, as is permitted, the appeal relates to some part only of the premises which would have been covered by the registration certificate, the same person should be named as respondent even if he did not actually object to the registration in respect of the premises which are the subject of the appeal.[1]

[1]   Section 50(3).

SURRENDER OF CERTIFICATE

8.52   A club registration certificate may be surrendered by lodging with the chief executive to the licensing justices a notice of surrender and the original club registration certificate. Sufficient copies must be provided to enable the chief executive to notify the police, fire authority and local authority.

CLUBS—GENERAL PROVISIONS

Other club premises

8.53 As indicated above, the Act defines club premises as premises which are 'occupied by and habitually used for the purposes of a club'.[1] A single registration certificate may relate to any number of premises of the same club.[2] On application, the registration certificate may be varied as regards the premises to which it relates.[3] If the club has other premises which are licensed, that may in itself (as indicated above) form a ground of refusal to a new grant or renewal if the court is of the opinion that because of the difference in permitted hours, or for some other reason, the situation is likely to give occasion for abuse.[4] The application for a registration certificate should, of course, identify the premises for which the certificate is sought, as well as indicate any other property which is to be used for the purposes of the club and not held by or in trust for the club absolutely. The application should also contain particulars of any premises which have been occupied and habitually used for the purpose of the club in the preceding 12 months.[5]

---

[1]   Section 39(6).
[2]   Section 52(1).
[3]   See para **8.45** as regards the procedure.
[4]   Section 43(3)(b).
[5]   See Sch 5, paras 5–7.

8.54 Intoxicating liquor may not be supplied by or on behalf of a registered club to a member or guest except at premises in respect of which the club is registered. An exception to this rule is when the club uses other premises on a *special occasion*. In that event, only members and guests may be permitted access to the premises.

Special occasion

8.55 There is no corresponding provision to the occasional licence (which entitles the holder of a justices' on-licence to trade elsewhere for a limited period) in relation to a registered club. However, as indicated above, the club is entitled, without application, on a special occasion to supply intoxicating liquor to members and guests at premises other than those in which the club is registered, provided all other persons are denied access. Off-sales are prohibited. There will be *no* restrictions as to the hours during which the supply of intoxicating liquor takes place.[1] Regular use of this provision would tend to suggest that the occasions were not 'special', so giving rise to a possible offence under s 39 and an application by the police for cancellation of the certificate.[2] During this 'special occasion' the club's other premises may also remain open.

[1]   Sections 39(3) and 59.
[2]   *Watson v Cully* [1926] 2 KB 270.

Permitted hours in clubs

8.56   Broadly speaking, the provisions as to permitted hours in licensed premises (see chapter 7) will apply, subject to the modifications as to Christmas Day outlined below.

Christmas day

8.57   On Christmas Day the hours will be those *fixed by or under the rules of the club* in accordance with the following provisions:

(1)   Commencement—not before 12.00 noon

       Termination—not after 10.30 pm

       Duration—not longer than six and a half hours.

(2)   Afternoon break—3.00 pm to 5.00 pm and any additional hours elected.

(3)   Second session—no more than three and a half hours after 5.00 pm.

The effect of these somewhat tortuous provisions is set out below. In summary, clubs are in a moderately privileged position as against licensed premises in that they can choose when to take the three and a half hours available to them between 5.00 pm and 10.30 pm, whereas licensed premises are fixed with the period following 7.00 pm.

8.58   As will be recalled, the application for the club registration certificate is obliged to state the hours (if any) fixed by or under the rules of the club as the permitted hours. If it is desired to change these hours the club must send a written notice (signed by the chairman or secretary of the club) to the chief executive to the justices fixing the new hours in accordance with these provisions.

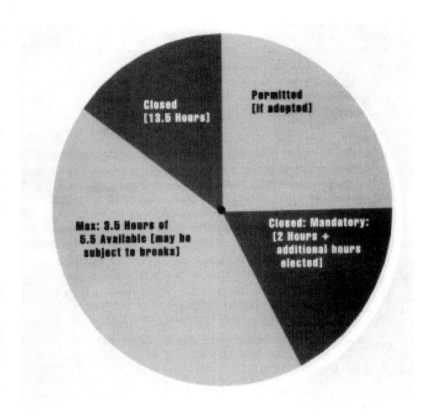

Section 68 (supper hour) certificates

8.59 The principles upon which a s 68 application should be heard and the effect of any certificate so granted will be the same for a registered club as it would be for licensed premises. Note, of course, that any such additional hours must be notified in writing to the chief executive to the justices in so far as they affect the hours on Christmas Day.[1]

[1] Section 62(3).

8.60 If, however, an alteration in permitted hours also requires an alteration in the rules notice needs to be given to the chief executive, the police and local authority.[1]

[1] Section 48.

8.61   As regards the notices to be given for an application for a s 68 certificate, the position is very different from that applicable to licensed premises. Section 92(4) provides that the procedure to be adopted will (subject to any necessary modifications) be that which applies to applications for the *issue* of a registration certificate. Accordingly, the following procedure should be observed:

(1)   The applicant lodges an original application together with the numbers of copies requested by the chief executive (not less than three) at the magistrates' court.

(2)   The notice is to be signed by the chairman or club secretary.

(3)   The chief executive must send copies to the chief officer of police, and the fire and local authorities.

(4)   Public notice is to be given, either by displaying the notice on or near the premises, in a place where it can be conveniently be read by the public, for the seven days beginning with the date of the application, or by advertisement on at least one of those days in a newspaper circulating in the place where the premises are situated.

(5)   Any objections are to be lodged with the chief executive to the justices (two copies) in writing within 28 days of the application.

(6)   Copies of any objection must be submitted by the clerk to the justices to the person signing the application.

(7)   Any objection must specify the grounds of the objection and the particulars of the matters relied upon to make it out.

Note that the application may be dealt with in the absence of the club, but only if it is to be granted, and that the court is able to award costs.

Section 70 (extended hours) orders

8.62   The operation of the provisions of the Act applicable to extended hours orders is identical to those relating to licensed premises, save that the procedure for making application is again governed by the provisions in Sch 6,[1] as set out above for supper hour certificates.

[1]   Section 92(4).

Special orders of exemption (extensions)

8.63   The same procedures and principles apply to registered clubs as they do to licensed premises (see chapter 7).

Section 77 (special hours) certificates

8.64 The principal difference here between licensed premises and registered clubs is that prior to making the application a club must obtain from the local authority, not a public entertainments licence (because the public are not, in general, admitted), but instead a certificate of suitability. There is no specific procedure for making application for a certificate of suitability, although it would seem sensible for local authorities to adopt a similar procedure to that which operates in respect of public entertainments licences. The local authority may attach conditions or restrictions to the certificate. The duration of the certificate will be fixed by the local authority, which *may* also accept applications for renewal. Conditions or restrictions may be varied upon application. If there is evidence of non-compliance written notice may be given to the club secretary by the local authority of an intention to revoke upon specified grounds. The club must then be given an opportunity to state its case to a person duly delegated by the authority to hear such representations. At least seven days after serving its notice and, if appropriate, hearing the representations of the club (as incorporated in the report of the person delegated to hear those representations), the authority may revoke the certificate. The authority is entitled to require payment of a reasonable fee on any application for the grant, renewal, waiver, modification or restriction of a certificate of suitability.[1]

[1] Section 79.

8.65 All other provisions as to special hours certificates apply equally to licensed premises and registered clubs, save in respect of applications for their grant (where Sch 6 again will apply—see above) and revocation. The latter should proceed by way of complaint against the club.[1] It would seem reasonable for the same procedure to be adopted in relation to an application under s 81A to impose limitations as to hours.

[1] Section 92(2).

Offences

8.66 As indicated above, the operation of registered clubs is far less subject to the sanction of criminal penalties than is the case for licensed premises.

Liability of committee members

8.67 Certain offences under the Act applying to registered clubs[1] also provide that a person committing a particular act by himself or by his servant or agent is liable to be convicted of the offence. Such provisions expose the members of the club committee employing the person who actually committed the act to prosecution as principals even though they had no knowledge of the incident in question.[2] It seems that trustees of a club will not, however, be liable; nor will members of a committee of a club which has been incorporated.[3]

[1]   Eg ss 59(1)(a), (b), 165 and 186.
[2]   *Anderton v Rodgers* (1981) 145 JP 181.
[3]   *Newman v Jones* (1886) 17 QBD 132; *Phipps v Hoffman* [1976] Crim LR 315.

Licensed clubs

8.68   As has been seen, there are a number of benefits to be derived by a members' club from holding a club registration certificate and the vast majority of such clubs are operated in this way. Proprietary clubs (that is, clubs where the profits accrue to the benefit of an individual, rather than for the membership as a whole) invariably operate under justices' on-licences, subject to conditions which principally restrict sales to members of the club, their bona fide guests and such other categories of persons as are agreed by the licensing committee. In between these two most common categories of clubs, there lies the hybrid 's 55 licence'.

8.69   Under this particular provision a club which does not qualify for some reason[1] for registration under Part II of the Act may still receive a justices' licence notwithstanding the fact that it remains substantially a members' club. Such a licence will be granted in the name of a duly nominated officer of the club. For most purposes that person will be treated as the licensee, entitled to exercise the same rights as a licensee and subject to the same obligations. There are, however, a number of disadvantages. If the same club is registered in respect of other premises it will not be able to take advantage of the provision authorising relocation to other premises for a special occasion.[2] Further, the original application will not be granted if the licensing committee considers that a club registration certificate would in fact serve the purpose, or that there is likely to be abuse because of the difference in permitted hours in the premises, or for some other reason.[3] A very modest benefit is that, if the licence is subject to conditions forbidding or restricting sales to non-members, the licensee may be excused the display of a notice bearing his name and the nature of the licence held.[4] It has been held that the holder of a s 55 licence is *not* entitled to make application for an occasional licence.[5]

[1]   See eg s 41.
[2]   Section 39(3).
[3]   Section 55(4).

4   Section 183.
5   *Birt v Swansea Justices* [1963] 2 All ER 769.

8.70 There does, in fact, seem little benefit in resorting to the s 55 procedure from the point of view of the club. If the framework of a club registration certificate is not found to be suitable, the most attractive alternative for most clubs will be a full on-licence, with conditions adapted to the precise requirements of the organisation and its members. See Part II for examples of the condition that might be adopted.

Registration under Part III of the Gaming Act 1968

Application

8.71 Members' clubs are entitled to seek registration under Part III of the Gaming Act 1968. If granted, registration will entitle the club to have up to two jackpot machines available for gaming at times when the public do not have access to the premises.[1]

1   Gaming Act 1968, s 31(8).

8.72 The procedure for the application is straightforward. Whilst there are no specific statutory time limits for lodging the application, reasonable notice should be given in advance of the meeting of the Betting and Gaming Licensing Committee of the local magistrates. Within seven days the applicant should serve a copy on the police. A form is prescribed by regulations made under the Act.[1]

1   The Gaming Act (Registration under Part III) Regulations 1969.

8.73 The application may be granted in the absence of the applicant if there are no police objections.

Grounds of refusal

8.74 The committee is *obliged* to refuse the application for registration if it is apparent that the premises are frequented wholly or mainly by persons under 18.

8.75 The committee *may* refuse the application if it finds that the club:

(a)   is not a bona fide members' club;[1] or

(b)   has less than 25 members; or

(c)   is of a merely temporary character.

¹   It follows from this provision that a proprietary club will need to persuade the committee to exercise its discretion. Factors that might be considered include the nature of the club's management, the extent of the similarity with a members' club and (of most significance) whether the profits from the machines are to be used directly or indirectly for the benefit of the club members. See *Miriam Walters v Chief Constable of Nottingham* (4 October 1975, unreported) and *Chief Constable, Strathclyde v Pollockshaws Road Snooker Centre* 1977 SLT (Sh Ct) 72. Both decisions are reported briefly in *Paterson's Licensing Acts* (110th edn), para 5.290.

8.76   Further, the grant of a certificate *may* be refused if an offence under certain provisions in the Gaming Act 1968 has been committed in respect of the premises, or a previous registration has been cancelled or refused upon renewal.

8.77   There is a right of appeal to the Crown Court against refusal to grant or renew. Registration may be cancelled following an application by the police and a formal hearing. A certificate will be of five years' duration from the date of first registration or renewal.

CHAPTER 9

THE EUROPEAN UNION AND OTHER LOCAL JURISDICTIONS

9.01 With the further development of the European Union it seems likely that the legislature will continue to look to the continent for examples of social systems which (whilst recognising the different environments in which they obtain) might provide a model for reform in the United Kingdom. The controlled admission of children into bars and a proposal (long since abandoned) for a new café-bar style licence expressly derived some of their inspiration from their continental counterparts. Closer to home, many of the procedures (including the children's certificate) already operating in Scotland have provided a model for a similar system introduced south of the border and the Isle of Man has now set the pace in terms of 24-hour licensing. It is likely that such models will in part be followed in this country, where convenient, in relation to the abandonment of the concept of permitted hours and a new system for the administration of the licensing process itself. The sole purpose of this chapter is to highlight some of the principal features of the legislation operating in the other Member States and local jurisdictions, which might in due course provide the basis for reform. Each entry is a very brief summary of certain elements of the relevant law only and legal advice should be sought from the practices named in the introduction to this work, or other local specialists, on specific licensing issues.

AUSTRIA

9.02 There are three levels of regulation: federal, provincial and local. At federal level the Trade Code (*Gewerbeordnung*) distinguishes between retail sales for consumption on the premises (hotels, restaurants, bars etc) and off-sales (food retailing). There are no special licensing requirements and procedures for businesses that also (or only) sell alcoholic (as opposed to non-alcoholic) beverages. The Trade Code does make specific provisions covering on-sales, for example compliance with provincial statutes and the requirement that retailers may *not* sell alcoholic beverages only: they must offer at least two non-alcoholic beverages at prices below the cheapest alcoholic drink available.

9.03   The different statutes of the Austrian provinces (*Länder*) and the local ordinances address issues such as the protection of children and young persons and permitted opening hours—these will also include provisions concerning the sale of alcoholic beverages. According to a local statute applicable to the Federal Province of Vienna persons under the age of 17 are not allowed to consume alcoholic beverages or tobacco in public. Persons under the age of 15 are not allowed to visit day or night bars or any night club. Those aged 15 or over may, however, stay in other establishments (eg cafes or guest houses) until 12 pm according to this statute.

9.04   The opening hours vary from province to province. In Vienna, for example, the permitted hours for a bar are currently until 4 am and for a cafe until 2 am.

9.05   Additional restrictions on the sale of alcoholic beverages may be imposed by local ordinances. These would usually cover specific local occasions, needs etc. There is no co-ordinated system governing such ordinances.

9.06   The general district administrative authorities act as licensing authorities, both in respect of alcoholic beverages and for all other businesses.

9.07   The Trade Code contains general requirements that apply to all businesses (is there a history of bankruptcy, for example?) as well as those specifically applicable to individuals running a hotel, restaurant or bar (*Gastgewerbe*: on-sales) or retailing foodstuffs (*Handel mit Lebensmitteln*: off-sales). Requirements for the latter are less burdensome. An applicant must merely show that he meets the relevant criteria (education, professional experience, examination etc). However, not only the conduct of a certain business but also the operation of the business on certain premises is subject to a permit. The grant of the latter permit depends on the suitability of the premises and its likely effect on neighbours. There is no limit on the numbers of licenses for the operation of restaurants, bars, nightclubs etc which can be granted.

9.08   Licences, once granted, run for an unlimited period. In certain situations, however, they may be revoked.

9.09 A retailer with an on-licence may also sell alcoholic beverages (eg in bottles) for consumption off the premises. In addition, retailers of foodstuffs have a general ancillary right to sell beer for consumption off their premises, albeit in limited quantities only. A comparable right exists for certain other types of retailers (butchers, for example) to sell beer in limited quantities for consumption off the premises.

9.10 There are no specific measures dealing with inspecting and overseeing retailers of alcoholic beverages. The rules specifically governing hotels, restaurants and bars do, however, provide for an inspection regime.

BELGIUM

9.11 The retail sale of alcohol in Belgium is regulated by a number of separate statutes which were co-ordinated in 1953 by the Royal Decree of 3 April. The Royal Decree contains the basic requirements which have to be complied with by the operators of outlets. Other requirements are set out in other laws such as those on drunkenness (Law of 14 November 1939) and on young people (Law of 15 July 1960). Additional regulations are issued by the local authorities, which have a general regulatory power to strengthen or to extend the basic requirements (Royal Decree, art 5) and to preserve law and order (New Municipality Law of 24 June 1988).

9.12 The control over outlets and their operators is exercised mainly by the local municipalities. To open premises the operator needs a certificate of hygiene and a certificate of morality, each of which is issued by the local authorities. The certificate of hygiene aims to control the sanitation of the premises (situation, ceiling height, ventilation, lighting, etc). The certificate of morality confirms that the operator has, for example, not been convicted of conducting illegal games, or of selling spirits without having paid the appropriate taxes.

9.13 The operator must also obtain from the Customs Tax Authorities a tax licence, the cost of which may vary from €300 to €1,000 (formerly 12,000 to 40,000 Belgian francs). The operator is further required to pay an opening tax amounting to three times the annual rental value of the premises being opened. Every five years another tax is due (after an initial period of 15 years) from operators of outlets run by a legal person and selling fermented drinks. This tax is equal to 50 per cent of the annual rental value of the premises. As from 1 January 2002, such taxes are no longer due from operators of the Flemish Region following a decision of the Flemish government of 7 December 2001.

9.14 The nature and extent of the detailed requirements of the local municipalities vary widely, as each is empowered to regulate opening hours, safety standards, etc. However, following a decision of the Administrative Supreme Court[1], local authorities may not impose standard closing hours for all outlets within a certain area as these have been judged as being contrary to the right of the individual to free trade. The right to open early in the morning and to remain open late at night can thus not be restricted by the local authorities which have the power only to close any particular premises as an individual sanction (eg in order to maintain law and order in the neighbourhood and avoid night disturbance).

[1]   Conseil d'Etat, 16 December 1992, JLMB, 1993, p 404.

9.15 Premises are kept under general police surveillance. There is no yearly renewal of a licence. The licence is granted for an indefinite period as long as the operator complies with the statutory, local and tax regulations.

9.16 Before 1983 spirits could be sold for consumption on the premises only within private clubs. Establishments open to the public could sell only beer for on-consumption and were forbidden to have any quantity of spirits in their premises. Since the law of 28 December 1983 all establishments may sell beer and spirits if they pay a tax authorising them to sell spirits, if they comply with the regulations and if they are not located on a motorway or in a school or hospital premises.

9.17 It is an offence for operators of premises or their employees to serve spirits to under 18s. In general, a child under 16 years of age may not enter premises where liquor is consumed and where people are dancing, without being accompanied by a parent. By special order of the Court of First Instance on request of the Public Prosecutor, an outlet where people dance can also be prohibited from entertaining children under 18 years for a maximum period of two years when it appears that the outlet is dangerous for the health, security or morality of the young persons.

DENMARK

9.18 Any commercial sale of liquor in Denmark is subject to The Danish Act on Catering and Hotel Business of 6 May 1993 (Act No 256). The Act is administered by the Danish Ministry of Business and Industry and the Danish Commerce and Companies Agency. Pursuant to this Act, a trade licence is required for the following activities:

(a)   independent trading related to the serving of food and beverages;

(b)   overnight accommodation with catering facilities;

(c)   serving of food and beverages at isolated events;
(d)   serving of alcoholic drinks for enjoyment at or near the premises.

9.19   Any person who is a Danish resident, is of full age and legal capacity, has not given notice that he or she intends to suspend payments or is subject to compulsory liquidation proceedings, has a legal claim for such trade licence. The granting of a trade licence may be withheld if the applicant has unpaid debts to public authorities exceeding DKK 50,000. The trade licence lapses if the conditions precedent are no longer fulfilled. It is issued by the chief of police.

9.20   A business may only serve alcohol if it holds a liquor licence. Such licence is granted and renewed by the local authority subject to the approval of the police or a licence committee appointed by the local authority. The licence to serve alcohol may only be issued to a person who holds a trade licence, is 25 years old or more and has not been declared legally incompetent. When deciding whether to grant a liquor licence, the local authority shall take into consideration the social context as well as law and order.

9.21   The liquor licence, which is granted for a period of eight years, can only be used by the place of business to which it is granted. The liquor licence can be granted conditionally and/or made subject to limitations.

9.22   The liquor licence lapses if the licensee ceases to use it. Furthermore, the local authority may withdraw the licence at the request of the police, if the business is being neglected or is carried out in a manner that allows drunkenness, prostitution, indecency or criminal acts.

9.23   As a general rule, restaurants and other refreshment outlets shall be closed between 2 am and 5 am. Subject to the consent of the police, the local authority may give permission for longer opening hours, most often until 5 am. Such permission is given at the discretion of the local authority.
The rules on closing time apply to all refreshment outlets irrespective of the availability of food.

9.24   Persons below the age of 18 may not buy alcoholic drinks. Generally, children of all ages are allowed in premises serving alcohol, but in special circumstances the police may forbid persons below the age of 18 entering particular premises.

9.25   As regards the sale of alcohol from shops, supermarkets and the like no liquor licence is required. The sale of alcohol from such establishments is not permitted between 8 pm and 6 am or to children under the age of 15.

EIRE

9.26   In 1902 it was decided that there should be no further new publican's licenses granted. If one has a publican's licence, one holds it under s 2(1) of the Licensing (Ireland) Act 1902, but if one has an hotel licence, one holds it under s 2(2). For an owner of a hotel licence to continue to have the benefit thereof, the owner must maintain the required number of bedrooms, ie 10 in the country and 20 in a city.There are two reasons for the confusion which exists in relation to these two forms of licence. One is that to enable an hotel owner to actually have a physical bar counter on his or her premises, one must extinguish a publican's licence anywhere in the country, pursuant to s 19 of the 1960 Licensing Act. The second difficulty is that on the face of the document one cannot establish which particular licence one has. The result of this has been that people have thought they had publican's licences for their hotels and when the need for the bedrooms decreased, or ceased to be a viable proposition, they ceased to maintain the required number, as they were, in many instances, receiving an adequate income from the bar of the hotel. They dropped the bedrooms and they then effectively had no licence whatsoever. This would come to light when they went to sell their property or mortgage it, as the case may be.

9.27   Under the Intoxicating Liquor Act 2000 a licence may be granted by the court for new premises if an existing licence for other premises is offered for surrender with the consent of the existing licensee.

9.28   Further, a restricted licence (ie a publican's licence which is not a full licence or a 'beerhouse licence' within the meaning of the Finance (1909–10) Act 1910) may be upgraded to a full licence upon payment of £2,500 to the Revenue Commissioners, if the applicant can show that he or she held the licence for a period of five years prior, or, inherited, received as a gift, leased or purchased the premises within that period. Such premises may then not be sold, nor the licence disposed of within a further five years.

9.29   Under the Intoxicating Liquor Act 2000 no alcohol may be sold on Christmas Day (save in an hotel or restaurant, where the hours will be noon to 10.00 pm) or Good Friday and there are restricted hours specified for the Eve of each day as well as Saint Patrick's Day and the 23 December (if a Sunday). Hours on Sundays generally are 12.30 pm to 11 pm. On Mondays, Tuesdays and Wednesdays the hours are 10.30 am to 11.30 pm, whilst for the remainder of the week it is 10.30 am to 12.30 am the following day. Off licences attached to a non-licensed business may open from 7.30 am on any weekday.

9.30 A special restaurant licence was introduced, despite the prohibition contained in the Licensing (Ireland) Act 1902 against the grant of further licences, and the holder of a special restaurant licence is entitled to sell spirits, wine, beer and cider on the premises in the quantity specified in Sch 1 to the Finance (1909–10) Act 1910. The special restaurant licence authorises the following:

(1) the supply of intoxicating liquor for consumption on licensed premises;

(2) the consumption of intoxicating liquor on these premises.

9.31 Such supply and consumption may only be taken where the intoxicating liquor is:

(a) ordered by or on behalf of the person for whom a substantial meal has been ordered;

(b) supplied in either the waiting area or the dining area, of the restaurant;

(c) consumed in the waiting area of the restaurant, prior to a meal, by the person for whom the meal has been ordered, or is consumed by that person in the dining area of the restaurant, either during the meal or at any time not later than thirty minutes after the meal has ended; or

(d) paid for at the same time as the meal is paid for.

The holder of this licence is also obliged to ensure that suitable beverages other than intoxicating liquor, including drinking water, are also available for consumption.

A person who does not propose to eat a substantial meal on the premises cannot therefore be served with intoxicating liquor.

9.32 The sale and supply of intoxicating liquor on a premises to which a special restaurant licence attaches, is not permitted during the following times:

(1) on a weekday before 12.30 pm and after 12.30 am;

(2) on a Sunday before 12.30 pm and between 3 and 6 pm;

(3) after 11 pm on a Sunday.

There are also special provisions relating to Christmas Day and Good Friday, and Sundays which fall on 23 and 24 December.

9.33 The holder of a special restaurant licence is entitled to open the premises at any time, for non-licensed business. There are no circumstances under which the holder of a special restaurant licence can obtain special exemption orders.

9.34 The following are the differences between a special restaurant licence and a publican's licence:

(i)   the holder of a special restaurant license is expressly prohibited from having a bar on the premises;

(ii) the holder of a special restaurant licence is not entitled to apply for an occasional licence;

(iii) in the application for a publican's licence, or an off-licence, it is not possible to tender for extinguishment a special restaurant licence or licences;

(iv) an applicant for a special restaurant licence is not entitled to apply for a declaration as to the fitness and convenience of his proposed premises for use as a restaurant;

(v)   a person who wishes to apply for a special restaurant licence must first obtain a certificate from the circuit court, entitling him to receive a special restaurant licence in respect of the restaurant premises, on payment of €3800 (formerly £3,000).

9.35 Under the Intoxicating Liquor Act 2000 where a person is convicted of selling to minors the court is obliged to make a closure order for a period of up to 7 days and between 7 and 30 days for any subsequent offence. The fines for various offences were also increased substantially.

FINLAND

9.36 The retail sale of alcohol is governed by the Alcohol Act (statute No 1143/1994), which provides the main guidelines for the retail sale and wholesale of alcohol, and by the Decree on Alcoholic Beverages and Spirits (statute No 1344/1994), which regulates the wholesale and retail sale of alcohol in detail. Both the Act and the Decree entered into force on 1 January 1995.

9.37 The Ministry of Social Affairs and Health is the highest authority controlling the sale of alcohol in Finland. A special division of the ministry, the National Product Control Agency for Welfare and Health (NPCA) is the authority that decides on the licences for the retail sale of alcohol. Local county governments may grant licences for the sale of alcoholic beverages with a low alcohol content.

9.38 In order to be able to serve alcohol at restaurants, bars, cafes, etc, the seller has to apply for a licence from the NPCA. A licence for serving alcoholic beverages having an alcohol content of no more than 4.7 per cent by volume is granted by the competent county government.

9.39 A licence to serve alcohol may be granted provided that the local council has allowed the serving of alcoholic beverages in the municipality. The licence may be granted to an applicant who is deemed reliable and qualified for the activity. Furthermore, the serving of alcohol may take place only in premises which are approved by the authority granting the licence and which are appropriate with regard to location, facilities and operations. The serving area may be altered only with the consent of the licensing authority.

9.40 Pursuant to the Alcohol Act, the licensing authority may reject the application or decide on certain requirements for the licence if it is deemed necessary for attaining the purpose of the Alcohol Act: the prevention of social and health hazards by influencing the consumption of alcohol. However, according to a recent decision of the Supreme Administrative Court, the appellate court for licensing matters, a licence may not be denied on the grounds that there is no need for new licensed premises in the area.

9.41 The licensing authority may refuse or limit the licence if the licensee has violated the rules regarding the serving of alcohol, no longer fulfills the requirements of the licence or the requirement of reliability, or disturbances have occurred at the premises of the licensee.

9.42 In licensed premises, alcohol may not be served to a person under 18 years of age. There are no statutory age limits for entrance to licensed premises, but owners may impose such age limits as they deem appropriate.

9.43 Alcohol may be served every day until 1.30 am and it may not generally be served earlier than 9 am. The authority granting the licence may issue a permit allowing alcohol to be served earlier than 9 am or later than 1.30 am but no later than 3.30 am. Food need not be available at the licensed premises.

9.44 Only the State Alcohol Company has the right to sell liquor in a shop. Alcoholic beverages with an alcohol content of no more than 4.7 per cent by volume may be sold at a grocer's if the local county government has granted a licence for the retail sale of such beverages. In addition, the sale of home-made wine and beer having an alcohol content of no more that 13 per cent by volume may be conducted in the immediate vicinity of the production site by someone who has obtained an NPCA licence for the production of such wine or beer.

9.45 In retail shops, alcohol may not be sold to a person under 20 years of age, save that alcoholic beverages having an alcohol content of no more the 22 per cent by volume may be sold to persons 18 or over.

9.46   Permitted selling hours for the State Alcohol Company and for a holder of a licence allowing for production and sale of home-made wine and beer are from Monday to Friday 9 am to 8 pm, and 9 am to 12 noon on Saturdays and some holiday eves. Retail sale is allowed on Sundays 9 am to 6 pm only for a holder of a licence allowing for production and sale of home-made wine and beer, provided that the place of production and the place of sales are located in close connection or in close vicinity to each other.

9.47   Alcoholic beverages with an alcohol content of no more than 4.7 per cent by volume may be sold at retail stores during their general opening hours, but in no case between 9 pm and 7 am.

FRANCE

9.48   The law in France governing the retail sale of alcoholic beverages in drinking establishments (débit de boissons) such as bars, cafes, etc is contained principally in the *Code des Débits de Boissons*, which grants local authorities considerable powers.

9.49   Control over drinking establishments and their operators is exercised pursuant to divided authority attributed to the mayor (*maire*) of the local municipality (*commune*), the prefect (*préfet*) of the territorial department, and, for Paris, the *Préfet de Police*.

9.50   The opening of a new drinking establishment requires the operator to hold the appropriate licence in accordance with the strength of alcoholic beverages served. In order to serve all types of alcoholic drinks, an operator must apply for a full licence (known as type IV licence) before the local prefect.

9.51   Pursuant to the Law of November 9, 1915 the new issue of full licences is in principle prohibited, though existing licences remain freely transferable and are valid indefinitely. Nevertheless, special legislation has been passed which authorises the granting of a certain number of new full licences in order to satisfy the particular needs in tourist areas or in newly created urban zones. There is in any case, however, an overall limitation of one full licence establishment per 3,000 local residents within a given municipality.

9.52   As a general matter, most openings of drinking establishments occur as the replacement of a previous establishment at the same site. Where the ownership or operation of the business is sold or leased, the licence may be, and generally is, included among the transferred or leased assets. In this case, the opening is subject merely to the filing of a prior declaration before the mayor of the municipality in which the establishment is located. This declaration must contain specific information regarding the new operator who must satisfy certain legal requirements relating to age, nationality, profession, criminal record, and moral character. Failure to observe the necessary formalities or satisfy the required conditions constitutes an offence punishable by a fine and/ or prison.

Relocation of an existing establishment is subject to a separate procedure which is somewhat more complex and strictly regulated.

9.53 The opening of an establishment is prohibited in certain geographical zones, which generally consist of areas surrounding hospitals, schools, sports arenas or industrial sites.

9.54 Opening hours are not subject to national regulation, but rather are established by local authorities (mayor and prefect) according to social, economic and cultural factors within the municipality. As a general matter, closing hours most often fall between 12 am and 2 am.

9.55 In total, there are four types of licences corresponding to the strength of alcohol in the beverages served. There is no requirement to serve food in connection with such licences.

(1) Licence I is required for the sale of non-alcoholic drinks. Such a licence is held, for instance, by milk bars, tea salons, or ice cream shops.

(2) Licence II is required for the sale of low strength alcoholic drinks such as wine, beer and cider.

(3) Licence III is required for the sale of alcoholic drinks up to 36 proof (18) such as aperitifs and liqueurs.

(4) Licence IV (full licence) allows for the sale of all alcoholic drinks.

9.56 The general prohibition outlined above regarding the issue of new full licences only applies in the case of granting new Licences II or III where the number of such establishments in a given municipality attains or exceeds the proportion of one per 450 residents.

9.57 In regard to consumer restrictions, minors below the age of 16 must be accompanied by an adult in order to enter the establishment but may not be served any alcoholic drinks whatsoever. Minors above the age of 16 may be served outside the company of an adult but only beer or wine. There are no nationwide entry time restrictions concerning minors, but the local mayor has the authority to issue such restrictions for the municipality if necessary.

9.58   It should be noted that restaurants, though permitted to serve alcoholic drinks, are subject to separate legislation and regulations.

GERMANY

9.59   In Germany the right to sell alcoholic beverages on the premises is dealt with in the *Gaststättengesetz* (German Licensing Act) and the *Jugendschutzgesetz* (Protection of Young Persons Act) of the Federal government and the relevant implementing laws of the federal states. The sale of alcoholic beverages on the premises principally requires a licence to operate a bar, restaurant or inn to be issued by the local governmental authorities. The grant of a licence may only be refused for the reasons set out in § 4 of the German Licensing Act, in particular in cases where the applicant does not have the reliability required for the proper operation of a bar, a restaurant or inn or where the premises or location are not suitable. Even though a formal licence is not required for wine produced for on-premise sale during certain times of the year in Bavaria and Rhineland-Palatinate, notification must be given. The permit can be issued for a limited period of time, be made subject to conditions and be revoked in case of non-observance of the legal provisions.

9.60   In addition to alcoholic beverages the keeper of the licensed premises must also sell non-alcoholic beverages, one of which must not be more expensive than the cheapest alcoholic beverage. The sale of liquor and beverages containing distilled spirits to persons under 18 is prohibited. Other alcoholic beverages, such as beer and wine, can be sold to persons aged 16 and over, and to young persons aged 14 and over if they are accompanied by a person having parental power. The keeper of the licensed premises has to check the person's age in case of doubt. Alcohol must not be sold to persons aged 18 or over if it is obvious that they are drunk.

9.61   The closing time is regulated differently in the federal states, and those, in turn, may delegate the regulatory power on to local authorities. In Bavaria, for instance, the period during which the licensed premises must remain closed starts at 1 am and ends at 6 am, and local exceptions apply. There are no such restrictions on New Year's Eve. The period during which individual licensed premises have to be closed can be extended or reduced if there are public requirements or special local conditions, that is to say it is possible to fix a closing period starting at

7 pm or ending at 8 am. Persons under 16 must not stay in licensed premises if they are not accompanied by a person having parental power, and persons under 18 must only stay until midnight. Persons under 18 are not allowed to stay in night bars, night clubs or similar premises. As regards discothèques, young persons are only allowed to stay if they are aged 16 or over and only until midnight.

9.62 Violations of the statutory provisions are punished by a fine of up to €5,000. Violations of the Protection of Young Persons Act are punished by a fine of up to €7,600 (formerly DM 15,000) or imprisonment of up to one year.

GREECE*

9.63 Presidential Decree No 180 of 10 March 1979, as amended by Presidential Decree No 231 of 2 May 1989, is the main statute governing the operation of retail shops selling alcoholic drinks for consumption on the premises. It should be noted that the rules governing the operation of shops, such as cellars and supermarkets, where alcoholic drinks are sold for consumption off the premises, are not included in this legislation.

* The law is stated as at June 1998.

9.64 Article 1 of the Presidential Decree No 180/1979 stipulates that the licence for the opening of shops where alcoholic drinks are offered for consumption, such as bars, restaurants and music halls, is granted by the local municipal authorities provided that the person interested in obtaining the licence submits to the said authorities: (i) a criminal record certificate, and (ii) a certificate of ownership of the premises or any other documentation establishing a legal right to occupy the premises.

9.65 Pursuant to Article 2, subsection 1 of the Presidential Decree No 180/1979 it is prohibited to grant a licence for the opening of retail outlets selling alcohol in the name of:

(i) persons condemned for a number of offences including manslaughter, rape, robbery, theft, fraud, drug related offences, etc;

(ii) persons under the age of 18 years;

(iii) persons who have been deprived of their civil rights; and

(iv) persons who are considered to represent a risk to public order.

9.66 Additionally, under Article 3, subsection 1 of the Presidential Decree 180/1979 local municipal authorities may refuse to grant a licence if the premises where consumption will take place is located less than 50 metres from a church, school, hospital, kindergarten, library, orphanage, conservatory, sports ground, barracks or industrial site.

9.67   The licence granted may be revoked by the local municipal authorities if the owner is convicted for an offence relating to drugs trafficking, public order, sanitary conditions or opening hours. If the licence has been revoked, the owner can reapply for the issue of a new one after a period of three years (Article 2, subsection 2 of the Presidential Decree No 180/1979).

9.68   The opening hours of retail outlets selling alcoholic drinks are regulated by the Ministerial Decree No 1011/22/19/20.21-12-1995. Accordingly, from Sundays to Thursdays, the opening hours are:

(i)   from 1 October to 31 March, until 3.00am; and

(ii)   from 1 April to 30 September, until 3.30am

On Fridays, Saturdays and public holidays, there is no time limit.

9.69   Admission of persons aged under 18 into shops where alcoholic beverages are sold and consumed is not controlled and no provisions restricting the sale of alcohol to young persons have been adopted to date.

ISLE OF MAN

9.70   Although part of the British Isles, the Isle of Man is an entirely separate legal jurisdiction being neither part of the United Kingdom nor a member of the EC. Nevertheless, the law on the Isle of Man follows the pattern of the United Kingdom law in many respects including liquor licensing. The present legislation is the Licensing Act 1995 (an Act of Tynwald) the Isle of Man Legislative Assembly, which is a consolidating and amending statute.

9.71   The power to grant liquor licenses and music and entertainment licenses is vested in the Licensing Court which consists of the High Bailiff or Deputy High Bailiff (a stipendiary magistrate) together with four other lay justices from among the licensing committee of the local magistrates.

9.72   Application for a new licence (and most other types of application) is made by giving a minimum of 10 days' notice in a prescribed form to the Court, the Police, and in appropriate cases the Fire Service with a notice also being advertised in two local papers. Plans must be included with most applications, drawn to a scale of not less than 1 to 50 containing details of all structural work identifying all areas where liquor is to be supplied or consumed, identifying all means of egress from the premises in case of fire and such other details as the High Bailiff may direct. Types of licence are similar to those available in the United Kingdom, that is to say a full on-licence, an on-licence limited by conditions (in particular restaurant conditions or residential conditions) and an off-licence. These are renewable every three years. Available are the provisional grant of a licence and a grant of temporary licences occasional licenses and charitable function licenses.

As in the United Kingdom the licensing court also deals with the registration of members' clubs.

9.73 In determining an application for licence, the court considers the suitability of the premises, the fitness and character of the applicant (including any previous convictions whether or not under the enactments relating to licensing) whether the requirements of the Act and any relevant Rules have been complied with, the requirements and circumstances of the neighbourhood in which the premises are situated, the requirements of visitors to the island, the adequacy of any notice of the application given and such other matters as the court may think relevant to the application. This means that the court has a wide discretion, and will usually require some convincing before granting a new licence, particularly a full licence. The holder of a licence must normally be the person or company entitled to possession of the property to be licensed, with a proviso that where this is a company, an individual must then be approved by the court to act as a 'designated official' taking personal responsibility for the conduct of the licensed premises. The applicant or designated official must produce three written character references and a declaration as to previous convictions.

9.74 The holder of an on-licence or off-licence can determine the hours between which he intends to sell or supply liquor. In the case of on-licences this is done by giving notice in writing to the Chief Constable with a requirement that the holder of the on-licence display a notice specifying the normal opening hours during which liquor is sold or supplied on the licensed premises. The notice must be displayed in prominent positions both within the premises so as to be clearly visible and legible by persons to whom liquor is sold or supplied and outside the premises so as to be clearly visible and legible by the public. The choice of hours is subject to the Licensing Court having the power to suspend or cancel the licence or restrict the hours.

Entertainment licensing is also dealt with by the Licensing Court on similar issues to on-licence applications.

9.75 There must be no sale of alcohol to anyone under the age of 18 years. When granting an on-licence the court will consider whether it should impose a condition prohibiting or restricting persons under the age of 16 from any room in the premises.

ITALY

9.76   The sale and distribution of alcohol in Italy (where 'distribution' means for consumption at the point of sale) are governed by Legislative Decree dated 31 March 1998, No 114 and Law dated 25 August 1991, No 287 respectively.

9.77   In order to sell alcoholic beverages, it is no longer necessary to enter the Shopowners' Trade Register (STR), as it was abolished for most of the product categories. On the contrary, a food sale authorisation is required to be issued by the municipality through different procedures according to the size of the retail area. This is possible if the following requirements are met by the applicant:

(i)   he must alternatively have passed the chamber of commerce examination, completed a professional business course, practised food sale activity on a professional basis for at least two years or been enrolled for the last five years in the STR;

(ii)   he must not have been convicted of an offence relating to sanitation, commercial practice (eg bribery, corruption) or food or alcohol; and

(iii) he must not be a person under penal supervision or a known delinquent.

9.78   As far as distribution of alcoholic beverages is concerned, the mandatory registration into the STR is still essential. As a consequence, applicants need to comply with the requisites set forth under Article 2 of Law No 287/1991, in order to obtain from the municipality the authorisation to exercise distribution activity.

9.79   Moreover, according to Article 86 of Royal Decree No 377 dated 18 June 1931, a specific licence, to be issued by the local Police chief (*Questore*), must be obtained in order to retail alcoholic beverages to the public. Such licence, however, is not required where alcoholic drinks are sold in closed containers with a capacity exceeding 0.2 litres, to be carried away from the retail area before consumption (Article 176 of Royal Decree No 635 dated 6 May 1940, enacting Royal Decree No 377/1931).

9.80   Opening hours are now freely decided by each retailer, in accordance with the criteria established by the relevant municipality. However, shops can stay open to the public every day from 7.00 am to 10.00 pm, and in no case for more than 13 hours a day.

9.81   According to Legislative Decree No 504/1995, operators selling alcohol beverages are obliged to have a so-called 'fiscal licence' granted by the local office of the Ministry of Finance, provided that they have not been convicted of offences relating to illegal production of alcoholic beverages, or of any of the offences listed under Legislative Decree No 504/1995. Enacting documents circulated by the Ministry have made clear that the above described obligation binds all parties exercising retailing activity of alcoholic beverages carrying the fiscal mark.

9.82   Inspections of public retail stores and verification of documents are carried out by police and municipal officers (both have the power to revoke or suspend any licence). Inspection and verification of distributors are the responsibility of the provincial office of commerce and industry. Verification on the alcohol content and composition of liquor on sale is assigned to the public health authority.

JERSEY

9.83   The retail of alcohol in Jersey is governed primarily by the Licensing (Jersey) Law 1974. Alcohol cannot be sold without a licence. Persons interested in applying for a licence must satisfy certain residency requirements. Usually the person must have been ordinarily resident in Jersey in the three years immediately preceding the application. There is, however, also a discretion to waive this requirement if a suitable official from the applicant's actual place of residence opines that the applicant would be a fit and proper person to hold the licence. This discretion only applies where the applicant has been resident either in the British Commonwealth or the European Community for the three years immediately preceding the application.

9.84   The application will be considered firstly by an assembly of the relevant parish, and then by the Licensing Assembly. At both assemblies objections can be voiced. The Licensing Assembly have the power to grant the licence and will take the recommendations of the parish assembly into account but will not be bound by them.

9.85   The decision of the Licensing Assembly is discretionary and will be influenced by the following factors:

(1)   the interests of the public in general;

(2)   the suitability of the premises for the proposed business.

The licence may be granted subject to any conditions the Licensing Assembly sees fit to impose in the circumstances.

9.86   An on-licence is open between 9 am and 11 pm. No person under the age of 18 years is allowed in the public bar during these opening hours. It is offence to sell alcohol to a person under the age of 18 years or to allow them to consume alcohol. In the cases of restaurants and nightclubs, the opening hours are extended, whilst the consumption of certain alcoholic beverages by persons under the age of 18 in restaurants is permitted in the presence of a supervising adult.

9.87   The licence can be renewed annually between 5 October and 5 November inclusive.

LUXEMBOURG

9.88   In the Grand Duchy of Luxembourg retail sale of alcoholic beverages (0.5 per cent or more by volume) is essentially governed by tax provisions. Local authorities do not issue specific regulations in this field.

9.89   In order to run an inn ('café') retailing alcohol, it is required to obtain an 'Innkeeper's Licence'. Obtaining that licence is subject to fulfilling the following procedural steps.

9.90   First, under the Law of December 28, 1988, any industrial or trade activity requires a business licence. The business licence is granted for an unlimited period of time by the Ministry of Middle Classes ('Ministère des Classes Moyennes') and is strictly personal, but may be revoked at any time by the competent authorities (eg if the applicant does not discharge his social or fiscal obligations). The applicant must demonstrate his good standing and his professional qualifications.

9.91   Second, under the law of June 29, 1989 on Inns, the applicant shall apply for an Innkeeper's Licence with the Ministry of Finance. The applicant must also advise the tax authorities of his intention to open the shop. This is then registered by the chamber of commerce and a VAT number is issued.

9.92   If the applicant is not a national of a Member State of the EU, he must furnish a certificate of five years' residence in Luxembourg. The applicant must pay an annual tax and an opening tax to the locality's tax authorities. The amount of the latter varies with the number of inhabitants of that locality.

9.93   The Ministry of Finance will grant the authorisation by taking into account the number of existing licenses; generally there can be no more than one retail outlet per 500 inhabitants. Nevertheless, it is possible to obtain a licence in disrespect of these conditions (for example for seasonal retail shops). Therefore, a special request has to be made to the Ministry of Finance, who can issue the licence or permit even if the 500 inhabitants limit is not reached. The licence is only valid on the territory of the locality for which it has been granted.

9.94 Normal opening hours are from 6am to 1am. Individual extensions until 3am are possible provided authorisation is obtained from the relevant mayor. Inside this period, at any moment, a bar or café can provide the customers with a minimal quantity of food.

9.95 Police and customs officers shall have access to the retail facility's records during legal and de facto opening times provided certain conditions are met.

9.96 Any person who intends to sell alcohol for off-consumption has to make a special declaration before commencing and certain special conditions must be met.

9.97 Minors under the age of 16 are not authorised to enter shops that sell alcohol without a person aged at least 18 exercising control over them. It is forbidden to serve alcohol to people under 16 years old.

THE NETHERLANDS

9.98 In the Netherlands the law pertaining to the retail sale of alcohol is contained in a number of separate statutes as well as in detailed regulations made by local authorities under general regulatory powers.

9.99 The main statute is the so called *Drank-en horecawet* (Act on Liquor and the Hotel and Catering Industry). This statute not only establishes certain basic principles, but also forms the basis for the delegation of regulatory powers to local authorities. This has resulted in several orders in council and official circulars.

9.100 The central features of the system are as follows. Hotels, bars or restaurants where alcohol is served 'for immediate use' on a commercial basis, retail stores, and places where alcohol is served on non-commercial basis, must obtain a licence for pouring alcohol. This licence is to be granted by the mayor of the town where the alcohol is served. A permit will be granted if:

(1) the applicant has sufficient knowledge of/or experience in the field and has executive abilities;

(2) the applicant is over 21 years of age;

(3) the applicant has not been convicted of certain criminal offences;

(4) the location complies with a number of requirements mainly concerning sanitary conditions and has sufficient knowledge of sanitary conditions.

9.101 Liquor may not be sold or given to people under 16 years of age. For spirits the minimum age is 18. These minimum ages have to be clearly shown in the premises. Local authorities may vary the minimum ages but only by fixing a *higher* age.

9.102 The person who is pouring the alcohol has to be certain that the user has reached the required age. In doubt he or she is obliged to verify the user's age by demanding valid identification. Alcohol may not be served when it is obvious that a glass of alcohol is immediately being passed on to a person under age. In case it cannot be determined whether a person is older than 16 years, this person is allowed in the premises where alcohol is served, provided that they are accompanied by someone over 21 years of age.

9.103 The closing time of bars etc is regulated by the local authorities. The closing time does not depend on the quantity of food served but rather on factors related to the location of the premises (eg noise nuisance for neighbours).

9.104 The Minister of Social Affairs and Public Health appoints an inspector and a number of officials for the supervision of public health. These officials are responsible for the enforcement of the statutes and the regulations relating to the sale of alcohol.

9.105 A seller of alcohol who doesn't observe important statutory provisions is liable on grounds of the Act on Economical Offences. The Dutch Penal Code also contains provision for other offences in relation to liquor.

NORTHERN IRELAND

9.106 The governing legislation is the Licensing (Northern Ireland) Order 1996 and the Registration of Clubs (Northern Ireland) Order 1996, both of which came into force on 20 February 1997.

9.107 Under the Licensing Order only the following premises may be licensed for the retail sale of intoxicating liquor:

(a) premises in which the business carried on is the business of selling intoxicating liquor by retail for consumption either in or off the premises ('the public house');

(b) premises in which the business carried on is the business of selling intoxicating liquor by retail for consumption off the premises ('the off-licence');

(c) an hotel;

(d) a guest house;

(e) a restaurant;

(f) a conference centre;

(g) a higher education institution;

(h) a place of public entertainment;

(i) a refreshment room in public transport premises;

(j) a seaman's canteen; and

(k) non-sea-going vessels.

9.108 A licence may be granted to an individual, a body corporate or to a partnership. The person to whom a licence is granted should be the owner of the business proposed to be carried on under the licence. A court must be satisfied of the following criteria before granting a licence:

(a) compliance with the statutory procedure;

(b) the fitness of the applicant;

(c) the premises are of the kind specified in the application;

(d) the suitability of the premises;

(e) in the case of a public house or an off-licence, the inadequacy of the number of certain existing licensed premises.

Procedure

9.109 A person who intends to make an application for the grant of a licence shall:

(a) not more than six weeks nor less than two weeks before the opening of the court sitting at which the application is to be made, publish the application at least once in two newspapers circulating in the vicinity of the premises for which the application is to be sought;

(b) during the weeks before that time, cause notice of that application to be displayed on or near the premises for which the licence is to be sought;

(c) not less than three weeks before that time, serve notice of the application upon the chief clerk of the county court and upon:

  (i) the sub-divisional commander of the police sub-division in which the premises are situated;

  (ii) where the applicant resides in some other police sub-division upon the sub-divisional commander of that sub-division (in practice this also includes England);

  (iii) the district council for the district in which the premises are situated.

9.110 The applications which are served must also have attached to them the following:

(a) a plan of the premises showing the area to be licensed;

(b) a copy of the planning permission.

9.111 Licensing matters are dealt with in the county court once every two months so that the timing of the application can be critical.

9.112 The application is usually initially for a 'provisional' grant of licence because the application may be refused.

9.113 An application for a final grant is made to the court when the store has been fitted out and is ready to trade. Such an application for final grant does not require to be advertised but notice must be served on the same parties as mentioned above adhering to the same time scales.

The fitness of the applicant

9.114 A licence may be granted to an individual, to a body corporate or to two or more persons carrying on business in partnership. The person to whom a licence is granted must be the owner of the business proposed to be carried on under the licence.

9.115 In considering the fitness of a person to hold a licence for any premises, the court shall have regard to:

(a) his character, reputation and financial standing;

(b) his qualifications and experience in respect of managing the business which is proposed to be carried on under the licence, or that of any person who is to be employed by him in that regard;

(c) the extent to which, by virtue of any estate vested in him, he is entitled to possession and control of the premises.

(a) and (b) are fairly self-explanatory but it should be noted that some care is required in the acquisition of premises to strike the balance between ensuring that if the licensing application is not successful the applicant is not left with premises for which he has no use and inserting a condition precedent which might lead a court to determine that possession and control had not passed into the hands of the applicant before the final grant, in which case the applicant would be deemed not to be a fit person.

The suitability of the premises

9.116 It was generally regarded that the judge principally looked at the premises themselves—that is to say the structure, safe access and egress and an ability to be easily supervised by the Police. However, a recent decision of the court indicates that suitability might extend to the effect that locating off-licence premises in a particular place will have on the locality.

The inadequacy of the number of certain existing licensed premises

9.117 The court cannot grant a licence for either a public house or an off-licence unless it is satisfied that the number of licensed premises of the kind specified in the application which are in the vicinity of the premises is, and will be inadequate, having regard to:

(a) any licence provisionally granted; or

(b) any sites approved for development as licensed premises by a housing authority.

'Vicinity' and 'inadequate' are the two key words in this provision.

Vicinity

9.118 The area to be regarded as the vicinity of the premises is a question of fact in each case. This is always the source of great debate in contested cases and it is impossible to lay down any general rule as to the extent of an area indicated by the word 'vicinity'. In country areas, people may be said to be neighbours, that is to say they live in the same neighbourhood, but they may live many miles apart. The same cannot be said of city dwellers where a single square may constitute a neighbourhood. Physical features may determine the boundary or boundaries of a neighbourhood as, for example, a river, a railway or a range of hills. In an urban area lacking such physical features the layout of the streets and the nature, character and use of the buildings need to be looked at, as well as the size and distribution of the population, whether residing or working in the area.

Adequacy

9.119   The test as to adequacy is objective and appears to involve four factors:
(a)   the character of the area as a whole;
(b)   the number of persons in that area;
(c)   the number of existing licensed premises of the same type in that area; and
(d)   the transient trade.

9.120   The character of the area would include such factors as housing developments, shopping facilities, whether urban or rural area, parking facilities and office accommodation.

9.121   The court will consider not just the number of existing off-licences but also the kind of service that they provide—it will therefore have regard to:
(a)   choice of commodity offered;
(b)   competition as to price;
(c)   situation of premises;
(d)   purchasing potential;
(e)   quality of service.

However, adequacy remains the paramount consideration and selection and competition are subordinate matters to be taken into account.

9.122   The court is not precluded from taking into consideration the number of public house premises in the vicinity which also have an off-sale facility. It must also assess the whole of the actual or expected demand for facilities and not just the demand which might come from the residents of the vicinity.

9.123   The adequacy test does not apply where the proposed public house or off-licence is in a redevelopment area or falls within one of the categories set out in the Licensing Order, Sch 2, para 2(a), eg premises destroyed by fire or where the tenancy has come to an end.

Opposition

9.124　Persons such as competitors can object to the grant of a licence or any of the court orders available based on the grounds that the application fails to fulfil the criteria laid down by the statute and the court.

Renewals

9.125　The licence, unless suspended, will remain in force for five years. After this time an application must be made to the magistrates' court for a renewal.

Transfer

9.126　Where the owner of the business selling intoxicating liquor by retail in the licensed premises has or is about to change then the new/proposed owner must make an application to the magistrates' court for the transfer of the licence.

Alterations

9.127　Licence holders must apply to the court for consent to certain alterations to the licensed premises. If such alterations are major then a new application for a licence may have to be made to the county court.

Hours of opening

9.128　The general permitted hours for all licensed premises except off-licences and places of public entertainment are:

(a)　on weekdays, other than Good Friday or Christmas Day, from 11.30 am to 11.00 pm; and

(b)　on Good Friday from 5.00 pm to 11.00 pm; and

(c)　on Sundays and on Christmas Day from 12.30 pm to 10.00 pm.

9.129　The general permitted hours for an off-licence are:

(a)　on weekdays, other than Christmas Day, from 8.00 am to 11.00 pm; and

(b)　on Sunday, not being Christmas Day or Easter Day, from 10.00 am to 10.00 pm.

9.130   As regards places of public entertainment, the general permitted hours are limited to the period of the entertainment and the half hours which immediately precede and succeed same during the hours:

(a)   on weekdays, other than Good Friday or Christmas Day, from 11.30 am to 11.00 pm; and

(b)   on Good Friday from 5.00 pm to 11.00 pm.

Suitability for functions

9.131   The holder of a licence for a public house, hotel, restaurant, conference centre or higher education institution may apply for an order that part of his premises be declared suitable for functions. Once such an order is in force the licensee may then apply for an extension licence as and when it is proposed to hold a function in the specified part of the licensed premises. However, such a suitability order would only be granted if the relevant part of the premises are structurally adapted or used, or intended to be used for the purposes of providing persons frequenting the premises with a main table meal. A main table meal is, or includes, a main course which is eaten by a person seated at a table or a counter. The specified hours are:

(a)   on weekdays between 11.30am and 1.00am in the morning of the day next following;

(b)   on Sunday, not being 31 December, between 12.30 pm in the afternoon and 12 midnight;

(c)   on Sunday, being 31 December, between 12.30 pm in the afternoon and 1.00 am in the morning of the day next following.

9.132   A public house licensee may apply on not more than 20 occasions during the course of year to the police for authority to sell intoxicating liquor during the hours:

(a)   on weekdays from 11.00 am to 1.00 am in the morning of the day next following; or

(b)   on Sunday, not being 31 December, from 10.00 pm to 12 midnight; or

(c)   on Sunday, being 31 December, from 10.00 pm to 1.00 am in the morning of the day next following.

Additional hours

9.133   In addition to the above permitted hours an additional hours order may in certain circumstances be obtained by the licence holder of the following licensed premises:

(a) an hotel;

(b) a restaurant;

(c) a conference centre;

(d) a higher education institution;

(e) a public house where substantial refreshment is to be habitually provided and the relevant power to structurally adapt it and used, or intended to be used, for the purpose of providing persons frequenting the premises with a main table meal.

9.134 An additional hours order allows the sale of liquor on such days as may be specified in the order. The hours are:

(a) on weekdays from 11.00 pm to 1.00 am in the morning of the day next following; or

(b) on Sunday, not being 31 December, from 10.00 pm to 12 midnight; or

(c) on Sunday, being 31 December, from 10.00 pm to 1.00 am in the morning of the day next following.

9.135 For such an application to be successful the court has to be satisfied that the relevant part of the licensed premises is structurally adapted and used, or intended to be used, for the purpose of providing:

(a) musical or other entertainment; or

(b) substantial refreshment; or

(c) both such entertainment and refreshment.

Children

9.136 During the permitted hours a person under the age of 18 must not be in:

(a) an off-sales part of a public house, which is not connected by any internal means of passage open to customers with the part used for the sale of liquor for consumption in the premises:

(b) any part of an off-licence;

(c) any part of any other licensed premises which:

    (i) contains a bar; or

    (ii) is used exclusively or mainly for the sale and consumption of intoxicating liquor.

The prohibitions in respect of the off-sales part of the public house or the off-licence do not apply if the young person is accompanied by a person who is over the age of 18.

9.137   The licence holder of any licensed premises which has either an open bar in a particular part of the licensed premises or which has a part used exclusively or mainly for the sale and consumption of intoxicating liquor may apply for a children's certificate. A children's certificate may be operational at any time up to 9.00 pm and the licence holder must display the notice. The court will not make such an order unless it is satisfied:

(a)   the specified part constitutes an environment in which it is suitable for a person under the age of 18 to be present;

(b)   meals and suitable beverages other than intoxicating liquor (including drinking water) will be made available for consumption in the specified part when the certificate is operational;

(c)   the specified part is equipped and furnished with an adequate number of tables and chairs;

(d)   there has been compliance with the conditions prescribed by the regulations.

No regulations have yet been made.

Supermarkets

9.138   Previously, in Northern Ireland, it was against the law to sell liquor along with other products (other than a very small specified number such as tobacco and crisps). Supermarket chains were forced to sell liquor on premises totally unconnected with and outside the main shopping area. The Licensing (Conditions for Mixed Trading) Regulations (Northern Ireland) 1997 now allow mixed trading if certain criteria are met. Liquor can now be sold on the same premises if the part of the premises selling liquor (the specified area) is separated from all other parts by a physical barrier made of solid material. Any means of passage between that area and the other parts of the premises should be controlled by a gate or a turnstile. The premises must also be sited so that a person may leave and enter the premises and have access to all other parts of the premises without passing through the parts selling alcohol. Any products (other than intoxicating liquor) available for purchase in any specified area shall also be available for purchase in the parts of the premises outside the specified areas. All purchases for the specified area must be paid for at a point of sale within the specified area.

Clubs

9.139   The Registration of Clubs (Northern Ireland) Order 1996 provides for the registration of clubs. In order to be successfully registered as a club, the club must apply to a county court. A preliminary notice of the application should be made one year prior to the opening of the court sittings at which the application is to be made, although a county court has a discretion to permit an abridgment of that time. The club rules must comply with the provisions of the Registration of Clubs Order. The court will have to be satisfied that the premises are suitable having regard to the objects of the club, the estimated maximum number of members, the location of the premises and the accommodation and facilities provided by the club premises. A children's certificate can also be obtained for a club.

9.140 The permitted hours are:

(a) on weekdays, other than Good Friday or Christmas Day, from 11.30 am to 11.00 pm; and

(b) on Good Friday from 5.00 pm to 11.00 pm; and

(c) on Sunday or Christmas Day from 12.30 pm to 10.00 pm.

9.141 The hours can be extended on an application to the police. The club may be granted a maximum of 52 such authorisations in any year. Such an authorisation permits the supply of intoxicating liquor:

(a) on weekdays from 11.00 pm to 1.00 am of the day next following;

(b) on Sunday, not being 31 December, from 10.00 pm to 12 midnight;

(c) on Sunday 31 December from 10.00 pm to 1.00 am of the day next following.

Such an authorisation will not allow the supply of intoxicating liquor on Christmas Day, Easter Day or Good Friday in any club.

PORTUGAL*

9.142 Regulations on alcohol apply throughout Portugal. However, vineous and non-vineous alcoholic drinks are regulated separately as follows:

(1) The distribution and sale to the consumer of vineous drinks are subject to the seller being registered with the Portuguese Institute of Vineyards and Wine. This Institute makes regular inspections of the premises in which wine is sold and may even confiscate bottles that show any sign of non-compliance with the legal requirements.

(2) The sale of non-vineous drinks (such as vodka, whisky, brandy and the like) depends on the issue of a sanitary licence regarding the

premises. However, the Ministry of Internal Trade does not issue any licence or authorisation to someone who intends to sell spirits.

*   The law is stated as at June 1998.

9.143   Alcoholic drinks may not be traded and sold to consumers save in bottles bearing a marketing stamp. The consumption of alcoholic drinks is freely authorised in restaurants, bars, etc, irrespective of the age of the consumer.

9.144   Some of the rules concerning the sale of spirits are provided for in legislation which also regulates the special taxation of alcoholic drinks (this tax applies equally to imported alcohol and domestic alcohol). The provisions referred to do not relate to matters such as drunkenness (which may, in certain cases, be punished under the Portuguese Penal Code).

9.145   The legal state monopoly over alcohol was abolished in 1992 (Decree Law No 117/92, dated 22 June 1992) in order to comply with the rules safeguarding fair competition, provided for in Art 208 of the Treaty of Accession of Portugal to the EC. Under the former regime, a State undertaking named AGA (General Administration for Sugar and Alcohol) held exclusive rights to import and market alcohol. These rights were eliminated by the Decree Law and private operators may now import and sell alcohol.

SCOTLAND

Introduction

9.146   The law regulating the sale and supply of alcoholic liquor in Scotland is contained in the Licensing (Scotland) Act 1976, as amended (principally by the Law Reform (Miscellaneous Provisions) (Scotland) Act 1990).

9.147   The administration of the licensing system is entrusted to licensing boards constituted for each local authority (council or islands) area or for separate divisions therein. Board members are locally-elected councillors. Legal advice is provided by a clerk, who must be legally qualified. Meetings must be held four times a year, in January, March, June and October (so-called 'quarterly meetings'). Major items of business, such as applications for new licences, may only be considered at such a meeting. Boards may also hold such other meetings as appear appropriate, while the disposal of certain types of applications (for example, for the temporary transfer of a licence) may be delegated to the clerk and/or one or more board members.

Types of licences

9.148 The types of licences which may be granted and the authority which they confer for the sale or supply of alcoholic liquor may be summarised as follows:

(a) a *public house* licence authorises the holder to sell alcoholic liquor for consumption on or off the premises;

(b) an *hotel licence* permits the sale of alcohol in an hotel for consumption on or off the premises, while a *restricted hotel licence* is effectively a hybrid between an hotel and restaurant licence with the supply of alcohol to the public generally limited to residents, their private friends and those taking meals;

(c) an *off-sale licence* allows the sale of alcohol for consumption off the premises only, although free tastings are permitted;

(d) a *restaurant licence* authorises the sale of alcohol to persons taking table meals; off-sales are prohibited;

(e) a *refreshment licence* is appropriate for premises used for public entertainment, such as cinemas, theatres, proprietary snooker clubs and discothèques. The consumption of alcohol must be ancillary to the entertainment provided. Conditions may be attached to that end. Off-sales are not permitted.

The application procedure

9.149 Licences may be granted to either (i) an individual alone, or (ii) a non-natural person, such as a limited company or partnership with an individual nominated as having day-to-day control of the premises.

9.150 Where premises have yet to be constructed or it is intended to make substantial alterations to premises which are already licensed, application is made for the provisional grant of a new licence. In rare cases where the premises are ready to trade, an application for the grant of a new licence will be appropriate. Except in the case of off-sale applications, the board may not entertain the application unless it is supported by certificates of suitability issued by local authority departments in relation to planning consent, building warrant approval and food hygiene matters; but an 'outline' provisional grant, which must later be affirmed, only requires a planning certificate.

9.151 Applications may only be considered at a quarterly meeting and must be lodged five weeks in advance. Plans of the premises are required although, strictly speaking, no plans need be lodged in support of an application for the grant of an off-sale licence. The board has a discretionary power to consider an application lodged late through 'inadvertence or misadventure'.

9.152   Notice of the application must be given in a newspaper advertisement, arranged by the clerk. The applicant must post a notice giving details of the application at the premises or site and serve a similar notice upon an adjoining occupiers.

9.153   The board is bound to grant an application unless it finds that one or more of four specified grounds of refusal applies.

(a)   The applicant, his intended manager or the person for whose benefit the applicant will manage the premises, is not 'a fit or proper person' to be the holder of a licence. Normally, fitness will only become an issue if exception to the applicant is taken by the Chief Constable.

(b)   The premises are not suitable or convenient for the sale of alcoholic liquor, having regard to their location, character and condition, the nature and extent of the proposed use and the persons likely to resort to the premises. This ground is now commonly invoked in relation to off-sale applications by petrol station operators (but note that premises primarily used for the sale of motor fuels are not statutorily disqualified from being licensed).

(c)   The use of the premises for the sale of alcohol is likely to cause undue public nuisance or a threat to public order or safety (because, for example, of their proximity to a school or football stadium).

(d)   The grant of the application would result in the over provision of licensed premises in the area. Recent judicial decisions have made it clear that the determination of over provision falls very squarely within the board's discretion, based on its local knowledge and licensing experience.

The refusal of an application may be appealed to the sheriff; and thereafter to the Court of Session.

9.154   A provisional grant must be finalised to allow the full licence to come into effect. Finalisation will be granted if the finished premises confirm to the approved plan. Minor deviations are permitted.

Transfers of licences

9.155   Where a licence has been granted to a non-natural person and a nominated manager, and the latter ceases to be responsible for the day-to-day control of the premises, a substitute must be approved by the board within eight weeks; the licence ceases to have effect until that step has been accomplished. The substitution must be confirmed at the next meeting of the board.

9.156 Otherwise, transfers may take place where:

(1) the transferee is a new or existing tenant or occupant of the premises;

(2) the present licence holder has died or become bankrupt, insolvent or incapable.

9.157 The transfer may be accomplished by one of two methods: either as a temporary transfer between board meetings followed by a permanent transfer at the next appropriate board meeting, or as a single-step transfer at a quarterly meeting. The consent of the current licence holder will normally be required. The board is bound to refuse the application if it considers that the proposed transferee is not a fit and proper person. The licence is transferred upon the terms and conditions attaching when it was granted and the renewal date is not affected.

Objections

9.158 Objections to various applications may be made by:

(a) the Chief Constable;

(b) the local community council;

(c) owners and occupiers of property in the neighbourhood or any organisation which in the board's opinion represents such persons;

(d) the fire authority;

(e) the local authority;

(f) an organised church which the board considers to represent a significant body of persons residing in the neighbourhood.

Additionally, the Chief Constable is empowered to submit observations in relation to certain types of application.

The permitted hours

9.159 Subject to exceptions explained below, alcoholic liquor may only be sold, supplied or consumed in licensed premises and registered clubs during the permitted hours, as follows:

(a) Mondays to Saturdays from 11 am to 11 pm;

(b) Sundays from 12.30 pm to 2.30 pm and 6.30 pm to 11 pm.

9.160 In the case of public house and refreshment licensed premises, specific permission to open for the sale or supply of alcohol on Sundays must be obtained when the licence is first granted and when it is renewed.

9.161   There are no special hours on Good Friday or Christmas Day, but byelaws enacted by a board may impose restrictions on New Year's Day and, where 1 January falls on a Sunday, on 2 January.

9.162   Customers who have purchased drink prior to the conclusion of permitted hours are allowed 15 minutes' drinking-up time. This is increased to 30 minutes where the alcohol was supplied at the same time as, and for consumption with, a meal.

9.163   The permitted hours are the subject of a number of other exceptions. Principally, they do not apply to consumption on the premises by:

(a) residents;

(b) private friends of a resident bona fide entertained by him at his own expense;

(c) private friends of the licence holder bona fide entertained by him at his own expense. Boards are empowered to modify the permitted hours in a number of ways, shown below;

(d) off-sale licensed premises have 'trading' hours rather than 'permitted' hours as follows:

— Mondays to Saturdays from 8 am to 10 pm, and

— on Sundays from 12.30 pm to 10 pm.

Regular extensions

9.164   The basic hours operated by on-licensed premises and registered clubs may be extended for a period of up to one year. Applications must be considered at a quarterly meeting and lodged five weeks in advance. A copy is to be sent to the Chief Constable by the applicant. Account is to be taken of the 'social circumstances' of the locality, the 'need' for extended hours and whether the benefit of an extension will outweigh any detriment to the locality. The refusal of an application is not susceptible to appeal but may be the subject of judicial review proceedings. Boards have evolved guidelines which set out the maximum hours likely to be granted, although each case must be examined on its own merits. Typically, guidelines will take account of the type of licence and whether the premises are situated in a residential or commercial environment. Public houses may not be granted extensions for any period before 12.30 pm on Sundays. Conditions may be attached; many boards prohibit entry or re-entry to premises after a certain time and there is often a requirement that adequate stewarding arrangements are in place.

Occasional extensions

9.165 These are granted for specific events such as local festivals, birthday parties and so on. They may not exceed a period of one month. The application time limit varies from area to area.

Table meal extensions

9.166 Premises with proper restaurant facilities may benefit from extended hours as follows:

(a) each evening from 11 pm until 1 am;
(b) Sundays from 2.30 pm to 4 pm;
(c) Sundays from 5 pm to 6.30 pm (but not in the case of entertainment licences).

9.167 The sale or supply of alcohol must be ancillary to the taking of a meal in a section of the premises set apart for that purpose. In the case of public houses and hotels, the board must first be satisfied that the premises are structurally adapted and bona fide used for the provision of meals.

9.168 Whether or not the board's declaration of satisfaction is initially required, the extended hours may not be operated until the licence holder has first given the Chief Constable 14 days' written notice of his intention so to do. A notice must be displayed at the premises explaining that a particular extension applies and the effect of that extension.

9.169 The permitted hours may be limited by means of a restriction order. A police officer of the rank of chief inspector or above may apply for a temporary restriction order. The board is empowered to close premises to the public for up to three hours on a specified day or days if it considers such a course desirable in the interests of public order or safety. This rarely-used provision is intended to cater for events such as football matches which could give rise to serious disturbance. The licence holder has no right to object.

9.170 Afternoon, evening and Sunday restriction orders may be imposed upon receipt of a complaint by a qualified objector (see above). A hearing requires to take place at a quarterly board meeting. An appeal lies to the sheriff and has the effect of placing the order in abeyance until abandoned or determined.

Duration and suspension of licences

9.171   Licences normally last for three years from the date of original grant or last renewal; but the provisional grant of a new licence subsists for one year only. The renewal application must be lodged not later than five weeks before the relevant quarterly meeting. Provision is made for the consideration of late application where failure to apply timeously was due to 'inadvertence or misadventure'.

Applications for the renewal of public house and refreshment licences should state whether it is intended to sell or supply alcohol on Sundays.

9.172   Boards may suspend licences for a fixed period not exceeding one year or the unexpired portion of the licence, whichever is less, following a hearing to consider a complaint from a competent objector (see above). Suspension is possible on one or all of the following grounds:

(a)   the licence holder is no longer a fit and proper person to be the holder of a licence;

(b)   the use of the premises has caused undue public nuisance or a threat to public order or safety;

(c)   there has been a breach of conditions attached to the licence designed to protect the health and safety of persons attending dance events where drug offences may be committed.

9.173   A closure order may be imposed where a board considers that the premises are no longer suitable for the sale of alcoholic liquor having regard to their character and condition and the nature and extent of their use. The licence ceases to have effect during the period of the order, which may be cancelled if remedial steps have been taken.

Suspension and closure orders may be appealed to the sheriff and are of no effect during that process.

Children in licensed premises

9.174   Children under the age of 14 are not permitted to be in a bar of licensed premises during the permitted hours, unless they are:

(a)   children of the licence holder;

(b)   resident in the premises but not employed there;

(c)   passing through the bar from one part of the premises to another where there is no other convenient way;

(d)   present in the bar by virtue of a children's certificate being in operation (see below).

9.175   The holder of a public house or hotel licence may apply to the board for a children's certificate which allows children under 14 to be in a bar: (i) for the purpose of consuming a meal, and (ii) accompanied by an adult aged 18 or over. The board requires to be satisfied that the premises (or the relevant part) constitute a suitable environment. Certificates may not be operated beyond 8 pm. Conditions may be attached, including a condition fixing an earlier finishing time.

9.176   The sale to and consumption of alcohol by persons under 18 is circumscribed in a variety of ways. It is an offence:

(a)   for a licence holder or his employee to sell alcohol to such a person or allow such a person to consume alcohol in a bar;

(b)   for such a person to buy or attempt to buy alcohol or to consume alcohol in the bar;

(c)   for anyone to act as agent for such a person in the purchase of alcohol or knowingly buy or attempt to buy alcohol for consumption by such a person in a bar.

Outwith bar areas, consumption is surprisingly unregulated. Above the age of five, a child may consume alcohol in any other part of licensed premises provided the purchase was made by an adult.

Registered clubs

9.177   Bona fide members' (as opposed to proprietary) clubs are not licensed but obtain a certificate of registration from the sheriff.

9.178   An application for a certificate must be supported by two copies of the club rules; a list containing the name and address of each official and each member of the management committee; and a certificate granted by two licence board members to the effect that the club is bona fide in nature and not mainly conducted for the supply of liquor.

9.179   The club rules must contain provisions regulating inter alia voting procedures and meetings. Visitors may only be supplied with alcohol on the invitation and in the company of a member. A visitors' book must be maintained.

9.180   Certificates last for three years and provision is made for cancellation on various grounds.

SPAIN

9.181   There are some restrictions regarding consumers. It is prohibited throughout Spain to serve or sell alcoholic drinks to anyone under the age of 16. In addition to this there are also restrictions upon the sale and ervice of alcoholic drinks of more than 23° proof, to persons under the age of 18.

9.182   Opening hours are regulated by the *Real Decreto Ley* 22/1993 of 29 December 1993, which establishes the hours for premises. This law delegates to local authorities the opening and closing hours for bars, cafeterias and dance halls. In this area, local authorities are entitled to enforce restrictions concerning the hours of opening. Local authorities therefore have the power to close any particular premises as an individual sanction if hours of opening are not observed.

9.183   The basic hours permitted in law for other kinds of establishments such as supermarkets, hypermarkets and food stores where alcoholic drinks are sold are between 8 am and 8 pm during weekdays. Additional restrictions on the sale of alcoholic beverages may be added by local ordinances. On the other hand, during weekends, working hours for these types of stores are more flexible.

9.184   Normal openings hours for pubs, music bars, etc are from 5 pm until 2.30 am although on Friday, Saturday and some holidays there can be a half an hour respite. The Decree makes no specific reference to the opening hours for bars, cafeterias or dance halls.

9.185   The control over outlets and their operators is exercised mainly by the local municipalities. To open premises the operator needs an authority or licence, granted by the local municipal authorities dealing mainly with town planning, health and safety regulations. There are no special licensing requirements for those markets and supermarkets that also sell alcoholic beverages.

9.186   Licences, once granted, run for an unlimited period. In certain situations, however, they may be revoked by the local authority.

9.187   The Spanish Ministry of Culture dictates (Orden 31 January of 1980) that entry into music bars, pubs and discos is not allowed for minors under age of 16 at any time. In other premises such as cafés or bars, minors are allowed to enter but they cannot be served any alcoholic drink. In these kinds of bars, minors can only enter with a parent or guardian. During evening town parties, popular festivals etc at night minors can attend public events without a parent or a guardian.

Such protection for minors is not new. Since 1928 the Spanish Penal Code has restricted those premises which may sell alcoholic drinks to minors.

9.188 Finally, the Spanish government is working on new legislation that establishes further limitations to the sale and service of alcoholic drinks. The Bill is still at the Ministerio del Interior (the Spanish equivalent of the UK Home Office), and is intended to apply to anyone under 18 years old. This Bill is expected to come before the Spanish Congress this year.

SWEDEN

9.189 Sweden has traditionally held a very restrictive public policy towards the sale of alcoholic beverages. This position still prevails in Sweden and has recently been approved by the European Court of Justice in the much debated *Franzén* ruling.[1] Harry Franzen had sold alcoholic beverages in his shop in breach of the Alcohol Act . The ECJ came to the conclusion that the aim of the Act—to reduce the harmful effects of the consumption of alcoholic beverages—justified the retail monopoly. However, the ECJ criticised the system of permits for import and wholesale, which has led to the lowering of permit fees and further review of the system.

[1]   C-189/95 *Re Franzén* [1997] ECR I-5909, ECJ.

9.190 The retail sale of alcohol is subject to a monopoly held by Systembolaget, a State-owned corporation. Consumers have to purchase alcoholic beverages (spirits, spiritous liquors, wine, strong beer and beer) at special 'Systembolaget' shops at 384 different locations around the country.

9.191 Manufacture and wholesale of alcoholic beverages is subject to permission in accordance with the Alcohol Act (SW: Alkohollgen SFS 1994:1738). Beer and wine may be produced without permit if produced for private use only. The supervising authority in accordance with the Alcohol Act is the National Alcohol Board (SW: Alkoholinspektionen). The Board issues permits and supervises the manufacturing and wholesale permit holders. The National Alcohol Board also actively monitors and evaluates the need for changes in order to achieve government alcohol policy objectives.

9.192 Foreign companies wishing to enter the Swedish market to sell alcoholic beverages are free to do so, however, subject to the same conditions as Swedish wholesalers. There are no special requirements in relation to foreign legal entities, although there are many practical issues that need to be resolved, eg with regard to the acceptance of delivery in Sweden.

9.193   Rules relating to the marketing of alcoholic beverages are found in the Alcohol Act and the Act on Restrictions on Marketing of Alcoholic Beverages (SW: Lag med vissa bestammelser om marknadsforing av alkoholdryker SFS 1978: 763). Marketing practice in relation to alcoholic beverages shall, according to the relevant statutes, be moderate and shall not encourage the use of alcohol. The rules on the marketing of alcoholic beverages are currently under revision by a special government commission.

9.194   Serving of alcoholic beverage in public places is allowed only after the municipality, where the premises are situated, has issued a special licence. Conditions for obtaining a serving licence are, for example, that the applicant is law abiding and suitable for the important role of serving alcohol. The authorities may impose special restrictions in connection with the permit. The requirement for the applicant to be a fit and proper person gives an element of discretion to the authorities' decision. There are no formal restrictions as to the number of outlets in a given area.

9.195   There are a number of requirements to be met by the premises where the alcoholic beverages are served. The municipality is in charge of supervision of the permit holder's compliance with restrictions and requirements.

9.196   The normal hours, where exceptions have not been granted by the municipality, for the sale of alcoholic beverages are 11am to 1am. The Alcohol Act requires that food be served at all times when alcoholic beverages are sold. Children are allowed in the premises at all times; the restrictions are only in regard to sale. The sale of alcoholic beverages is only permitted to persons 20 years of age and older when sold at Systembolaget shops, and from 18 years when sold in public places.

9.197   Finally, it might be of interest to readers that Sweden at the time of entering the EU retained the right to maintain quantitative limits for imports of cigarettes and other tobacco products, spirits, wines and beer from other Member States.

9.198   The import of quantities exceeding the permitted levels is subject to high excise duty. The restrictions have been authorised until 30 June 2000 and permit the importation of alcohol in the following quantities:

(1)   1 litre of spirits (alcoholic beverage with an alcohol content exceeding 22 per cent by volume) or 3 litres of fortified wine (alcohol content exceeding 15 by volume; refers also to sparkling wine);

(2)   5 litres of wine (other than fortified wine and also other alcoholic beverages with an alcohol content exceeding 3.5 per cent by volume but not exceeding 15 per cent by volume and which are not strong beer);

(3)   15 litres of strong beer (alcohol content exceeding 3.5 per cent by volume).

9.199   The tax exemption only applies to travellers who are not resident in Sweden, or residents who enter Sweden by air on a commercial flight, or where the time spent outside Sweden exceeds 20 hours, or tax has been levied on the goods in another EU country.

CHAPTER 10

OCCASIONAL LICENCES AND OCCASIONAL PERMISSIONS

10.01 There are three circumstances in which a place in respect of which there is no authority to sell or supply intoxicating liquor may be conferred with such authority on a temporary basis:

(1) occasional permission;

(2) occasional licence;

(3) 'occasional club'.

10.02 Which application is the most appropriate to the circumstances will depend largely upon the nature of the organisation wishing to hold the event, although there are other factors, such as the timing of notices, which may ultimately influence the decision. Each type of authority will now be considered in turn.

OCCASIONAL PERMISSION

10.03 This is a relatively new creature of statute,[1] which was introduced so as to enable organisations *not carried on for private gain* to seek a limited number of authorities in each year to sell intoxicating liquor at functions with their activities. This facility enables those organisations to retain the profits arising from such sales, which can be a valuable addition to their general fund-raising activities. Not surprisingly, the occasional permission has proved extremely popular, there being a 40 per cent increase in applications between 1986 and 1992, by which time approximately 36,000 applications were being made per annum.

1 Licensing (Occasional Permissions) Act 1983 as amended by the Deregulation (Occasional Permissions) Order 1997, SI 1997/1133, which introduced new provisions from 22 March 1997.

The applicant

10.04 The application must be submitted by a *member*[1] of an eligible organisation or a branch of such an organisation. Applications previously often failed at this first hurdle when the person appearing before the licensing committee was unable to satisfy it that he or she was an officer of the organisation, rather than merely a member, as is now the requirement.

1   Previous requirement was for the application to be made by an officer of the organisation. Amendments introduced by the Deregulation (Occasional Permissions) Order 1997, SI 1997/1133 included provisions concerning notice periods and the number of applications that might be made in any one year.

10.05   The Act of 1983 defines an eligible organisation as one which is not carried on for the purposes of private gain. The mere fact that an individual might derive some benefit from the fulfilment of the organisation's purpose will not be regarded as a private gain, unless the organisation is a commercial undertaking. The most common examples of eligible organisations are parents' and teachers' associations, local political associations etc.

Notices

10.06   A written application should be submitted (in duplicate) to the chief executive to the licensing justices at least 21 days[1] before the date of the function in respect of which the application is made. However, if there is a licensing session within 15 days of the receipt of the notice, the chief executive *must* adjourn the application to the next sessions.[2] It is absolutely crucial therefore, that as soon as these events are contemplated steps be taken to ascertain the dates of the relevant sessions and ensure that application is made in good time, so as to comply with *both* notice requirements.

1   Licensing (Occasional Permissions) Act 1983, s 2(2).
2   Licensing (Occasional Permissions) Act 1983, s 2(4).

10.07   The written application should contain the following particulars:

(a)   applicant's name;

(b)   applicant's address;

(c)   applicant's date of birth;

(d)   place of applicant's birth;

(e)   details of the organisation—name, purposes for which carried on, name of branch (if any) holding the particular function;

(f)   nature of the applicant's office in the organisation (where applicable);

(g)   details of the function—date, nature and place where it is to be held;

(h)   the kinds of intoxicating liquor to be sold;

(i)   timing—hours during which intoxicating liquor needs to be sold (note that no single permission may exceed 24 hours' duration);

(j)   details of any occasional permissions granted to the organisation in the 12 months preceding the date of the application.

10.08   The applicant's records may be checked with the court office before the hearing. No more than 12 occasional permissions may be granted in any 12-month period in respect of functions organised by a particular organisation.

10.09   Where the applicant is not an officer in the relevant organisation then the application must contain a signed statement by such an officer confirming that the application is made with his approval *and* indicating the nature of his office.[1]

1   Licensing (Occasional Permissions) Act 1983, s 2(1A).

10.10   Following receipt of the application, the chief executive will serve a copy on the chief officer of police. He will also send to the applicant notice of the date, time and place of the licensing sessions at which the application is to be heard.

The hearing

10.11   It is not a requirement of the 1983 Act that the applicant attend in person, although the court has the power to require such attendance and, in practice, most courts wish to see applicants to ensure that they are familiar with the laws concerning the sale of intoxicating liquor.

10.12   Where justices do require the attendance of an applicant who has been granted such a permission within the past 12 months then the committee is required to inform the applicant in writing of its reason or reasons for making such a request.

10.13   Applications *must* be refused if the licensing justices are not satisfied that:

(1)   the member is a fit and proper person to sell intoxicating liquor;

(2)   the place where the function is to be held is a suitable place for intoxicating liquor to be sold and *is situated in their licensing district*; and

(3)   the sale of intoxicating liquor at the function is not likely to result in disturbance or annoyance being caused to residents in the neighbourhood of that place, or in any disorderly conduct.

Having satisfied themselves as to these matters they must then consider whether to exercise their discretion and grant a permission.

10.14   In granting the application, the licensing justices must specify:
(1)   the place where liquor is to be sold;
(2)   the kinds of intoxicating liquor that may be sold;[1]
(3)   the hours and dates when the liquor may be so sold;
(4)   any condition that they think proper to impose.

1   See the Licensing Act 1964, s 1(1)(a) for the five categories of liquor that may be sold under a justices' on-licence.

Offences

10.15   The principal offences under the 1983 Act (and the prescribed penalties) are as follows:[1]
(1)   making false statements in the application (fine: level 3);
(2)   failure to comply with a condition attached to the permission (fine: level 3);
(3)   failure to produce the permission to a police constable upon being ordered to, within a reasonable time (fine: level 1);
(4)   selling liquor to under 18s—this offence is substantially the same as that under the main 1964 Act (see chapter 6) (fine: level 2 or 3, according to the nature of the offence);
(5)   permitting drunkenness—for the holder of an occasional permission it is an offence to permit 'drunkenness or any violent, quarrelsome or riotous conduct'. Further, where a drunken person is found on the premises the onus is upon the holder of the permission to establish that he (and his agents) took all reasonable steps to prevent drunkenness on the premises (fine: level 2).

1   Section 3 and Schedule.

10.16   The 1983 Act contains powers similar to those conferred upon a licensee for the holder of the occasional permission to exclude drunken or disorderly persons. Those who fail to leave at the request of a constable commit an offence (punishable by a fine: level 1). The police have power to enter the premises covered by an occasional permission for the purpose of detecting the commission of offences.

OCCASIONAL LICENCE

10.17   This was the traditional means whereby organisations were authorised to sell intoxicating liquor at fetes, garden parties, etc. The procedure is very straightforward, requiring no more than 24 hours' notice to be given to the police. The disadvantage to those organising the function, which gave rise to the procedure for occasional permissions outlined in the previous section, is that liquor is sold under the authority of a licensee, who will not unnaturally be seeking to make a profit on the exercise. The occasional licence is also an invaluable device for overcoming a loss of trade following the lapse of a club registration certificate, justices' on- or off-licence or even a special hours certificate.

The applicant

10.18   The applicant for an occasional licence is a holder of a justices' on-licence. The application is made to magistrates within the petty sessional division where the function is to take place, which need not necessarily be the same as the division where the licensed premises to which the justices' on-licence attaches are situated.

Notices

10.19   The only requirement is that the applicant serve upon the chief officer of police at least 24 hours' notice of his intended application, containing the following details:

(a)   name and address of applicant;

(b)   place and occasion for which the occasional licence is required;

(c)   the period for which it is required;

(d)   the hours to be specified.

In practice, it is usual to give rather more notice than this. It is also convenient for the chief executive to the licensing justices to be served so that the matter can be included in the court list for that day.

10.20   If two copies of the application are lodged with the chief executive to the licensing justices at least one month before the earliest day for which the application is made, the magistrates may, if they see fit, grant the application without a hearing. In practice, again, many courts will grant applications in the absence of the applicant, even though a lesser period of notice has been given, provided no difficulties are anticipated.

10.21   Where the applicant seeks to take advantage of the one-month rule the chief executive will send a copy of the notice of application upon receipt to the chief officer of police. If, within seven days, the police lodge two copies of a notice of objection with the chief executive to the licensing justices magistrates may not grant the application without a hearing, unless the objection is subsequently withdrawn. Any such notice of objection will be forwarded to the applicant by the chief executive.

Refusal

10.22   The justices have a general discretion as regards the grant of an occasional licence. Contrary to the impression created by some courts, they are *not* required to be satisfied that the occasion is a *special* occasion. For example, as indicated above, occasional licences have been used to cover periods where 'other' licences or certificates have lapsed and it would otherwise be necessary to cease trading. For example:

(1)   where a registered club failed to apply for renewal;[1]

(2)   on failure to apply for a renewal of a justices' on-licence;[2]

(3)   to permit off-sales.[3] Although a grant for this purpose was quashed by the Divisional Court, it seems generally to be held that the effect of *R v Bow Street Justices*, which was determined subsequently, has been to confirm that an occasional licence may be granted in such circumstances. Great care should be taken, however, to ensure that the licensee is either paid for the service that he is providing, or receives a share of the profits. It is not sufficient that he merely attends the event, even if he has general conduct of the bar itself. He is the person who is authorised under the justices' licence to sell intoxicating liquor and if, in practice, he receives no benefit for the service, it is likely that the courts will hold such an arrangement to be a sham, rendering the beneficiaries liable to prosecution.[4]

1   *R v Woolwich Justices, ex p Arnold* [1987] Crim LR 572.
2   *R v Bow Stipendiary Magistrate, ex p Metropolitan Police Comr* [1983] 2 All ER 915.
3   *R v Brighton Justices, ex p Jarvis* [1954] 1 All ER 197.
4   See *Dunning v Owen* [1907] 2 KB 237.

10.23   Occasional licences may be granted for periods of up to three weeks. Indeed, such licences can be granted on one occasion for consecutive periods, if the justices so determine.

10.24   Justices may grant an occasional licence for *other* licensed premises so as, for example, to overcome the temporary loss of a special hours certificate. In such circumstances it would be necessary to satisfy the justices that in all other respects the requirements of a special hours certificate would be met.

10.25   However, they may not grant a licence in respect of the premises to which the 'parent' justices' on-licence attached (so as to circumvent any conditions of that particular licence); nor may they grant an occasional licence to an applicant who holds only a residential licence.

10.26 If the applicant holds either a restaurant licence or a residential and restaurant licence, the justices may grant the occasional licence only if they are satisfied that the sale of intoxicating liquor under the authority of the occasional licence will be ancillary to the provision of substantial refreshment.[1]

1   Section 180(6).

Hours

10.27 An occasional licence may be granted for any hours that the magistrates consider to be appropriate, although not on Christmas Day, Good Friday or any day appointed for public fast or thanksgiving. An occasional licence is granted *in addition* to the justices' licence already held by the licensee and so there is no requirement for the 'parent' licensed premises to cease trading while the occasional licence is being exercised. There is no right of appeal against the refusal to grant an occasional licence, other than the usual entitlement to apply to the High Court in respect of procedural flaws or evident bias.

Offences

10.28 The definition of 'licensed premises' in s 200(1) of the 1964 Act includes any place where intoxicating liquor is sold under an occasional licence. Accordingly, those offences which relate to activities taking place on licensed premises may also be committed where an occasional licence has been granted. Note, however, that s 59(3) specifically excludes the provisions as to permitted hours in relation to premises operated under an occasional licence, and proceedings brought in the alternative for selling intoxicating liquor 'without holding a justices' licence ... authorising ... the sale of that liquor' are equally likely to fail.[1]

1   *Southall v Haime* (1979) 143 JP 245.

'OCCASIONAL CLUB'

10.29 This is not a term recognised in the Act; it merely describes the situation where a club seeks to supply intoxicating liquor to its members or guests on a special occasion.[1] In that event, there is no requirement to give notice, or even to observe any particular hours. However, only members and their guests may be admitted to the event and there must be no off-sales. Bars at the club's registered premises may remain open throughout this period.

1   Section 39(3). See also para **8.55**.

CHAPTER 11

LICENSING AND THE HUMAN RIGHTS ACT 1998

EXISTING CONTROLS

11.01   The Human Rights Act 1998 (HRA 1998), which came into force on 2 October 2000, imported into UK statute law many of the key provisions of the European Convention on Human Rights. For the purposes of this work such rights include:

— the right to a fair hearing;
— the right to a public hearing;
— the independence of the tribunal;
— the impartiality of the tribunal;
— a public determination of the issues;
— recognition of a private life;
— peaceful enjoyment of possessions.

11.02   In this chapter we will deal in turn with each of these rights and the impact of the HRA 1998 upon licensing practice and procedure. In the excitement to play with these new toys, however, lawyers and others involved in the process should not overlook those existing authorities and statutory provisions which to a significant degree already recognised such rights. These will be touched upon in the following paragraphs.

THE NEW REGIME

Background

11.03   During the Second Reading of the Bill The Lord McCluskey expressed a view that the HRA 1998 would be:

'A field day for crackpots, a pain in the neck for judges and a goldmine for lawyers'.

Experience has already shown that this light-hearted comment may not have been so very wide of the mark.

11.04   Previously, individuals of Member States could only complain about interference with their Convention rights by lodging an application with the European Court of Human Rights in Strasbourg. Once lodged, such an application was passed to a Committee of three judges who decided upon its admissibility. If that criteria was satisfied it would then be passed to a Chamber of seven judges who determined the application on its merits. If the application raised issues affecting the interpretation of the Convention it was passed to a Grand Chamber of 11 judges.

11.05   From 2 October 2000 individuals in the UK have been able to assert their Convention rights directly in our national courts and tribunals, thereby making the Convention an effective and legitimate part of UK law.

General principles

11.06   All UK legislation, whenever enacted, must be interpreted if possible so as to be compatible with the Convention. As from 2 October 2000, 'courts' have been obliged to interpret statutes and statutory instruments on the basis that Parliament intended legislation to be compatible with the Convention, unless it has been impossible to the construe the relevant provision in that way. Where it is impossible to construe the legislation in this way, the courts have the power to strike down or disregard subordinate legislation. Where primary legislation is concerned this is not the case. In such instances the higher courts, including the Court of Appeal and the High Court are able to make a 'declaration of incompatibility' which, whilst not affecting the validity or continuing operation of the legislation, is intended to operate as a signal to Parliament that legislative change is required. It is intended that where such change is promoted it is dealt with by way of a 'remedial order' which is a statutory instrument amending the offending provision of the primary legislation. A 'fast track' procedure allows for the laying of the order for 60 days after which it is approved by both Houses.

11.07   Individuals who believe their Convention rights have been violated by a 'public authority' can rely on those rights as a defence in criminal proceedings, in judicial review or, where no other avenue is open, in civil proceedings for damages. There are limitations in respect of judicial acts carried out in good faith.

11.08   A court or tribunal must take into consideration the case law of the European Court of Human Rights, the European Commission and the Committee of Ministers. Thus Strasbourg jurisprudence, whilst not binding in member courts, will be influential. However, the HRA 1998 specifies that rights provided by the Convention may only be asserted in the national courts where an individual (who falls within the definition of 'victim' for the purpose of the HRA 1998, s 7) is in dispute with a 'public authority bound to act in a way compatible with Convention rights'. Section 6 of the HRA 1998 provides a broad definition of 'public authorities', which includes local government, courts and tribunals, the police and any other 'person certain of whose functions are functions of a public nature.' Clearly licensing committees fall well within the scope of this definition.

11.09   A 'victim' is a person (including a company) who can show that their rights have been violated or whose rights run the risk of being directly affected by the decision or action in issue. Only a 'victim' can take action under or rely on the rights contained in the Convention.

Qualified rights

11.10   The European Convention for the Protection of Human Rights and Fundamental Freedoms is simply a treaty which has been ratified by the Member States of the Council of Europe and which contains what might be considered the essential civil liberties required for any democratic society.

11.11   Article 1 of the Convention details the rights and freedoms. Some of these rights are absolute in that they cannot be restricted in any circumstances. Others are qualified so that the rights protected are balanced against the public interest. However any restrictions upon individual freedoms must be justifiable by the body attempting to use them. The Convention seeks to ensure that any limitations placed upon an individual's inherent rights are not excessive, and it is now established that for the State, and consequently any 'public authority', to be able to justify any interference it must be able to show that the action:

— is prescribed by law;

— serves one of the legitimate aims provided for in the relevant Article; and

— is proportionate and necessary in a democratic society.

Prescribed by law

11.12   In order for any interference to be considered legitimate, it must be based upon a specific legal rule. This means that interference cannot be arbitrary. In addition to this, that legal rule must be readily available, in the public domain and formulated in such a manner as to enable any person reading it to understand how that law might be applied. In the case of *Malone v United Kingdom*,[1] Mr Malone had his phone tapped by the police and at that time the only regulation dealing with phone tapping was an internal guidance document produced by the police which was not available to members of the public. The European Court of Human Rights took the view that Mr Malone, as he did not have access to the document, was unable to either assess whether his telephone was likely to be listened into or on what basis a decision to listen-in would be made. Thus his complaint was justified. This could be applicable in a licensing context if a local authority had an internal unwritten 'policy' about the number of late night premises it would allow in a particular area. Any decision based on such a 'policy' would, as far as one is able to anticipate such things, be contrary to the Convention rights.

[1]   (1984) 7 EHRR 14, ECtHR.

Legitimate aim

11.13   The legitimate aim is quite simply what the State hopes to achieve through the legislation or action which is being challenged and which it believes justifies the interference. The Articles themselves contain the list of legitimate aims, which include national security, and the protection of the rights and freedom of others.

'Necessary in a democratic society'—the proportionality principle

11.14   This can be summed up quite simply as the 'sledgehammer and nut' test. All it means is that any interference with a right granted under the Convention must be proportionate to the intended objective. Thus even if an action of the State which interferes with a Convention right is pursuing a legitimate aim (for example, crime prevention), if the means to achieve that aim are excessive in the circumstances then the interference will not be justified. The burden of proof in such cases is on the State once an interference is established.

11.15   For example, whilst it may be considered wrong to allow a licensed premises to open until 4.00am if it has the potential to cause a nuisance to those in the surrounding area, a decision not grant a licence to such a premises, or to revoke an existing licence, *could* be regarded as disproportionate on account of the potential impact upon the owner, the proposed or existing employees, on those who wish to attend such a premises.

ARTICLE 6: THE RIGHT TO A FAIR HEARING

11.16   Article 6 (para 1) of the Convention, which appears in the HRA 1998, Sch 1 is likely to continue to feature in many licensing applications. The Article provides that:

'In the determination of his civil rights and obligations or of any criminal charge against him, everyone is entitled to a fair and public hearing within a reasonable time by an independent and impartial tribunal established by law. Judgement shall be pronounced publicly ... *(save in certain limited circumstances, for which, refer to the Schedule).*'

11.17   Historically, of course there have been specific controls upon justices designed to prevent specific abuses which were perhaps more common in previous ages when, as a rule, those in authority tended to be less accountable than they are today. The current control may be found in the Licensing Act 1964, s 193 which disqualifies justices from acting in the context of that legislation where they hold certain occupations, particularly those in the brewing trade.

11.18   Prior to the HRA 1998 the High Court has always been prepared to intervene where there has been a clear breach of natural justice. For example, simply because the Local Government (Miscellaneous Provisions) Act 1982 did not provide for the applicant for an entertainment licence to receive notice of objections or representations, did not mean that such a requirement should be dispensed with; the rules of natural justice demanded that such notice should be given.[1]

---

[1]   See *R v Huntingdon District Council, ex p Cowan* [1984] 1 All ER 58, [1984] 1 WLR 501.

11.19   There is generally little argument that the magistrates' court provides an independent and impartial hearing and thus licensing applications before them complies with Article 6. However, the practice specified by the Crown Court Rules 1982, r 3(2) of including within the appellate tribunal two justices from the petty sessional division from which the appeal had been brought, very quickly fell foul of this provision and was struck out from the Rule by the Administrative Court in the case of *Gosling* (see chapter 2 for further details).

11.20   The question is whether a hearing before a licensing committee of the local authority falls within the same category? It could be argued in a particular case that the committee will consist of elected members whose decisions might be tainted by their desire to be re-elected. Alternatively, the members may also either sit on or be influenced by those who sit on the planning committee which may be working to a different agenda based upon changing an area from essentially leisure uses to more residential and may therefore wish applications for licences and/or renewals to be refused. In such a situation it could be difficult to argue that the licensing committee is impartial within the meaning of the HRA 1998. The solution to that difficulty lies within the appeal provisions provided within the relevant legislation. Where there is a right of appeal from the local authority to the courts, then this will provide the impartiality required by the Article.

11.21   This was confirmed in the case of *Bryan v United Kingdom.*[1] Here the UK's planning appeal procedure was challenged before the ECtHR on the basis that the appeal to an inspector of the Planning Inspectorate from the decision of a local planning committee was not sufficiently impartial, as the Secretary of State had the power to 'call in' the appeal to determine it himself (and therefore taking it back into government hands). The court held that in the circumstances of that particular case, as there was a further right of appeal to the High Court, this was sufficient to provide an independent hearing for the purposes of the Article.

[1]   (1995) 21 EHRR 342, [1996] 1 PLR 47.

11.22   As indicated, Article 6 includes a right to a reasoned judgment. In the case of *Stefan v General Medical Council,*[1] it was said that the provisions of Article 6 'will require closer attention to be paid to the duty to give reasons, at least in relation to those cases where a person's civil rights and obligations are being determined'.

[1]   [1999] 1 WLR 1293, [1999] Lloyd's Rep Med 90.

11.23   In all cases a hearing must be 'fair'. In criminal proceedings there is a further right (Article 6(3)) to hear the case one has to answer and to cross-examine.

11.24   There is an inherent right in all judicial and quasi-judicial proceedings that an applicant should know in advance and be able to question the content of objections, so in requiring hearings to be fair Article 6 simply preserves the position as it currently exists. In the case of *R v Licensing Justices of East Gwent,*[1] licensing justices refused to consider written statements of objectors (which the police authority wished to have put before them) on the basis the applicant licensee did not have the opportunity to cross-examine the objectors. The High Court found that the justices *were* obliged to take such evidence into account, but how much weight they attached to it was a matter for them taking into account the fact that the makers had not given oral evidence and that such evidence had not been tested by cross-examination.

¹ (1999) 164 JP 339.

ARTICLE 8: RIGHT TO RESPECT FOR PRIVATE AND FAMILY LIFE

11.25 Article 6 is concerned with the mechanics of the judicial process; Article 8 addresses the substance. The latter Convention right is likely to be that most frequently cited in licensing proceedings by those seeking to protect their personal amenity against the intrusion of further development or business activity.

11.26 Article 8 provides:

'(1) Everyone has the right to respect for his private and family life, his home and his correspondence.

(2) There shall be no interference by a public authority with the exercise of this right except such as is in accordance with the law and is necessary in a democratic society in the interests of national security, public safety or the economic well being of the country, for its prevention of disorder or crime, for the protection of health or morals, or for the protection of the rights and freedoms of others.'

As can be seen, Article 8(2) contains the exceptions to the right guaranteed in Article 8(1).

11.27 The European Commission and the European Court of Human Rights have considered a number of applications concerning nuisance suffered by individuals of Member States, including that caused by a nuclear power station, air traffic noise connected with an airport, road traffic noise and nuisance resulting from a military shooting range. It is one of the most open-ended—and thus potentially the most useful—of the Articles for objectors. The right is, however, subject to the qualification that it can be interfered with if the limitations are 'in accordance with the law' and 'necessary in a democratic society' in the interest of the matters which are specified. Those most likely to be relied upon by an applicant in the context of licensing applications are:

— public safety—eg the inclusion of certain safety features for premises to which a neighbour might object;

— the economic well-being of the country—presumably this is intended to mean that orders *of this type* are necessary for a healthy economy;

— for its prevention of disorder or crime—again, might cover, eg lighting to which a neighbour has objected;

— for the protection of the rights and freedoms of others—this final qualification of the Convention 'right' is likely to be the one upon which reliance is most frequently made. The right to respect for the householder's family life may, in an appropriate case, be subject to 'interference' by a licensing authority which permits, for example, a nightclub to trade in the vicinity. Such a decision may be made in favour of an applicant on the grounds that one person's right to peaceful evenings may legitimately be compromised (to a limited degree) by the right of a large number of people in the locality freely to meet and socialise.

11.28   It may be helpful to consider briefly several recent cases where the application of Article 8 has been in issue. In *Powell and Rayner v United Kingdom*[1] the applicants complained of noise pollution from night-flights out of Heathrow airport. The court held that Article 8 was material as:

'The quality of the applicants private life and the scope for enjoying the amenities of his home had been adversely affected by the noise generated by aircraft using Heathrow Airport. Article 8 is therefore a material provision in relation to both Mr Powell and Mr Rayner.'

The court then considered whether the interference was justifiable:

'... regard must be had to the fair balance that has to be struck between the competing interests of the individual and of the community as a whole ...'

[1]   (1990) 12 EHRR 355, ECtHR.

11.29   They then considered the benefits derived from having an airport and the steps undertaken by the airport to minimise its impact:

'... the existence of large international airports, even in densely populated urban areas ... have without question become necessary in the interests of a country's economic well-being.
A number of measures have been introduced ... to control, abate and compensate for aircraft noise ... including restrictions on night jet movements, noise monitoring ... and runway alteration'.

11.30   On that basis the court concluded:

'... there is no serious ground for maintaining that either the policy approach to the problem or the content of the particular regulatory measures adopted by the United Kingdom authorities gives rise to a violation of Article 8 ...'

11.31   Thus, the operation of the airport was a legitimate aim and it was accepted that, despite the government having taken certain measures, one could not entirely eliminate negative repercussions on the environment.

11.32   *Lopez Ostra v Spain*[1] is probably the most celebrated environmental protection case under the Convention. The facts of it were as follows: a waste treatment plant which belonged to a private company and which was developed with the assistance of a subsidy provided by the State, was located some 12 metres from the applicant's home. In addition, the plant began to operate without the requisite authorisation. Due to the release of gas fumes, smells and pollution, the town council evacuated the local residents who were rehoused elsewhere before the council eventually closed down one of the plant's activities.The applicant took action in the Spanish courts based upon the effects of pollution on her health but was unsuccessful. She subsequently took action in the European Court of Human Rights under Article 8.

[1]   (1994) 20 EHRR 277, ECtHR.

11.33   Whilst acknowledging that the plant had caused a serious nuisance to the residents, the Spanish government argued that the applicant was no longer a victim since she and her family had been rehoused at the municipality's expense. They also argued that the plant had been closed in 1993 (the year prior to the matter coming before the court) and consequently all nuisances had come to an end. This second argument was partially accepted by the court who stated:

'At all events, if the applicant could now return to her former home following the decision to close the plant, this would be a factor to be taken into account in assessing the damage she sustained but would not mean that she ceased to be a victim.'

The court went on:

'Neither Mrs Lopez Ostra's move nor the waste treatment plant's closure ... alters the fact that the applicant and her family lived for years only 12 metres away from a source of smells, noise and fumes.'

11.34   So far as the pollution itself was concerned the court said:

'Naturally, severe environmental pollution may have some effect on an individual's well-being and prevent them from enjoying their home in such a way as to affect their private and family life adversely, without, however, seriously endangering their health.'

This is an important part of the judgment as it indicates that there is no requirement to show that human health has been seriously endangered by an industrial activity that pollutes the environment in order to allege that the right to private and family life has been affected. Thus, taking this to its logical conclusion, one could argue that public authorities should not allow activities to be undertaken which, whilst not seriously affecting human health, do cause environmental pollution. This would obviously be subject to the qualifications considered above.

11.35   The applicant also alleged that the situation complained of had been prolonged by the municipality's failure to act. The court found that:

'Regard must be had to the fair balance that has to be struck to the competing interest of the individual and the community as a whole'.

11.36   The court accepted that this particular waste treatment plant had been built to solve a serious pollution problem and that the Spanish authorities were not directly responsible for the emission produced as it was a private enterprise. However the court held that the balance had not been fairly struck between the public interest and the applicant's right to respect for her home and her private and family life. Consequently, in allowing such interference the authorities had therefore been in breach of Article 8. The court considered it relevant that although the public authorities were not directly responsible for the emissions, the town council had allowed the plant to be built on its land, the State had subsidised the construction and the various public authorities failed to shut the plant down. The court awarded the applicant 400 million pesetas compensation.

11.37   What do these cases mean in respect of the use of Article 8 by objectors to licensed premises? First it is clear that a public authority may interfere with the right to respect for family life and home under certain circumstances including economic well-being and 'for the protection of the rights and freedoms of others'.

11.38   One could use the decision in the *Powell and Rayner* case to argue that it is for the public authority to decide policy in relation to issues such as land-use and whether premises should be licensed, especially where there are procedures in place to mitigate any interference.

11.39   Secondly, the only cases that have been successful before the European Court of Human Rights are those where there has been significant damage. In the *Lopez Ostra* case local residents were evacuated from their homes and in a similar case[1] 150 persons were affected by arsenic poisoning. Thus for an objector to be successful under Article 8 the disturbance or threat of disturbance would have to be significant.

[1]   *Guerra v Italy* (1998) 26 EHRR 357, ECtHR.

11.40   Thirdly, the *Lopez Ostra* case suggests the possibility of a new cause of action for what would effectively be damage sustained due to a breach of Convention rights, for example, where a licensing authority fails to take action to require the abatement of a nuisance or fails to impose sufficiently stringent conditions. Contrast *R v Lam and Brennan (t/a Namesakes of Torbay) and Torbay Borough Council*[1] (decided before the HRA 1998 came into force) where the Court of Appeal held that the authority did not have a duty of care to the owner of the restaurant whose family and business was severely affected by fumes from a nearby workshop which the authority did nothing to prevent.

[1]   [1997] 3 PLR 22, [1998] PLCR 30.

11.41   Whether this will mean we will see actions being taken by objectors against licensing authorities for damages for the loss of enjoyment of their home due to the authority granting or renewing a licence is uncertain. To justify such awards the objectors, it would seem, would have to demonstrate a major interference with their right under Article 8, with the authority being unable to establish that such interference fell within Article 8(2) in that it was protecting the rights and freedoms of others.

ARTICLE 1 OF THE FIRST PROTOCOL: PROTECTION OF PROPERTY

11.42   This important safeguard provides:

'Every natural or legal person is entitled to peaceful enjoyment of his possessions. No one shall be deprived of his possessions except in the public interest and subject to the conditions provided for by law and by the general principles of international law.

The preceding provisions shall not, however, in any way impair the right of a State to enforce such laws as it deems necessary to control the use of property in accordance with the general interest or to secure the payment of taxes or other contributions or penalties'.

Possessions

11.43   The question of what 'possessions' fall within Article 1 of the First Protocol is an important one as any such 'possessions' are protected from interference, subject to the stated qualifications. Is a licence a possession? The leading authority on this point is *Tre Traktörer Aktiebolag v Sweden*.[1] The case concerned the removal of a licence to sell alcohol from premises in Sweden. The licence holders made an application to the European Court of Human Rights on a number of grounds including an allegation of violation of Article 1 of the First Protocol.

[1]   (1989) 13 EHRR 309, ECtHR.

11.44   The State initially argued that the licence was not a possession within the Article. The court disagreed stating:

'... the economic interests connected with the running of (the premises) were possessions for the purposes of Article 1 of the Protocol. Indeed, the court has already found that the maintenance of the licence was one of the principal conditions for the carrying on of the applicant company's business, and that its withdrawal had adverse effects on the goodwill and value of the restaurant. Such withdrawal thus constitutes ... interference with (the applicants) right to the peaceful enjoyment of its possessions'.

11.45   The court then continued,

'Severe though it may have been, the interference at issue does not fall within the ambit of the second sentence of the first paragraph (namely deprivation of possessions).The applicant company, although it could no longer open as a restaurant business, kept some economic interest represented by the leasing of the premises and the property assets contained therein which it finally sold in June 1984. There was accordingly no deprivation of property in terms of Article 1 of the Protocol.

The court finds, however, that the withdrawal of the licence to serve alcoholic beverages constituted a measure of control of the use of the property which falls to be considered under the second paragraph of Article 1 of the Protocol'.

11.46   The court then considered whether the control of the premises was in 'the general interest' and 'proportionate' to the effect on the licence holder. Unfortunately for the applicants the court concluded:

' ... having regard to the legitimate aim of Swedish social policy concerning the consumption of alcohol ... the State did not fail to strike a fair balance between the economic interest of the applicant company and the general interest of Swedish society'.

11.47   The licence holder's claim under Article 1 of the First Protocol was therefore dismissed. *Catscratch Ltd v Glasgow Licensing Board (No 2)*[1] followed the decision in *Tre Tractörer v Sweden*[2] by holding that the possession of an entertainment licence *was* a right protected by Article 1 of the First Protocol and consequently interference with it (in this case the interference being the refusal of extensions to the licence which effectively closed the business) was capable of being in breach of Article 1. Again, in *Catscratch* such interference was held to be justified for the protection of the environment and the pursuance of the aims of the licensing legislation—these being considered to be 'in the public interest' and 'subject to the conditions provided for by law'.

[1]   2002 SLT 503
[2]   (1989) 13 EHRR 309.

11.48   Note that the Article draws a distinction which the court noted in *Tre Tractörer* between *deprivation* of a possession and the right of the State to enforce the law to *control* a possession.

11.49   Any steps taken by the enforcing authority (for example a licensing authority) to interfere with a licence must recognise that a balance should be drawn between the requirements and demands of the general population and the protection of the licence holder's individual rights. In other words, in balancing the interest of the community against the interest of the licence holder, has the licence holder who has been deprived of a licence, or whose licence is being controlled by conditions, suffered an excessive burden?

11.50   Another case of interest, from the environmental sphere, which may also be relevant in relation to licensing, is that of *Fredin v Sweden*.[1] In *Fredin* the applicant owned a number of gravel pits that had been licensed and exploited for a number of years. The State served notice of its intention to revoke the permit, thereby effectively closing the business. Whilst finding that the permit was a possession, the court held that its removal was 'control' and not 'deprivation', and that as 'in today's society the protection of the environment is an increasingly important consideration', the steps taken were justifiable and there was no violation of the Article. Significantly perhaps, the court bore in mind the fact that a three-year notice period had been given to the applicant.

[1]   (1991) 13 EHRR 784, ECtHR.

11.51   Yet another Swedish case which considered interference with possessions was *Sporrong and Lönnroth v Sweden*.[1] Mr Sporrong owned substantial property in Stockholm that had a rateable value of some 600,000 Swedish Crowns. The city council obtained orders which had the effect of requiring the compulsory purchase of the land together with orders preventing any further construction taking place. The orders and the construction bans were in force for over 20 years. Mr Sporrong argued that as he had been unable to sell or develop the site, this was equivalent to depriving him of his right to property contrary to the First Protocol. The Swedish government argued that such orders and prohibitions were an intrinsic feature of town planning and did not impair Mr Sporrong's right to the peaceful enjoyment of his possessions.

[1]   (1982) 5 EHRR 35, ECtHR.

11.52   The European court rejected the government's contention, finding that the orders and prohibitions did impair Mr Sporrong's right to peaceful enjoyment. However, the real question was whether the interference was justified. As the court, said the issue was whether:

> 'a fair balance was struck between the demands of the general interests of the community and the requirements of the protection of the individual's fundamental rights ... the search for this balance is inherent in the whole of the Convention and is also reflected in the structure of Article 1'.

11.53   The court held that there *had been* a violation of Article 1 of the First Protocol. The construction prohibitions were characterised as matters which 'controlled' the use of the property within the second rule mentioned above, whilst the compulsory purchase orders (although being accepted to be an interference with the applicants possessions) were determined not to fall within the definition of 'deprivation' as they could in theory still be sold. The fair balance between the protection of the right of property and requirements of general interest had been upset by the prolonged extension of the orders and prohibitions. In this case it was the time period that offended rather than the control itself. An award equivalent to £100,000 was provided.

11.54   Equating this to a licensing issue, it appears that revocation of a licence would be seen as control rather than deprivation due to the fact that the premises could continue to be used. Any such controls must be seen as being in the public interest and not disproportionate to the aim to be achieved

11.55   Where does all this leave us in terms of the security of licences? It is probably too early to say. We do not know yet how the courts are going to interpret the Convention rights in the UK. However, although the courts are only required to 'have regard' to existing human rights case law, the indications to date are that such authorities are likely to prove extremely persuasive. Consequently it is clear that Article 1 of the First Protocol is unlikely to be of much assistance to licence holders who have had their licence revoked or curtailed in some way due to the breadth of the qualifying provision within the Article which allows the licensing authority to control the use of premises where the balance of interest is in favour of the general public.

Remedies

11.56   If an individual does take action by way of an appeal against an unlawful act and is successful, what can he recover? Section 8(1) of the HRA 1998 states;

> 'in relation to any act ... of a public authority which the court finds is ... unlawful, it may grant such relief or remedy, or make such order ... as it considers just and appropriate'.

11.57   An injunction to prohibit or require a certain action will, be a potent remedy in licensing challenges, as it may for example:

— prohibit premises from being licensed;

— restrict opening hours;

— require noise insulation works to be undertaken.

11.58   Damages will only be awarded where the court is satisfied that it is necessary to do so having taken into account any other relief granted. Such damages can only be awarded by a court or tribunal that has the power to award damages in civil proceedings. The damages that may be awarded in respect of a judicial act done in good faith are limited by the Convention.

PART II
APPENDICES

Licensing Act 1964

PART I   THE GENERAL LICENSING SYSTEM

Justices' licences and provisions as to licensing justices

[A.1]

1   Justices' licences (1) In this Act ... 'justices' licence' means a licence under this Part of this Act authorising ... the sale by retail of intoxicating liquor (and also, in the case of a licence granted to a club for club premises, for its supply to or to the order of members otherwise than by way of sale).

(2) In this Act 'justices' on-licence' and 'justices' off-licence' mean respectively—
(a)   a justices' licence ... authorising sale for consumption either on or off the premises for which the licence is granted; and
(b)   a justices' licence ... authorising sale for consumption off those premises only.

(3) A justices' licence shall be in such form as the Secretary of State may prescribe [and—
(a)   in the case of a justices' on-licence may authorise the sale—
   (i)   of intoxicating liquor of all descriptions; or
   (ii)   of beer, cider and wine only; or
   (iii)   of beer and cider only; or
   (iv)   of cider only; or
   (v)   of wine only;
(b)   in the case of a justices' off-licence, may authorise the sale—
   (i)   of intoxicating liquor of all descriptions; or
   (ii)   of beer, cider and wine only].

Amendment
Sub-ss (1), (2): words omitted repealed by the Finance Act 1967, ss 5(1)(a), 45(8), Sch 16, Part I.
Sub-s (3): words in square brackets substituted by the Finance Act 1967, s 5(1)(b), Sch 7, para 7.

[A.2]

2   Licensing justices and districts [(1) The licensing districts for the purposes of this Act shall be the petty sessions areas. ...]

[(2) The licensing justices for any petty sessions area shall be a committee (which shall be known as the area licensing committee) of the justices acting for that area.]

[(2A) ...]

(3) For the purpose of carrying out their functions under this Act the licensing justices for each district shall hold licensing sessions as follows, that is to say,—

(a)　a general annual licensing meeting, and

(b)　not less than four ... transfer sessions,

in the twelve months beginning with February in every year.

(4) Except where this Act otherwise provides, all powers exercisable by licensing justices under this Act may be exercised at any licensing sessions, but this subsection shall not affect the operation of any enactment in so far as it expressly authorises licensing justices to act otherwise than at a licensing sessions.

(5) Part I of Schedule 1 to this Act shall have effect with respect to the constitution and procedure of licensing committees and Part II thereof with respect to the holding of licensing sessions.

Amendment

Sub-s (1): substituted by the Local Government Act 1972, s 204(4), Sch 25, Pt I, para 1; words omitted repealed by the Access to Justice Act 1999, s 106, Sch 15, Pt V, Table (1).

Sub-s (2): substituted by the Access to Justice Act 1999, s 76(2), Sch 10, paras 23, 24.

Sub-s (2A) (as originally inserted by SI 1985/1383, art 8, Schedule, para 2): repealed by the Access to Justice Act 1999, s 106, Sch 15, Pt V, Table (1).

Sub-s (3): words omitted repealed by the Licensing Act 1988, ss 14(1), 19, Sch 4.

Grant of justices' licence

[A.3]

3　Grant of justices' licence (1) Licensing justices may grant a justices' licence to any such person, not disqualified under this or any other Act for holding a justices' licence, as they think fit and proper.

(2) A justices' licence may be granted as a new licence or by way of renewal, transfer or, subject to section 93(4) of this Act, removal.

(3) In this Act—

(a)　renewing a justices' licence means granting a justices' licence for any premises to the holder of a similar licence in force for those premises;

(b)　removing a justices' licence means taking it from the premises for which it was granted and granting it for other premises;

(c)   transferring a justices' licence means granting it for any premises to a person in substitution for another person who holds or has held a licence for those premises.

(4) Schedule 2 to this Act shall have effect with regard to the procedure to be followed in relation to applications for the grant of a justices' licence.

[A.4]

4   New licences (1) Subject to the provisions of Part IV of this Act, licensing justices granting a new justices' on-licence, other than a licence for the sale of wine alone . . . may attach to it such conditions governing the tenure of the licence and any other matters as they think proper in the interests of the public; but no payment may be required in pursuance of a condition attached under this subsection.

(2) Subject to section 113 of this Act, licensing justices shall not grant a new justices' on-licence for premises unless the premises are in their opinion structurally adapted to the class of licence required.

Amendment
Sub-s (1): words omitted repealed by the Finance Act 1967, ss 5(1)(a), 45(8), Sch 16, Part I.

[A.5]

5   Removals   (1) Subject to the following provisions of this Act, licensing justices shall have the same power to grant a removal of a justices' licence as they have to grant a new licence.

(2) Licensing justices may grant an ordinary removal to premises in their licensing district from any other premises, whether in that district or not.

(3) An application for a removal shall be made by the person wishing to hold the licence after the removal.

(4) Subject to sections 113, 122 and 126 of this Act, licensing justices shall not grant the removal of a justices' on-licence to any premises unless in their opinion the premises are structurally adapted to the licence.

(5) Licensing justices shall not grant an ordinary removal unless they are satisfied that no objection to the removal is made—
(a)   where the licence is a justices' on-licence, by the owner of the premises from which it is sought to remove the licence or by the holder of the licence,
(b)   where the licence is a justices' off-licence, by the holder of the licence,

or by any person other than the owner of the said premises and the holder of the licence or, as the case may be, other than the holder of the licence, whom the justices consider to have a right to object to the removal.

(6) In this Act, 'ordinary removal' means a removal which is neither a special removal (as defined in section 15(2) of this Act) nor a planning removal or temporary premises removal (as defined in sections 121(2) and 126(2) of this Act respectively).

[A.6]

6 Provisional grant of new licence or removal (1) Where licensing justices are satisfied, on application made by a person interested in any premises which are—
(a) about to be constructed or in the course of construction for the purpose of being used as a house for the sale of intoxicating liquor (whether for consumption on or off the premises); or
(b) about to be altered or extended or in the course of alteration or extension for that purpose (whether or not they are already used for that purpose);

that the premises, if completed in accordance with plans deposited under this Act, would be such that they would have granted a justices' on-licence or a justices' off-licence for the premises, they may make a provisional grant of such a licence for those premises.

(2) Any such application may be made either for the provisional grant of a new licence or for a provisional removal of a licence to the premises, and the grant may be made accordingly.

(3) On an application by the holder of a provisional licence, licensing justices may consent to any modifications of the deposited plans where, in their opinion, the premises, if completed in accordance with the modified plans, will be fit and convenient for their purpose.

(4) Licensing justices shall, after such notice has been given as they may require, declare a provisional grant final on being satisfied—
(a) that the premises have been completed in accordance with the plans deposited, or in accordance with those plans with modifications consented to under the preceding subsection; and
(b) that the holder of the provisional licence is not disqualified by this or any other Act for holding a justices' licence and is in all other respects a fit and proper person to hold a justices' licence;

...

[(4A) The holder of a provisional licence may also apply to have a provisional grant declared final before the premises have been completed if it is likely that they will be completed as mentioned in paragraph (a) of subsection (4) of this section before the date appointed for the next licensing sessions; and the licensing justices, if they are satisfied that the premises are likely to be so completed and are further satisfied of the matters mentioned in paragraph (b) of that subsection, may direct that the declaration may be made before the next licensing sessions by a single licensing justice.

(4B) In a case where a direction has been given under subsection (4A) of this section, a single licensing justice, after such notice has been given as he may require, shall declare the provisional grant final if he is satisfied that the premises have been completed as mentioned in paragraph (a) of subsection (4) of this section. `

(4C) Until a provisional grant has been declared final under subsection (4) or (4B) of this section it shall not be valid.]

(5) If on an application for the provisional grant of a justices' licence the applicant deposits, instead of plans of the premises, a plan sufficient to identify the site of the premises, together with such description of the premises as will give a general indication of their proposed size and character (with reference in particular to the sale of intoxicating liquor), then—

(a) the licensing justices shall deal with the application as if the site plan and description deposited instead were the deposited plans, and shall assume that the premises will be fit and convenient for their purpose; but

(b) any provisional grant of a licence made on the application shall become ineffective unless affirmed under subsection (6) of this section in pursuance of an application made at a licensing sessions held within the twelve months following the date of the grant (or, where there is an appeal, the date the appeal is disposed of).

(6) Where licensing justices make a provisional grant of a licence by virtue of subsection (5) of this section the holder of the provisional licence may apply for the grant to be affirmed, and shall give notice of the application and deposit plans, as if he were applying (otherwise than under that subsection) for the grant of the licence; and the licensing justices shall affirm the provisional grant if satisfied that the premises, if completed in accordance with the plans deposited, will be fit and convenient for their purpose.

Amendment
Sub-s (4): words omitted repealed by the Licensing Act 1988, s 19, Sch 4.
Sub-ss (4A)–(4C): inserted by the Licensing Act 1988, s 9.

[A.7]

7 Renewals (1) Licensing justices may not renew a justices' licence at transfer sessions, except where the licence was due for renewal at the preceding general annual licensing meeting and the justices are satisfied that the applicant had reasonable cause for not applying for renewal at that meeting.

(2) A person intending to oppose an application for the renewal of a justices' licence shall give notice in writing of his intention to the applicant [and the clerk to the licensing justices], specifying in general terms the grounds of the opposition, not later than seven days before the commencement of the licensing sessions at which the application is to be made, and unless notice has been so given the licensing justices shall not entertain the objection, ...

(3) ...

(4) Evidence given on an application for the renewal of a justices' licence shall be given on oath.

(5) Where the holder of a justices' licence fails to apply for its renewal at the general annual licensing meeting at which it is due for renewal, and the licence expires in consequence of his failure, an application by him for a similar licence for the same premises shall be treated as an application for renewal, and the grant of the licence applied for shall be treated as a renewal of the expired licence, if the application is made not later than the next general annual licensing meeting and the licensing justices are satisfied that he had reasonable cause for his failure.

Amendment
Sub-s (2): words in square brackets inserted and words omitted repealed by the Licensing Act 1988, s 19, Sch 3, para 1, Sch 4.
Sub-s (3): repealed by the Licensing Act 1988, s 19, Sch 4.

[A.8]

8   Transfers   (1) Subject to sections 138 and 145 of this Act, licensing justices shall not grant a transfer of a justices' licence except in the following cases and to the following persons, that is to say—
(a)   where the holder of the licence has died, to his representatives or the new tenant or occupier of the premises;
(b)   where the holder of the licence becomes incapable through illness or other infirmity of carrying on business under the licence (and notwithstanding that the licence may have ceased to be in force before the transfer), to his assigns or the new tenant or occupier of the premises;
[(c)   where the holder of the licence has been adjudged bankrupt, or a [voluntary arrangement proposed by the holder of the licence has been approved under Part VIII of the Insolvency Act 1986], or a trustee has been appointed under a deed of arrangement within the meaning of the Deeds of Arrangement Act 1914 for the benefit of the creditors of the holder of the licence, to the trustee of the bankrupt's estate or under the deed or the supervisor of the [voluntary arrangement] or the new tenant or occupier of the premises;]

(d) where the holder of the licence has given up or is about to give up, or his representatives have given up or are about to give up, occupation of the premises, to the new tenant or occupier of the premises or the person to whom the representatives or assigns have, by sale or otherwise, bona fide conveyed or made over the interest in the premises;

(e) where the occupier of the premises, being about to quit them, has wilfully omitted or neglected to apply for the renewal of the licence, to the new tenant or occupier of the premises;

(f) where the owner of the premises or some person on his behalf has been granted a protection order under section 10(3) of this Act and application for the transfer is made at the first or second licensing sessions begun after the making of that order, to the owner or person applying on his behalf.

(2) For the purposes of paragraph (d) of the preceding subsection, a person occupying premises for the purpose of carrying on business under a licence shall be treated as giving up occupation on his giving up the carrying on of the business, notwithstanding that he remains temporarily in occupation of the premises or part of them.

(3) The foregoing provisions of this section, except paragraphs (e) and (f) of subsection (1), shall apply in relation to the transfer of a provisional licence, as if the licence were in force, and shall, as so applying, be construed as if 'occupation' included intended occupation, and similarly as respects other expressions.

(4) Licensing justices may, at their general annual licensing meeting, make regulations determining the time that must elapse after the hearing of an application for transfer before another such application may be made in respect of the same premises; but licensing justices may in any particular case dispense with the observance of regulations made under this subsection.

Amendment
Sub-s (1): para (c) substituted by the Insolvency Act 1985, s 235, Sch 8, para 12, words in square brackets therein substituted by the Insolvency Act 1986, s 439(2), Sch 14.

[A.9]

[8A Approval of prospective licensees (1) If, on an application made to licensing justices with respect to any licensed premises, the justices are satisfied that the applicant—

(a) is a fit and proper person, and

(b) is not disqualified under this or any other Act for holding a justices' licence,

the justices may, subject to subsection (3) of this section, approve him as a prospective licensee of the premises.

(2) Where the power of licensing justices to transfer a justices' licence for any premises is exercisable by virtue of section 8(1) of this Act, any person who has been approved as a prospective licensee of the premises may, by notice in writing—

(a) to the [chief executive] to the licensing justices, and

(b) to the chief officer of police,

elect that the enactments relating to the sale of intoxicating liquor and to licensed premises shall apply as if the licence were transferred to him immediately after the giving of the notice; and any election so made shall have effect accordingly.

(3) Licensing justices shall not approve a person as a prospective licensee of any licensed premises if, in their opinion, there is a likelihood that, if he became a licensee of the premises under subsection (2) of this section, he would be prevented by other commitments from properly discharging his functions as such a licensee.

(4) Licensing justices approving any person as a prospective licensee of any licensed premises shall cause a memorandum of the approval to be endorsed on the justices' licence for the premises or, where a copy of the licence is admissible in evidence, on a copy of the licence.

(5) Paragraphs 1(a) and (c), 4(a) and (b) and 5 to 8 of Schedule 2 to this Act (application for justices' licence) shall apply in relation to an application for approval under this section as they apply to an application for the grant of a justices' licence.]

Amendment
Inserted by SI 1998/114, art 2.
Sub-s (2): in para (a) words 'chief executive' in square brackets substituted by the Access to Justice Act 1999, s 90(1), Sch 13, paras 36, 37(a).

[A.10]

9 Persons and premises disqualified for holding or receiving justices' licence   (1) Without prejudice to the provisions of this or any other Act whereby a person may be disqualified for holding a justices' licence, the following persons shall be so disqualified, that is to say—

(a) a sheriff's officer or officer executing the legal process of any court;

(b) a person convicted, whether under this Act or otherwise, of forging a justices' licence or making use of a forged justices' licence knowing it to have been forged;

(c) a person convicted, whether under this Act or otherwise, of permitting to be a brothel premises for which at the time of the conviction he held a justices' licence.

(2) Where within a period of two years two persons severally holding a justices' licence for any premises forfeit their licences, the premises shall

be disqualified for receiving a justices' licence for a period of twelve months following the second forfeiture.

(3) Premises shall be disqualified for receiving a justices' licence if they are situated on land acquired or appropriated by a special road authority, and for the time being used, for the provision of facilities to be used in connection with the use of a special road provided for the use of traffic of class I (with or without other classes).

(4) For the purposes of subsection (3) of this section—

(a) 'special road' and 'special road authority' have the same meanings as in [the Highways Act 1980] except that 'special road' includes a trunk road to which by virtue of [paragraph 3 of Schedule 23 to that Act] the provisions of that Act apply as if the road were a special road; and

(b) 'class I' means class I in Schedule 4 to that Act as varied from time to time by any order under [section 17] of that Act, but if that Schedule is amended by such an order so as to add to it a further class of traffic, the order may adapt the reference in subsection (3) of this section to traffic of class I so as to take account of the additional class.

[(4A) Premises shall be disqualified for receiving a justices' licence if they are primarily used as a garage or form part of premises which are primarily so used.

(4B) In subsection (4A) of this section, the reference to use as a garage is a reference to use for any one or more of the following purposes, namely, the retailing of petrol or derv or the sale or maintenance of motor vehicles.]

(5) The provisions ... of this section shall be without prejudice to the disqualification under any other Act of premises for receiving a justices' licence.

(6) A justices' licence purporting to be held by any person disqualified for holding a licence, or attached to premises disqualified for receiving a licence, shall be void.

Amendment

Sub-s (4): words in square brackets substituted by the Highways Act 1980, s 343(2), Sch 24, para 12.

Sub-ss (4A), (4B): inserted by the Licensing Act 1988, s 10(1).

Sub-s (5): words omitted repealed by the Licensing Act 1988, s 19, Sch 3, para 2, Sch 4.

[Interim authorities]

[A.11]

[9A Interim authorities (1) This section applies where the power of licensing justices to transfer a justices' licence for any premises is exercisable by virtue of section 8(1) of this Act.

(2) If the licensing justices are satisfied, on application made by notice in writing to the [chief executive] to the licensing justices and to the chief officer of police, that the applicant—

(a)   is a fit and proper person, and

(b)   is not disqualified under this or any other Act for holding a justices' licence,

the justices may grant him an authority (in this Act referred to as an 'interim authority') conferring in respect of the premises the same authority as that conferred by the justices' licence.

(3) An interim authority shall be granted for a period of 28 days beginning with such date as may be specified in it.

(4) If during the period for which an interim authority granted to any person is in force, an application for the transfer of the justices' licence is made (whether by him or by any other person), the interim authority shall continue in force until the application is disposed of.

(5) While an interim authority in respect of any premises is in force, the enactments relating to the sale of intoxicating liquor and to licensed premises (other than those relating to the renewal or transfer of licences or to protection orders) shall apply to the person granted the authority as if he were the holder of the justices' licence.

(6) The power conferred on licensing justices by subsection (2) of this section—

(a)   shall not be exercisable in relation to premises which are already the subject of an interim authority, and

(b)   shall not be exercisable more than twice in relation to each occasion on which the power to transfer a justices' licence becomes exercisable as mentioned in subsection (1) of this section.]

Amendment
Inserted by SI 1998/114, art 3(1).
Sub-s (2): words 'chief executive' in square brackets substituted by the Access to Justice Act 1999, s 90(1), Sch 13, paras 36, 37(b).

[A.12]

[9B   Supplementary provisions relating to interim authorities   (1) Where an application for an interim authority is made under section 9A of this Act within seven days of the power of the licensing justices to transfer a justices' licence becoming exercisable by virtue of section 8(1) of this Act—

(a)   an interim authority shall be deemed to have been granted in respect of the premises; and

(b)   subject to subsection (2) of this section, that authority shall remain in force for a period of 14 days beginning with the date of the application.

(2) An interim authority deemed to have been granted by virtue of subsection (1) of this section shall cease to have effect if, within the period of 14 days mentioned in that subsection—

(a)   the chief officer of police, or

(b)   an officer of police designated by him,

by notice in writing served on the applicant and the licensing justices, objects to the granting of an interim authority under section 9A of this Act.

(3) The power conferred on licensing justices by section 9A of this Act—

(a)   may be exercised by a single justice, and

(b)   may be exercised otherwise than at licensing sessions.

(4) A justice to whom application is made under section 9A of this Act for an interim authority may examine the applicant on oath.]

Amendment
Inserted by SI 1998/114, art 3(1).

Protection orders

[A.13]

10   Protection orders   (1) A person who proposes to apply for the transfer of a justices' licence for any premises may apply to justices of the peace acting for the petty sessions area in which the premises are for the grant of an authority, in this Act referred to as a 'protection order', to sell intoxicating liquor on the premises, and the justices may grant the protection order if they are satisfied that the applicant is a person to whom the licensing justices could grant a transfer of the licence.

(2) The authority conferred by a protection order in respect of any premises shall be the same as that conferred by the justices' licence in force (or last in force) for those premises; and, while the order is in force, the enactments relating to the sale of intoxicating liquor and to licensed premises (other than those relating to the renewal or transfer of licences or to protection orders) shall apply to the person granted the order as if he were the holder of that licence …

(3) Where—

(a)   a justices' licence for any premises is forfeited for the first time by virtue of a second or subsequent conviction under section 160 of this Act or of a conviction under section 184 thereof, or

(b)   a justices' licence for any premises is forfeited by order of a magistrates' court made on complaint under section 20(3) of this Act, or

(c)   a justices' licence for any premises is forfeited by order of a court under section [169H(2)] of this Act, or

(d)   a justices' licence for any premises is forfeited by virtue of a disqualification order made under section 100 of this Act, or

(e)   the holder of a justices' licence for any premises becomes disqualified for the first time for holding such a licence by reason of being convicted as mentioned in section 9(1) of this Act,

justices of the peace may grant a protection order to any owner of the premises or any other person authorised by an owner of the premises, notwithstanding the forfeiture or the previous licence holder's disqualification; but not more than one protection order may be granted under this subsection on any such forfeiture or disqualification.

(4) A protection order shall remain in force until the conclusion of the second licensing sessions begun after the date of the order (and until any application made at the sessions for a transfer of the justices' licence has been disposed of) except that it shall cease to have effect before that time on the coming into force of a justices' licence granted by way of transfer or removal of the licence for the premises, or the coming into force of a further protection order for the premises.

[(5) Where the holder of a justices' licence has died or has been adjudged bankrupt, or a [voluntary arrangement proposed by the holder of a justices' licence has been approved under Part VIII of the Insolvency Act 1986], or a trustee has been appointed under a deed of arrangement within the meaning of the Deeds of Arrangement Act 1914 for the benefit of the creditors of the holder of a justices' licence, the personal representatives or the person who is for the time being the trustee of the bankrupt's estate or under the deed or the supervisor of the [voluntary arrangement] shall be in the same position as regards carrying on business under the licence as a person to whom a protection order had been validly granted on the date of the death, or, as the case may be, the date on which he became trustee or supervisor.]

Amendment
Sub-s (2): words omitted repealed by the Finance Act 1967, ss 5(1)(a), 45(8), Sch 16, Part I.
Sub-s (3): in para (c) reference '169H(2)' in square brackets substituted by the Licensing (Young Persons) Act 2000, s 2(1).
Sub-s (5): substituted by the Insolvency Act 1985, s 235(1), Sch 8, para 12(3); words in square brackets substituted by the Insolvency Act 1986, s 439(2), Sch 14.

[A.14]

11   Supplementary provisions relating to protection orders   (1) A protection order may be made for any premises so as to supersede a previous protection order (other than one made under section 10(3) of this Act), if the justices making the order are satisfied that the person granted the previous protection order consents to its being superseded, or that he no longer proposes to apply for a transfer of the licence or is not qualified to do so, or that he is for any reason unable to carry on business under the protection order.

(2) Justices of the peace to whom application is made for a protection order may examine on oath the applicant or any person giving evidence before them.

(3) Justices of the peace shall not grant a protection order unless the applicant has, not less than seven days before the application, given notice in writing to the chief officer of police, signed by the applicant or his authorised agent, and stating his name and address and his trade or calling during the six months preceding the giving of the notice; or, in an urgent case, unless the applicant has given such notice to the police as the justices think reasonable.

(4) Justices of the peace granting a protection order shall cause a memorandum of the order to be endorsed on the licence, or, where a copy of the licence is admissible in evidence, on a copy of the licence; and a majority of the justices shall sign the memorandum or the justices shall cause the clerk to the justices to seal or stamp it with the official seal or stamp of the magistrates' court of which he is clerk and to verify the seal or stamp by his signature.

(5) A memorandum purporting to be made under subsection (4) of this section shall be received in evidence.

(6) ...

(7) The power of justices of the peace to grant protection orders shall be exercisable by the number of justices, and in the place, required by the [Magistrates' Courts Act 1980] for the hearing of a complaint.

Amendment
Sub-s (6): repealed by the Finance Act 1967, ss 5(1)(a), 45(8), Sch 16, Part I.
Sub-s (7): words in square brackets substituted by virtue of the Magistrates' Courts Act 1980, s 154, Sch 8, para 5.

Old on-licences

[A.15]

12 Restricted power of licensing justices to refuse renewal or transfer of old on-licences (1) In this Act—

'old on-licence' means a justices' on-licence, other than one for the sale of wine alone ... granted by way of renewal from time to time of a licence in force on 15th August 1904, or of a licence that before that day had been provisionally granted and confirmed under section 22 of the Licensing Act 1874 where the grant and confirmation have been subsequently declared final, except that it does not include a licence varied under section 37 of this Act or granted by way of renewal from time to time of a licence so varied; and

'old beerhouse licence' means an old on-licence for the sale of beer or cider, with or without wine, granted by way of renewal from time to time of a licence for premises for which a corresponding excise licence was in force on 1st May 1869;

no account being taken of any transfer nor, except for the purpose of determining whether a licence is an old beerhouse licence, of any removal.

(2) Subject to any disqualification of the applicant or of the premises to which the application relates, licensing justices shall not refuse an application for the renewal of an old on-licence except on one or more of the following grounds, that is to say—

(a)   in the case of an old beerhouse licence, those specified in subsection (3) of this section;

(b)   in the case of any other old on-licence, those specified in subsection (4) of this section;

and, in either case, the ground that there has been entered in the register of licences a conviction of bribery or treating made in pursuance of [section 168(7) of the Representation of the People Act 1983].

(3) The renewal of an old beerhouse licence may be refused on the ground—

(a)   that the applicant has failed to produce satisfactory evidence of good character; or

(b)   that the house or shop to which the application relates, or any adjacent house or shop owned or occupied by him, is of a disorderly character, or frequented by thieves, prostitutes or persons of bad character; or

(c)   that a licence previously held by the applicant for the sale of wine, spirits, beer or cider has been forfeited for his misconduct, or that he has previously been adjudged for his misconduct disqualified for receiving such a licence or for selling wine, spirits, beer or cider.

(4) The renewal of an old on-licence other than an old beerhouse licence may be refused on the ground—

(a)   that the applicant is not a fit and proper person to hold the licence; or

(b)   that the licensed premises have been ill-conducted or are structurally deficient or structurally unsuitable,

and for the purposes of paragraph (b) of this subsection, premises shall be deemed to have been ill-conducted if, among other things, the holder of the licence has persistently and unreasonably refused to supply suitable refreshment, other than intoxicating liquor, at a reasonable price, or has failed to fulfil any reasonable undertaking given to the justices on the grant of the licence.

(5) Where an application is made for the renewal of an old on-licence and the licensing justices ask the applicant to give an undertaking, they shall adjourn the hearing of the application and cause notice of the undertaking for which they ask to be served on the registered owner of the premises and shall give him an opportunity of being heard.

(6) Licensing justices refusing to renew an old on-licence shall specify to the applicant in writing the grounds of their refusal.

(7) Subsections (2) to (6) of this section shall apply to the transfer of an old on-licence as they apply to the renewal of such a licence, except that the transfer of an old beerhouse licence may also be refused on the ground that the applicant is not a fit and proper person to hold the licence.

Amendment
Sub-s (1): words omitted repealed by the Finance Act 1967, ss 5(1)(a), 45(8), Sch 16, Part I.
Sub-s (2): words in square brackets substituted by the Representation of the People Act 1983, s 206, Sch 8, para 7.

13–14 (*Repealed by the Licensing (Alcohol Education and Research) Act 1981.*)

15 (*Not reproduced*)

16–18 (*Repealed by the Licensing (Alcohol Education and Research) Act 1981.*)

Control of licensing justices over structure of licensed premises

[A.16]
19   Power to require structural alterations on renewal of on-licence
(1) On an application for the renewal of a justices' on-licence the licensing justices may require a plan of the premises to be produced to them and deposited with their [chief executive], and on renewing such a licence the licensing justices may order that, within a time fixed by the order, such structural alterations shall be made in the part of the premises where intoxicating liquor is sold or consumed as they think reasonably necessary to secure the proper conduct of the business.

(2) The [chief executive] to the licensing justices shall serve on the registered owner of the premises notice of any order made under this section.

(3) Where an order under this section is complied with, licensing justices shall not make a further order under this section within the five years following the first-mentioned order.

(4) If the holder of the licence makes default in complying with an order under this section he shall be guilty of an offence; and he shall be guilty of a further offence for every day on which the default continues after the expiration of the time fixed by the order.

(5) A person guilty of an offence under this section shall be liable to a fine not exceeding [level 1 on the standard scale].

(6) The preceding provisions of this section shall apply in relation to a transfer whereby the duration of the licence is extended as they apply in relation to a renewal.

Amendment
Sub-ss (1), (2): words 'chief executive' in square brackets substituted by the Access to Justice Act 1999, s 90(1), Sch 13, paras 36, 37(c).
Sub-s (5): maximum fine increased by the Criminal Law Act 1977, s 31(6), (9), and converted to a level on the standard scale by the Criminal Justice Act 1982, ss 37, 46.

[A.17]
20   Consent required for certain alterations to on-licensed premises
(1) No alteration shall be made to premises for which a justices' on-licence is in force if the alteration—
(a)   gives increased facilities for drinking in a public or common part of the premises; or
(b)   conceals from observation a public or common part of the premises used for drinking; or
(c)   affects the communication between the public part of the premises where intoxicating liquor is sold and the remainder of the premises or any street or other public way;

unless the licensing justices have consented to the alteration or the alteration is required by order of some lawful authority.

(2) Before considering an application for their consent under this section, the licensing justices may require plans of the proposed alteration to be deposited with their [chief executive] at such time as they may determine.

(3) If subsection (1) of this section is contravened, a magistrates' court may by order on complaint declare the licence to be forfeited or direct that within a time fixed by the order the premises shall be restored to their original condition.

(4) The [justices' chief executive for] the court that makes an order under subsection (3) of this section shall, if he is not the [chief executive to] the licensing justices, serve notice of the order on the [chief executive to] the licensing justices; and the [chief executive to] the licensing justices shall serve notice of the order on the registered owner of the premises.

(5) A person aggrieved by an order under subsection (3) of this section may appeal to [the Crown Court].

(6) In this section—

(a) 'public part' means a part open to customers who are not residents or guests of residents; and

(b) 'common part' means a part open generally to all residents or to a particular class of them.

Amendment
Sub-s (2): words 'chief executive' in square brackets substituted by the Access to Justice Act 1999, s 90(1), Sch 13, paras 36, 38(1), (2).
Sub-s (4): words 'justices' chief executive for' in square brackets substituted by the Access to Justice Act 1999, s 90(1), Sch 13, paras 36, 38(1), (3)(a); words 'chief executive to' in square brackets in each place they occur substituted by the Access to Justice Act 1999, s 90(1), Sch 13, paras 36, 38(1), (3)(b).
Sub-s (5): words in square brackets substituted by the Courts Act 1971, s 56, Sch 9, Part I.

[Revocation of justices' licences]

[A.18]

[20A Revocation   (1) Licensing justices may revoke a justices' licence at any licensing sessions, other than licensing sessions at which an application for renewal of the licence falls to be considered, either of their own motion or on the application of any person.

(2) The power to revoke a justices' licence under this section is exercisable on any ground on which licensing justices might refuse to renew a justices' licence or a justices' licence of that description.

(3) Licensing justices may only exercise the power conferred by this section if, at least twenty-one days before the commencement of the licensing sessions in question, notice in writing of the proposal to exercise the power or, as the case may be, to make the application has been given to the holder of the licence and, in the case of a proposed application, to the [chief executive] to the licensing justices, specifying in general terms the grounds on which it is proposed the licence should be revoked.

(4) Evidence given for the purposes of proceedings under this section shall be given on oath.

(5) A decision under this section to revoke a justices' licence shall not have effect—

(a)   until the expiry of the time for appealing against the decision; or

(b)   if the decision is appealed against, until the appeal is disposed of.]

Amendment
Inserted by the Licensing Act 1988, s 12(1).
Sub-s (3): words 'chief executive' in square brackets substituted by the Access to Justice Act 1999, s 90(1), Sch 13, paras 36, 39.

Appeals

[A.19]

21   Appeals   (1) Subject to subsection (2) of this section, any person aggrieved by any of the following decisions of licensing justices, that is to say—
(a)   a decision granting or refusing to grant a new justices' licence or an ordinary removal of a justices' licence;
(b)   a decision refusing the renewal, transfer or special removal of a justices' licence;
(c)   a refusal to declare a provisional grant final or to affirm a provisional grant or to give consent, on the application of the holder of a provisional licence, to a modification of plans;
(d)   the making of an order under section 19 of this Act;
(e)   the refusal of a consent required under section 20 of this Act; . . .
[(ee) the revocation of a justices' licence; or]
(f)   any decision as to the conditions of a justices' on-licence;
may appeal to [the Crown Court] against that decision.

(2) A person may not appeal against the grant of a justices' licence unless he has appeared before the licensing justices and opposed the grant; and no person may appeal against a refusal to attach conditions to a licence or to vary or revoke conditions previously attached, except the person (if any) whose application or request is required for the justices to have jurisdiction to attach or to vary or revoke the conditions.

(3) ...

[(4) Where the holder of a justices' licence gives notice of appeal against a refusal by the licensing justices to renew that licence [or a decision by the licensing justices to revoke it], the licensing justices or the [Crown Court] having jurisdiction to hear the appeal may, on such conditions as they think fit, order that the licence shall continue in force until the determination of the appeal notwithstanding that the appeal is not determined until after the date when the licence would otherwise cease to have effect.]

Amendment
Sub-s (1): word omitted from para (e) repealed, and para (ee) substituted, by the Licensing Act 1988, s 19, Sch 3, para 3(a); final words in square brackets substituted by the Courts Act 1971, s 56, Sch 9, Part I.
Sub-s (3): repealed by the Courts Act 1971, s 56(4), Sch 11, Part IV.
Sub-s (4): inserted by the Finance Act 1967, s 5(1)(c), Sch 7, para 3; first words in square brackets inserted by the Licensing Act 1988, s 19, Sch 3, para 3(b); second words in square brackets substituted by the Courts Act 1971, s 56, Sch 9, Part I.

[A.20]

22 Procedural provisions as to appeals (1) An appeal under section 21 of this Act shall be commenced by notice of appeal given by the appellant to the [chief executive] to the licensing justices within [twenty-one days] after the decision appealed against.

(2) On an appeal against the grant of a justices' licence the applicant for the licence and not the licensing justices shall be respondent, and notice of appeal must be given to him as well as to the [chief executive] to the licensing justices.

(3) On an appeal against a refusal to grant a justices' licence, or against, a decision as to conditions given on the grant of a justices' licence, any person who appeared before the licensing justices and opposed the grant shall be respondent in addition to the licensing justices; ...

[(3A) On an appeal against a decision to revoke a justices' licence, any person on whose application the licence was revoked shall be respondent in addition to the licensing justices.]

(4) On any appeal under section 21 of this Act the [chief executive to] the licensing justices shall transmit the notice of appeal to [the appropriate officer of the Crown Court], and the appeal shall be entered and notice thereof given to [the appropriate officer of the Crown Court] ...; and [section 109(1) of the Magistrates' Courts Act 1980] shall apply accordingly with respect to the abandonment of the appeal.

(5) Where a person appears before licensing justices and opposes the grant of a justices' licence, his name and address shall be recorded by the [chief executive] to the licensing justices and, in the event of an appeal against a refusal of the grant or against a decision as to conditions given on the grant, shall be transmitted to [the appropriate officer of the Crown Court] with the notice of appeal.

(6) Where the same application to licensing justices gives rise to more than one appeal to [the Crown Court], [the Crown Court] may give such directions as they think fit for the appeals to be heard together or separately, and where two or more appeals are heard together, [the Crown Court] may deal with the costs of the appeals, so far as those costs are in their discretion, as if they were a single appeal.

(7) A justice shall not act in the hearing or determination of an appeal under section 21 of this Act from any decision in which he took part.

Amendment
Sub-s (1): words 'chief executive' in square brackets substituted by the Access to Justice Act 1999, s 90(1), Sch 13, paras 36, 40(1), (2); words 'twenty-one days' in square brackets substituted by SI 1982/1109, r 6(2), Sch 3, Pt II, para 3.
Sub-s (2): words 'chief executive' in square brackets substituted by the Access to Justice Act 1999, s 90(1), Sch 13, paras 36, 40(1), (2).

Sub-s (3): words omitted repealed by SI 1971/1292, r 24, Sch 3.

Sub-s (3A): inserted by the Licensing Act 1988, s 19, Sch 3, para 4.

Sub-s (4): words 'chief executive to' in square brackets substituted by the Access to Justice Act 1999, s 90(1), Sch 13, paras 36, 40(1), (3); words 'the appropriate officer of the Crown Court' in square brackets in both places they occur substituted by the Courts Act 1971, s 56(1), Sch 8, Pt I, para 2; words omitted repealed by the Access to Justice Act 1999, s 106, Sch 15, Pt V, Table (7); words 'section 109(1) of the Magistrates' Courts Act 1980' in square brackets substituted by the Magistrates' Courts Act 1980, s 154, Sch 7, para 45.

Sub-s (5): words 'chief executive' in square brackets substituted by the Access to Justice Act 1999, s 90(1), Sch 13, paras 36, 40(1), (4); words 'the appropriate officer of the Crown Court' in square brackets substituted by the Courts Act 1971, s 56, Sch 8, Pt I, para 2.

Sub-s (6): words 'the Crown Court' in square brackets in each place they occur substituted by the Courts Act 1971, s 56, Sch 9, Pt I.

[A.21]

23   Powers of [the Crown Court] on appeals   (1), (2) …

(3) The judgment of [the Crown Court] on any such appeal shall be final.

[(4) Where the Crown Court allows an appeal against the revocation of a justices' licence which has been continued in force under section 21(4) of this Act, it may order that the licence shall further continue in force until the date of the next licensing sessions for the district in which the licence is granted.]

Amendment

Section heading: words in square brackets substituted by the Courts Act 1971, s 56, Sch 9, Part I.

Sub-ss (1), (2): repealed by the Courts Act 1971, s 56, Sch 11, Part IV.

Sub-s (3): words in square brackets substituted by the Courts Act 1971, s 56, Sch 9, Part I.

Sub-s (4): inserted by the Licensing Act 1988, s 19, Sch 3, para 5.

24 (*Repealed by SI 1971/1292.*)

[A.22]

25   Award of costs of licensing justices out of local funds (1) Where—

(a)   an appeal under section 21 of this Act, other than an appeal against the grant of a justices' licence, is allowed, or

(b)   [the Crown Court] have, … , awarded costs against the appellant and are satisfied that the licensing justices cannot recover those costs from him,

the court shall order payment out of [central funds] of such sums as appear to the court sufficient to indemnify the licensing justices from all costs and charges whatever to which they have been put in consequence of the appellant's notice of appeal.

(2)–(4) …

Amendment

Sub-s (1): words omitted repealed by SI 1971/1292, r 24, Sch 3; words in square brackets substituted by the Courts Act 1971, ss 51(2), 56(2), Sch 6, para 7, Sch 9, Part I.

Sub-ss (2)–(4): repealed by the Courts Act 1971, s 56(4), Sch 11, Part III.

Duration of licences

[A.23]

26   Duration of licences   (1) Subject to the following provisions of this section and to sections 27, 133(3) and 142(3) of this Act, a justices' licence—

[(a) if granted before 5th January 1989, shall be granted to have effect from the time of the grant until 4th April 1989;

(b) if granted after 4th January and before 5th April 1989, shall be granted to have effect from the time of the grant until 4th April 1992; and

(c) if granted after 4th April 1989, shall be granted to have effect from the time of the grant until the expiry of the current licensing period or, if granted in the last three months of that period, until the end of the next licensing period;

but shall be superseded on the coming into force of a licence granted by way of renewal, transfer or removal of it].

(2) A justices' licence granted by way of transfer or removal may be granted to have effect from a time specified in the grant (not being earlier, where it is granted before the coming into force of the licence transferred or removed, than the time of the coming into force of that licence).

(3) In the case of a licence granted provisionally, subsection (1) of this section shall apply as if the licence were granted at the time when it is declared final, but a transfer of such a licence may be granted so as to have effect for the purpose of superseding that licence from a date before it is declared final, and, if so granted, shall as regards its duration and coming into force be subject to the same provisions as it if were the licence transferred.

(4) Where on the renewal or transfer of a licence the licensing justices attach new conditions (whether in addition to or in substitution for any conditions previously attached) the justices may, on such terms as they think just, suspend the operation of those conditions in whole or in part pending the determination of any appeal against the decision to attach them or pending the consideration of the question of bringing such an appeal.

[(5) In this Act 'licensing period' means a period of three years beginning with 5th April 1989 or any triennial of that date.]

Amendment
Sub-s (1): words in square brackets substituted by the Licensing Act 1988, s 11(1).
Sub-s (5): substituted by the Licensing Act 1988, s 11(1).

[A.24]

27   Effect on duration of opposition to grant of licence   (1) The provisions of this section shall have effect where on an application to licensing justices for the grant of a new justices' licence, or for the grant of a licence by way of ordinary removal of a justices' licence, a person appears before the licensing justices and opposes the grant, but the justices grant the licence.

(2) Until the expiry of the time for bringing an appeal against the grant and, if such an appeal is brought, until the appeal has been disposed of,—
(a) the licence granted shall not come into force;
(b) where the grant is by way of ordinary removal and the licence which it is sought to remove is in force at the time of the grant, the licence shall not expire unless the licensing justices otherwise direct.

(3) If on appeal the grant is confirmed or if the appeal is abandoned, the time when the appeal is disposed of shall be substituted for the time of the grant for the purpose of determining the period for which the licence is to have effect and [the Crown Court] shall (if need be) amend the licence accordingly.

(4) If there is an appeal against the grant of an ordinary removal, and the licence which it is sought to remove is in force on the day when notice of appeal is given to the applicant for the removal, then—
(a) he may within seven days of that day give notice in writing to [the appropriate officer of the Crown Court] of his desire that the expiry of that licence shall be postponed for a specified period (not exceeding three weeks) after the appeal is disposed of, and if he does so, subsection (2) of this section shall apply until the expiry of that period;
(b) whether or not he gives such a notice, [the Crown Court], if they confirm the grant and if he so requests, may by their order direct that that subsection shall continue to apply for such further period as they think fit;
(c) if [the Crown Court] refuse to confirm the grant, and at the time of their decision it is too late to renew that licence at the general annual licensing meeting at which it was due for renewal, then—
    (i)   the holder of the licence shall be treated as having had reasonable cause for not applying for renewal at that meeting, and the licence may be renewed at transfer sessions accordingly; and
    (ii) if notice has been given under paragraph (a) of this subsection, and within the period for which the licence is continued in force by that paragraph notice is given to the [chief executive] to the licensing justices of an application for the renewal of the licence at the first licensing sessions held not less than twenty-one days after the notice is given, the licence shall not expire until the application is disposed of or those sessions end without its being made.

Amendment
Sub-ss (3), (4): words 'the Crown Court' in square brackets in each place they occur substituted by the Courts Act 1971, s 56, Sch 9, Pt I.
Sub-s (4): in para (a) words 'the appropriate officer of the Crown Court' in square brackets substituted by the Courts Act 1971, s 56, Sch 8, Pt I, para 2; in para (c)(ii) words 'chief executive' in square brackets substituted by the Access to Justice Act 1999, s 90(1), Sch 13, paras 36, 41.

28–31 (*Not reproduced*)

[A.25]

32   Registration of owner, etc   (1) Every person applying for a new justices' licence, or the renewal of a justices' licence, shall state the name of the person for the time being entitled to receive, either on his own account or as mortgagee or other incumbrancer in possession, the rack-rent of the premises for which the licence is granted; and the [chief executive] to the licensing justices shall enter that name in the register of licences as the name of an owner of the premises, and endorse the name on the licence.

(2) The [chief executive] to the licensing justices shall also, on the application of any person whose name is not entered under the preceding subsection, and who has an estate or interest in the premises, whether as owner, lessee or mortgagee, prior or paramount to that of the occupier, enter that person's name in the register of licences as an owner of the premises.

Where any such estate or interest is vested in two or more persons jointly, one only of those persons shall be registered as representing that estate or interest.

(3) Any reference in this Act to the registered owner of premises shall be construed as a reference to any person whose name is for the time being entered in the register of licences under this section.

Amendment
Sub-ss (1), (2): words 'chief executive' in square brackets substituted by the Access to Justice Act 1999, s 90(1), Sch 13, paras 36, 45.

33 (*Not reproduced*)

[A.26]

34   Inspection of register   (1) The following persons shall be entitled at any reasonable time to inspect the register of licences for a licensing district on payment of the fee chargeable, that is to say—
(a)   any person rated in respect of a hereditament in the district;
(b)   any owner of licensed premises situated in the district;
(c)   any holder of a justices' licence granted in the district.

(2) Any constable or any officer of Customs and Excise shall, without payment, be entitled at any reasonable time to inspect the register of licences.

(3) If the [chief executive] to the licensing justices or any other person refuses inspection of the register of licences under this section or obstructs any person attempting to inspect the register under this section or receives or demands any unauthorised charge for permitting the register to be inspected under this section, he shall be liable to a fine not exceeding [level 1 on the standard scale].

Amendment
Sub-s (3): words 'chief executive' in square brackets substituted by the Access to Justice Act 1999, s 90(1), Sch 13, paras 36, 47; maximum fine increased by the Criminal Law Act 1977, s 31(6), (9), and converted to a level on the standard scale by the Criminal Justice Act 1982, ss 37, 46.

35–37 (*Not reproduced*)

38 (*Repealed by the Licensing (Alcohol Education and Research) Act 1981.*)

PART II SALE AND SUPPLY OF INTOXICATING LIQUOR IN CLUB PREMISES
Conditions for supply of intoxicating liquor by clubs

[A.27]

39   Conditions for supply of intoxicating liquor by clubs   (1) No intoxicating liquor shall on any club premises be supplied by or on behalf of the club to a member or guest, unless the club is registered under this Act in respect of those premises or the liquor is supplied under the authority of a justices' licence held by the club for the premises.

(2) No intoxicating liquor shall, on any premises in respect of which a club is registered, be supplied by or on behalf of the club for consumption off the premises except to a member in person.

(3) Intoxicating liquor shall not be supplied by or on behalf of a registered club to a member or guest except at premises in respect of which the club is registered or at any premises or place which the club is using on a special occasion for the accommodation of members and to which persons other than members and their guests are not permitted access; and at any premises or place other than premises in respect of which the club is registered intoxicating liquor shall be so supplied only for consumption in the premises or place.

(4) A person supplying or authorising the supply of intoxicating liquor in contravention of subsection (1) of this section shall be liable to imprisonment for a term not exceeding six months, or to a fine not exceeding [level 4 on the standard scale], or to both; and a person supplying or obtaining intoxicating liquor in contravention of subsection (2) or subsection (3) of this section shall be liable to a fine not exceeding [level 1 on the standard scale].

(5) If intoxicating liquor is kept in any premises or place by or on behalf of a club for supply to members or their guests in contravention of this section, every officer of the club shall be liable to a fine not exceeding [level 1 on the standard scale], unless he shows that it was so kept without his knowledge or consent.

(6) In this Act 'club premises' means premises which are occupied by and habitually used for the purposes of a club.

Amendment
Sub-s (4): first-mentioned maximum fine increased and converted to a level on the standard scale by the Criminal Justice Act 1982, ss 37, 38, 46; second-mentioned maximum fine increased by the Criminal Law Act 1977, s 31(6), (9), and converted to a level on the standard scale by the Criminal Justice Act 1982, ss 37, 46.
Sub-s (5): maximum fine increased and converted to a level on the standard scale by the Criminal Justice Act 1982, ss 37, 38, 46.

Registered clubs

[A.28]
40 Registration of clubs (1) A club is registered, within the meaning of this Act, in respect of any premises if and so long as it holds for those premises a certificate under this Part of this Act of a magistrates' court (in this Act referred to as a registration certificate).

(2) Subject to the provisions of this section and of section 50(4) of this Act, a registration certificate shall have effect for twelve months, but may be from time to time renewed, and may at any time be surrendered by the club.

(3) Any renewal of a registration certificate shall be for one year from the expiry of the period for which the certificate was issued or last renewed, except that on the second or any subsequent renewal the certificate may, if the court thinks fit, be renewed for such number of years, not exceeding ten, from the expiry of that period as may be requested in the application for renewal or for any less number of years.

(4) An application by a club for the issue or renewal of a registration certificate shall be made to a magistrates' court and shall comply with the requirements of Schedule 5 to this Act; and the provisions of Schedule

6 to this Act shall have effect as regards the procedure for registration and related matters.

(5) Where an application for the renewal of a registration certificate is made not less than twenty-eight days before the certificate is due to expire, the certificate shall continue in force until the application is disposed of by the magistrates' court or the court otherwise orders under paragraph 10 of Schedule 6 to this Act.

(6) Where an application is duly made in accordance with this Part of this Act for the issue or renewal of a registration certificate, the magistrates' court shall not, in the absence of an objection duly made in accordance with this Part of this Act, refuse the application except as provided by the following provisions of this Part of this Act; and a magistrates' court shall state in writing the grounds of any refusal to issue or renew a registration certificate.

[A.29]

41   Qualifications for registration   (1) A club shall only be qualified to receive a registration certificate (whether in the first instance or by way of renewal), if under the rules of the club—

(a)   persons may not be admitted to membership or be admitted as candidates for membership to any of the privileges of membership, without an interval of at least two days between their nomination or application for membership and their admission; and

(b)   persons becoming members without prior nomination or application may not be admitted to the privileges of membership without an interval of at least two days between their becoming members and their admission.

(2) A club shall be qualified to receive a registration certificate for any premises (whether in the first instance or by way of renewal), only if—

(a)   it is established and conducted in good faith as a club and has not less than twenty-five members; and

(b)   intoxicating liquor is not supplied, or intended to be supplied, to members on the premises otherwise than by or on behalf of the club; and

(c)   the purchase for the club, and the supply by the club of intoxicating liquor (so far as not managed by the club in general meeting or otherwise by the general body of members) is managed by an elective committee, as defined in Schedule 7 to this Act; and

(d)   no arrangements are or are intended to be made—

(i)   for any person to receive at the expense of the club any commission, percentage or similar payment on or with reference to purchases of intoxicating liquor by the club; or

(ii) for any person directly or indirectly to derive any pecuniary benefit from the supply of intoxicating liquor by or on behalf of the club to members or guests, apart from any benefit accruing to the club as a whole and apart also from any benefit which a person derives indirectly by reason of the supply giving rise or contributing to a general gain from the carrying on of the club.

(3) Subject to subsection (4) of this section, in determining whether a club is established and conducted in good faith as a club a magistrates' court may have regard—

(a) to any arrangement restricting the club's freedom of purchase of intoxicating liquor; and

(b) to any provision in the rules, or arrangement, under which money or property of the club, or any gain arising from the carrying on of the club, is or may be applied otherwise than for the benefit of the club as a whole or for charitable, benevolent or political purposes; and

(c) to the arrangements for giving members proper information as to the finances of the club, and to the books of account and other records kept to ensure the accuracy of that information; and

(d) to the nature of the premises occupied by the club.

(4) Subject to section 49(2) of this Act, where the rules of a club applying for the issue or renewal of a registration certificate conform with Schedule 7 to this Act, the court shall assume, as regards any matters not raised by an objection duly made in accordance with this Part of this Act, that the club satisfies the conditions of paragraphs (a) to (c) of subsection (2) of this section and, in the case of a renewal, also the conditions of paragraph (d) of that subsection, except that the court may, if it sees fit, inquire whether there is any such arrangement or provision in the rules as is referred to in paragraph (a) or (b) of subsection (3) of this section, and, if so, whether it is such that the club ought not to be treated as established and conducted in good faith as a club.

[A.30]

42 Modification of registration qualifications for certain clubs (1) In the case of a club which is a registered society within the meaning of the Industrial and Provident Societies Act 1893 or the Friendly Societies Act 1896—

(a) any requirement of paragraph (c) of subsection (2) of section 41 of this Act that a matter shall be managed by an elective committee shall be treated as satisfied so long as the matter is under the control of the members or of a committee appointed by the members (and references in this Act to that subsection shall be taken as referring to it as modified by this paragraph); and

(b) the rules of the club shall be treated as conforming with Schedule 7 to this Act so long as they conform with that Schedule as regards voting at general meetings and as regards election or admission to membership.

(2) Where the rules of a club make provision for a class of members to have limited rights or no rights of voting in relation to the affairs of the club, any question whether the requirements of the said paragraph (c) are satisfied in relation to the club, or whether the rules of the club conform with Schedule 7 to this Act shall, if the court determining the question so directs, be determined as if the exclusion of that class from voting to the extent provided for by the rules were authorised by the provisions of that Schedule as to voting at general meetings or elections; but the court shall not so direct unless satisfied that the provision so made by the rules is part of a bona fide arrangement made in the interests of the club as a whole and of that class of members for facilitating the membership of persons who are precluded by distance or other circumstances from making full use of the privileges of membership, and is not designed to secure for a minority of the members an unfair measure of control over the affairs of the club.

[A.31]

43 Disqualification for and refusal of registration certificate (1) A registration certificate shall not be issued or renewed, nor have effect, for premises disqualified by an order under section 47 of this Act for use for the purposes of a registered club, nor for licensed premises, nor for premises which include or form part of premises so disqualified or licensed premises; but this subsection does not prevent the issue or renewal for any premises of a registration certificate to take effect on their ceasing to be, include or form part of premises so disqualified or licensed premises.

(2) A magistrates' court may refuse an application for the issue or renewal of a registration certificate, if it is proved that a person who, if a certificate is granted, will or is likely to take any active part in the management of the club during the currency of the certificate, is not a fit person, in view of his known character as proved to the court, to be concerned in the management of a registered club.

(3) A magistrates' court may refuse an application for the issue or renewal of a registration certificate—

(a) if the premises or any premises including or forming part of them have been licensed premises within the twelve months preceding the making of the application but have ceased to be licensed premises by the forfeiture [or revocation] of the licence or by the refusal of an application to renew it; or

(b) if the club has other club premises which are licensed premises and the court is of opinion that the issue or renewal of the registration certificate is likely to give occasion for abuse by reason of any difference in the permitted hours in the premises or otherwise.

Amendment
Sub-s (3): words in square brackets inserted by the Licensing Act 1988, s 19, Sch 3, para 6.

[A.32]

44 Objections to and cancellation of registration certificate (1) Objection to an application for the issue or renewal of a registration certificate for any premises may be made by the chief officer of police, by the local authority or by any person affected by reason of his occupation or interest in other premises, and may be made on any one or more of the following grounds, that is to say—

(a) that the application does not give the information required by this Part of this Act, or the information is incomplete or inaccurate, or the application is otherwise not in conformity with this Part of this Act;

(b) that the premises are not suitable and convenient for the purpose in view of their character and condition and of the size and nature of the club;

(c) that the club does not satisfy the conditions of subsections (1) and (2) of section 41 of this Act, or that the application must or ought to be refused under section 43 of this Act;

(d) that the club is conducted in a disorderly manner or for an unlawful purpose, or that the rules of the club are habitually disregarded as respects the admission of persons to membership or to the privileges of membership or in any other material respect;

(e) that the club premises or any of them (including premises in respect of which the club is not registered or seeking registration) are habitually used for an unlawful purpose, or for indecent displays, or as a resort of criminals or prostitutes, or that in any such premises there is frequent drunkenness, or there have within the preceding twelve months been illegal sales of intoxicating liquor, or persons not qualified to be supplied with intoxicating liquor there are habitually admitted for the purpose of obtaining it;

and the court, if satisfied that the ground of objection is made out, may refuse the application and, in the case of an objection made on any of the grounds mentioned in paragraphs (a) to (c) of this subsection, shall do so unless in the case of an objection made on the ground mentioned in paragraph (b) the court thinks it reasonable not to, having regard to any steps taken or proposed to be taken to remove the ground of objection.

(2) A complaint against a club for the cancellation of a registration certificate held by the club for any premises may be made in writing to a magistrates' court by the chief officer of police or by the local authority, and may be made on any ground on which objection might be made under paragraph (c), (d) or (e) of the preceding subsection to an application for the renewal of the certificate; and the court, if satisfied that on such an objection the application for renewal must or ought to be refused on that ground, shall cancel the certificate.

[A.33]

45   Inspection of premises before first registration   (1) Where a club applies for the issue of a registration certificate in respect of any premises, an officer of the local authority authorised in writing by that authority may, on giving not less than forty-eight hours' notice to the person signing the application and, if the premises are not occupied by the club, to the occupier, and on production of his authority, enter and inspect the premises at any reasonable time on such day, not more than fourteen days after the making of the application, as may be specified in the notice; and a constable authorised in writing by the chief officer of police shall have the like right to enter and inspect the premises, but a chief officer of police shall not so authorise a constable unless in his opinion special reasons exist making it necessary that the premises should be inspected for the proper discharge of his functions in relation to the registration of clubs.

(2) Any person obstructing a constable or officer of a local authority in the exercise of the power conferred by this section shall be liable to a fine not exceeding [level 1 on the standard scale].

(3) If on an application by the chief officer of police or by the local authority it is made to appear to a magistrates' court that, after reasonable steps had been taken by and on behalf of the applicant to inspect the premises in good time under subsection (1) of this section, it was not possible to do so within the time allowed, the court may extend the time allowed.

(4) Where a club applies for the renewal of a registration certificate in respect of different, additional or enlarged premises, the foregoing subsections shall have effect as if the application were, so far as relates to those premises, an application for the issue of a registration certificate.

Amendment
Sub-s (2): maximum fine increased and converted to a level on the standard scale by the Criminal Justice Act 1982, ss 37, 38, 46.

[A.34]

46 Rights of fire authorities in connection with registration of clubs (1) As regards any matter affecting fire risks the local authority, if they are the fire authority, shall have the like rights in relation to the inspection of premises under section 45 of this Act on any application for the renewal of a registration certificate for the premises as they have in the case of an application for the issue of a certificate.

(2) Where the local authority is not the fire authority, the [chief executive] to the justices shall as soon as may be give the fire authority written notice of the making of an application for the issue or renewal of a registration certificate for any premises.

(3) As regards any matter affecting fire risks a fire authority other than the local authority shall have the like rights—

(a) in relation to the inspection of premises under section 45 of this Act, and

(b) in relation to the making of objections, on the ground mentioned in paragraph (b) of section 44(1) of this Act, to the issue or renewal of a registration certificate,

as the authority would have if they were the local authority.

(4) In this section 'fire authority' means, in relation to any premises, the authority discharging in the area where the premises are situated the functions of fire authority under the Fire Services Act 1947.

Amendment
Sub-s (2): words 'chief executive' in square brackets substituted by the Access to Justice Act 1999, s 90(1), Sch 13, paras 36, 48.

[A.35]

47 Power to order disqualification of premises (1) Subject to the following provisions of this section, where a club is registered in respect of any premises, and a magistrates' court cancels or refuses to renew the registration certificate for those premises on any ground mentioned in paragraph (c), (d) or (e) of section 44(1) of this Act, the court may order that, for a period specified in the order, the premises shall not be occupied and used for the purposes of any registered club.

(2) The period specified in an order under this section shall not exceed one year unless the premises have been subject to a previous order under this section or to a similar order under any previous enactment about clubs, and shall not in any case exceed five years.

(3) At any time while an order under this section is in force, a magistrates' court, on complaint made by any person affected by the order, may revoke the order or vary it by reducing the period of disqualification specified in it.

(4) Any summons granted on a complaint under subsection (3) of this section for the revocation or variation of an order as respects any premises shall be served on the chief officer of police and on the local authority.

(5) The foregoing provisions of this section do not apply where the premises in respect of which the club is registered are situated in the city of Oxford and the club is mainly composed of past or present members of the University of Oxford.

[A.36]

48   Notification of alteration in rules of registered club   (1) Where any alteration is made in the rules of a club registered in respect of any premises, the secretary of the club shall give written notice of the alteration to the chief officer of police and to the clerk of the local authority.

(2) If the notice required by this section is not given within twenty-eight days of the alteration, the secretary shall be liable to a fine not exceeding [level 1 on the standard scale].

(3) Notwithstanding anything in [section 127(1) of the Magistrates' Courts Act 1980], proceedings under this section for failing to give notice of an alteration of rules may be brought at any time within the twelve months following the date on which the alteration is made.

Amendment
Sub-s (2): maximum fine increased and converted to a level on the standard scale by the Criminal Justice Act 1982, ss 37, 38, 46.
Sub-s (3): words in square brackets substituted by the Magistrates' Courts Act 1980, s 154, Sch 7, para 47.

[A.37]

49   Sale of intoxicating liquor by registered clubs   (1) Notwithstanding anything in any enactment, where a club is registered in respect of any premises, and the rules of the club provide for the admission to the premises of persons other than members and their guests and for the sale of intoxicating liquor to them by or on behalf of the club for consumption on the premises, then subject to the following provisions of this section the authority of a licence shall not be required for such a sale, and intoxicating liquor may be supplied to those persons and their guests for consumption on the premises as it may to members and their guests.

(2) In determining for the purposes of this Part of this Act whether a club is established and conducted in good faith as a club, a magistrates' court may, notwithstanding anything in subsection (4) of section 41 of this Act, have regard to any provision made by the rules for the sale of intoxicating liquor by or on behalf of the club, and to the use made or intended to be made of any such provision; and paragraphs (c) and (d)(ii) of subsection

(2) of that section shall apply in relation to the sale of intoxicating liquor by or on behalf of a club as they apply in relation to its supply to members of the club.

(3) Subject to subsection (4) of this section, a magistrates' court, on the issue or renewal of a registration certificate for any premises, may attach to the certificate such conditions restricting sales of intoxicating liquor on those premises as the court thinks reasonable (including conditions forbidding or restricting any alteration of the rules of the club so as to authorise sales not authorised at the time of the application to the court), and subsection (1) of this section shall not authorise a sale in breach of any such condition.

(4) No condition shall be attached to a registration certificate under subsection (3) of this section so as to prevent the sale of intoxicating liquor to a person admitted to the premises as being a member of another club, if—

(a)   the other club is registered in respect of premises in the locality which are temporarily closed; or

(b)   both clubs exist for learned, educational or political objects of a similar nature; or

(c)   each of the clubs is primarily a club for persons who are qualified by service or past service, or by any particular service or past service, in Her Majesty's forces and are members of an organisation established by Royal Charter and consisting wholly or mainly of such persons; or

(d)   each of the clubs is a working men's club (that is to say, a club which is, as regards its purposes, qualified for registration as a working men's club under the Friendly Societies Act 1896 and is a registered society within the meaning of that Act or of the Industrial and Provident Societies Act 1893).

(5) A registration certificate may, at the time of its renewal, or on the application of the club, or on complaint in writing made against the club by the chief officer of police or the local authority, be varied by imposing, varying or revoking any conditions authorised by subsection (3) of this section.

(6) At the hearing of an application for the issue or renewal of a registration certificate, or of an application by a club under subsection (5) of this section, the chief officer of police or the local authority shall be entitled, on giving written notice of intention to do so, to make representations as to the conditions which ought to be attached to the certificate under this section.

(7) Where the rules of a club registered in respect of any premises are altered so as to authorise at those premises sales of intoxicating liquor

not authorised by the rules at the time of the application or last application by the club for the issue or renewal of a registration certificate for those premises, the alteration shall not be effective for the purposes of subsection (1) of this section until notice of it has been given in accordance with section 48 of this Act.

[A.38]

50 Appeal to [the Crown Court] (1) A club may appeal to [the Crown Court] against any decision of a magistrates' court refusing to issue or renew a registration certificate, or cancelling a registration certificate, or against any decision of a magistrates' court as to the conditions of a registration certificate relating to sales of intoxicating liquor, or against any order of a magistrates' court under section 47 of this Act.

(2) Where the decision appealed against relates to two or more premises, the appeal may be brought in respect of any of those premises without the others.

(3) Where the decision appealed against was given on an application to the magistrates' court by the club, no person shall be made a party to the appeal except a person who appeared before the magistrates' court to make an objection to or representations on the application, but any such person shall be a party to the appeal, whether or not his objection related to the same premises as the appeal.

(4) Where a magistrates' court refuses an application for the renewal of a registration certificate, the court may, on such conditions as it thinks fit, order that the certificate (as in force at the time of the application) shall continue in force pending the determination of an appeal against the refusal, or pending the consideration of the question of bringing such an appeal.

Amendment
Section heading: words in square brackets substituted by the Courts Act 1971, s 56, Sch 9, Part I.
Sub-s (1): words in square brackets substituted by the Courts Act 1971, s 56, Sch 9, Part I.

[A.39]

51 Register of clubs (1) The [chief executive] to the justices for any petty sessions area shall keep a register of clubs holding registration certificates for premises in the area.

(2) The register shall show for the premises in respect of which a club is registered the hours [on Christmas Day], if any, fixed as the permitted hours by or under the rules of the club (as notified to the [chief executive] of the justices), and shall contain such other particulars, and shall be in such form, as may be prescribed by regulations of the Secretary of State.

Any regulations under this subsection shall be made by statutory instrument, which shall be subject to annulment in pursuance of a resolution of either House of Parliament.

(3) The register shall at all reasonable times be open to inspection on payment of the appropriate fee (if any) by any person, and without payment by any officer of police, by any officer of Customs and Excise, or by any officer of the local authority who is authorised in writing to inspect it on their behalf.

(4) Written notice, signed by the chairman or secretary of the club, shall be given to the [chief executive] to the justices of any change in the particulars of the club which are contained or required to be contained in the register by virtue of regulations under this section; and if the notice required by this subsection is not given within forty-two days of the change, the chairman and secretary shall each be liable to a fine not exceeding [level 3 on the standard scale].

Amendment

Sub-s (1): words 'chief executive' in square brackets substituted by the Access to Justice Act 1999, s 90(1), Sch 13, paras 36, 49(1), (2).

Sub-s (2): words 'on Christmas Day' in square brackets (originally inserted by the Licensing Act 1988, s 1, Sch 1, para 1) substituted by the Licensing (Sunday Hours) Act 1995, s 4(1), Sch 1, para 2; words 'chief executive' in square brackets substituted by the Access to Justice Act 1999, s 90(1), Sch 13, paras 36, 49(1), (3).

Sub-s (4): words 'chief executive' in square brackets substituted by the Access to Justice Act 1999, s 90(1), Sch 13, paras 36, 49(1), (4); maximum fine increased and converted to a level on the standard scale by the Criminal Justice Act 1982, ss 37, 38, 46.

[A.40]

52   Provisions as to different premises of same club   (1) A single registration certificate may relate to any number of premises of the same club, and on an application duly made a registration certificate may, at the time of renewal or otherwise, be varied as regards the premises to which it relates.

(2) Where a variation of a registration certificate would result in the club being registered in respect of different, additional or enlarged premises, and is to be made otherwise than at the time of renewal, the provisions of this Act shall apply as they apply in the case of a renewal, except that the variation shall not extend the duration of the certificate.

(3) Where a club seeks or holds a registration certificate for two or more premises not contiguous to one another, the court on an objection to the issue or renewal of the certificate or complaint for its cancellation may refuse to issue or renew it or may cancel it for some only of the premises, if the ground of objection or complaint relates only to those premises or is only made out for those premises, and the court is of opinion that it is

in the circumstances reasonable for the club to be or remain registered in respect of the other premises.

(4) No order shall be made under section 47 of this Act in relation to any premises unless the ground of objection or complaint relates to and is made out for those premises or contiguous premises.

53–58 (*Not reproduced*)

PART III PERMITTED HOURS

Prohibition of sale, etc of intoxicating liquor outside permitted hours

[A.41]

59   Prohibition of sale, etc of intoxicating liquor outside permitted hours   (1) Subject to the provisions of this Act, no person shall, except during the permitted hours—

(a)   himself or by his servant or agent sell or supply to any person in licensed premises or in premises in respect of which a club is registered any intoxicating liquor, whether to be consumed on or off the premises; or

(b)   consume in or take from such premises any intoxicating liquor.

(2) If any person contravenes this section he shall be liable to a fine not exceeding [level 3 on the standard scale].

(3) This section does not apply in relation to intoxicating liquor sold under an occasional licence.

Amendment
Sub-s (2): maximum fine increased and converted to a level on the standard scale by the Criminal Justice Act 1982, ss 37, 38, 46.

General provisions as to permitted hours

[A.42]

60   Permitted hours in licensed premises   (1) Subject to the following provisions of this Part of this Act [and the Regulatory Reform (Special Occasions Licensing) Order 2001], the permitted hours in licensed premises shall be—

(a)   on weekdays, other than Christmas Day[, Good Friday or New Year's Eve, or 3rd June 2002], the hours from eleven in the morning to [eleven] in the evening, …; and

[(b)   on Sundays, other than Christmas Day [or New Year's Eve], and on Good Friday, the hours from twelve noon to half past ten in the evening; …

(c) on Christmas Day, the hours from twelve noon to half past ten in the evening, with a break of four hours beginning at three in the afternoon;] [and

(d) on any New Year's Eve and on 3rd June 2002, the hours set out in article 3 of the Regulatory Reform (Special Occasions Licensing) Order 2001.]

(2), (3) ...

(4) The licensing justices for any licensing district, if satisfied that the requirements of the district make it desirable, may by order modify for the district the hours specified in subsection (1)(a) of this section, [so that the permitted hours begin at a time earlier than eleven, but not earlier than ten, in the morning].

(5) In this Act 'the general licensing hours' means, in relation to any licensing district, the hours specified in paragraphs [(a) to (c)] of subsection (1) of this section, with any modification applying in the district by virtue of [subsection] (4) of this section.

(6) In premises licensed for the sale of intoxicating liquor for consumption off the premises only the permitted hours on weekdays, other than Christmas Day ..., shall begin at ... eight in the morning ... [and the permitted hours on Sundays, other than Christmas Day, shall begin at ten in the morning].

(7) References in this Act to the permitted hours shall, except in so far as the context otherwise requires, be construed in relation to any licensed premises where the permitted hours are restricted by any conditions attached to the licence, as referring to the hours as so restricted.

Amendment

Sub-s (1): words 'and the Regulatory Reform (Special Occasions Licensing) Order 2001' in square brackets inserted by SI 2001/3937, art 2(1), (2); in para (a) words ', Good Friday or New Year's Eve, or 3rd June 2002' in square brackets substituted by SI 2001/3937, art 2(1), (3); in para (a) word 'eleven' in square brackets substituted by the Licensing Act 1988, s 1(1)(a); in para (a) words omitted repealed by the Licensing Act 1988, ss 1(1)(b), 19, Sch 4; paras (b), (c) substituted, for sub-para (b) as originally enacted, by the Licensing (Sunday Hours) Act 1995, s 1(2); in para (b) words 'or New Year's Eve' in square brackets inserted by SI 2001/3937, art 2(1), (4)(a); in para (b) word omitted repealed by SI 2001/3937, art 2(1), (4)(b); para (d) and word 'and' immediately preceding it inserted by SI 2001/3937, art 2(1), (5).

Sub-ss (2), (3): repealed by the Licensing Act 1988, s 19, Sch 4.

Sub-s (4): words from 'so that the' to 'in the morning' in square brackets substituted by the Licensing Act 1988, s 1(3).

Sub-s (5): words '(a) to (c)' in square brackets substituted by the Licensing (Sunday Hours) Act 1995, s 4(1), Sch 1, para 3; word 'subsection' in square brackets substituted by the Licensing Act 1988, s 1(7), Sch 1, para 2.

Sub-s (6): first words omitted repealed by the Licensing (Sunday Hours) Act 1995, s 1(3); second and final words omitted repealed by the Licensing Act 1988, ss 1(4), 19, Sch 4; words from 'and the permitted' to 'in the morning' in square brackets inserted by the Licensing (Sunday Hours) Act 1995, s 1(3).

[A.43]

61   Orders varying permitted hours   (1) The power of licensing justices to make orders under [subsection] (4) of section 60 of this Act shall be exercised by them at their general annual licensing meeting in accordance with such procedure as may be prescribed by rules made by the Secretary of State.

(2) An order under [that subsection] may make different provision for different periods of the year or for different weekdays in every week of the year or of any such period, or may make provision to take effect for particular periods only, or for particular weekdays in every week of the year or of any such period, but no alteration of the general licensing hours shall take effect within eight weeks of another.

(3) The power of licensing justices to make an order under [that subsection] shall include power to vary or revoke an order so made by a subsequent order.

(4) An order made under [that subsection] shall be published in such manner as the Secretary of State may direct.

(5) A document purporting to be an order made by licensing justices under [that subsection] and to be issued by them shall be received in evidence.

Amendment
Words in square brackets substituted by the Licensing Act 1988, s 1(7), Sch 1, para 3.

[A.44]

62   Permitted hours in clubs   [(1) The permitted hours in premises in respect of which a club is registered shall be—
[(a) on days other than Christmas Day, the general licensing hours;]
(b) on [Christmas Day], the hours fixed by or under the rules of the club in accordance with the following conditions—
  (i)   the hours fixed shall not be longer than [six] and a half hours and shall not begin earlier than twelve noon nor end later than half past ten in the evening;
  (ii) there shall be a break in the afternoon of not less than two hours which shall include the hours from three to five; and
  (iii) there shall not be more than three and a half hours after five.]
(2) ...

(3) Written notice (signed by the chairman or secretary of the club) of the hours [on Christmas Day] fixed as the permitted hours for any club premises by or under the rules of the club shall be given to the [chief executive] to the justices for the petty sessions area in which the premises are; and no decision fixing those hours shall be effective until notice is so given, but the hours previously fixed and notified, if any, shall continue to apply.

Amendment
Sub-s (1): substituted by the Licensing Act 1988, s 1; sub-para (a) substituted by the Licensing (Sunday Hours) Act 1995, s 2(1)(a); in sub-para (b) first words in square brackets substituted by the Licensing (Sunday Hours) Act 1995, s 2(1)(b), final word in square brackets substituted by the Licensing (Amendment) Act 1989, s 1.
Sub-s (2): repealed by the Licensing Act 1988, s 19, Sch 4.
Sub-s (3): words 'on Christmas Day' in square brackets (originally inserted by the Licensing Act 1988, s 1, Sch 1, para 4) substituted by the Licensing (Sunday Hours) Act 1995, s 2(2); words 'chief executive' in square brackets substituted by the Access to Justice Act 1999, s 90(1), Sch 13, paras 36, 50(a).

Exceptions

[A.45]

63 Exceptions from prohibition of sale, etc of intoxicating liquor outside permitted hours (1) Where any intoxicating liquor is supplied in any premises during the permitted hours, section 59 of this Act does not prohibit or restrict—

(a) during the first [twenty minutes] after the end of any period forming part of those hours, the consumption of the liquor on the premises, nor, unless the liquor was supplied or is taken away in an open vessel, the taking of the liquor from the premises;

(b) during the first half hour after the end of such a period, the consumption of the liquor on the premises by persons taking meals there, if the liquor was supplied for consumption as an ancillary to their meals.

(2) Section 59 of this Act does not prohibit or restrict—

(a) the sale or supply to, or consumption by, any person of intoxicating liquor in any premises where he is residing;

(b) the ordering of intoxicating liquor to be consumed off the premises, or the despatch by the vendor of liquor so ordered;

(c) the sale of intoxicating liquor to a trader for the purposes of his trade, or to a registered club for the purposes of the club; or

(d) the sale or supply of intoxicating liquor to any canteen or mess.

(3) Section 59 of this Act does not prohibit or restrict as regards licensed premises—

(a) the taking of intoxicating liquor from the premises by a person residing there; or

(b) the supply of intoxicating liquor for consumption on the premises to any private friends of a person residing there who are bona fide entertained by him at his own expense, or the consumption of intoxicating liquor by persons so supplied; or

(c) the supply of intoxicating liquor for consumption on the premises to persons employed there for the purposes of the business carried on by the holder of the licence, or the consumption of liquor so supplied, if the liquor is supplied at the expense of their employer or of the person carrying on or in charge of the business on the premises.

(4) In subsection (2) of this section, as it applies to licensed premises, and in subsection (3) of this section, references to a person residing in the premises shall be construed as including a person not residing there but carrying on or in charge of the business on the premises.

Amendment
Sub-s (1): words in square brackets substituted by the Licensing Act 1988, s 2.

Restrictions on permitted hours in licensed premises

[A.46]

64   Seasonal licences (1) The licensing justices for any licensing district, if satisfied that the requirements of the district make it desirable, may at the request of the person applying for the grant of a justices' on-licence, or on an application by the holder of such a licence, insert in the licence a condition that, during such part or parts of the year as may be specified in the condition, there shall be no permitted hours in the premises.

(2) A licence in which such a condition is inserted is in this Act referred to as a seasonal licence.

(3) Licensing justices may vary or revoke such a condition either on an application by the holder of the licence or on the renewal, transfer or removal of the licence and at the request of the person applying for the renewal, transfer or removal.

[A.47]

65   Six-day and early-closing licences   (1) Licensing justices shall, at the request of the person applying for the grant of a justices' on-licence[, or on an application by the holder of such a licence,] insert in the licence—
(a)   a condition that on Sundays there shall be no permitted hours in the premises; or
(b)   a condition that the permitted hours shall end one hour earlier in the evening than the general licensing hours.

(2) A licence in which a condition is inserted under subsection (1) of this section is in this Act referred to as a six-day licence if the condition is as mentioned in paragraph (a), and as an early-closing licence if the condition is as mentioned in paragraph (b) of that subsection.

[(3) Licensing justices shall revoke a condition inserted under subsection (1) of this section on an application by the holder of the licence requesting them to do so.]

Amendment
Sub-s (1): words in square brackets inserted by the Licensing Act 1988, s 19, Sch 3, para 7(a).
Sub-s (3): substituted by the Licensing Act 1988, s 19, Sch 3, para 7(b).

66–67D (*Not reproduced*)

Extension of permitted hours in licensed premises and clubs

[A.48]

68   Extension of permitted hours in restaurants, etc   (1) In any premises to which either of the following paragraphs applies there shall be added to the permitted hours (so far as not otherwise comprised in them) for the purpose and in the part of the premises mentioned in subsection (2) of this section—

(a)   where this paragraph applies, the period[, on [Christmas Day,] between the first and second parts of the general licensing hours;]

(b)   where this paragraph applies, the hour following the general licensing hours;

but for other purposes, or in other parts of the premises, the permitted hours shall be the same as if that paragraph did not apply to the premises.

(2) The addition shall be for the purpose of the sale or supply to persons taking table meals in the premises, and the consumption, of intoxicating liquor which is supplied—

(a)   in a part of the premises usually set apart for the service of such persons; and

(b)   for consumption by such a person in that part of the premises as an ancillary to his meal.

(3) Either or both paragraphs of subsection (1) of this section may be applied, in accordance with section 69 of this Act, to licensed premises or to premises in respect of which a club is registered, if the licensing justices for the district in which the licensed premises are situated are satisfied or, in the case of premises in respect of which a club is registered, the magistrates' court is satisfied, that the premises are structurally adapted and bona fide used, or intended to be used for the purpose of habitually providing, for the accommodation of persons frequenting the premises, substantial refreshment to which the sale and supply of intoxicating liquor is ancillary.

Amendment
Sub-s (1): first words in square brackets substituted by the Licensing Act 1988, s 1, Sch 1, para 5, words in square brackets therein substituted by the Licensing (Sunday Hours) Act 1995, s 4(1), Sch 1, para 4.

[A.49]

69 Application of paragraph (a) or (b) of s 68(1) (1) Each paragraph of section 68(1) of this Act may be applied by the holder of the licence or, as the case may be, the secretary of the club, as from such day as he may fix by notice to the chief officer of police served not less than fourteen days before that day and, if so applied, shall continue to apply until its application is terminated under subsection (2) of this section or—

(a) in the case of licensed premises, the licensing justices cease to be satisfied as mentioned in subsection (3) of the said section 68;

(b) in the case of premises in respect of which a club is registered, the magistrates' court declares that it is no longer so satisfied.

(2) The holder of the licence or, as the case may be, the secretary of the club may terminate the application of either or both of the said paragraphs on 4th April in any year by notice to the chief officer of police served not less than fourteen days before that day.

[A.50]

70 Extended hours in restaurants, etc providing entertainment (1) Subject to the provisions of this section, where any licensed premises or premises in respect of which a club is registered are structurally adapted and bona fide used, or intended to be used, for the purpose of habitually providing, for the accommodation of persons frequenting them, musical or other entertainment as well as substantial refreshment, and the sale and supply of intoxicating liquor is ancillary to that refreshment and entertainment, then if—

(a) paragraph (b) of section 68(1) of this Act applies to the premises, and

(b) an order under this section is in force with respect to them,

the time added by the said section 68(1) to the permitted hours on [days] on which the entertainment is provided and the purpose for which the time is added shall, in any part of the premises habitually set apart for the provision of the refreshment and entertainment, be as mentioned in subsection (2) [or (2A)] of this section.

(2) [Subject to subsection (2A),] in any such part of the premises the time so added shall, ... , extend until one o'clock in the morning following, ...; and the purpose for which it is added shall be—

(a) the sale and supply, before the provision of the entertainment or the provision of substantial refreshment has ended, of intoxicating liquor for consumption in any such part of the premises; and

(b) the consumption of intoxicating liquor so supplied;

but this section does not authorise any sale or supply to a person admitted to the premises either after midnight or less than half an hour before the entertainment is due to end, except in accordance with subsection (2) of section 68 of this Act.

[(2A) If the order under this section applies to the permitted hours on a Sunday, subsection (2) has effect in relation to those permitted hours as if—

(a)   for 'one o'clock' there were substituted 'half an hour past midnight', and

(b)   for 'midnight' there were substituted 'half past eleven in the evening'.]

(3) Where in any premises or part of premises the time added to the permitted hours by section 68(1) of this Act is so added for the purpose mentioned in subsection (2) of this section, section 59 of this Act does not restrict the consumption in the premises or part, during the first half hour after the entertainment ends, of intoxicating liquor supplied before it ends.

(4) In this section 'entertainment' does not include any form of entertainment given otherwise than by persons actually present and performing; and, subject to the provisions of this Act, no premises or part shall be treated for the purposes of this section as used or intended to be used for the purpose of habitually providing refreshment and entertainment or as habitually set apart for that purpose, unless it is used or intended to be used, or is set apart, for the purpose of providing them after, and for a substantial period preceding, the end of the general licensing hours on every [day] or on particular [days] in every week, subject to any break for a period or periods not exceeding two weeks in any twelve successive months or on any special occasion or by reason of any emergency.

(5) The power to make an order under this section shall be exercisable—

(a)   with respect to licensed premises, by licensing justices in accordance with section 71 of this Act; and

(b)   with respect to premises in respect of which a club is registered, by the magistrates' court in accordance with section 72 of this Act.

Amendment
Sub-s (1): word 'days' in square brackets substituted by SI 2001/920, art 2, Schedule, para 2(1), (2)(a); words 'or (2A)' in square brackets inserted by SI 2001/920, art 2, Schedule, para 2(1), (2)(b).
Sub-s (2): words 'Subject to subsection (2A), ' in square brackets inserted by SI 2001/920, art 2, Schedule, para 2(1), (3); words omitted repealed by Licensing (Amendment) Act 1985, s 1(2).
Sub-s (2A): inserted by SI 2001/920, art 2, Schedule, para 2(1), (4).
Sub-s (4): word 'day' in square brackets substituted by SI 2001/920, art 2, Schedule, para 2(1), (5)(a); word 'days' in square brackets substituted by SI 2001/920, art 2, Schedule, para 2(1), (5)(b).

[A.51]

71   Orders of licensing justices under s 70   (1) Licensing justices may make an order under section 70 of this Act with respect to any premises on the application of a person applying for or holding a justices' licence for the premises.

(2) Any such order—

[(a)   shall lapse when the licence ceases to be in force otherwise than on its being superseded on renewal or transfer; and

(b)   may be varied by a further such order.]

(3) Before making an application for an order under section 70 of this Act ... , a person shall give notice of the application to the persons, in the manner and at the times required by Schedule 2 to this Act on an application for a new justices' licence for the premises; but if through inadvertence or misadventure he fails to do so paragraph 7 of that Schedule shall apply.

[(3A) In the case of an order under section 70 of this Act which would extend the permitted hours on a Sunday, subsections (3B) to (3D) apply.

(3B) Before making an application at a licensing sessions for such an order in respect of premises in Greater London, a person shall, not less than twenty-one days before the day of the licensing sessions, give to the relevant local authority notice in writing of the application.

(3C) In considering whether to make such an order the licensing justices shall take account of—

(a)   the special nature of Sunday, and

(b)   any guidance on that special nature issued by the Secretary of State.

(3D) Where the licensing justices make such an order with respect to any premises in spite of an objection from a relevant local authority which is based on the residential character of the area in which the premises are situated, they shall state their reasons for doing so.]

(4) Where licensing justices make an order under section 70 of this Act with respect to any premises, the holder of the justices' licence for the premises shall within fourteen days give notice of the making of the order to the chief officer of police, and shall send with the notice a copy of the order; and if he fails to do so he shall be liable to a fine not exceeding [level 1 on the standard scale].

[(5) In this section 'relevant local authority'—

(a)   if the premises are in England outside Greater London, means the district council;

(b)   if the premises are in Wales, means the county or county borough council;

(c)   if the premises are in the City of London, means the Common Council of the City of London; and

(d)   if the premises are in a London borough, means the council of that
      borough.]

Amendment
Sub-s (2): words in square brackets substituted by the Licensing Act 1988, s 4(1)(a).
Sub-s (3): words omitted repealed by the Licensing Act 1988, ss 4(1)(b), 19, Sch 4.
Sub-ss (3A)–(3D): inserted by SI 2001/920, art 2, Schedule, para 3(1), (2).
Sub-s (4): maximum fine increased and converted to a level on the standard scale by the
Criminal Justice Act 1982, ss 37, 38, 46.
Sub-s (5): inserted by SI 2001/920, art 2, Schedule, para 3(1), (3).

[A.52]

72   Orders of magistrates' court under s 70   (1) The magistrates'
court may make an order under section 70 of this Act with respect to any
premises on the application of the club which is registered in respect of
the premises.

(2) Any such order shall lapse on the club's registration certificate ceasing
to be in force [without being renewed], but may be ... varied by a further
such order.

[(2A) In the case of an order under section 70 of this Act which would
extend the permitted hours on a Sunday, subsections (2B) to (2C) apply.

(2B) In considering whether to make such an order the magistrates' court
shall take account of—
(a)   the special nature of Sunday, and
(b)   any guidance on that special nature issued by the Secretary of State.

(2C) Where the magistrates' court makes such an order with respect to
any premises in spite of an objection from a relevant local authority which
is based on the residential character of the area in which the premises are
situated, they shall state their reasons for doing so.]

(3) Where the magistrates' court makes an order under section 70 of this
Act with respect to any premises the secretary of the club which is
registered in respect of the premises shall within fourteen days give
written notice of the making of the order to the chief officer of police,
and shall send with the notice a copy of the order; and if he fails to do so
he shall be liable to a fine not exceeding [level 1 on the standard scale].

[(4) In this section 'relevant local authority' has the same meaning as in
section 71(5) of this Act.]

Amendment
Sub-s (2): words in square brackets substituted, and words omitted repealed, by the
Licensing Act 1988, ss 4(2), 19, Sch 4.
Sub-ss (2A)–(2C): inserted by SI 2001/920, art 2, Schedule, para 4(1), (2).
Sub-s (3): maximum fine increased and converted to a level on the standard scale by the
Criminal Justice Act 1982, ss 37, 38, 46.
Sub-s (4): inserted by SI 2001/920, art 2, Schedule, para 4(1), (3).

[A.53]

73   Supplementary provisions as to orders under s 70   (1) An order under section 70 of this Act shall not be made unless it is shown that the condition of subsection (1) of that section as to the use or intended use of the premises is satisfied in relation to the premises or part of the premises, to the periods, to the [days] and to the times for which the order is to have effect, and that the premises or part of the premises is structurally adapted for the purpose; but in making an order by way of variation ... of a previous order licensing justices or the magistrates' court may assume, unless they see reason to the contrary, that the conditions for the making of the previous order were and still are satisfied.

(2) Licensing justices or the magistrates' court may refuse to make an order under the said section 70, or may in such an order limit the operation of that section to a particular part of the premises or to particular periods of the year or to particular [days] or to a time earlier than one o'clock in the morning [or, in the case of the morning following Sunday, half an hour past midnight] (and may impose different limitations in relation to different parts of the premises, different periods or different [days]), if it appears to them reasonable to do so having regard to all the circumstances and in particular to the comfort and convenience of the occupiers and inmates of premises in the neighbourhood.

(3) Where the use of any premises or part of premises for the purpose specified in subsection (1) of section 70 of this Act is, or is intended to be, limited to a particular period or periods of the year, an order under that section may be made to have effect for the whole or part of the period or periods in question, but excluding any period of less than four weeks.

(4) Licensing justices or, as the case may be, the magistrates' court shall revoke an order under section 70 of this Act if they are satisfied on an application made by or on behalf of the chief officer of police for the police area in which the premises are situated, either—

(a)   that use has not been made for the purposes specified in subsection (1) of that section of the premises or part of the premises for which the order has effect; or

(b)   that it is expedient to revoke the order either by reason of the occurrence of disorderly or indecent conduct in the premises or part, or by reason of the conduct of persons resorting to the premises and any annoyance resulting or likely to result from it to the occupiers or inmates of premises in the neighbourhood, or by reason of the premises having been in any way ill-conducted.

Amendment
Sub-s (1): word 'days' in square brackets substituted by SI 2001/920, art 2, Schedule, para 5(1), (2); words omitted repealed by the Licensing Act 1988, s 19, Sch 4.

Sub-s (2): word 'days' in square brackets in both places it occurs substituted by SI 2001/
920, art 2, Schedule, para 5(1), (3)(a); words from 'or, in the case' to 'an hour past
midnight' in square brackets inserted by SI 2001/920, art 2, Schedule, para 5(1), (3)(b).

[A.54]

74   Exemption orders   (1) Subject to the following provisions of this
section, justices of the peace may—
(a)   on an application by the holder of a justices' on-licence for premises
      situated in the immediate neighbourhood of a public market or place
      where people follow a lawful trade or calling, or
(b)   on an application by the secretary of a club registered in respect of
      any premises so situated,
make an order (in this Act referred to as a general order of exemption)
adding, either generally or for such days as may be specified in the order,
such hours as may be so specified to the permitted hours in those premises.

(2) Justices of the peace shall not make a general order of exemption
unless satisfied, after hearing evidence, that it is desirable to do so for
the accommodation of any considerable number of persons attending the
public market, or following the trade or calling.

(3) Justices of the peace may revoke or vary a general order of exemption;
but, unless it is proved that the holder of the justices' on-licence or, as
the case may be, the secretary of the club had notice of the revocation or
variation, a person shall not be guilty of an offence under section 59 of
this Act in doing anything that would have been lawful had the revocation
or variation not been made.

(4) Justices of the peace may—
(a)   on an application by the holder of a justices' on-licence for any
      premises, or
(b)   on an application by the secretary of a club registered in respect of
      any premises,
make an order (in this Act referred to as a special order of exemption)
adding such hours as may be specified in the order to the permitted hours in
those premises on such special occasion or occasions as may be so specified.

(5) Any power conferred by this section to add to the permitted hours in
any premises may be exercised in either or both of the following manners,
that is to say, by adding to them any hour not comprised in them or by
adding to them for all purposes any hour comprised in them for limited
purposes by virtue of section 68 or section 70 of this Act.

(6) In its application to premises in the City of London or the metropolitan
police district [subsection (4) of] this section shall have effect as if for
[the reference] to justices of the peace there were substituted—

(a)   if the premises are in the City of London, [a reference] to the Commissioner of Police for the City of London acting with the approval of the Lord Mayor;

(b)   if the premises are in the metropolitan police district, [a reference] to the Commissioner of Police for the Metropolis acting with the approval of the Secretary of State

[and the Commissioner of Police for the City of London and the Commissioner of Police for the Metropolis shall have the same power as justices' clerks to charge fees in respect of matters arising under this section].

Amendment
Sub-s (6): words in square brackets inserted or substituted by the Licensing Act 1988, ss 6, 7.

[A.55]

75   Procedural provisions as to exemption orders outside metropolitan area   (1) Any power of justices of the peace under section 74 of this Act shall be exercisable by justices acting for the petty sessions area in which the premises are situated, and by the number of justices, and in the place, required by the [Magistrates' Courts Act 1980] for the hearing of a complaint.

(2) Subject to subsection (3) of this section, the justices may, if they see fit, make a special order of exemption without a hearing, if written application for the order is made by lodging two copies of the application with the [chief executive] to the justices not less than one month before the day or earliest day for which application is made.

(3) Where such an application is made—

(a)   the [chief executive] on receipt of the application shall serve notice of it on the chief officer of police by sending him a copy of the application; and

(b)   if, not later than seven days after the day he sends it, written notice of objection is given by or on behalf of the chief officer to the [chief executive] by lodging two copies with him, the application shall not be granted without a hearing, unless the objection is afterwards withdrawn by a further notice given in the same way; and

(c)   the [chief executive], on receipt of any such notice of objection or notice withdrawing an objection, shall send a copy to the applicant.

Amendment
Sub-s (1): words in square brackets substituted by virtue of the Magistrates' Courts Act 1980, s 154, Sch 8, para 5.
Sub-ss (2), (3): words 'chief executive' in square brackets in each place they occur substituted by the Access to Justice Act 1999, s 90(1), Sch 13, paras 36, 50(b).

Special hours certificates

[A.56]

76 Permitted hours where special hours certificate in force (1)
This section applies to licensed premises or premises in respect to which
a club is registered, or part of any such premises, during the time that—
(a) there is in force for the premises or part a special hours certificate
     granted under the following provisions of this Part of this Act; and
(b) the section is applied, under subsection (7) of this section, to the
     premises or part, by the holder of the licence or, as the case may be,
     the secretary of the club.

(2) Subject to the following provisions of this section, the permitted hours
on weekdays ... in any premises or part of premises to which this section
applies shall [extend until] two o'clock in the morning following, except
that—
(a) the permitted hours shall end at midnight ... on any day on which
     music and dancing is not [or, in the case of casino premises, gaming
     facilities are not] provided after midnight; and
(b) on any day that music and dancing end [or, in the case of casino
     premises, gaming ends] between midnight and two o'clock in the
     morning, the permitted hours shall end when the music and dancing
     end [or, as the case may be, when the gaming ends][; and
[(c) in any premises or part for which a certificate is in force subject to
     a limitation imposed in pursuance of section 78A or 81A of this Act,
     the permitted hours on any day to which the limitation relates shall
     not extend beyond the time specified in the certificate].]

[(2A) In relation to the morning on which summer time begins, subsection
(2) of this section shall have effect—
(a) with the substitution of references to three o'clock in the morning
     for references to two o'clock in the morning; and
(b) where the permitted hours in any premises or part of premises extend
     to a time between one o'clock and two o'clock in the morning by
     virtue of a limitation in the special hours certificate imposed pursuant
     to section 78A or 81A of this Act, as if the permitted hours extended
     to one hour after that specified in the certificate.]

(3) In relation to premises which are situated in any part of the metropolis
outside the City of London which is specified for the purposes of this
subsection by an order of the Secretary of State, subsection (2) of this
section shall have effect—
[(a) except in relation to the morning on which summer time begins,]
     with the substitution of references to three o'clock in the morning
     for the references to two o'clock in the morning[, and

(b)   in relation to that morning, with the substitution of references to four o'clock in the morning for the references to two o'clock in the morning.]

[(3A) Subject to the following provisions of this section, the permitted hours on Sundays in any premises or part of premises to which this section applies shall extend until thirty minutes past midnight in the morning following, except that—

(a)   the permitted hours shall end at midnight on any Sunday on which music and dancing is not or, in the case of casino premises, gaming facilities are not provided after midnight;

(b)   where music and dancing end or, in the case of casino premises, gaming ends between midnight on any Sunday and thirty minutes past midnight, the permitted hours on that Sunday shall end when the music and dancing end or, as the case may be, when the gaming ends; and

(c)   in any premises or part for which a certificate is in force subject to a limitation imposed in relation to Sundays in pursuance of section 78A or 81A of this Act, the permitted hours shall not extend beyond the time specified in the certificate.

(3B) In relation to any Sunday which falls immediately before a day which is a bank holiday in England and Wales under the Banking and Financial Dealings Act 1971, other than Easter Sunday, subsection (3A) shall have effect—

(a)   in the case of premises which are situated as mentioned in subsection (3), with the substitution for the references to thirty minutes past midnight in the morning following of references to three o'clock in the morning following; and

(b)   in the case of any other premises, with the substitution for the references to thirty minutes past midnight in the morning following of references to two o'clock in the morning following.]

(4) Where the permitted hours are fixed by this section, section 63(1) of this Act shall apply to the consumption of liquor on the premises as if in paragraph (a) thereof half an hour were substituted for [twenty] minutes and paragraph (b) thereof were omitted.

(5) ...

(6) Where a special hours certificate for any premises or part of premises is limited to particular days in every week, this section does not affect the permitted hours in the premises on days on which the certificate does not apply.

[(6A) Subsections (3A) and (3B) shall not apply to a certificate granted before the coming into force of those subsections or to a certificate granted after that time that does not extend to Sundays; but any such certificate may be varied by the licensing justices or, as the case may be, magistrates' court on the application of the licensee or club.]

(7) The holder of the licence or, as the case may be, the secretary of the club, may apply this section, or terminate its application, from such day as he may fix by notice in writing to the chief officer of police served not less than fourteen days before that day.

[(8) In this section, references to summer time are to the period of summer time for the purposes of the Summer Time Act 1972.]

Amendment
Sub-s (2): words omitted repealed by the Licensing (Amendment) Act 1985, s 1(3); words 'extend until' in square brackets substituted by the Licensing Act 1988, s 1; in para (a) words 'or, in the case of casino premises, gaming facilities are not' in square brackets inserted by SI 1997/950, art 4(2); in para (b) words 'or, in the case of casino premises, gaming ends' in square brackets inserted by SI 1997/950, art 4(2); in para (b) words 'or, as the case may be, when the gaming ends' in square brackets inserted by SI 1997/950, art 4(2); para (c) and word 'and' immediately preceding it inserted by the Licensing (Amendment) Act 1980, s 2; para (c) substituted by the Licensing Act 1988, s 19, Sch 3, para 8(a).
Sub-s (2A): inserted by SI 1996/977, art 2(2), (4).
Sub-s (3): paras (a), (b) inserted by SI 1996/977, art 2(3).
Sub-ss (3A), (3B): inserted by SI 2001/920, art 2, Schedule, para 6(1), (2).
Sub-s (4): word in square brackets substituted by the Licensing Act 1988, s 19, Sch 3, para 8(b).
Sub-s (5): repealed by the Licensing (Amendment) Act 1976, s 1.
Sub-s (6A): inserted by SI 2001/920, art 2, Schedule, para 6(1), (3).
Sub-s (8): inserted by SI 1996/977, art 2(2), (4).

[A.57]
77 Special hours certificates for licensed premises If, on an application made to the licensing justices with respect to licensed premises … , the justices are satisfied—

[(a) that the premises are—
  (i)   casino premises, or
  (ii) premises for which a music and dancing licence is in force, and
(b) that the whole or any part of the premises is structurally adapted, and bona fide used, or intended to be used, for the purpose of providing for persons resorting to the premises—
  (i)   in the case of casino premises, gaming facilities and substantial refreshment, and
  (ii) in the case of any other premises, music and dancing and substantial refreshment,
to which the sale of intoxicating liquor is ancillary,]

the licensing justices [may] grant[, with or without limitations,] a special hours certificate for the premises or, if they are satisfied that part only of the premises is adapted or used or intended to be used as mentioned in paragraph (b) of this section, for that part.

Amendment
Words omitted repealed by the Local Government (Miscellaneous Provisions) Act 1982, ss 1, 47, Sch 1, para 19, Sch 7, Part I; paras (a) and (b) substituted by SI 1997/950, art 2; second word in square brackets substituted and final words in square brackets inserted by the Licensing Act 1988, s 5(1).

[A.58]

[77A   Provisional grant of special hours certificates by licensing justices   (1) Where, on an application made by a person interested in any premises of in respect of which a grant or provisional grant of a justices' licence has been made and which are to be, or are in the course of being, constructed, altered or extended, the licensing justices are satisfied—

[(a) that the premises are—
  (i) casino premises, or
  (ii) premises for which a music and dancing licence is in force,]
(b) that the whole or any part of the premises is intended to be used, and, if completed in accordance with plans deposited with the licensing justices, will be structurally adapted, for the purpose of providing for persons resorting to the premises,
  [(i) in the case of casino premises, gaming facilities and substantial refreshment, and
  (ii) in the case of any other premises, music and dancing and substantial refreshment,
  to which the sale of intoxicating liquor is ancillary.]

(2) Where a special hours certificate has been granted under subsection (1) of this section, the licensing justices may, on application by the person who applied for the certificate, consent to any modification of the deposited plans if, in their opinion, the premises to which the certificate relates will, if completed in accordance with the modified plans, be structurally adapted for the purpose mentioned in paragraph (b) of that subsection.

(3) Where a special hours certificate has been granted under subsection (1) of this section, the licensing justices shall, after such notice has been given as they may require, declare the provisional grant final on being satisfied, in relation to the premises to which the certificate relates—
(a) that they are, or are part of, licensed premises;
[(b) that they are, or are part of—
  (i) casino premises, or
  (ii) premises for which a music and dancing licence is in force;]
(c) that they have been completed in accordance with the deposited plans.

(4) Until a provisional grant under subsection (1) of this section has been declared final under subsection (3) of this section, the certificate to which the provisional grant relates shall not be valid.

(5) Where licensing justices—

(a)   refuse to make a provisional grant of a special hours certificate;

(b)   make a provisional grant of such a certificate with limitations;

(c)   refuse to declare a provisional grant of such a certificate final; or

(d)   refuse to give consent, on the application of the person who applied for the certificate, to any modification of the deposited plans,

they shall specify in writing to the applicant their reasons for doing so.

(6) In subsection (1) of this section, references to premises for which a music and dancing licence is in force include premises for which a person holds a music and dancing licence which is subject to a condition that it shall be of no effect until confirmed.

(7) In this section and sections 78ZA and 81B of this Act—

(a)   'deposited plans', in relation to a special hours certificate, means the plans deposited in connection with the application for the certificate; and

(b)   references to completion in accordance with the deposited plans are, where any modification of those plans has been consented to under subsection (2) of this section or section 78ZA(2) of this Act, to completion in accordance with those plans with that modification.]

Amendment
Inserted by SI 1996/977, art 3.
Sub-s (1): words in square brackets substituted by SI 1997/950, art 3(1)–(3).
Sub-s (3): para (b) substituted by SI 1997/950, art 3(1), (4).

[A.59]

78   Special hours certificates for clubs   If, on an application made to the magistrates' court with respect to premises in respect of which a club is or is to be registered ... , the court is satisfied—

(a)   that a certificate granted under section 79 of this Act is in force for the premises, and

(b)   that the whole or any part of the premises is structurally adapted, and bona fide used, or intended to be used, for the purpose of providing for the members of the club music and dancing and substantial refreshment to which the supply of intoxicating liquor is ancillary,

the court [may] grant[, with or without limitations,] a special hours certificate for the premises or, if the court is satisfied that part only of the premises is adapted or used or intended to be used as mentioned in paragraph (b) of this section, for that part.

Amendment

Words omitted repealed by the Local Government (Miscellaneous Provisions) Act 1982, ss 1, 47, Sch 1, para 19, Sch 7, Part I; words in square brackets substituted or inserted by the Licensing Act 1988, s 5.

[A.60]

[78ZA Provisional grant of Special Hours Certificates by Magistrates Court (1) Where, on an application made to the magistrates' court with respect to premises in respect of which a club is or is to be registered and which are to be, or are in the course of being altered or extended, the court is satisfied—

(a) that a certificate granted under section 79 of this Act is in force for the premises; and

(b) that the whole or any part of the premises is intended to be used, and, if completed in accordance with plans deposited with the court, will be structurally adapted, for the purpose of providing for the members of the club music and dancing and substantial refreshment to which the supply of intoxicating liquor is ancillary,

the court may make a provisional grant, with or without limitations, of a special hours certificate for the premises or, if the court is satisfied that part only of the premises is intended to be used or will be adapted as mentioned in paragraph (b) of this subsection, for that part.

(2) Where a special hours certificate has been granted under subsection (1) of this section, the magistrates' court may, on application by the person who applied for the certificate, consent to any modification of the deposited plans if, in its opinion, the premises to which the certificate relates will, if completed in accordance with the modified plans, be structurally adapted for the purpose mentioned in paragraph (b) of that subsection.

(3) Where a special hours certificate has been granted under subsection (1) of this section, the magistrates' court shall, after such notice has been given as it may require, declare the provisional grant final on being satisfied, in relation to the premises to which the certificate relates—

(a) that they are, or are part of, premises in respect of which a club is or is to be registered;

(b) that they are, or are part of, premises for which a certificate granted under section 79 of this Act is in force; and

(c) deposited plans.

(4) Until a provisional grant under subsection (1) of this section has been declared final under subsection (3) of this section, the certificate to which the provisional grant relates shall not be valid.

(5) Where a magistrates' court—

(a) refuses to make a provisional grant of a special hours certificate;

(b) makes a provisional grant of such a certificate with limitations;

(c) refuses to declare a provisional grant of such a certificate final; or

(d) refuses to give consent, on the application of the person who applied for the certificate, to any modification of the deposited plans,

it shall specify in writing to the applicant its reasons for doing so.]

Amendment
Inserted by SI 1996/977, art 4.

[A.61]

[**78A Limitations on special hours certificates**   (1) On an application for a special hours certificate the licensing justices or, as the case may be, the magistrates' court may grant a certificate under section 77[, 77A, 78 or 78ZA] of this Act limited in any of the following respects.

(2) The limitations referred to are limitations—

(a) to particular times of the day;

(b) to particular days of the week;

(c) to particular periods of the year.

(3) Different limitations may be imposed by virtue of subsection (2)(a) above for different days.

(4) Where a special hours certificate is subject to limitations under this section the licensing justices or, as the case may be, the magistrates' court may, on the application of the licensee or the club, vary any limitation to which it is so subject.

[(5) Subsections (6) to (9) apply to an application to the licensing justices or, as the case may be, the magistrates' court for the grant of a special hours certificate which extends to Sundays or for the variation of a limitation so as to affect the operation of a special hours certificate in relation to Sundays.

(6) Not less than twenty-one days before making such an application to licensing justices, a person shall give notice to the relevant local authority.

(7) In considering whether to grant or vary a certificate in the manner described in subsection (5), the licensing justices or, as the case may be, the magistrates' court shall (without prejudice to other functions in relation to the grant or variation) consider the exercise of the power to limit the certificate—

(a) to days not including Sunday, or

(b) to different times of the day on Sundays and on other days.

(8) In discharging their function under subsection (7), the licensing justices or, as the case may be, the magistrates' court shall take account of—

(a) the special nature of Sunday, and

(b) any guidance on that special nature issued by the Secretary of State.

(9) Where the licensing justices or, as the case may be, the magistrates' court grant a special hours certificate which extends to Sundays or vary a limitation so as to affect the operation of such a certificate in relation to Sundays in spite of an objection from a relevant local authority which is based on the residential character of the area in which the premises are situated, they shall state their reasons for doing so.

(10) In this section 'relevant local authority' has the same meaning as in section 71(5) of this Act.]]

Amendment
Inserted by the Licensing Act 1988, s 5(2).
Sub-s (1): words in square brackets substituted by SI 1996/977, art 5(2).
Sub-ss (5)–(10): inserted by SI 2001/920, art 2, Schedule, para 7.

[A.62]

79   Licensing authority's certificate of suitability of club premises for music and dancing   (1) If, on an application by the secretary of a club with regard to any premises in respect of which the club is or proposes to be registered [, the licensing authority under the statutory regulations for music and dancing] are satisfied that the premises (whether or not they are kept or intended to be kept for dancing, music or other public entertainment of the like kind) in all other respects fulfil the authority's requirements for the grant of a music and dancing licence, the authority may grant a certificate for the premises under this section.

(2) The authority may grant a certificate under this section on such terms, and subject to such conditions or restrictions, as they think fit; and, subject to the following provisions of this section, the certificate shall remain in force for such period as may be specified therein.

(3) The authority may, on the application of the secretary of the club, from time to time renew a certificate granted under this section; and subsections (1) and (2) of this section shall apply to the renewal as they apply to the grant of a certificate.

(4) The authority may, on the application of the secretary of the club, waive or modify any condition or restriction subject to which a certificate has been granted or renewed under this section.

(5) If, while a certificate under this section is in force, it appears to the authority—

(a)   that any condition or restriction subject to which the certificate was granted or last renewed, as the case may be, has not been complied with or, in the case of a condition or restriction that has been modified under subsection (4) of this section, that the condition or restriction as so modified has not been complied with, and

(b)   that the condition or restriction has not been waived under that subsection, the authority may give the secretary of the club notice in writing that they propose to revoke the certificate, specifying the ground upon which they propose to revoke it, and shall give him an opportunity of being heard by a person appointed to the authority for the purpose.

(6) The authority may, not less than seven days after the giving of a notice under subsection (5) of this section and, if the secretary avails himself of the opportunity of being heard, after considering the report of the person appointed to hear the secretary, revoke the certificate.

[(7) On any application for the grant or renewal of a certificate, or the waiver or modification of a condition or restriction in a certificate, under this section, the applicant shall pay a reasonable fee determined by the authority.]

Amendment
Sub-s (1): words in square brackets substituted by the Local Government (Miscellaneous Provisions) Act 1982, s 1, Sch 1, para 19, Sch 2, para 5.
Sub-s (7): original sub-s (7) repealed by the Local Government (Miscellaneous Provisions) Act 1982, ss 1, 47, Sch 1, para 19, Sch 7, Part I; new sub-s (7) inserted by the Licensing Act 1988, s 6(2).

[A.63]
80 Special hours certificates limited to particular days or parts of the year (1) Where a special hours certificate is granted for any premises or part of premises which are used or intended to be used only on particular [days] for the provision of music and dancing and substantial refreshment the certificate shall be limited to those days in the week on which it is shown to the satisfaction of the licensing justices or magistrates' court granting it that music and dancing and refreshment are, or are intended to be, provided as required by section 77[, 77A, 78 or 78ZA] of this Act.

[(1A) Where a special hours certificate is granted for any premises or part of premises which—
(a) are, or are part of, casino premises; and
(b) are used or intended to be used only on particular [days] for the provision of gaming facilities and substantial refreshment,

the certificate shall be limited to those days in the week on which it is shown to the satisfaction of the licensing justices that gaming facilities and refreshment are, or are intended to be, provided as required by section 77 or 77A of this Act.]

(2) ...

(3) So long as the justices' licence in force for any premises is a seasonal licence, any special hours certificate for those premises or any part of them shall be taken, except in so far as it is granted for a more restricted period under [section 78A of this Act], to extend, but only to extend, to

the season during which there are permitted hours in the premises under the condition attached to the licence under section 64 of this Act.

(4) On the variation or revocation of the condition referred to in subsection (3) of this section, the licensing justices shall, if need be, vary the special hours certificate so as to secure that it does not operate except as respects any period or periods during which it is shown to their satisfaction that it is intended to use the premises or part in question as mentioned in section 77 [or, as the case may be, 77A] of this Act.

Amendment

Sub-s (1): word 'days' in square brackets substituted by SI 2001/920, art 2, Schedule, para 8; words ', 77A, 78 or 78ZA' in square brackets substituted by SI 1996/977, art 5(3)(a).

Sub-s (1A): inserted by SI 1997/950, art 4(3); in para (b) word 'days' in square brackets substituted by SI 2001/920, art 2, Schedule, para 8.

Sub-s (2): repealed by the Licensing Act 1988, ss 5(3)(a), 19, Sch 4.

Sub-s (3): words in square brackets substituted by the Licensing Act 1988, s 5(3)(b).

Sub-s (4): words in square brackets inserted by SI 1996/977, art 5(3)(b).

[A.64]

81 Revocation of special hours certificates (1) If at any time while a special hours certificate is in force [there is not also in force for the premises to which or part of which the certificate relates—
(a) where the special hours certificate is granted by virtue of section 77(a)(i) or 77A(3)(b)(i) of this Act, a licence under the Gaming Act 1968, and
(b) where the special hours certificate is granted by virtue of section 77(a)(ii) or 77A(3)(b)(ii) of this Act, a music and dancing licence or, as the case may be, a certificate under section 79 of this Act,
the special hours certificate shall thereby be revoked.]

[(1A) Where a special hours certificate is revoked under subsection (1) above as a consequence of—
(a) an application for the renewal of a licence being refused under paragraph 6A(2) of Schedule 1 to the Local Government (Miscellaneous Provisions) Act 1982 or paragraph 2A(2) of Schedule 12 to the London Government Act 1963; or
(b) a licence being revoked under paragraph 11A(2) or 12(5) of Schedule 1 or paragraph 9A(2) or 10(4A) of Schedule 12,
the certificate shall be reinstated if the licence is subsequently renewed under paragraph 17 of Schedule 1 or paragraph 19 of Schedule 12 or if the licence is subsequently reinstated under paragraph 11A(4) or 17 of Schedule 1 or paragraph 9A(4) or 19 of Schedule 12.]

(2) At any time while a special hours certificate for any premises or part of premises is in force, the chief officer of police may apply to the

licensing justices or, if it was granted under section 78 [or 78ZA] of this Act, to the magistrates' court, for the revocation of the certificate on the ground that, while the certificate has been in force—
(a) the premises have not, or the part has not, been used as mentioned in section 77[, 77A, 78 or, as the case may be, 78ZA] of this Act; or
(b) a person has been convicted of having at those premises or that part contravened section 59 of this Act;

or that on the whole the persons resorting to the premises or part are there, at times when the sale or supply of intoxicating liquor there is lawful by virtue only of the certificate, for the purpose of obtaining intoxicating liquor rather than for [an appropriate purpose]; and if the licensing justices or magistrates' court are satisfied that the ground of the application is made out they may revoke the certificate.

[(2A) For the purposes of subsection (2) of this section, the following are appropriate purposes—
(a) in the case of casino premises, gaming and the obtaining of refreshments other than intoxicating liquor,
(b) in the case of any other premises, dancing and the obtaining of such refreshments.]

(3) Where a special hours certificate is revoked under subsection (2) of this section in consequence of a contravention of section 59 of this Act, no special hours certificate shall be valid in relation to the premises or part in question, if it is issued on an application made earlier than two months after the date of the revocation or made earlier than such later time, if any (not being more than twelve months after that date) as may be specified in the order revoking the certificate.

[(4) At any time while a special hours certificate for any premises or for part of any premises is in force, the chief officer of police may apply to the licensing justices or, if it was granted under section 78 [or 78ZA]of this Act, to the magistrates' court, for the revocation of the certificate on the ground that the revocation is expedient by reason of the occurrence of disorderly or indecent conduct in the premises or part to which the certificate relates; and if the licensing justices or the magistrates' court, as the case may be, are satisfied that the ground of the application is made out, they shall revoke the certificate.]

Amendment
Sub-s (1): words in square brackets substituted by SI 1997/950, art 4(4)(a).
Sub-s (1A): inserted by the Public Entertainments Licences (Drug Misuse) Act 1997, s 3.
Sub-s (2): first words in square brackets inserted, and second words in square brackets substituted, by SI 1996/977, art 5(4)(a); final words in square brackets substituted by SI 1997/950, art 4(4)(b).
Sub-s (2A): inserted by SI 1997/950, art 4(4)(c).

Sub-s (4): substituted by the Licensing (Amendment) Act 1981, s 1; words in square brackets inserted by SI 1996/977, art 5(4)(b).

[A.65]

[81A Special hours certificates: further powers to impose limitations as to hours (1) Limitations to particular times of the day may also be attached to special hours certificates by licensing justices or, as the case may be, a magistrates' court as provided by subsections (2) and (3) below; and different limitations may be imposed under this section for different days.

(2) On an application for revocation of such a certificate under section 81(2) of this Act, the justices or court may, instead of revoking the certificate, attach any limitation authorised by subsection (1) above or vary any such limitation to which the certificate is subject under section 78A of this Act.

(3) At any time while such a certificate is in force (other than for any premises situated as mentioned in section 76(3) of this Act) the justices or court may, on the application of the chief officer of police, attach any limitation authorised by subsection (1) above or vary any such limitation to which the certificate is subject under section 78A of this Act.

(4) Where a special hours certificate is subject to limitations under subsection (2) or (3) above, the licensing justices or, as the case may be, the magistrates' court may, on the application of the licensee or the club, vary any limitation to which it is so subject.

[(5) Not less than twenty-one days before making an application under subsection (4) to licensing justices to vary a limitation under this section so as to affect the operation of a special hours certificate in relation to Sundays, the person making the application shall give notice to the relevant local authority.

(6) In considering under subsection (2) or (3) whether to attach any limitation authorised by subsection (1) or, under those subsections or subsection (4), whether to vary any limitation to which a special hours certificate is subject, the licensing justices or, as the case may be, the magistrates' court shall consider the exercise of the power to limit the certificate—

(a)   to days not including Sundays, or

(b)   to different times of the day on Sundays and on other days.

(7) In discharging their function under subsection (6), the licensing justices or, as the case may be, the magistrates' court shall take account of—

(a)   the special nature of Sunday, and

(b)   any guidance on that special nature issued by the Secretary of State.

(8) Where the licensing justices or, as the case may be, the magistrates' court vary a limitation so as to affect the operation of a special hours

certificate in relation to Sundays in spite of an objection from a relevant local authority which is based on the residential character of the area in which the premises are situated, they shall state their reasons for doing so.

(9) In this section 'relevant local authority' has the same meaning as in section 71(5) of this Act.]]

Amendment
Inserted by the Licensing (Amendment) Act 1980, s 3.
Substituted by the Licensing Act 1988, s 5.
Sub-ss (5)–(9): inserted by SI 2001/920, art 2, Schedule, para 9.

[A.66]

[81AA Special hours certificates: exclusion of Sundays in case of disturbance etc (1) At any time while there is in force for any premises or for part of any premises a special hours certificate which extends to Sundays, a person or authority mentioned in subsection (3) may apply to the licensing justices or, if it was granted under section 78 or 78ZA of this Act, to the magistrates' court, for the imposition of a limitation excluding Sundays on the following grounds.

(2) The grounds referred to are that such a limitation is desirable to avoid or reduce on Sundays—
(a) any disturbance of or annoyance to—
  (i) persons living or working in the neighbourhood, or
  (ii) customers or clients of any business in the neighbourhood; or
(b) the occurrence in the vicinity of the premises of disorderly conduct on the part of persons resorting to the premises or part of the premises.

(3) The persons and authorities referred to in subsection (1) are—
(a) a person falling within sub-paragraph (i) of subsection (2)(a);
(b) the chief officer of police; or
(c) a relevant local authority within the meaning of section 71(5) of this Act.

(4) If on an application under this section the licensing justices or, as the case may be, the magistrates' court are satisfied that the grounds of the application are made out, they shall attach a limitation to the special hours certificate which has the effect of excluding Sundays.]

Amendment
Inserted by SI 2001/920, art 2, Schedule, para 10.

[A.67]

[81B Special hours certificates: appeals (1) Subject to subsection (2) of this section, any person aggrieved by a decision of licensing justices or a magistrates' court—

[(a)   not to grant a special hours certificate under section 77[, 77A, 78 or 78ZA] of this Act;]

[(aa)]to revoke or not to revoke a special hours certificate on an application under subsection (2) or (4) of section 81 of this Act,

[(b)   to attach or not to attach limitations under section 78A of this Act,

. . .

(c)   to attach or not to attach limitations under section 81A [or 81AA] of this Act,]

[(d)   to refuse to declare the provisional grant of a special hours certificate final, or

(e)   to refuse to give consent, on the application of the person who applied for the certificate, to any modification of the deposited plans.]

may appeal to the Crown Court against that decision.

[(2) Only the chief officer of police may appeal against a decision not to revoke a certificate as mentioned in paragraph (aa) of subsection (1) of this section or not to attach a limitation under section 81A(3) of this Act; and a person may appeal against a decision not to attach a limitation under section 81A(2) [or 81AA] of this Act only if he has appeared before the licensing justices or magistrates' court and made representations that the limitation be attached.]

[(2A) Subsection (2C) applies where the condition in subsection (2B) is satisfied and the effect of the Crown Court allowing or dismissing an appeal under this section is that—

(a)   a special hours certificate which extends to Sundays is granted,

(b)   a special hours certificate which extends to Sundays is varied so as to relax a limitation in respect of Sundays, or

(c)   a special hours certificate not extending to Sundays is varied so as to extend to Sundays.

(2B) The condition referred to in subsection (2A) is that a relevant local authority made to the licensing justices or, as the case may be, the magistrates' court an objection to the grant or variation of the certificate on grounds based on the residential character of the area in which the premises to which the certificate relates are situated.

(2C) Where this subsection applies, the Crown Court shall state the reasons for their decision.]

(3) A person other than the appellant shall be a party to an appeal under this section if, and only if, he has appeared before the licensing justices or magistrates' court and made representations on the application to which the decision appealed against relates.

(4) Licensing justices shall have the same power to make an order for the payment of costs on the abandonment of an appeal under this section

as a magistrates' court has by virtue of [section 109 of the Magistrates' Courts Act 1980] on the abandonment of an appeal to which that section relates.]

[(5) In this section 'relevant local authority' has the same meaning as in section 71(5) of this Act.]

Amendment
Inserted by the Licensing (Amendment) Act 1980, s 3.
Sub-s (1): para (a) inserted by the Licensing Act 1988, s 5(5); in para (a) words ', 77A, 78 or 78ZA' in square brackets substituted by SI 1996/977, art 5(a); para (aa) (originally para (a)) renumbered as para (aa) by the Licensing Act 1988, s 5(5); paras (b), (c) substituted by the Licensing Act 1988, s 19, Sch 3, para 9; word omitted from para (b) repealed by SI 1996/977, art 5(1), (5); in para (c) words 'or 81AA' in square brackets inserted by SI 2001/920, art 2, Schedule, para 11(1), (2); paras (d), (e) inserted by SI 1996/977, art 5(1), (5).
Sub-s (2): substituted by the Licensing Act 1988, s 19, Sch 3, para 9(b); words 'or 81AA' in square brackets inserted by SI 2001/920, art 2, Schedule, para 11(1), (3).
Sub-ss (2A)–(2C): inserted by SI 2001/920, art 2, Schedule, para 11(1), (4).
Sub-s (4): words in square brackets substituted by virtue of the Magistrates' Courts Act 1980, s 154, Sch 8, para 5.
Sub-s (5): inserted by SI 2001/920, art 2, Schedule, para 11(1), (5).

[A.68]

82 Special hours certificate and extension or exemption orders in respect of same premises (1) Where section 76 of this Act applies to part only of any premises the part to which it applies and the part to which it does not apply shall be treated as separate premises for the purposes of section 68(1)(b) of this Act and for the purpose of general and special orders of exemption.

(2) Section 68(1)(b) and section 76 of this Act may both be applied to the same premises or part of premises, so that section 68(1)(b) has effect on days on which the permitted hours are not affected by section 76.

[A.69]

83 Supplementary provisions as to special hours certificates (1) In sections 76 to 81 of this Act 'music and dancing licence' means a licence granted by the licensing authority under the statutory regulations for music and dancing and authorising the keeping or using of any premises for public dancing, singing, music or other public entertainment.

(2) References in those sections to providing music and dancing and refreshment [or, as the case may be, gaming facilities and refreshment,] shall be construed as references to providing them on every [day] or on particular [days] in every week, subject to any break for a period or periods not exceeding two weeks in any twelve successive months or on

any special occasion or by reason of any emergency; and references in those sections to providing dancing shall be construed as references to providing facilities for dancing that are adequate having regard to the number of persons for whose reception in the premises or part of premises in question provision is made.

[(3) References in those sections to gaming are to gaming within the meaning of the Gaming Act 1968, otherwise than by means of any machine to which Part III of that Act applies.

(4) For the purposes of those sections, premises are casino premises if a licence under the Gaming Act 1968 is in force in relation to them and they are not premises to which section 20 of that Act applies (bingo club premises).]

Amendment
Sub-s (2): words 'or, as the case may be, gaming facilities and refreshment,' in square brackets inserted by SI 1997/950, art 4(5); word 'day' in square brackets substituted by SI 2001/920, art 2, Schedule, para 12(a); word 'days' in square brackets substituted by SI 2001/920, art 2, Schedule, para 12(b).
Sub-ss (3), (4): inserted by SI 1997/950, art 4(6)

83A (*Repealed by SI 2001/3937.*)

84–88 (*Not reproduced*)

Supplementary provisions

[A.70]
89 Duty of licensee to post notice where permitted hours modified (1) Where the permitted hours in any licensed premises or part of licensed premises depend to any extent on a general order of exemption[, an order under section 87A of this Act] or on any provision of section 68, 70 or 76 of this Act, the holder of the licence shall keep posted in some conspicuous place there a notice stating the effect of the order or provision applying and, if it applies on certain days only, stating the days on which it applies.

(2) A person contravening this section shall be liable to a fine not exceeding [level 1 on the standard scale].

Amendment
Sub-s (1): words in square brackets inserted by the Licensing Act 1988, s 19, Sch 3, para 10.
Sub-s (2): maximum fine increased and converted to a level on the standard scale by the Criminal Justice Act 1982, ss 37, 38, 46.

90–92 (*Not reproduced*)

PART IV RESTAURANTS AND GUEST HOUSES

[A.71]

93 Provisions as to grant of certain licences for restaurants, guest houses, etc   (1) In this Act 'Part IV licence' means a justices' on-licence which—

(a) is granted for such premises and is subject to such conditions as are mentioned in section 94 of this Act; and

(b) is not subject to any other condition, except—

    (i) conditions required to be attached to it under section 95 or 96 of this Act, or

    (ii) a condition by virtue of which it is a six-day licence, early-closing licence or seasonal licence, or

    (iii) in the case of a licence for club premises, conditions prohibiting or restricting sales of intoxicating liquor to non-members.

(2) A Part IV licence is a restaurant licence, a residential licence or a residential and restaurant licence, according as it falls within subsection (1), (2) or (3) of section 94 of this Act.

(3) Licensing justices shall not refuse an application duly made for the grant of a new Part IV licence or for the renewal or transfer of a Part IV licence, except on one or more of the grounds specified in section 98 of this Act; but this subsection shall not affect—

(a) the operation of any enactment relating to the disqualification of persons or premises for holding or receiving a justices' licence; or

(b) the application to any club premises of section 55(4) of this Act.

(4) No licence shall be granted by way of removal of a Part IV licence.

(5) Nothing in section 4(1) of this Act shall be taken to prevent the granting of a licence for wine alone ... as a Part IV licence.

Amendment
Sub-s (5): words omitted repealed by the Finance Act 1967, ss 5(1)(a), 45(8), Sch 16, Part I.

[A.72]

94 Conditions attached to Part IV licences for restaurants, guest houses, etc   (1) In this Act 'restaurant licence' means a Part IV licence which—

(a) is granted for premises structurally adapted and bona fide used, or intended to be used, for the purpose of habitually providing the customary main meal at midday or in the evening, or both, for the accommodation of persons frequenting the premises; and

(b) is subject to the condition that intoxicating liquor shall not be sold or supplied on the premises otherwise than to persons taking table meals there and for consumption by such a person as an ancillary to his meal.

(2) In this Act 'residential licence' means a Part IV licence which—

(a) is granted for premises bona fide used, or intended to be used, for the purpose of habitually providing for reward board and lodging, including breakfast and one other at least of the customary main meals; and

(b) is subject to the condition that intoxicating liquor shall not be sold or supplied on the premises otherwise than to persons residing there or their private friends bona fide entertained by them at their own expense, and for consumption by such a person or his private friend so entertained by him either on the premises or with a meal supplied at but to be consumed off the premises.

(3) In this Act 'residential and restaurant licence' means a Part IV licence which—

(a) is granted for premises falling within both paragraph (a) of subsection (1) and paragraph (a) of subsection (2) of this section; and

(b) is subject to the condition that intoxicating liquor shall not be sold or supplied otherwise than as permitted by the conditions of a restaurant or supplied otherwise than as permitted by the conditions of a restaurant licence or by those of a residential licence.

(4) The conditions as to the sale and supply of intoxicating liquor set out in subsection (1)(b) and subsection (2)(b) of this section—

(a) shall not extend to the supply for consumption on the premises of intoxicating liquor (whether inside or outside the permitted hours) in any case in which section 59 of this Act does not prohibit liquor being so supplied outside the permitted hours;

(b) shall not extend to the sale of intoxicating liquor, or supply of liquor, sold on the premises under the authority of an occasional licence;

(c) subject to paragraph (b) of this subsection, shall extend to all sales of intoxicating liquor, whether or not requiring the authority of a justices' licence.

(5) It shall be an implied condition of any Part IV licence that suitable beverages other than intoxicating liquor (including drinking water) shall be equally available for consumption with or otherwise as an ancillary to meals served in the licensed premises.

[A.73]

95 Permitted hours in premises for which restaurant or residential and restaurant licence is in force (1), (2) …

(3) … [Paragraphs (a) and (b)] of section 68(1) of this Act shall apply to any premises for which a restaurant licence or residential and restaurant licence is for the time being in force.

Amendment
Sub-ss (1), (2): repealed by the Licensing Act 1988, s 19, Sch 3, para 12, Sch 4.
Sub-s (3): words omitted repealed by the Licensing Act 1988, s 19, Sch 4; words
'Paragraphs (a) and (b)' in square brackets substituted by SI 2002/493, art 2.

[A.74]

96   Requirement of sitting accommodation for residential licence or residential and restaurant licence (1) Where licensing justices grant a new residential licence or residential and restaurant licence, they shall, unless it appears to them that in the particular circumstances of the case there is good reason not to do so, attach to the licence a condition that there shall be afforded in the premises, for persons provided with board and lodging for reward, adequate sitting accommodation in a room not used or to be used for sleeping accommodation, for the service of substantial refreshment or for the supply or consumption of intoxicating liquor.

(2) Where such a licence is granted without the condition required by subsection (1) of this section, licensing justices shall, on the renewal or transfer of the licence, attach the condition if by reason of any change of circumstances it appears to them that the requirement ought no longer to be dispensed with.

[A.75]

97   Restrictions concerning justices' licences for restaurants and guest-houses, etc   (1) Licensing justices shall not attach to any new justices' on-licence—

(a)   any conditions calculated to restrict the sale or supply of intoxicating liquor to a sale or supply in connection with the service of meals, other than such condition as is required to be attached to a restaurant licence (modified, if need be, to allow for any sale or supply which it is desired to authorise in addition to the sale or supply in connection with the service of table meals); or

(b)   any conditions calculated to restrict the sale or supply of intoxicating liquor to a sale or supply to persons residing in the licensed premises, other than such condition as is required to be attached to a residential licence (modified, if need be, to allow for any sale or supply which it is desired to authorise in addition to a sale or supply to persons residing in the premises).

(2) No justices' licence other than a restaurant licence shall be granted for a restaurant carried on under the powers of the Civic Restaurants Act 1947.

(3) Paragraphs (a) to (c) of subsection (4) of section 94 of this Act shall apply also to any conditions which are in the same terms as those set out in subsection (1)(b) or subsection (2)(b) of that section but are attached to a justices' licence which is not a Part IV licence.

[A.76]

98 Grounds for refusing applications for Part IV licences (1)
Licensing justices may refuse an application for the grant of a Part IV
licence on any of the following grounds, that is to say,—

(a) that the applicant is not of full age, or is in any other respect not a fit
and proper person to hold one;

(b) that the premises do not fall within paragraph (a) of subsection (1),
(2) or (3), as the case may be, of section 94 of this Act, or are not
suitable and convenient for the use contemplated by that paragraph,
having regard to their character and condition, to the nature and
extent of the proposed use and (where it applies) to the condition as
to sitting accommodation required by section 96 of this Act or as to
the supply of intoxicating liquor for consumption as an ancillary to
a table meal only;

(c) that within the twelve months preceding the application—

(i) a justices' on-licence for the premises has been forfeited; or

(ii) the premises have been ill-conducted while a justices' on-
licence or a licence under the Refreshment Houses Act 1860
was in force for them; or

(iii) the condition as to sitting accommodation required by section
96 of this Act has been habitually broken while a residential
licence or a residential and restaurant licence, or other licence
with the like condition, was in force for the premises; or

(iv) the condition implied by section 94(5) of this Act as to the
availability of beverages other than intoxicating liquor has been
habitually broken while a Part IV licence, or other licence with
the like condition, was in force for the premises.

(2) Licensing justices may also refuse an application for the grant of a
restaurant licence or residential and restaurant licence on the ground that
the trade done in the premises in providing refreshment to persons
resorting there (but not provided with board and lodging) does not
habitually consist to a substantial extent in providing table meals of a
kind to which the consumption of intoxicating liquor might be ancillary.

(3) Licensing justices may also refuse an application for the grant of a
Part IV licence on the ground that the sale or supply of intoxicating liquor
on the premises is undesirable either because it would be by self-service
methods, that is to say, methods allowing a customer to help himself on
payment or before payment, or because—

(a) in the case of a residential licence or a residential and restaurant
licence, a large proportion of the persons provided with board and
lodging for reward;

(b) in the case of a restaurant licence or a residential and restaurant
licence, a large proportion of the persons resorting to the premises
but not provided with board and lodging;

is habitually made up of persons under the age of eighteen who are not accompanied by others (whether parents or persons of full age) who pay for them.

(4) If on an application for the grant of a Part IV licence for any premises it is made to appear to the licensing justices on behalf of any such authority as is mentioned in subsection (5) of this section—

(a)   that the authority or an officer designated in that behalf by the authority desired in connection with the application to have the premises inspected as to the matters mentioned in paragraph (b) of subsection (1) of this section; and

(b)   that after reasonable steps had been taken by or on behalf of the authority or officer for the purpose it was not possible to have the premises so inspected;

the licensing justices may refuse the application.

(5) The authorities referred to in subsection (4) of this section are—

(a)   (according to the situation of the premises) the Common Council of the City of London or the council of the county borough, London borough or county district [or, in Wales, the council of the county or county borough]; and

(b)   the authority (if not included in paragraph (a) of this subsection) discharging in the area where the premises are situated the functions of fire authority under the Fire Services Act 1947; and

(c)   the chief officer of police for the police area where the premises are situated.

(6) Licensing justices refusing an application for the grant of a Part IV licence shall specify in writing to the applicant the grounds of their refusal.

Amendment
Sub-s (5): words in square brackets inserted by the Local Government (Wales) Act 1994, s 66(6), Sch 16, para 22(4).

[A.77]

99   Application for Part IV licence in place of other on-licence   (1) Where licensing justices refuse an application duly made for the grant of a new justices' on-licence other than a Part IV licence, they shall at the request of the applicant treat him as having also duly made an alternative application for such Part IV licence, relating to such descriptions of intoxicating liquor, as he may specify in the request.

(2) Where on appeal [the Crown Court] refuse to confirm the grant of a new justices' on-licence other than a Part IV licence, they shall at the request of the holder of the licence treat the appeal as an appeal against the grant of such Part IV licence, relating to such descriptions of intoxicating liquor, as he may specify in the request and, if they dismiss

that appeal, shall, on confirming the grant, attach to the licence the conditions required by the foregoing provisions of this Part of this Act.

(3) On the renewal, transfer or removal of a justices' on-licence licensing justices may, at the request of the applicant made with the consent of the registered owner (if any) of the licensed premises, vary the licence by attaching the conditions required for it to be granted as a Part IV licence of the description specified in the request (in substitution for any conditions previously attached), and the renewal, transfer or removal of a justices' on-licence with such a variation shall not be refused except on the grounds on which a renewal may be refused of a licence of the description so specified.

(4) Where under subsection (3) of this section conditions are attached to a justices' on-licence, the applicant for the renewal, transfer or removal may appeal notwithstanding that it is done at his request.

Amendment
Sub-s (2): words in square brackets substituted by the Courts Act 1971, s 56(1), Sch 8, Part I, para 2.

100–159 (*Not reproduced*)

PART XI GENERAL PROVISIONS REGULATING SALE, ETC, POSSESSION AND DELIVERY OF INTOXICATING LIQUOR

[A.78]

160   Selling liquor without licence   (1) Subject to the provisions of this Act, if any person—

(a)   sells or exposes for sale by retail any intoxicating liquor without holding a justices' licence or canteen licence [or occasional permission] authorising ... the sale of that liquor, or

(b)   holding a justices' licence [an occasional licence] or a canteen licence [or occasional permission] sells or exposes for sale by retail any intoxicating liquor except at the place for which that licence [or permission] authorises ... the sale of that liquor,

he shall be guilty of an offence under this section.

(2) Where intoxicating liquor is sold in contravention of this section on any premises, every occupier of the premises who is proved to have been privy or consenting to the sale shall be guilty of an offence under this section.

(3) A person guilty of an offence under this section shall be liable to imprisonment for a term not exceeding six months or to a fine not exceeding [level 4 on the standard scale], or to both.

(4) The holder of a justices' licence or a canteen licence shall, on his second or subsequent conviction of an offence under this section, forfeit the licence.

(5) The court by or before which a person is convicted of an offence under this section committed after a previous conviction of such an offence may order him to be disqualified for holding a justices' licence—
(a)   on a second conviction, for a period not exceeding five years;
(b)   on a third or subsequent conviction, for any term of years or for life.

(6) The court by or before which the holder of a justices' licence [an occasional licence] or a canteen licence is convicted of an offence under this section may declare all intoxicating liquor found in his possession, and the vessels containing it, to be forfeited.

[(7) In subsection (1) of this section 'occasional permission' means a permission granted under the Licensing (Occasional Permissions) Act 1983.]

Amendment
Sub-s (1): words omitted repealed, and second words in square brackets inserted, by the Finance Act 1967, ss 5(1), 45(8), Sch 7, para 12, Sch 16, Part I; other words in square brackets inserted by the Licensing (Occasional Permissions) Act 1983, s 4.
Sub-s (3): maximum fine increased and converted to a level on the standard scale by the Criminal Justice Act 1982, ss 37, 38, 46.
Sub-s (6): words in square brackets inserted by the Finance Act 1967, s 5(1), Sch 7, para 12.
Sub-s (7): inserted by the Licensing (Occasional Permissions) Act 1983, s 4.

[A.79]
161   Selling liquor in breach of conditions of licence   (1) If the holder of a justices' on-licence knowingly sells or supplies intoxicating liquor to persons to whom he is not permitted by the conditions of the licence to sell or supply it he shall be guilty of an offence under this section.

(2) If the holder of a Part IV licence knowingly permits intoxicating liquor sold in pursuance of the licence to be consumed on the licensed premises by persons for whose consumption there he is not permitted by the conditions of the licence to sell it, he shall be guilty of an offence under this section.

(3) A person guilty of an offence under this section shall be liable to imprisonment for a term not exceeding six months or to a fine not exceeding [level 4 on the standard scale] or to both.

Amendment
Sub-s (3): maximum fine increased and converted to a level on the standard scale by the Criminal Justice Act 1982, ss 37, 38, 46.

[A.80]

162 Keeping on premises of liquor of kind not authorised by licence If without reasonable excuse the holder of a justices' licence [an occasional licence] or a canteen licence has in his possession on the premises in respect of which the licence is in force any kind of intoxicating liquor which he is not authorised to sell, he shall be liable [to a fine not exceeding level 2 on the standard scale] and shall forfeit the liquor and the vessels containing it.

Amendment

First words in square brackets inserted by the Finance Act 1967, s 5(1)(c), Sch 7, para 13; enhanced penalty on a subsequent conviction abolished and pecuniary penalty on any conviction now a fine not exceeding level 2 on the standard scale by virtue of the Criminal Law Act 1977, s 31(6), (9), and the Criminal Justice Act 1982, ss 35, 37, 46.

[A.81]

163 Delivery from vehicles, etc (1) A person shall not, in pursuance of a sale by him of intoxicating liquor, deliver that liquor, either himself or by his servant or agent, from any van, barrow, basket or other vehicle or receptacle unless the quantity, description and price of the liquor and the name and address of the person to whom it was to be supplied had been entered, before the liquor was dispatched—

(a) in a day book kept on the premises from which the liquor was dispatched, and

(b) in a delivery book or invoice carried by the person delivering the liquor.

(2) A person shall not, himself or by his servant or agent—

(a) carry in any van, barrow, basket or other vehicle or receptacle, while in use for the delivery of intoxicating liquor in pursuance of a sale by that person, any intoxicating liquor that is not entered in a day book and delivery book or invoice under subsection (1) of this section;

(b) deliver in pursuance of a sale by him any intoxicating liquor at any address not entered as aforesaid.

(3) A person shall not, himself or by his servant or agent, refuse to allow a constable to examine any van, barrow, basket or other vehicle or receptacle while in use for the distribution or delivery of any intoxicating liquor or to examine a delivery book or invoice carried, or day book kept, under subsection (1) of this section.

(4) The holder of a justices' licence shall not be guilty of an offence under this section committed by his servant or agent if he proves that the offence was committed without his knowledge or consent.

(5) Nothing in this section shall prohibit or restrict the delivery of intoxicating liquor to a trader for the purposes of his trade, or to a registered club for the purposes of the club.

(6) If any person contravenes this section he shall be liable to a fine not exceeding [level 2 on the standard scale].

Amendment
Sub-s (6): maximum fine increased by the Criminal Law Act 1977, s 31(6), (9), and converted to a level on the standard scale by the Criminal Justice Act 1982, ss 37, 46.

[A.82]
164 Penalty for breach of terms of off-licence (1) Where a person, having purchased intoxicating liquor from the holder of a justices' licence which does not cover the sale of that liquor for consumption on the premises, drinks the liquor—

(a) in the licensed premises, or
(b) in premises which adjoin or are near the licensed premises and which belong to the holder of the licence or are under his control or used by his permission, or
(c) on a highway adjoining or near those premises,

then, if the drinking is with the privity or consent of the holder of the licence, the holder of the licence shall be liable [to a fine not exceeding level 2 on the standard scale].

(2) If the holder of a justices' off-licence, with intent to evade the terms of the licence, takes, or suffers any other person to take, any intoxicating liquor from the licensed premises for the purpose of its being sold on his account or for his benefit or profit, he shall be liable [to a fine not exceeding level 2 on the standard scale].

(3) For the purposes of subsection (2) of this section, if liquor is taken for the purpose of its being drunk in any house, tent, shed or other building belonging to the holder of the licence, or hired, used or occupied by him, the burden of proving that he did not intend to evade the terms of the licence shall lie upon him.

[(4) If the holder of a justices' off-licence sells any spirits or wine in an open vessel, he shall be liable [to a fine not exceeding level 1 on the standard scale].]

Amendment
Sub-ss (1), (2): enhanced penalty on a subsequent conviction abolished and penalty on any conviction now a fine not exceeding level 2 on the standard scale by virtue of the Criminal Law Act 1977, s 31(6), (9), and the Criminal Justice Act 1982, ss 35, 37, 46.
Sub-s (4): inserted by the Finance Act 1967, s 5(1)(c), Sch 7, para 14; enhanced penalty on a subsequent conviction abolished, maximum fine on any conviction increased and converted to level 1 on the standard scale by the Criminal Justice Act 1982, ss 35, 37, 38, 46.

165 (*Repealed by SI 1996/1339.*)

[A.83]

166   Restriction on credit sales   (1) Subject to the following provisions of this section, a person shall not in any licensed premises, licensed canteen or the premises of a registered club—

(a)   himself or by his servant or agent sell or supply intoxicating liquor for consumption on the premises, or

(b)   consume intoxicating liquor,

unless it is paid for before or at the time when it is sold or supplied; and if any person contravenes this subsection he shall be liable to a fine not exceeding [level 2 on the standard scale].

(2) Subsection (1) of this section does not apply—

(a)   if the liquor is sold or supplied for consumption at a meal supplied at the same time, is consumed with the meal and is paid for together with the meal; or

(b)   if, in the case of licensed premises, the liquor is sold or supplied for consumption by a person residing in the premises or his guests and is paid for together with his accommodation.

(3) Nothing in this section shall prohibit or restrict the sale or supply of intoxicating liquor to any canteen or mess.

Amendment
Sub-s (1): maximum fine increased by the Criminal Law Act 1977, s 31(6), (9), and converted to a level on the standard scale by the Criminal Justice Act 1982, ss 37, 46.

[A.84]

167   Saving for liqueur chocolates   (1) No provision of this Act as to the sale, supply, purchase, delivery or consumption of intoxicating liquor, except subsection (2) of this section, and no enactment requiring the authority of an excise licence for the sale or supply of intoxicating liquor, shall have effect in relation to intoxicating liquor in confectionery which—

(a)   does not contain intoxicating liquor in a proportion greater than one fiftieth of a gallon of liquor [(containing a quantity of ethyl alcohol amounting to 57 per cent of the volume of the liquor inclusive of the alcohol contained in it as at 20 degrees C)] per pound of the confectionery; and

(b)   either consists of separate pieces weighing not more than one and a half ounces or is designed to be broken into such pieces for the purposes of consumption.

(2) Intoxicating liquor in confectionery shall not be sold to a person under sixteen, and if any person knowingly contravenes this subsection he shall be liable [to a fine not exceeding level 2 on the standard scale].

Amendment
Sub-s (1): words in square brackets substituted by SI 1979/1476, reg 2.
Sub-s (2): enhanced penalty on a subsequent conviction abolished, maximum fine on any conviction increased and converted to level 2 on the standard scale by the Criminal Justice Act 1982, ss 35, 37, 38, 46.

PART XII PROTECTION OF PERSONS UNDER EIGHTEEN AND OTHER PROVISIONS AS TO CONDUCT OF LICENSED PREMISES AND LICENSED CANTEENS

Persons under eighteen

[A.85]

168   Children prohibited from bars   (1) The holder of a justices' licence shall not allow a person under fourteen to be in the bar of the licensed premises during the permitted hours.

(2) No person shall cause or procure, or attempt to cause or procure, any person under fourteen to be in the bar of licensed premises during the permitted hours.

(3) Where it is shown that a person under fourteen was in the bar of any licensed premises during the permitted hours, the holder of the justices' licence shall be guilty of an offence under this section unless he proves either—

(a)   that he [exercised all] due diligence to prevent the person under fourteen from being admitted to the bar, or

(b)   that the person under fourteen had apparently attained that age.

[(3A) No offence shall be committed under subsection (1) of this section if—

(a)   the person under fourteen is in the bar in the company of a person who is eighteen or over,

(b)   there is in force a certificate under section 168A(1) of this Act relating to the bar, and

(c)   the certificate is operational or subsection (3B) of this section applies.

(3B) This subsection applies where—

(a)   the person under fourteen, or a person in whose company he is, is consuming a meal purchased before the certificate ceased to be operational, and

(b)   no more than thirty minutes have elapsed since the certificate ceased to be operational.

(3C) No offence shall be committed under subsection (2) of this section if the person causes or procures, or attempts to cause or procure, the person under fourteen to be in the bar in the circumstances mentioned in paragraphs (a) to (c) of subsection (3A) of this section.]

(4) No offence shall be committed under this section if the person under fourteen—

(a)   is the licence-holder's child, or

(b)   resides in the premises, but is not employed there, or

(c)   is in the bar solely for the purpose of passing to or from some part of the premises which is not a bar and to or from which there is no other convenient means of access or egress.

(5) No offence shall be committed under this section if the bar is in any railway refreshment-rooms or other premises constructed, fitted and intended to be used bona fide for any purpose to which the holding of a justices' licence is merely ancillary.

(6) If any person contravenes this section he shall be liable [to a fine not exceeding level 1 on the standard scale].

(7) A local education authority may institute proceedings for an offence under this section.

(8) Where in any proceedings under this section it is alleged that a person was at any time under fourteen, and he appears to the court to have then been under that age, he shall be deemed for the purposes of the proceedings to have then been under that age, unless the contrary is shown.

Amendment
Sub-s (3): words in square brackets substituted by the Licensing Act 1988, s 19, Sch 3, para 16.
Sub-ss (3A)–(3C): inserted by the Deregulation and Contracting Out Act 1994, s 19(1).
Sub-s (6): maximum fines on first or subsequent convictions increased to the same amount by the Criminal Law Act 1977, s 31(6), (9), and converted to level 1 on the standard scale by the Criminal Justice Act 1982, ss 37, 46.

[A.86]

[168A   Children's certificates   (1) The holder of a justices' licence may apply to the licensing justices for the grant of a certificate in relation to any area of the premises for which the licence is in force which consists of or includes a bar.

(2) Licensing justices may grant an application for a certificate under subsection (1) of this section ('a children's certificate') if it appears to them to be appropriate to do so, but shall not do so unless they are satisfied—

(a)   that the area to which the application relates constitutes an environment in which it is suitable for persons under fourteen to be present, and

(b) that meals and beverages other than intoxicating liquor will be available for sale for consumption in that area.

(3) Where a children's certificate is in force, the holder of the justices' licence for the licensed premises to which the certificate relates shall keep posted in some conspicuous place in the area to which the certificate relates a notice which—
(a) states that a children's certificate is in force in relation to the area, and
(b) explains the effect of the certificate and of any conditions attached to it.

(4) A person who fails to perform the duty imposed on him by subsection (3) of this section shall be guilty of an offence and liable on summary conviction to a fine of an amount not exceeding level 1 on the standard scale.

(5) In any proceedings for an offence under subsection (4) of this section, it shall be a defence for the accused to prove that he took all reasonable precautions, and exercised all due diligence, to avoid the commission of the offence.

(6) Schedule 12A to this Act (supplementary provisions) shall have effect.

(7) Subsection (1) of this section shall apply to an applicant for a justices' licence as it applies to the holder of a justices' licence, and, in its application by virtue of this subsection, shall have effect as if the reference to the premises for which the licence is in force were to the premises which are the subject of the application for a justices' licence.]

Amendment
Inserted by the Deregulation and Contracting Out Act 1994, s 19(2).

[A.87]

[169A   Sale of intoxicating liquor to a person under 18   (1) A person shall be guilty of an offence if, in licensed premises, he sells intoxicating liquor to a person under eighteen.

(2) It is a defence for a person charged with an offence under subsection (1) of this section, where he is charged by reason of his own act, [to prove—
(a) that he believed that the person was not under eighteen; and
(b) either that he had taken all reasonable steps to establish the person's age or that nobody could reasonably have suspected from his appearance that the person was under eighteen.

(2A) For the purposes of subsection (2) of this section a person shall be treated as having taken all reasonable steps to establish another person's age if he asks the other person for evidence of his age unless it is shown that the evidence was such that no reasonable person would have been convinced by it].

(3) It is a defence for a person charged with an offence under subsection (1) of this section, where he is charged by reason of the act or default of some other person, to prove that he exercised all due diligence to avoid the commission of an offence under that subsection.

(4) Subsection (1) of this section has effect subject to section 169D of this Act.]

Amendment
Substituted, together with ss 169B–169H, for s 169 as originally enacted, by the Licensing (Young Persons) Act 2000, s 1.
Sub-ss (2), (2A): words from 'to prove—' to 'convinced by it' in square brackets substituted by the Criminal Justice and Police Act 2001, s 30(1).

[A.88]

[169B   Allowing the sale of intoxicating liquor to a person under 18 (1) A person to whom this subsection applies shall be guilty of an offence if, in licensed premises, he knowingly allows any person to sell intoxicating liquor to a person under eighteen.

(2) Subsection (1) of this section applies to a person who works in the licensed premises in a capacity, whether paid or unpaid, which gives him authority to prevent the sale.

(3) Subsection (1) of this section has effect subject to section 169D of this Act.]

Amendment
Substituted, together with ss 169A, 169C–169H, for s 169 as originally enacted, by the Licensing (Young Persons) Act 2000, s 1.

[A.89]

[169C   Purchase of intoxicating liquor by or for a person under 18 (1) A person under eighteen shall be guilty of an offence if, in licensed premises, he buys or attempts to buy intoxicating liquor.

[(1A) Subsection (1) of this section does not apply where the person under eighteen buys or attempts to buy the intoxicating liquor at the request of—
(a)   a constable, or
(b)   an inspector of weights and measures appointed under section 72(1) of the Weights and Measures Act 1985 (c 72),
who is acting in the course of his duty.]

(2) A person shall be guilty of an offence if, in licensed premises, he buys or attempts to buy intoxicating liquor on behalf of a person under eighteen.

(3) A person shall be guilty of an offence if he buys or attempts to buy intoxicating liquor for consumption in a bar in licensed premises by a person under eighteen.

(4) It is a defence for a person charged with an offence under subsection (2) or (3) of this section to prove that he had no reason to suspect that the person was under eighteen.

(5) Subsections (1) and (2) of this section have effect subject to section 169D of this Act.]

Amendment
Substituted, together with ss 169A, 169B, 169D–169H, for s 169 as originally enacted, by the Licensing (Young Persons) Act 2000, s 1.
Sub-s (1A): inserted by the Criminal Justice and Police Act 2001, s 31(1).

[A.90]

[169D   Exception to the section 169A–C offences   Sections 169A(1), 169B(1), and 169C(1) and (2) of this Act do not apply where—
(a)   the person under eighteen has attained the age of sixteen,
(b)   the intoxicating liquor in question is beer, porter or cider, and
(c)   its sale or purchase is for consumption at a meal in a part of the licensed premises which is not a bar and is usually set apart for the service of meals.]

Amendment
Substituted, together with ss 169A–169C, 169E–169H, for s 169 as originally enacted, by the Licensing (Young Persons) Act 2000, s 1.

[A.91]

[169E   Consumption of intoxicating liquor by a person under 18   (1) A person under eighteen shall be guilty of an offence if, in a bar in licensed premises, he consumes intoxicating liquor.

(2) A person to whom this subsection applies shall be guilty of an offence if, in licensed premises, he knowingly allows a person under eighteen to consume intoxicating liquor in a bar.

(3) Subsection (2) of this section applies to a person who works in the licensed premises in a capacity, whether paid or unpaid, which gives him authority to prevent the consumption.]

Amendment
Substituted, together with ss 169A–169D, 169F–169H, for s 169 as originally enacted, by the Licensing (Young Persons) Act 2000, s 1.

[A.92]

[169F   Delivery of intoxicating liquor to a person under 18   (1) A person who works in licensed premises, whether paid or unpaid, shall be guilty of an offence if he knowingly delivers to a person under eighteen intoxicating liquor sold in those premises for consumption off the premises.

(2) A person to whom this subsection applies shall be guilty of an offence if he knowingly allows any person to deliver to a person under eighteen intoxicating liquor sold in licensed premises for consumption off the premises.

(3) Subsection (2) of this section applies to a person who works in the licensed premises in a capacity, whether paid or unpaid, which gives him authority to prevent the delivery.

(4) Subsections (1) and (2) of this section do not apply where—
(a)   the delivery is made at the residence or working place of the purchaser, or
(b)   the person under eighteen works in the licensed premises in a capacity, whether paid or unpaid, which includes the delivery of intoxicating liquor.]

Amendment
Substituted, together with ss 169A–169E, 169G, 169H, for s 169 as originally enacted, by the Licensing (Young Persons) Act 2000, s 1.

[A.93]

[169G   Sending a person under 18 to obtain intoxicating liquor   (1) A person shall be guilty of an offence if he knowingly sends a person under eighteen for the purpose of obtaining intoxicating liquor sold or to be sold in licensed premises for consumption off the premises.

(2) Subsection (1) of this section applies regardless of whether the liquor is to be obtained from the licensed premises or from other premises from which it is delivered in pursuance of the sale.

(3) Subsection (1) of this section does not apply where the person under eighteen works in the licensed premises where the sale has been or is to be made, in a capacity, whether paid or unpaid, which includes the delivery of intoxicating liquor.

[(4) Subsection (1) of this section does not apply where the person under eighteen is sent by—
(a)   a constable, or
(b)   an inspector of weights and measures appointed under section 72(1) of the Weights and Measures Act 1985 (c 72),
who is acting in the course of his duty.]]

Amendment
Substituted, together with ss 169A–169F, 169H, for s 169 as originally enacted, by the Licensing (Young Persons) Act 2000, s 1.
Sub-s (4): inserted by the Criminal Justice and Police Act 2001, s 31(2).

[A.94]

[169H   Penalty for offences   (1) A person guilty of an offence under section 169A, 169B, 169C, 169E, 169F, or 169G of this Act shall be liable to a fine not exceeding level 3 on the standard scale.

(2) Where the holder of a justices' licence is convicted of any of the offences referred to in subsection (1) and the licence is held in respect of the licensed premises in relation to which the offence was committed, the court may order that he shall forfeit the licence if—

(a)   he already has one or more convictions of that or any other offence referred to in subsection (1) of this section, or

(b)   he already has one or more convictions of an offence under section 169 of this Act.]

Amendment
Substituted, together with ss 169A–169G, for s 169 as originally enacted, by the Licensing (Young Persons) Act 2000, s 1.

[A.95]

[169I   Enforcement role for weights and measures authorities in relation to certain offences   (1) It is the duty of every local weights and measures authority in England and Wales to enforce within their area the provisions of sections 169A and 169B of this Act.

(2) A local weights and measures authority shall have power to make, or to authorise any person to make on their behalf, such purchases of goods as may appear expedient for the purpose of determining whether or not the provisions of section 169A or 169B of this Act are being complied with.

(3) In this section 'local weights and measures authority' has the meaning given by section 69 of the Weights and Measures Act 1985 (local weights and measures authorities).]

Amendment
Inserted by the Criminal Justice and Police Act 2001, s 31(3).

[A.96]

170   Persons under 18 not to be employed in bars   (1) If any person under eighteen is employed in any bar of licensed premises at a time when the bar is open for the sale or consumption of intoxicating liquor, the holder of the licence shall be liable [to a fine not exceeding level 1 on the standard scale].

[(1A) Subsection (1) of this section shall not apply where—

(a)   the person employed is of or over the age of sixteen; and

(b)   the employment is under a training scheme approved for the purposes of section 170A of this Act by the Secretary of State.]

(2) For the purposes of this section a person shall not be deemed to be employed in a bar by reason only that in the course of his employment in some other part of the premises he enters the bar for the purpose of giving or receiving any message or of passing to or from some part of the premises which is not a bar and to or from which there is no other convenient means of access or egress.

(3) For the purposes of this section a person shall be deemed to be employed by the person for whom he works notwithstanding that he receives no wages for his work.

(4) Where in any proceedings under this section it is alleged that a person was at any time under eighteen, and he appears to the court to have then been under that age, he shall be deemed for the purposes of the proceedings to have then been under that age unless the contrary is shown.

Amendment
Sub-s (1): enhanced penalty on a subsequent conviction abolished, maximum fine on any conviction increased and converted to level 1 on the standard scale by the Criminal Justice Act 1982, ss 35, 37, 38, 46.
Sub-s (1A): inserted by SI 1997/957, art 2(1).

[A.97]

[170A Employment in bars under approved training schemes (1) The Secretary of State may approve for the purposes of this section any training scheme which relates to the employment in bars of licensed premises of persons under eighteen if he is satisfied—

(a) that the scheme includes satisfactory arrangements for the approval—
  (i) of the persons to whom training is provided under it ('trainees'), and
  (ii) of licensed premises participating in it;
(b) that, in relation to any person or premises approved under the arrangements mentioned in paragraph (a) of this subsection, the scheme includes satisfactory arrangements for the provision of documentary evidence of the approval to that person or, as the case may be, the holder of the justices' licence for those premises;
(c) that the scheme includes satisfactory arrangements for monitoring—
  (i) the quality of training provided under it, and
  (ii) the progress of trainees;
(d) that, in relation to the provision under the scheme of training in a bar, the scheme includes satisfactory arrangements for ensuring that there is adequate supervision of trainees;
(e) that, in relation to the supervision mentioned in paragraph (d) of this subsection, the scheme includes arrangements for the provision to

the holder of the justices' licence for the licensed premises of a statement of—

    (i)   the criteria to be used by the holder of the licence in determining whether persons are fit to supervise trainees, and

    (ii) the duties of persons supervising trainees; and

(f)   that the scheme provides that licensed premises shall cease to be approved for participation in the scheme if trainees are not adequately supervised in their training in any bar of the premises.

(2) A scheme shall not be taken for the purposes of paragraph (d) of subsection (1) of this section to include satisfactory arrangements for ensuring that there is adequate supervision of trainees if it fails to provide—

(a)   that supervision is to be undertaken by the holder of the licence or a person of or over the age of eighteen who acts on his behalf, or

(b)   that, when the trainee is present in a bar which is open for the sale or consumption of intoxicating liquor, the person supervising the trainee must be present on the licensed premises and must be present in the bar unless his absence from the bar is—

    (i)   unavoidable,

    (ii) necessary for carrying on the licence holder's business, or

    (iii) necessary to facilitate the trainee's development under the scheme.

(3) Where a person under eighteen is employed under a training scheme approved for the purposes of this section in any bar of licensed premises at a time when the bar is open for the sale or consumption of intoxicating liquor, and

(a)   the time falls outside—

    (i)   the general licensing hours, and

    (ii) any period during which the consumption of intoxicating liquor is permitted by virtue of section 63(1) of this Act; or

(b)   the holder of the licence has not notified the chief officer of police that the licensed premises will be participating in the scheme,

the holder of the licence shall be liable to a fine not exceeding level 1 on the standard scale.]

Amendment
Inserted by SI 1997/957, art 2(2).

[A.98]

171   Exclusion from sections 168 to 170 of bars while in regular use for service of table meals   References in the foregoing provisions of this Part of this Act to a bar do not include a bar at any time when it is usual in the premises in question for it to be, and it is,—

(a)　set apart for the service of table meals; and
(b)　not used for the sale or supply of intoxicating liquor otherwise than to persons having table meals there and for consumption by such a person as an ancillary to his meal.

[A.99]

[171A　Prohibition of unsupervised off-sales by persons under 18　(1) In any premises which are licensed for the sale of intoxicating liquor for consumption off the premises only or any off-sales department of on-licensed premises, the holder of the licence shall not allow a person under eighteen to make any sale of such liquor unless the sale has been specifically approved by the holder of the licence or by a person of or over the age of eighteen acting on his behalf.

(2) The reference in subsection (1) of this section to an off-sales department of on-licensed premises is a reference to any part of premises for which a justices' on-licence has been granted which is set aside for use only for the sale of intoxicating liquor for consumption off the premises.

(3) A person guilty of an offence under this section shall be liable to a fine not exceeding level 1 on the standard scale.]

Amendment
Inserted by the Licensing Act 1988, s 18.

Preservation of order

[A.100]

172　Licence holder not to permit drunkenness, etc　(1) The holder of a justices' licence shall not permit drunkenness or any violent, quarrelsome or riotous conduct to take place in the licensed premises.

(2) If the holder of a justices' licence is charged under subsection (1) of this section with permitting drunkenness, and it is proved that any person was drunk in the licensed premises, the burden of proving that the licence holder and the persons employed by him took all reasonable steps for preventing drunkenness in the premises shall lie upon him.

(3) The holder of a justices' licence shall not sell intoxicating liquor to a drunken person.

(4) If any person contravenes this section he shall be liable [to a fine not exceeding [level 3] on the standard scale].

Amendment

Sub-s (4): enhanced penalty on a subsequent conviction abolished and penalty on any conviction now a fine not exceeding level 2 on the standard scale by virtue of the Criminal Law Act 1977, s 31(6), (9), and the Criminal Justice Act 1982, ss 35, 37, 46; words 'level 3' in square brackets substituted by the Criminal Justice and Police Act 2001, s 32(1).

[A.101]

[172A   Other persons in authority not to permit drunkenness etc   (1) A relevant person shall not permit drunkenness or any violent, quarrelsome or riotous conduct to take place in licensed premises

(2) If a relevant person is charged under subsection (1) of this section with permitting drunkenness, and it is proved that any person was drunk in the licensed premises, the burden of proving that the relevant person and any persons employed by him took all reasonable steps for preventing drunkenness in the premises shall lie upon him.

(3) A relevant person shall not, in licensed premises, sell intoxicating liquor to a drunken person.

(4) If any person contravenes this section he shall be liable to a fine not exceeding level 3 on the standard scale.

(5) This section is without prejudice to the liability under section 172 of this Act of the holder of a justices' licence for acts or omissions of persons other than himself.

(6) In this section 'relevant person' means any person (other than the holder of the justices' licence for the licensed premises concerned) who—

(a)   in a case falling within subsection (1) of this section, works in the licensed premises in a capacity, whether paid or unpaid, which gives him authority to prevent the drunkenness or (as the case may be) conduct concerned;

(b)   in a case falling within subsection (3) of this section, works in the licensed premises in a capacity, whether paid or unpaid, which gives him authority to sell the intoxicating liquor concerned.]

Amendment

Inserted by the Criminal Justice and Police Act 2001, s 32(2).

[A.102]

173   Procuring drink for drunken person   (1) If any person in licensed premises procures or attempts to procure any intoxicating liquor for consumption by a drunken person he shall be guilty of an offence under this section.

(2) If any person aids a drunken person in obtaining or consuming intoxicating liquor in licensed premises he shall be guilty of an offence under this section.

(3) A person guilty of an offence under this section shall be liable to imprisonment for a term not exceeding one month or to a fine not exceeding [level 1 on the standard scale].

Amendment
Sub-s (3): maximum fine increased by the Criminal Law Act 1977, s 31(6), (9), and converted to a level on the standard scale by the Criminal Justice Act 1982, ss 37, 46.

[A.103]
174   Power to exclude drunkards, etc, from licensed premises   (1) Without prejudice to any other right to refuse a person admission to premises or to expel a person from premises, the holder of a justices' licence [or a relevant person] may refuse to admit to, or may expel from, the licensed premises any person who is drunken, violent, quarrelsome or disorderly, [and the holder of a justices' licence may refuse to admit to, or may expel from, the licensed premises any person] whose presence in the licensed premises would subject the licence holder to a penalty under this Act.

(2) If any person liable to be expelled from licensed premises under this section, when requested by the holder of the justices' licence or his agent or servant or [(as the case may be) the relevant person or any agent or servant of his or by] any constable to leave the premises, fails [without reasonable excuse] to do so, he shall be liable to a fine not exceeding [level 1 on the standard scale].

(3) Any constable shall, on the demand of the holder of a justices' licence or his agent or servant [or (as the case may be) a relevant person or any agent or servant of his], help to expel from the licensed premises any person liable to be expelled from them under this section, and may use such force as may be required for the purpose.

[(4) In this section 'relevant person' means any person who works in licensed premises in a capacity, whether paid or unpaid, which gives him authority to prevent such drunkenness or such conduct as is mentioned in section 172A(1) of this Act.]

Amendment
Sub-s (1): words 'or a relevant person' in square brackets inserted by the Criminal Justice and Police Act 2001, s 32(3)(a); words from 'and the holder' to 'any person' in square brackets substituted by the Criminal Justice and Police Act 2001, s 32(3)(b).
Sub-s (2): words from '(as the case' to 'his or by' in square brackets inserted by the Criminal Justice and Police Act 2001, s 32(4); words 'without reasonable excuse' in square brackets inserted by the Criminal Justice and Police Act 2001, s 18(2); maximum fine increased by the Criminal Law Act 1977, s 31, Sch 6, and converted to a level on the standard scale by the Criminal Justice Act 1982, ss 37, 46.
Sub-s (3): words from 'or (as the' to 'servant of his' in square brackets inserted by the Criminal Justice and Police Act 2001, s 32(5).
Sub-s (4): inserted by the Criminal Justice and Police Act 2001, s 32(6).

[A.104]

175   Prostitutes not to be allowed to assemble on licensed premises   (1) The holder of a justices' licence shall not knowingly allow the licensed premises to be the habitual resort or place of meeting of reputed prostitutes, whether the object of their so resorting or meeting is or is not prostitution; but this section does not prohibit his allowing any such persons to remain in the premises for the purpose of obtaining reasonable refreshment for such time as is necessary for that purpose.

(2) If the holder of a justices' licence contravenes this section he shall be liable [to a fine not exceeding level 2 on the standard scale].

Amendment
Sub-s (2): enhanced penalty on a subsequent conviction abolished and penalty on any conviction now a fine not exceeding level 2 on the standard scale by virtue of the Criminal Law Act 1977, s 31(6), (9), and the Criminal Justice Act 1982, ss 35, 37, 46.

[A.105]

176   Permitting licensed premises to be a brothel   (1) If the holder of a justices' licence permits the licensed premises to be a brothel, he shall be liable to a fine not exceeding [level 2 on the standard scale].

(2) If the holder of a justices' licence is convicted, whether under this section or under any other enactment, of permitting his premises to be a brothel, he shall forfeit the licence.

Amendment
Sub-s (1): maximum fine increased by the Criminal Law Act 1977, s 31(6), (9), and converted to a level on the standard scale by the Criminal Justice Act 1982, ss 37, 46.

[A.106]

177   Gaming on licensed premises   (1) If the holder of a justices' licence suffers any game to be played in the premises in such circumstances that an offence under [the Gaming Act 1968] is committed or a requirement or restriction for the time being in force under [section 6] of that Act is contravened, he shall be liable [to a fine not exceeding level 2 on the standard scale].

(2) The conviction of the holder of a justices' licence of an offence in connection with the licensed premises under section 1(1) of the Betting, Gaming and Lotteries Act 1963 shall for the purposes of this Act be deemed to be a conviction of an offence under this section.

Amendment
Sub-s (1): first and second words in square brackets substituted by the Gaming Act 1968, s 53(1)(b), Sch 11, Part III; enhanced penalty on a subsequent conviction abolished and penalty on any conviction now a fine not exceeding level 2 on the standard scale by virtue of the Criminal Law Act 1977, s 31(6), (9), and the Criminal Justice Act 1982, ss 35, 37, 46.

Offences in relation to constables

[A.107]

178   Offences in relation to constables   If the holder of a justices' licence—

(a)   knowingly suffers to remain on the licensed premises any constable during any part of the time appointed for the constable's being on duty, except for the purpose of the execution of the constable's duty, or

(b)   supplies any liquor or refreshment, whether by way of gift or sale, to any constable on duty except by authority of a superior officer of the constable, or

(c)   bribes or attempts to bribe any constable,

he shall be liable [to a fine not exceeding level 2 on the standard scale].

Amendment

Enhanced penalty on a subsequent conviction abolished and penalty on any conviction now a fine not exceeding level 2 on the standard scale by virtue of the Criminal Law Act 1977, s 31(6), (9), and the Criminal Justice Act 1982, ss 35, 37, 46.

Application to seamen's canteens and occasional licences

179 (*Not reproduced*)

PART XIII MISCELLANEOUS

[*Closure of certain licensed premises due to disorder or disturbance*]

[A.108]

[**179A   Closure order**   (1) A senior police officer may make a closure order in relation to relevant licensed premises if he reasonably believes that—

(a)   there is likely to be disorder on, or in the vicinity of and related to, the premises and the closure of the premises is necessary in the interests of public safety;

(b)   there is disorder on, or in the vicinity of and related to, the premises and the closure of the premises is necessary in the interests of public safety; or

(c)   a disturbance is being caused to the public by excessive noise emitted from the premises and the closure of the premises is necessary to prevent the disturbance.

(2) In this section and sections 179B to 179K of this Act—

'closure order' means an order requiring relevant licensed premises to be closed for a period not exceeding twenty-four hours beginning with the coming into force of the order; and

'relevant licensed premises' means licensed premises other than premises
for which a justices' off-licence only or an occasional licence is in
force and other than premises in respect of which a notice under
section 199(c) of this Act is in force.

(3) In determining whether to make a closure order the senior police
officer shall consider, in particular, any conduct of the holder of the
justices' licence for the premises or the manager of the premises in relation
to the disorder or disturbance.

(4) A closure order shall—
(a)   specify the premises which are to be closed;
(b)   specify the period for which the premises are to be closed;
(c)   specify the grounds for the making of the order; and
(d)   state the effect of sections 179B to 179E of this Act.

(5) A closure order shall come into force as soon as notice of the order is
given by a constable to—
(a)   the holder of the justices' licence for the premises; or
(b)   a manager of the premises.

(6) A person who, without reasonable excuse, permits relevant licensed
premises to be open in contravention of a closure order or any extension
of it shall be guilty of an offence and shall be liable to a fine not exceeding
£20,000 or to imprisonment for a term not exceeding three months or to
both.]

Amendment
Inserted by the Criminal Justice and Police Act 2001, s 17.

[A.109]

[179B   Consideration of closure order by certain justices   (1) The
responsible senior police officer shall, as soon as reasonably practicable
after the coming into force of a closure order, apply to relevant justices
for them to consider under this section the order and any extension of it.

(2) The relevant justices shall, as soon as reasonably practicable, consider
whether to exercise their powers under subsection (3) of this section in
relation to the order and any extension of it.

(3) The relevant justices may—
(a)   revoke the order and any extension of it if the order or extension is
      still in force;
(b)   order the relevant licensed premises to remain, or to be, closed until
      the matter is dealt with by an order of licensing justices at the next
      licensing sessions;
(c)   make any other order as they think fit in relation to the premises.

(4) In determining whether the premises will be, or will remain, closed
the relevant justices shall, in particular, consider whether—

(a)   in the case of an order made by virtue of section 179A(1)(a) or (b) of this Act, closure is necessary in the interests of public safety because of disorder or likely disorder on the premises or in the vicinity of, and related to, the premises;

(b)   in the case of an order made by virtue of section 179A(1)(c) of this Act, closure is necessary to ensure that no disturbance is, or is likely to be, caused to the public by excessive noise emitted from the premises.

(5) A person who, without reasonable excuse, permits relevant licensed premises to be open in contravention of an order made under subsection (3)(b) of this section shall be guilty of an offence and shall be liable to a fine not exceeding £20,000 or to imprisonment for a term not exceeding three months or to both.

(6) A person who, without reasonable excuse, fails to comply with, or does an act in contravention of, an order made under subsection (3)(c) of this section shall be guilty of an offence and shall be liable to a fine not exceeding level 5 on the standard scale or to imprisonment for a term not exceeding three months or to both.

(7) In this section and sections 179C to 179K of this Act 'relevant justices' means—

(a)   licensing justices for the licensing district in which the premises are situated; or

(b)   if no such justices are available within a reasonable time, justices of the peace acting for the petty sessions area in which the premises are situated.

(8) In this section and sections 179C to 179K of this Act 'the responsible senior police officer' means the senior police officer who made the closure order or, if another senior police officer is designated for this purpose by the chief officer of police for the police area in which the premises are situated, that other senior police officer.]

Amendment
Inserted by the Criminal Justice and Police Act 2001, s 17.

[A.110]

[179C   Extensions of closure order   (1) If, before the end of the period for which relevant licensed premises are to be closed under a closure order or any extension of it ('the closure period'), the responsible senior police officer reasonably believes that—

(a)   relevant justices will not have considered under section 179B of this Act the order and any extension of it by the end of the closure period; and

(b)   the conditions for an extension under this subsection are satisfied, he may extend the closure period for a further period, not exceeding twenty-four hours, beginning with the expiry of the previous closure period.

(2) For the purposes of subsection (1) of this section the conditions for an extension under that subsection are that—

(a)   in the case of an order made by virtue of section 179A(1)(a) or (b) of this Act, closure is necessary in the interests of public safety because of disorder or likely disorder on the premises or in the vicinity of, and related to, the premises;

(b)   in the case of an order made by virtue of section 179A(1)(c) of this Act, closure is necessary to ensure that no disturbance is, or is likely to be, caused to the public by excessive noise emitted from the premises.

(3) An extension under subsection (1) of this section shall, subject to subsection (4) of this section, come into force as soon as notice of it has been given by a constable to—

(a)   the holder of the justices' licence for the premises; or

(b)   a manager of the premises.

(4) No such extension shall come into force unless the notice has been given before the end of the previous closure period.]

Amendment
Inserted by the Criminal Justice and Police Act 2001, s 17.

[A.111]

[179D   Cancellation of closure order   (1) At any time—

(a)   after a closure order has been made; but

(b)   before the order and any extension of it has been considered by relevant justices under section 179B of this Act,

the responsible senior police officer may cancel the order and any extension of it.

(2) The responsible senior police officer shall cancel the closure order and any extension of it if he does not reasonably believe that—

(a)   in the case of an order made by virtue of section 179A(1)(a) or (b) of this Act, closure is necessary in the interests of public safety because of disorder or likely disorder on the relevant licensed premises or in the vicinity of, and related to, the premises;

(b)   in the case of an order made by virtue of section 179A(1)(c) of this Act, closure is necessary to ensure that no disturbance is, or is likely to be, caused to the public by excessive noise emitted from the premises.

(3) Where a closure order and any extension of it is cancelled under subsection (1) or (2) of this section, the responsible senior police officer

shall ensure that notice of the cancellation is given to—

(a)   the holder of the justices' licence for the premises; or

(b)   a manager of the premises.]

Amendment
Inserted by the Criminal Justice and Police Act 2001, s 17.

[A.112]

[179E   Revocation of justices' licence etc after closure order   (1) Where a closure order has come into force in relation to relevant licensed premises, licensing justices for the licensing district in which the premises are situated shall of their own motion consider, at the next licensing sessions, whether to exercise their powers under subsection (2) of this section.

(2) The licensing justices may—

(a)   revoke the justices' licence for the premises concerned; or

(b)   attach to it such conditions as they think fit (whether in substitution for any conditions previously attached or otherwise);

but no payment may be required in pursuance of a condition attached under paragraph (b) of this subsection.

(3) The power under subsection (2) of this section to revoke a justices' licence is exercisable on any ground on which licensing justices might refuse to renew a justices' licence or a justices' licence of that description.

(4) Licensing justices may only exercise their powers under subsection (2) of this section if, at least seven days before the commencement of the licensing sessions concerned, notice of the proposed exercise of the powers has been given to the holder of the licence specifying in general terms—

(a)   the grounds on which it is proposed that the licence should be revoked; or

(b)   (as the case may be) the conditions which are proposed to be attached to the licence and the reasons for them.

(5) Where licensing justices have decided at the next licensing sessions whether to exercise their powers under subsection (2) of this section, they may also make such order as they think fit in relation to the closure order and any extension of it or any order under section 179B of this Act.

(6) Where licensing justices have decided to revoke a justices' licence under subsection (2) of this section, the revocation shall, subject to subsection (7) of this section, not have effect—

(a)   until the expiry of the time given for appealing against the decision; or

(b)   if the decision is appealed against, until the appeal is disposed of.

(7) Where the premises to which the licence relates have been closed until the making of the decision to revoke the licence by virtue of an order under section 179B(3)(b) of this Act, the premises shall, subject to section 179G(5) of this Act, remain closed (but the licence otherwise in force)—

(a) until the expiry of the time given for appealing against the decision to revoke; or

(b) if the decision is appealed against, until the appeal is disposed of.

(8) A person who, without reasonable excuse, permits premises to be open in contravention of subsection (7) of this section shall be guilty of an offence and shall be liable to a fine not exceeding £20,000 or to imprisonment for a term not exceeding three months or to both.

(9) Where licensing justices have decided to attach conditions to a licence under subsection (2) of this section, the licensing justices may, on such terms as they think fit, suspend the operation of those conditions in whole or in part pending the determination of any appeal against the decision to attach them or pending the consideration of the question of bringing such an appeal.]

Amendment
Inserted by the Criminal Justice and Police Act 2001, s 17.

[A.113]

[179F Procedural requirements (1) Where an application under section 179B(1) of this Act is made to justices of the peace acting for the petty sessions area in which the premises concerned are situated, the responsible senior police officer shall give notice to the chief executive to the licensing justices for the licensing district in which the relevant licensed premises are situated—

(a) that a closure order has come into force;

(b) of the contents of the order and of any extension to the order; and

(c) of the application under section 179B(1) of this Act.

(2) The powers conferred on licensing justices by section 179B of this Act may be exercised by a single justice and may be exercised otherwise than at licensing sessions.

(3) The powers conferred on justices of the peace by section 179B of this Act shall be exercisable in the place required by the Magistrates' Courts Act 1980 (c 43) for the hearing of a complaint and may be exercised by a single justice.

(4) Evidence given for the purpose of proceedings under section 179B or 179E of this Act shall be given on oath.

(5) The Secretary of State may make regulations about the procedure and practice to be followed on and in connection with proceedings before licensing justices under sections 179B and 179E of this Act.]

Amendment
Inserted by the Criminal Justice and Police Act 2001, s 17.

[A.114]

[179G   Rights of appeal   (1) Any person aggrieved by a decision of relevant justices under section 179B of this Act or of licensing justices under section 179E of this Act may appeal to the Crown Court against the decision.

(2) An appeal under subsection (1) of this section shall be commenced by notice of appeal given by the appellant to the chief executive to the licensing justices or (as the case may be) to the justices' chief executive within 21 days after the decision appealed against.

(3) On an appeal against a decision under section 179E of this Act by licensing justices not to revoke a justices' licence, the holder of the licence shall be respondent in addition to the licensing justices.

(4) Where the holder of a justices' licence gives notice of appeal against a decision under section 179E of this Act by licensing justices to revoke the licence, the Crown Court may, on such conditions as it thinks fit, order that the licence shall continue in force until the determination of the appeal notwithstanding that the appeal is not determined until after the date when the licence would otherwise cease to have effect.

(5) Where—

(a)   the holder of a justices' licence gives notice of appeal against a decision under section 179E of this Act by licensing justices to revoke the licence; and

(b)   the premises are closed by virtue of section 179E(7) of this Act, the Crown Court may, on such conditions as it thinks fit, order that section 179E(7) of this Act shall not apply to the premises.

(6) Sections 21 and 22(3A) of this Act (appeals) do not apply to any decision of licensing justices which is subject to a right of appeal under subsection (1) of this section or to any appeal under subsection (1) of this section.

(7) Section 22(4), (6) and (7), section 23(3) and (4) and section 25(1) of this Act shall apply, with necessary modifications, to appeals under subsection (1) of this section against decisions of licensing justices as they apply to appeals under section 21 of this Act.

(8) Section 23(4) of this Act shall have effect, in its application by virtue of subsection (7) of this section, as if the reference to section 21(4) of this Act were a reference to subsection (4) of this section.]

Amendment
Inserted by the Criminal Justice and Police Act 2001, s 17.

[A.115]

[179H   Enforcement   (1) This section applies where a closure order or an order under section 179B(3)(b) of this Act has been made in relation to relevant licensed premises.

(2) Any person who without reasonable excuse fails to leave the premises when asked to do so, for the purposes of ensuring compliance with the order concerned (or with any extension of a closure order or with section 179E(7) of this Act), by the holder of the justices' licence for the premises or any manager of the premises shall be guilty of an offence and liable to a fine not exceeding level 1 on the standard scale.

(3) A constable shall, on the request of the holder of the justices' licence or any manager of the premises or any agent or servant of either of them, help to remove from the premises any person who is required to leave the premises by virtue of subsection (2) of this section.

(4) A constable may use such reasonable force as may be required for the purpose of giving help under subsection (3) of this section.]

Amendment
Inserted by the Criminal Justice and Police Act 2001, s 17.

[A.116]

[179I   Exemption from liability for certain damages   (1) A constable shall not be liable for relevant damages in respect of anything done or omitted to be done by him in the performance or purported performance of his functions in relation to a closure order or any extension of it.

(2) A chief officer of police shall not be liable for relevant damages in respect of anything done or omitted to be done by a constable under his direction or control in the performance or purported performance of the constable's functions in relation to a closure order or any extension of it.

(3) Neither subsection (1) of this section nor subsection (2) of this section applies—
(a)   if the act or omission is shown to have been in bad faith; or
(b)   so as to prevent an award of damages made in respect of an act or omission on the ground that the act or omission was unlawful as a result of section 6(1) of the Human Rights Act 1998 (c 42).

(4) This section is without prejudice to any other exemption from liability for damages (whether at common law or otherwise).

(5) In this section 'relevant damages' means damages in proceedings for judicial review or for the tort of negligence or misfeasance in public office.]

Amendment
Inserted by the Criminal Justice and Police Act 2001, s 17.

[A.117]

[179J Offences by body corporate (1) Where an offence under section 179A(6) or 179B(5) or (6) or 179E(8) of this Act committed by a body corporate is proved to have been committed with the consent or connivance of, or to be attributable to any neglect on the part of, a director, manager, secretary or other similar officer of the body corporate, he as well as the body corporate commits the offence and shall be liable to be proceeded against and punished accordingly.

(2) Where the affairs of a body corporate are managed by its members, subsection (1) of this section applies in relation to the acts and defaults of a member in connection with his functions of management as if he were a director of the body corporate.]

Amendment
Inserted by the Criminal Justice and Police Act 2001, s 17.

[A.118]

[179K Interpretation of sections 179A to 179K (1) In sections 179A to 179J of this Act and this section—
'chief officer of police' has the meaning given by section 101(1) of the Police Act 1996 (c 16);
'closure order' has the meaning given by section 179A(2) of this Act;
'manager' (except in section 179J(1) of this Act) means any person who works in relevant licensed premises in a capacity which gives him authority to close the premises;
'the next licensing sessions' means the first licensing sessions held not less than fourteen days after the day on which the closure order concerned was considered by relevant justices under section 179B of this Act;
'notice' means notice in writing;
'police area' means a police area provided for by section 1 of the Police Act 1996 (c 16);
'relevant justices' has the meaning given by section 179B(7) of this Act;
'relevant licensed premises' has the meaning given by section 179A(2) of this Act;
'the responsible senior police officer' has the meaning given by section 179B(8) of this Act; and
'senior police officer' means a police officer of or above the rank of inspector.

(2) For the purposes of sections 179A to 179J of this Act, relevant licensed premises are open if any person other than the holder of the justices' licence for the premises, a manager of the premises or any member of the family of either of them—

(a)   enters onto the premises; and
(b)   purchases, or is supplied with, any item of food or drink or any item
       which is usually sold on the premises.]

Amendment
Inserted by the Criminal Justice and Police Act 2001, s 17.

[*Other*]

[A.119]

180   Consent to grant of occasional licence   [(1) Justices of the peace
may, on the application of the holder of a justices' on-licence, grant him
a licence (in this Act referred to as an 'occasional licence') authorising
the sale by him of any intoxicating liquor to which his justices' on-licence
extends at such place other than the premises in respect of which his
justices' on-licence was granted, during such period not exceeding three
weeks at one time, and between such hours, as may be specified in the
occasional licence, but an occasional licence shall not authorise the sale
of intoxicating liquor thereunder—
(a)   in [any area] in Wales and Monmouthshire in which section 66(1)
       of this Act for the time being applies, on any Sunday; or
(b)   on Christmas Day, Good Friday, or any day appointed for public
       fast or thanksgiving.]

(2) Subject to the following provisions of this section, the justices shall
not hear an application for [an occasional licence] unless satisfied that
the applicant has served on the chief officer of police at least twenty-
four hours' notice of his intention to apply for [it], stating the name and
address of the applicant, the place and occasion for which [it] is required,
the period for which he requires it to be in force, and the hours to be
specified in [it].

(3) Subject to subsection (4) of this section, the justices may, if they see
fit, grant [an occasional licence] without a hearing if written application
for the grant is made by lodging two copies of the application with the
[chief executive] to the justices not less than one month before the day
or earliest day for which application is made, and the application gives
the particulars required for a notice under subsection (2) of this section.

(4) Where written application is made in accordance with subsection (3)
of this section—
(a)   the [chief executive] on receipt of the application shall serve notice
       of it on the chief officer of police by sending him a copy of the
       application; and
(b)   if, not later than seven days after the day he sends it, written notice
       of objection is given by or on behalf of the chief officer to the [chief
       executive] by lodging two copies with him, the application shall not

be granted without a hearing, unless the objection is afterwards withdrawn by a further notice given in the same way; and

(c) the [chief executive], on receipt of any such notice of objection or notice withdrawing objection, shall send a copy to the applicant.

(5) Where written application is made in accordance with subsection (3) of this section but the application is not granted without a hearing, the application may be heard without the applicant having served notice on the chief officer of police under subsection (2) of this section.

(6) Justices shall not grant [an occasional licence to an applicant who holds only a residential licence; and, if he holds only a restaurant licence or residential and restaurant licence, they shall not grant the occasional licence] unless satisfied that the sale of intoxicating liquor under the authority of the occasional licence is to be ancillary to the provision of substantial refreshment.

(7) The power of justices of the peace to grant [an occasional licence] shall be exercisable by justices acting for the petty sessions area in which the place to which the application relates is situated, and by the number of justices and in the place required by the Magistrates' Courts Act 1952 for the hearing of a complaint.

[(8) An occasional licence granted to the holder of a justices' on-licence in respect of any premises shall have effect as if granted to any person who is for the time being the holder of a justices' on-licence in respect of those premises and shall be of no effect at any time when no justices' licence is for the time being held in respect of those premises.]

Amendment

Sub-s (1): substituted by the Finance Act 1967, s 5(1)(c), Sch 7, para 15; words in square brackets in para (a) substituted by the Local Government (Wales) Act 1994, s 66(6), Sch 16, para 22(5).

Sub-ss (2), (3): words 'an occasional licence' in square brackets substituted by the Finance Act 1967, s 5(1)(c), Sch 7, para 15.

Sub-s (2): word 'it' in square brackets in each place it occurs substituted by the Finance Act 1967, s 5(1)(c), Sch 7, para 15.

Sub-s (3), (4): words 'chief executive' in square brackets in each place they occur substituted by the Access to Justice Act 1999, s 90(1), Sch 13, paras 36, 50(f).

Sub-s (6): words from 'an occasional licence' to 'the occasional licence' in square brackets substituted by the Finance Act 1967, s 5(1)(c), Sch 7, para 15.

Sub-s (7): words 'an occasional licence' in square brackets substituted by the Finance Act 1967, s 5(1)(c), Sch 7, para 15.

Sub-s (8): inserted by the Finance Act 1967, s 5(1)(c), Sch 7, para 15.

181 (*Repealed by the Licensing (Retail Sales) Act 1988.*)

[A.120]

[181A Sales to or by persons under 18 of intoxicating liquor on wholesale premises (1) In any premises from which he deals wholesale the wholesaler or his servant shall not sell intoxicating liquor to a person under eighteen.

(2) In any premises from which he deals wholesale the wholesaler shall not allow a person under eighteen to make any sale of intoxicating liquor unless the sale has been specifically approved by the wholesaler or by a person of or over the age of eighteen acting on his behalf.

(3) A person under eighteen shall not in premises from which intoxicating liquor is dealt in wholesale buy or attempt to buy such liquor.

(4) In proceedings for an offence under subsection (1) of this section—
(a)   where the person charged is charged by reason of his own act, it shall be a defence for him to prove—
  (i)   that he exercised all due diligence to avoid the commission of an offence under that subsection; or
  (ii)   that he had no reason to suspect that the other person was under eighteen; and
(b)   where the person charged is charged by reason of the act of some other person, it shall be a defence for him to prove that he exercised all due diligence to avoid the commission of an offence under that subsection.

(5) A person guilty of an offence under subsection (1) or (3) of this section shall be liable to a fine not exceeding level 3 on the standard scale.

(6) A person guilty of an offence under subsection (2) of this section shall be liable to a fine not exceeding level 1 on the standard scale.

(7) In this section 'wholesaler' and 'wholesale' have the same meaning as in section 4 of the Alcoholic Liquor Duties Act 1979.]

Amendment
Inserted by the Licensing Act 1988, s 17.

[A.121]

182   Relaxation with respect to licensed premises, of law relating to music and dancing licences and billiards   (1) No statutory regulations for music and dancing shall apply to licensed premises so as to require any licence for the provision in the premises of public entertainment by the reproduction of wireless (including television) broadcasts [or of programmes included in any programme service (within the meaning of the Broadcasting Act 1990) other than a sound or television broadcasting service], or of public entertainment by way of music and singing only which is provided solely by the reproduction of recorded sound, or by not more than two performers, or sometimes in one of those ways and sometimes in the other.

(2) ...

Amendment
Sub-s (1): words in square brackets substituted by the Broadcasting Act 1990, s 203(1), Sch 20, para 7.
Sub-s (2): repealed by the Billiards (Abolition of Restrictions) Act 1987, s 1, Schedule.

[A.122]

183   Name of holder of licence, etc, to be affixed to licensed premises
(1) Subject to section 55(5) of this Act, the holder of a justices' licence, other than a residential licence, shall keep painted on or affixed to the licensed premises in a conspicuous place, and in such form and manner as the licensing justices may direct, his name, and after the name the word 'licensed' followed by words sufficient to express the business for which the licence is granted, and in particular—

(a)   words expressing whether the licence is an on-licence or an off-licence;

(b)   if the licence is a six-day licence or an early-closing licence, words indicating that the licence is such.

(2) In the case of a restaurant licence or a residential and restaurant licence the nature of the business for which the licence is granted is sufficiently indicated for the purposes of subsection (1) of this section, so far as relates to the restrictions imposed by the conditions as to the sale and supply of intoxicating liquor, if the words express that the holder of the licence is licensed to sell for consumption on the premises with meals.

(3) A person shall not have on his premises words or letters importing that he is authorised, as the holder of a licence, to sell any intoxicating liquor that he is not authorised to sell.

(4) If any person contravenes this section he shall be liable [to a fine not exceeding level 2 on the standard scale].

Amendment
Sub-s (4): enhanced penalty on a subsequent conviction abolished and penalty on any conviction now a fine not exceeding level 2 on the standard scale by virtue of the Criminal Law Act 1977, s 31(6), (9), and the Criminal Justice Act 1982, ss 35, 37, 46.

[A.123]

184   Communication between licensed premises and places of public resort   (1) If any person makes or uses, or allows to be made or used, any internal communication between licensed premises and any premises, other than licensed premises, used for public resort, or as a refreshment house, he shall be guilty of an offence, and shall be guilty of a further offence for every day on which the communication remains open.

(2) A person guilty of an offence under this section shall be liable to a fine not exceeding ten pounds and, if he is the holder of a justices' licence, he shall on conviction forfeit the licence.

Amendment
Sub-s (2): maximum fine (apart from daily fine, which remains at £10) increased by the Criminal Law Act 1977, s 31(6), (9), and converted to level 1 on the standard scale by the Criminal Justice Act 1982, ss 37, 46.

[A.124]

185 Licence or exemption order to be produced on demand If the holder of a justices' licence, [an occasional licence] a canteen licence [, an order under section 87A of this Act] or a general or special order of exemption, on being ordered by a justice of the peace, [or constable] to produce it for examination, fails to do so within a reasonable time he shall be liable to a fine not exceeding [level 1 on the standard scale].

Amendment
First words in square brackets inserted, and third words in square brackets substituted, by the Finance Act 1967, s 5(1)(c), Sch 7, para 17; second words in square brackets inserted by the Licensing Act 1988, s 19, Sch 3, para 18; maximum fine increased by the Criminal Law Act 1977, s 31(6), (9), and converted to a level on the standard scale by the Criminal Justice Act 1982, ss 37, 46.

[A.125]

186 Right of constables to enter premises [(1) For the purpose of preventing or detecting the commission of any offence against this Act a constable may enter licensed premises, a licensed canteen or premises for which or any part of which a special hours certificate is in force under section 78 [or 78ZA] of this Act—
(a) at any time within the hours specified in relation to the premises in subsection (1A) of this section, and
(b) in the case of premises for which a justices' licence is in force or a licensed canteen, at any time outside those hours when he suspects, with reasonable cause, that such an offence is being or is about to be committed there.

(1A) The hours referred to in subsection (1)(a) of this section are—
(a) in the case of licensed premises (other than premises which are licensed premises by virtue only of an occasional licence) or a licensed canteen, the permitted hours and the first half hour after the end of any period forming part of those hours;
(b) in the case of premises for which an occasional licence is in force, the hours specified in the licence;
(c) in the case of premises for which, or any part of which, a special hours certificate is in force under section 78 [or 78ZA] of this Act, the hours beginning at eleven o'clock in the evening and ending thirty minutes after the end of the permitted hours fixed by section 76 of this Act;

and, in relation to premises within more than one paragraph of this subsection, the hours referred to in subsection (1)(a) are the hours specified in any of the relevant paragraphs.]

(2) If any person, himself or by any person in his employ or acting with his consent, fails to admit a constable who demands entry to premises in pursuance of this section he shall be liable [to a fine not exceeding level 1 on the standard scale].

Amendment
Sub-ss (1), (1A): substituted for sub-s (1), as originally enacted, by the Licensing (Amendment) Act 1977, s 1; words in square brackets inserted by SI 1996/977, art 5(8). Sub-s (2): maximum fines on first or subsequent convictions increased to the same amount by the Criminal Law Act 1977, s 31(6), (9), and converted to level 1 on the standard scale by the Criminal Justice Act 1982, ss 37, 46.

[A.126]

187   Search warrant   (1) If a justice of the peace is satisfied by information on oath that there is reasonable ground for believing that any intoxicating liquor is sold by retail or exposed or kept for sale by retail at any place in the [commission area] for which he is justice, being a place where that liquor may not lawfully be sold by retail, he may issue a search warrant under his hand to a constable authorising him at any time or times within one month from the date of the warrant to enter that place, which shall be named in the warrant, by force if need be, and search the place for intoxicating liquor and seize and remove any intoxicating liquor that the constable has reasonable grounds for supposing to be in the place for the purpose of unlawful sale there or elsewhere, and the vessels containing the liquor.

(2) If the owner or occupier of the place from which any intoxicating liquor has been removed under the preceding subsection is convicted of selling by retail, or of exposing for sale by retail, any intoxicating liquor that he is not authorised to sell by retail, or is convicted of having in his possession intoxicating liquor that he is not authorised to sell, any intoxicating liquor so removed, and the vessels containing it, shall be forfeited.

(3) Where a constable seizes any intoxicating liquor in pursuance of a warrant issued under this section, any person found in the place shall, unless he proves that he is there for a lawful purpose, be liable to a fine not exceeding [level 1 on the standard scale].

(4) Where a constable seizes any liquor as aforesaid, and any person so found, on being asked by a constable for his name and address—
(a)   refuses to give them, or
(b)   gives a false name or address, or

(c) gives a name or address that the constable has reasonable grounds for thinking to be false, and refuses to answer satisfactorily any questions put by the constable to ascertain the correctness of the name or address given,

he shall be liable to a fine not exceeding [level 1 on the standard scale].

(5) ...

Amendment
Sub-s (1): words 'commission area' in square brackets substituted by the Access to Justice Act 1999, s 76(2), Sch 10, paras 23, 26.
Sub-ss (3), (4): maximum fines increased by the Criminal Law Act 1977, s 31(6), (9), and converted to levels on the standard scale by the Criminal Justice Act 1982, ss 37, 46.
Sub-s (5): repealed by the Police and Criminal Evidence Act 1984, s 119, Sch 7, Part I.

188–192 (*Not reproduced*)

[A.127]

[192A Power of justices at licensing sessions to act in divisions (1) If a majority of the licensing justices present at a licensing sessions so resolve, they may for the purposes of that sessions constitute themselves into two or more divisions.

(2) A division constituted in accordance with this section may exercise all the powers exercisable by licensing justices under this Act and those powers shall be exercisable by a majority of the members present at a meeting of the division assembled for the purpose.

(3) The quorum of a division of justices constituted under this section shall be three.]

Amendment
Inserted by the Licensing Act 1988, s 14(2).

193 (*Not reproduced*)

[A.128]

[193A Power of clerk to licensing justices to grant unopposed renewals of justices' licences and canteen licences (1) This section has effect in relation to applications for the renewal of justices' licences and canteen licences made to the general annual licensing sessions immediately preceding the expiry of a licensing period.

(2) The clerk to licensing justices may exercise on behalf of the justices their powers with respect to an application for the renewal of a justices' licence or canteen licence if—

(a) the application is not opposed; or

(b) where under this Act the application may only be refused on specified grounds, it is not opposed on a ground on which renewal may be refused.

(3) An application may not be dealt with under this section if—
(a)   the justices so direct;
(b)   it is made in conjunction with any other application or request with respect to the licence sought to be renewed; or
(c)   in the case of an application for the renewal of a justices' licence, there is a relevant entry in the register of justices' licences maintained under this Act which relates to the applicant or the premises for which the licence is sought.

(4) An entry in the register of justices' licences is relevant for the purposes of this section if it is an entry made in pursuance of section 31 of this Act or section 163(1)(b) or 168(7)(a) of the Representation of the People Act 1983 (reports or convictions of bribery or treating to be entered in the register).]

Amendment
Inserted by the Licensing Act 1988, s 13.

[A.129]
[193AA   Power of clerk to licensing justices to grant certain transfers etc   (1) This section applies where—
(a)   the power of licensing justices to transfer a justices' licence for any premises is exercisable by virtue of section 8(1) of this Act, and
(b)   application is made for the transfer of the licence or the grant of an interim authority.

(2) If the applicant—
(a)   holds a justices' licence, or
(b)   has held such a licence at any time in the three years immediately preceding the date of the application,

the clerk to the licensing justices may grant the application on behalf of the justices unless he considers that there are circumstances which make it desirable for the matter to be considered by the justices.

(3) The functions of the clerk to the licensing justices under this section may be exercised otherwise than at licensing sessions.]

Amendment
Inserted by SI 1998/114, art 4.

[A.130]
[193B   Power of licensing justices to award costs   (1) On the hearing of any application under this Act relating to licensed premises or a seamen's canteen, the licensing justices may make such order as they think just and reasonable for the payment of costs to the applicant by any person opposing the application or by the applicant to any such person.

(2) For the purposes of enforcement an order for costs made under subsection (1) above shall be treated as an order for the payment of a sum enforceable as a civil debt.]

Amendment
Inserted by the Licensing Act 1988, s 15.

194–195 (*Not reproduced*)

[A.131]
196   Proof of sale or consumption of intoxicating liquor   (1) Evidence that a transaction in the nature of a sale of intoxicating liquor took place shall, in any proceedings relating to an offence under this Act, be evidence of the sale of the liquor without proof that money passed.

(2) Evidence that consumption of intoxicating liquor was about to take place shall in any such proceedings be evidence of the consumption of intoxicating liquor without proof of actual consumption.

(3) Evidence that any person, other than the occupier of licensed premises or a servant employed in licensed premises, [or, as the case may be, other than the occupier of a licensed canteen or a servant employed in such a canteen] consumed or intended to consume intoxicating liquor in the premises [or, as the case may be, canteen] shall be evidence that the liquor was sold by or on behalf of the holder of the justices' licence [occasional licence or canteen licence, as the case may be,] to that person.

Amendment
Sub-s (3): words in square brackets substituted by the Finance Act 1967, s 5(1)(c), Sch 7, para 18.

196A–198 (*Not reproduced*)

[A.132]
199   Exemptions and savings   Nothing in this Act shall—
(a) affect any privilege enjoyed by the University of Cambridge or by any person to whom any such privilege has been transferred in pursuance of any Act;
(b) affect the exemption from the requirement to take out a justices' licence enjoyed by the company of the master, warden and commonalty of Vintners of the City of London;
[(c) make unlawful the sale or exposure for sale by retail without a justices' licence of any intoxicating liquor at any premises in respect of which a licence under the Theatres Act 1968 is for the time being in force, or which by virtue of any letters patent of the Crown may lawfully be used for the public performance of plays without a

licence under that Act being held in respect thereof, if the proprietor of those premises has given to the [chief executive] to the licensing justices notice in writing of the intention to sell such liquor by retail at those premises and that notice has not been withdrawn;]

[(d) make unlawful the sale or exposure for sale by retail without a justices' licence to passengers in an aircraft, vessel or railway passenger vehicle of intoxicating liquor for consumption on board the aircraft, vessel or vehicle if the aircraft or vessel is employed for the carriage of passengers and is being flown or navigated from a place in the United Kingdom to another such place or from and to the same place in the United Kingdom on the same day or, as the case may be, if the vehicle is a vehicle in which passengers can be supplied with food;]

(e) prohibit the sale of medicated or methylated spirits;

(f) prohibit the sale by registered medical practitioners or registered pharmacists of spirits made up in medicine;

(g) prohibit the sale of intoxicating liquor by wholesale;

(h) affect any penalties recoverable by or on behalf of the Commissioners, or, except where the context requires it, any laws relating to excise; or

(i) apply to the sale or consumption of intoxicating liquor in canteens.

Amendment
Para (c) substituted by the Theatres Act 1968, s 19(1), Sch 2; in para (c) words 'chief executive' in square brackets substituted by the Access to Justice Act 1999, s 90(1), Sch 13, paras 36, 50(g); para (d) substituted by the Finance Act 1967, s 5(1)(c), Sch 7, para 20.

[A.133]

200   Meaning of 'licensed premises' in this Act and s 12 of Licensing Act 1872   (1) Any reference in this Act to licensed premises shall, unless the context otherwise requires, be construed as a reference to premises for which a justices' licence [or occasional licence is in force and as including a reference to any [premises] in respect of which a notice under section 199(c) of this Act is for the time being in force] ...

(2) In section 12 of the Licensing Act 1872 the expression 'licensed premises' shall include any place where intoxicating liquor is sold under an occasional licence.

Amendment
Sub-s (1): first words in square brackets substituted by the Finance Act 1967, s 5(1)(c), Sch 7, para 21, word in square brackets therein substituted by the Theatres Act 1968, s 19(1), Sch 2; words omitted repealed by SI 1979/977 and by the Licensing (Abolition of State Management) Act 1971, s 1.

[A.134]

201 Interpretation of other expressions (1) In this Act, unless the context otherwise requires—

'bar' includes any place exclusively or mainly used for the sale and consumption of intoxicating liquor;

'canteen', except in Part X of this Act and in the expressions 'canteen licence' and 'licensed canteen', means a canteen in which the sale or supply of intoxicating liquor is carried on under the authority of the Secretary of State;

'canteen licence' has the meaning assigned to it by section 148(1) of this Act;

['children's certificate' has the meaning assigned to it by section 168A(2) of this Act;]

['cider' includes perry;]

'club premises' has the meaning assigned to it by section 39(6) of this Act.

'the Commissioners' means the Commissioners of Customs and Excise;

...

'development corporation' has the same meaning as in the New Towns Act 1946;

'early-closing licence' has the meaning assigned to it by section 65(2) of this Act;

'enactment' includes an enactment contained in any order, regulation or other instrument having effect by virtue of an Act;

'the general licensing hours' has the meaning assigned to it by section 60 (5) of this Act;

'general order of exemption' has the meaning assigned to it by section 74 (1) of this Act;

'grant' in relation to a justices' licence includes a grant by way of renewal, transfer or removal and 'application' shall be construed accordingly;

['interim authority' has the meaning assigned to it by section 9A(2) of this Act;]

['intoxicating liquor' means spirits, wine, beer, cider, and any other fermented, distilled or spirituous liquor [but does not include—

   [(a) any liquor which is of a strength not exceeding 0.5 per cent at the time of the sale or other conduct in question;]

   (b) perfumes;

   (c) flavouring essences recognised by the Commissioners as not being intended for consumption as or with dutiable alcoholic liquor;

   (d) spirits, wine or made-wine so medicated as to be, in the opinion of the Commissioners, intended for use as a medicine and not as a beverage;

and expressions used in paragraphs (a) and (d) above shall have the same meaning as in the Alcoholic Liquor Duties Act 1979];]

'licensed canteen' means a canteen within the meaning of Part X of this Act in respect of which a canteen licence is in force;

['licensing period' has the meaning assigned to it by section 26(5) of this Act;]

'mess' means an authorised mess of members of Her Majesty's naval, military or air forces;

['the metropolis' means [the area consisting of the inner London boroughs and the City of London];]

'the Minister' means the Minister of Housing and Local Government;

['occasional licence' means a licence granted under section 180 of this Act;]

'old on-licence' has the meaning assigned to it by section 12(1) of this Act;

'ordinary removal' has the meaning assigned to it by section 5(6) of this Act;

'Part IV licence' has the meaning assigned to it by section 93 of this Act;

'planning removal' has the meaning assigned to it by section 121(2) of this Act;

'registered', in relation to a club, has the meaning assigned to it by section 40(1) of this Act;

'registered owner' has the meaning assigned to it by section 32(3) of this Act;

'residential licence', 'residential and restaurant licence' and 'restaurant licence' have the meanings assigned to them by section 94 of this Act;

['restriction order' has the meaning assigned to it by section 67A(2) of this Act;]

['sale by retail', in relation to any intoxicating liquor, means a sale of any such liquor at any one time to any one person, except where the sale is—

(a) to a trader for the purposes of his trade;

(b) to a registered club for the purposes of the club;

(c) to any canteen or mess;

(d) to the holder of an occasional permission within the meaning of the Licensing (Occasional Permissions) Act 1983 for the purposes of sales authorised by that permission; or

(e) of not less than the following quantities—

   (i) in the case of spirits, wine or made-wine, 9 litres or 1 case; or

   (ii) in the case of beer or cider, 20 litres or 2 cases,

   and is made from premises owned by the vendor, or occupied

by him under a lease to which the provisions of Part 2 of the
Landlord and Tenant Act 1954 apply.]
'seasonal licence' has the meaning assigned to it by section 64(2) of this
Act;
'secretary', in relation to a club, includes any officer of the club or other
person performing the duties of a secretary and, in relation to a
proprietary club where there is no secretary, the proprietor of the
club;
'six-day licence' has the meaning assigned to it by section 65(2) of this
Act;
'special hours certificate' means a certificate granted under section 77[,
77A, 78 or 78ZA] of this Act;
'special order of exemption' has the meaning assigned to it by section
74 (4) of this Act;
'special removal' has the meaning assigned to it by section 15(2) of this
Act;
'statutory regulations for music and dancing' means—
    [(i)   Schedule 12 to the London Government Act 1963; or
    (ii) Schedule 1 to the Local Government (Miscellaneous
          Provisions) Act 1982;]
'table meal' means a meal eaten by a person seated at a table, or at a
counter or other structure which serves the purpose of a table and is
not used for the service of refreshments for consumption by persons
not seated at a table or structure serving the purpose of a table;
'temporary premises removal' has the meaning assigned to it by section
126(2) of this Act;
['wine' means wine or made-wine as defined in section 1 of the Alcoholic
Liquor Duties Act 1979].

(2) For the purposes of this Act a person shall be treated as residing in
any premises, notwithstanding that he occupies sleeping accommodation
in a separate building, if he is provided with that accommodation in the
course of a business of providing board and lodging for reward at those
premises and the building is habitually used for the purpose by way of
annexe or overflow in connection with those premises and is occupied
and managed with those premises.

(3) ...

(4) Any provision in this Act requiring or authorising notice to be given
to the chief officer of police shall be construed as requiring or authorising
the notice to be given—
(a)   if the premises to which the notice relates (that is to say, in the case
      of an application for a licence, the premises to be licensed) are in
      the City of London, to the Commissioner of Police for the City;

(b)   if the premises are in the metropolitan police district, to the Commissioner of Police of the Metropolis;

(c)   if the premises are in any other police area to the chief constable for that area.

(5) Except where the context otherwise requires, references in this Act to any enactment are references to that enactment as amended, and include references thereto as extended or applied, by any other enactment, including this Act.

Amendment
Sub-s (1): definition 'children's certificate' inserted by the Deregulation and Contracting Out Act 1994, s 39, Sch 11, para 1(4); definition 'cider' inserted by the Finance Act 1967, s 5(1)(c), Sch 7, para 22; definition omitted repealed by the Licensing (Alcohol Education and Research) Act 1981, s 11, Sch 2, Pt I; definition 'interim authority' inserted by SI 1998/114, art 3(2); definition 'intoxicating liquor' substituted by the Finance Act 1967, s 5(1)(c), Sch 7, para 22; in definition 'intoxicating liquor' words from 'but does' to 'Act 1979' in square brackets substituted by the Finance Act 1981, s 11(1), Sch 8, Pt III, para 25; in definition 'intoxicating liquor' para (a) substituted by the Licensing (Low Alcohol Drinks) Act 1990, s 1; definition 'licensing period' inserted by the Licensing Act 1988, s 11(4); definition 'the metropolis' substituted by the Administration of Justice Act 1964, s 39(2), Sch 3, Pt II, para 31(4); in definition 'the metropolis' words from 'the area consisting' to 'City of London' in square brackets substituted by the Access to Justice Act 1999, s 76(2), Sch 10, paras 23, 29; definition 'occasional licence' substituted by the Finance Act 1967, s 5(1)(c), Sch 7, para 22; definition 'restriction order' inserted by the Licensing Act 1988, s 11(4); definition 'sale by retail' substituted by the Licensing (Retail Sales) Act 1988, s 1(1); in definition 'special hours certificate' words ', 77A, 78 or 78ZA' in square brackets substituted by SI 1996/977, art 5(9); in definition 'statutory regulations for music and dancing' paras (i), (ii) substituted by the Local Government (Miscellaneous Provisions) Act 1982, s 1, Sch 2, para 6; definition 'wine' substituted by the Alcoholic Liquor Duties Act 1979, s 92(1), Sch 3, para 5(3).
Sub-s (3): repealed by the Administration of Justice Act 1964, s 41(8), Sch 5.

202–204 (*Not reproduced*)

SCHEDULE 1   (*Not reproduced*)

SCHEDULE 2 APPLICATIONS FOR JUSTICES' LICENCES

Sections 3, 71

[A.135]

1   A person proposing to apply at a licensing sessions for the grant of a new justices' licence, or for the ordinary or special removal or the transfer of a justices' licence, shall give the following notices—

(a) not less than twenty-one days before the day of the licensing sessions he shall give notice in writing to the [chief executive] to the licensing justices, the chief officer of police and the proper local authority;

(b) in the case of a transfer he shall give the like notice to the holder of the licence (if any), and in the case of a removal he shall give the like notice to the registered owner of the premises from which it is sought to remove the licence and the holder of the licence (if any) unless he is also the applicant;

(c) except in the case of a transfer, he shall—

    (i) not more than twenty-eight days before the day of the licensing sessions display notice of the application for a period of seven days in a place where it can conveniently be read by the public on or near the premises to be licensed (or, in the case of an application for a provisional grant, on or near the proposed site of those premises); and

    (ii) not more than twenty-eight days nor less than fourteen days before the day of the licensing sessions (and, if the licensing justices so require, on some day or days outside that period but within such other period as they may require) advertise notice of the application in a newspaper circulating in the place where the premises to be licensed are situated.

2 A person proposing to apply at transfer sessions for the renewal of a justices' licence shall give notice in accordance with sub-paragraph (a) of paragraph 1 of this Schedule.

3 With the notice given under sub-paragraph (a) of paragraph 1 of this Schedule to the [chief executive] to the licensing justices there shall be deposited a plan of the premises to be licensed, if the application is—

(a) for the grant of a new justices' on-licence or of an ordinary removal of a justices' on-licence; or

(b) for the provisional grant of a new justices' off-licence or of an ordinary removal of a justices' off-licence;

and is not an application made in accordance with section 6(5) of this Act.

4 A notice under this Schedule—

(a) shall be signed by the applicant or his authorised agent;

(b) shall state the name and address of the applicant and, except in the case of a removal of a licence held by him or of a renewal, his trade or calling during the six months preceding the giving of the notice;

(c) shall state the situation of the premises to be licensed and, in the case of a removal, the premises from which it is sought to remove the licence;

(d) in the case of a new licence, shall state the kind of licence for which application is to be made.

5 The notice required by sub-paragraph (a) of paragraph 1 of this Schedule to be given to the proper local authority shall be given—

[(a) if the premises to be licensed are [in England but] outside Greater London, to the proper officer of the district council; and

[(aa) if the premises to be licensed are in Wales, to the proper officer of the county council or county borough council; and]

(b) if the premises to be licensed are in a parish, to the proper officer of the parish council or, where there is no parish council, to the chairman of the parish meeting; and

(c) if the premises are in a community where there is a community council, to the proper officer of that council];

and, in the case of a new licence or a removal, shall also be given to the authority discharging in the area where those premises are situated the functions of fire authority under the Fire Services Act 1947.

6 The [chief executive] to the licensing justices shall for each licensing sessions keep a list of the persons giving notice under this Schedule of their intention to apply for the grant of a justices' licence; and the list shall show the name and address of the applicant, the nature of the application and the situation of the premises to be licensed, and for the fourteen days preceding the sessions shall at all reasonable times be open to inspection, by any person on payment of the appropriate fee (if any) and, without payment, by any officer of Customs and Excise.

7 Where the applicant for the grant of a justices' licence has, through inadvertence or misadventure, failed to comply with the requirements of the preceding paragraphs of this Schedule, the licensing justices may, upon such terms as they think fit, postpone consideration of his application; and, if on the postponed consideration they are satisfied that any terms so imposed have been complied with, they may deal with the application as if the applicant had complied with those requirements.

8 On the consideration of an application for a justices' licence the applicant shall, if so required by the licensing justices, attend in person, and licensing justices may postpone consideration of an application until the applicant does so attend; but he shall not be required to attend in the case of a renewal unless objection is made to the renewal.

9 ...

Amendment
Para 1: in sub-para (a) words 'chief executive' in square brackets substituted by the Access to Justice Act 1999, s 90(1), Sch 13, paras 36, 51(a).
Para 3: words 'chief executive' in square brackets substituted by the Access to Justice Act 1999, s 90(1), Sch 13, paras 36, 51(b).
Para 5: para (a) substituted by the Local Government Act 1972, s 204, Sch 25, Part I, para 6, words in square brackets inserted by the Local Government (Wales) Act 1994, s 66(6), Sch 16, para 22(6); para (aa) inserted by the Local Government (Wales) Act 1994,

s 66(6), Sch 16, para 22(6); paras (b), (c) substituted by the Local Government Act 1972, s 204, Sch 25, Part I, para 6.
Para 6: words 'chief executive' in square brackets substituted by the Access to Justice Act 1999, s 90(1), Sch 13, paras 36, 51(c).
Para 9: repealed by the Licensing Act 1988, s 19, Sch 4.

SCHEDULES 3, 4 *(Repealed by the Licensing (Alcohol Education and Research) Act 1981.)*

SCHEDULE 5 REQUIREMENTS TO BE COMPLIED WITH BY CLUB'S APPLICATION FOR REGISTRATION CERTIFICATE

Section 40

[A.136]

1   The application shall specify the name, objects and address of the club, and shall state that there is kept at that address a list of the names and addresses of the members.

2   The application shall state, in terms of subsections (1) and (2) of section 41 of this Act, that the club is qualified under those subsections to receive a registration certificate for the premises, or will be so qualified if, as regards any provision of the rules specified in the application, the court sees fit to give a direction under section 42(2) of this Act.

3   The application shall set out, or shall incorporate a document annexed which sets out, the names and addresses of the members of any committee having the general management of the affairs of the club, and those of the members of any other committee concerned with the purchase for the club or with the supply by the club of intoxicating liquor, and those of other officers of the club.

4   (1) The application shall state, or shall incorporate a document annexed which states, the rules of the club or, in the case of an application for renewal, the changes in the rules made since the last application for the issue or renewal of the certificate.

(2) If, in the case of an application for renewal, there has been no such change as aforesaid, the application shall so state.

5   The application shall—
(a)   identify the premises for which the issue or renewal of the registration certificate is sought; and
(b)   state that those premises are or are to be occupied by and habitually used for the purposes of the club, the times at which they are or are

to be open to members and the hours (if any) fixed by or under the rules of the club as the permitted hours there; and

(c)   state the interest held by or in trust for the club in those premises and, if it is a leasehold interest or if the club has no interest, the name and address of any person to whom payment is or is to be made of rent under the lease or otherwise for the use of the premises.

6   (1) The application shall give, or shall incorporate a document annexed which gives—

(a)   particulars of any property not comprised in paragraph 5 of this Schedule which is or is to be used for the purposes of the club and not held by or in trust for the club absolutely, including the name and address of any person to whom payment is or is to be made for the use of that property;

(b)   particulars of any liability of the club in respect of the principal or interest of moneys borrowed by the club or charged on property held by or in trust for the club, including the name and address of the person to whom payment is or is to be made on account of that principal or interest;

(c)   particulars of any liability of the club or of a trustee for the club in respect of which any person has given any guarantee or provided any security, together with particulars of the guarantee or security given or provided, including the name and address of the person giving or providing it.

(2) An application for renewal, or document annexed to it, may give the particulars required by this paragraph by reference to the changes (if any) since the last application by the club for the issue or renewal of the registration certificate.

(3) If there is no property or liability of which particulars are required by any paragraph of sub-paragraph (1) of this paragraph, the application shall so state.

(4) In this paragraph, 'liability' includes a future or contingent liability.

7   (1) The application shall give, or shall incorporate a document annexed which gives, particulars of any premises not comprised in paragraph 5 of this Schedule, which have within the preceding twelve months been occupied and habitually used for the purposes of the club, and shall state the interest then held by or in trust for the club in those premises and, if it was a leasehold interest or if the club had no interest, the name and address of any person to whom payment was made of rent under the lease or otherwise for the use of the premises.

(2) If there are no premises of which particulars are required by this paragraph, the application shall so state.

8 Where the interest held by or in trust for the club in any land of which particulars are required by paragraph 5, 6 or 7 of this Schedule is or was a leasehold interest, and the rent under the lease is not or was not paid by the club or the trustees for the club, the application shall state the name and address of the person by whom it is or was paid.

SCHEDULE 6 PROCEDURE ON APPLICATIONS AND COMPLAINTS RELATING TO REGISTRATION CERTIFICATES

Sections 40, 44, 92

PART I ISSUE, RENEWAL AND SURRENDER OF REGISTRATION CERTIFICATES

Applications, etc

[A.137]

1 (1) An application by a club for the issue, renewal or variation of a registration certificate shall be made by lodging the application, together with the number of additional copies required under paragraph 4 of this Schedule, with the [chief executive] to the justices.

(2) The court may, on such conditions as the court thinks fit, allow such an application to be amended.

(3) An amended application shall be made by lodging with the [chief executive] to the justices the original application or the relevant parts of it altered so as to show the amendments, together with the number of additional copies required under paragraph 4 of this Schedule.

2 A registration certificate shall be surrendered by lodging with the [chief executive] to the justices a notice of surrender, together with the certificate and such number of additional copies of the notice as is required under paragraph 4 of this Schedule.

3 (1) Any such application or amended application and any such notice shall be signed by the chairman or by the secretary of the club.

(2) In the absence of objection the court shall not require proof that an application or amended application purporting to be so signed is duly signed.

4 On receipt of any such application or amended application or of any such notice the [chief executive to] the justices shall forthwith send a copy to any chief officer of police concerned and to the clerk of any local authority concerned, and the number of additional copies required to be lodged with the [chief executive is] the number necessary to provide the copies the [chief executive needs] for this purpose.

5   A club applying for the issue of a registration certificate for any premises, or for the renewal of a registration certificate in respect of different, additional or enlarged premises, shall give public notice of the application (identifying those premises and giving the name and address of the club) either—

(a)   by displaying the notice on or near the premises, in a place where it can conveniently be read by the public, for the seven days beginning with the date of the application; or

(b)   by advertisement on one at least of those days in a newspaper circulating in the place where the premises are situated.

Objections, etc

6   (1) Subject to sub-paragraph (2) of this paragraph, an objection to an application for the issue or renewal of a registration certificate shall be made by lodging with the [chief executive] to the justices two copies in writing of the objection not later than twenty-eight days after the making of the application or, if the application is amended, after the making of the amended application.

(2) If a magistrates' court extends the time allowed under section 45 of this Act to the chief officer of police, fire authority or local authority for inspecting premises to which the application relates, that court shall also extend the time in which the chief officer or authority may make objections to the application.

7   On receipt of an objection to an application for the issue or renewal of a registration certificate the [chief executive] to the justices shall forthwith send a copy to the person signing the application at any address furnished by him for communications relating to the application or, in default of such an address, at the address given in the application as that of the club.

8   Paragraphs 6 and 7 of this Schedule shall apply in relation to any notice of intention, on an application for the issue, renewal or variation of a registration certificate, to make representations as to conditions relating to the sale of intoxicating liquor as they apply to objections to an application for the issue or renewal of a registration certificate (with the substitution of references to giving the notice for references to making the objection).

9   Where any such objection is made or any such notice is given, the magistrates' court may make such order as it thinks just and reasonable for the payment of costs to the club by the person making the objection or giving the notice or by the club to that person; and for purposes of enforcement the order shall be treated as an order for the payment of a sum enforceable as a civil debt.

10 Where a club applies for a renewal of a registration certificate, and the magistrates' court under paragraph 6(2) of this Schedule extends the time for any person to make objection to the application, the court may order that the certificate to be renewed shall not continue in force by virtue of section 40(5) of this Act beyond a date specified in the order.

11 (1) Subject to sub-paragraph (2) of this paragraph, an objection to an application for the issue or renewal of a registration certificate shall specify the ground of objection with such particulars as are sufficient to indicate the matters relied on to make it out.

(2) Where objection is made to an application for the issue or renewal of a registration certificate on the ground that the application does not give the information required by this Act, or the information is incomplete or inaccurate, or the application is otherwise not in conformity with this Act, it shall be sufficient for the objection to state the ground as a matter of suspicion, and to indicate the reasons for the suspicion.

12 Where, on an objection to an application for the issue or renewal of a registration certificate, there appears to the court to be good reason to suspect that the application does not give the information required by this Act, or that the information is incomplete or inaccurate, or the application is otherwise not in conformity with this Act, it shall be for the applicant to satisfy the court that the ground of objection cannot be made out, unless the applicant desires and is permitted to amend the application so as to remove the ground of objection.

Amendment
Para 1: words 'chief executive' in square brackets in both places they occur substituted by the Access to Justice Act 1999, s 90(1), Sch 13, paras 36, 52(1), (2).
Para 2: words 'chief executive' in square brackets substituted by the Access to Justice Act 1999, s 90(1), Sch 13, paras 36, 52(1), (2).
Para 4: words 'chief executive to' in square brackets substituted by the Access to Justice Act 1999, s 90(1), Sch 13, paras 36, 52(1), (3)(a); words 'chief executive is' in square brackets substituted by the Access to Justice Act 1999, s 90(1), Sch 13, paras 36, 52(1), (3)(b);words 'chief executive needs' in square brackets substituted by the Access to Justice Act 1999, s 90(1), Sch 13, paras 36, 52(1), (3)(c).
Para 6: in sub-para (1) words 'chief executive' in square brackets substituted by the Access to Justice Act 1999, s 90(1), Sch 13, paras 36, 52(1), (4).
Para 7: words 'chief executive' in square brackets substituted by the Access to Justice Act 1999, s 90(1), Sch 13, paras 36, 52(1), (4).

PART II COMPLAINT FOR CANCELLATION OR VARIATION OF REGISTRATION CERTIFICATE

13 (1) A summons issued on a complaint made against a club for the cancellation or variation of a registration certificate shall be served on the chairman or secretary of the club or the person who signed the last application for the issue or renewal of the certificate, and that service shall be treated as service on the club.

(2) Any such summons shall, in addition to being served on the club, be served on such persons, if any, as the justices issuing the summons may direct.

14   Where it appears to a magistrates' court having jurisdiction to deal with any such complaint that the summons cannot be served on the club in accordance with paragraph 13 of this Schedule, or not without undue difficulty or delay, the court may order that service on the club may be effected by serving the summons on a person named in the order, being a person who appears to the court to have, or to have had, an interest in the club, or to be, or to have been, an officer of the club.

15   A complaint may be made against a club for the cancellation of a registration certificate on the ground that the club has not twenty-five members, notwithstanding that the complainant's case is that the club does not exist.

PART III   GENERAL

16   (1) A magistrates' court may deal with an application by a club for the issue, variation or renewal of a registration certificate without hearing the club, but—

(a)   before refusing such an application, or renewing a registration certificate for a shorter time than is requested in the application, shall give the club an opportunity to be heard; and

(b)   before renewing a registration certificate for a longer period than one year, may invite any chief officer of police or local authority concerned to make representations.

(2) In relation to any such application [sub-sections (1) and (3) of section 97 and section 121 of the Magistrates' Courts Act 1980] shall apply as they apply in relation to a complaint.

17   On any application or complaint made to a magistrates' court by or against a club under Part II of this Act, and on any appeal by a club under section 50 of this Act, the club, if not represented by counsel or a solicitor, shall be heard by the chairman or secretary, by any member of the committee having the general management of the affairs of the club or by any officer of the club duly authorised.

18   This Schedule in so far as it relates to matters about which there is power to make rules under [section 144 of the Magistrates' Courts Act 1980, shall have effect subject to any rules so made and to any rules made under section 15 of the Justices' of the Peace Act 1949 (which was re-enacted in the said section 144) after 3rd August 1961].

Amendment
Paras 16, 18: words in square brackets substituted by the Magistrates' Courts Act 1980, s 154, Sch 7, para 50.

SCHEDULE 7 PROVISIONS AS TO CLUB RULES

Sections 41, 42

Management of club

[A.138]

1   The affairs of the club, in matters not reserved for the club in general meeting or otherwise for the decision of the general body of members, must, under the rules, be managed by one or more elective committees; and one committee must be a general committee, charged with the general management of those affairs in matters not assigned to special committees.

General meetings

2   (1) There must, under the rules, be a general meeting of the club at least once in every year, and fifteen months must not elapse without a general meeting.

(2) The general committee must be capable of summoning a general meeting at any time on reasonable notice.

(3) Any members entitled to attend and vote at a general meeting must be capable of summoning one or requiring one to be summoned at any time on reasonable notice, if a specified number of them join to do so; and the number required must not be more than thirty nor more than one-fifth of the total number of the members so entitled.

(4) At a general meeting the voting must be confined to members, and all members entitled to use the club premises must be entitled to vote, and must have equal voting rights, except that—
(a)   the rules may exclude from voting, either generally or on particular matters, members below a specified age (not greater than twenty-one), women if the club is primarily a men's club, and men if the club is primarily a women's club, and
(b)   if the club is primarily a club for persons qualified by service or past service, or by any particular service or past service, in Her Majesty's forces, the rules may exclude persons not qualified from voting, either generally or on particular matters; and

(c) if the rules make special provision for family membership or family subscriptions or any similar provision, the rules may exclude from voting, either generally or on particular matters, all or any of the persons taking the benefit of that provision as being members of a person's family, other than that person.

Membership

3 (1) Ordinary members must, under the rules, be elected either by the club in general meeting or by an elective committee, or by an elective committee with other members of the club added to it for the purpose; and the name and address of any person proposed for election must, for not less than two days before the election, be prominently displayed in the club premises or principal club premises in a part frequented by the members.

(2) The rules must not make any such provision for the admission of persons to membership otherwise than as ordinary members (or in accordance with the rules required for ordinary members by sub-paragraph (1) of this paragraph) as is likely to result in the number of members so admitted being significant in proportion to the total membership.

Meaning of 'elective committee'

4 (1) In this Schedule 'elective committee' means, subject to the following provisions of this paragraph, a committee consisting of members of the club who are elected to the committee by the club in accordance with sub-paragraph (2) of this paragraph for a period of not less than one year nor more than five years; and paragraph 2(4) of this Schedule shall apply to voting at the election as it applies to voting at general meetings.

(2) Elections to the committee must be held annually, and if all the elected members do not go out of office in every year, there must be fixed rules for determining those that are to; and all members of the club entitled to vote at the election and of not less than two years' standing, must be equally capable of being elected (subject only to any provision made for nomination by members of the club and to any provision prohibiting or restricting re-election) and, if nomination is required, must have equal rights to nominate persons for election.

(3) Except in the case of a committee with less than four members, or of a committee concerned with the purchase for the club or with the supply by the club of intoxicating liquor, a committee of which not less than two-thirds of the members are members of the club elected to the

committee in accordance with sub-paragraphs (1) and (2) of this paragraph shall be treated as an elective committee.

(4) A sub-committee of an elective committee shall also be treated as an elective committee if its members are appointed by the committee and not less than two-thirds of them (or, in the case of a sub-committee having less than four members, or concerned with the purchase for the club or with the supply by the club of intoxicating liquor, all of them) are members of the committee elected to the committee in accordance with sub-paragraphs (1) and (2) of this paragraph who go out of office in the sub-committee on ceasing to be members of the committee.

(5) For the purposes of this paragraph a person who on a casual vacancy is appointed to fill the place of a member of an elective committee for the remainder of his term and no longer shall, however appointed, be treated as elected in accordance with sub-paragraphs (1) and (2) of this paragraph if the person whose place he fills was so elected or is to be treated as having been so elected.

SCHEDULES 8–12 (*Not reproduced*)

[SCHEDULE 12A CHILDREN'S CERTIFICATES: SUPPLEMENTARY PROVISIONS]

Section 168A

[Applications

[A.139]

1 (1) Licensing justices shall not entertain an application for a children's certificate unless the applicant has, at least 21 days before the commencement of the licensing sessions at which the application is to be made, given to the [chief executive] to the justices and to the chief officer of police notice of his intention to make the application.

(2) Notice under sub-paragraph (1) of this paragraph shall—
(a) be in writing and be signed by the applicant or his authorised agent, and
(b) state the situation of the premises where the area to which the application relates is to be found.

(3) If the premises mentioned in sub-paragraph (2)(b) of this paragraph include a bar which is not included in the area to which the application relates, licensing justices may decline to entertain the application until the applicant has lodged a plan of the premises indicating the area to which the application relates.

2   (1) Where a chief officer of police wishes to oppose an application for a children's certificate, he must give notice of his intention to do so to the applicant and to the [chief executive] to the licensing justices at least 7 days before the commencement of the licensing sessions at which the application is to be made.

(2) Notice under sub-paragraph (1) of this paragraph shall be in writing and specify in general terms the grounds of the opposition.

Refusal

3   Where licensing justices refuse an application for a children's certificate, they shall specify their reasons in writing to the applicant.

Conditions

4   (1) It shall be a condition of the grant of a children's certificate that meals and beverages other than intoxicating liquor are available for sale for consumption in the area to which the certificate relates at all times when the certificate is operational.

(2) Licensing justices may impose such other conditions on the grant of a children's certificate as they think fit.

(3) Without prejudice to the generality of sub-paragraph (2) of this paragraph, conditions under that sub-paragraph may restrict the hours during which, or days on which, the certificate is operational.

When operational

5   (1) Subject to any condition attached by the licensing justices and to sub-paragraph (2) of this paragraph, a children's certificate shall be operational at any time up to nine in the evening.

(2) Licensing justices may, in relation to a children's certificate, approve a later time than nine in the evening as the time when the certificate ceases to be operational, and may do so either generally or for particular days or periods.

(3) Licensing justices may only act under sub-paragraph (2) of this paragraph on the application of the appropriate person, but an approval under that provision need not correspond with the applicant's proposals.

(4) In sub-paragraph (3) of this paragraph, the reference to the appropriate person is—

(a)   in the case of an application with respect to an existing children's certificate, to the holder of the justices' licence for the licensed premises to which the certificate relates, and

(b)   in the case of an application made in conjunction with an application for a children's certificate, to the applicant for the certificate.

Duration

6   A children's certificate shall remain in force until revoked.

7   (1) Licensing justices may, on their own motion or on application by the chief officer of police, revoke a children's certificate if they are satisfied—

(a)   that the area to which the certificate relates does not constitute an environment in which it is suitable for persons under fourteen to be present, or

(b)   that there has been a serious or persistent failure to comply with one or more conditions attached to the certificate.

(2) When acting on their own motion, licensing justices may only revoke a children's certificate if, at least 21 days before the commencement of the licensing sessions at which they propose to revoke the certificate, they have given notice of their intention to do so to the holder of the justices' licence for the licensed premises to which the certificate relates.

(3) When acting on application by the chief officer of police, licensing justices may only revoke a children's certificate if, at least 21 days before the commencement of the licensing sessions at which the application is to be made, the chief officer of police has given—

(a)   to the [chief executive] to the licensing justices, and

(b)   to the holder of the justices' licence for the licensed premises to which the certificate relates,

notice of his intention to apply for the revocation of the certificate.

(4) Notice under sub-paragraph (2) or (3) of this paragraph shall be in writing and specify in general terms the grounds for the proposed revocation.

8   If the holder of the justices' licence for the licensed premises to which a children's certificate relates gives—

(a)   to the [chief executive] to the licensing justices, and

(b)   to the chief officer of police,

at least fourteen days notice in writing of a day on which he wishes the certificate to cease to be in force, it shall be treated as revoked on that day.

9   A children's certificate shall be treated as revoked on the day on which the area to which it relates ceases to be comprised in premises for which a justices' licence is in force.

Appeals

10 (1) Any applicant for a children's certificate who is aggrieved by a decision of licensing justices—

(a) refusing to grant a certificate, or

(b) as to the conditions attached to the grant of a certificate,

may appeal to the Crown Court against the decision.

(2) Any applicant for an extension of the time when a children's certificate is operational who is aggrieved by a decision of licensing justices with respect to his application may appeal to the Crown Court against the decision.

(3) Any holder of a justices' licence who is aggrieved by a decision of licensing justices revoking a children's certificate relating to the licensed premises may appeal to the Crown Court against the decision.

(4) The judgment of the Crown Court on any appeal under this paragraph shall be final.

11   Where the Crown Court—

(a) has awarded costs against an appellant under paragraph 10 of this Schedule, and

(b) is satisfied that the licensing justices cannot recover those costs from him,

it shall order payment out of central funds of such sums as appear to it sufficient to indemnify the licensing justices from all costs and charges whatever to which they have been put in consequence of the appellant's notice of appeal.]

Amendment
Inserted by the Deregulation and Contracting Out Act 1994, s 19(3), Sch 7.
Para 1: in sub-para (1) words 'chief executive' in square brackets substituted by the Access to Justice Act 1999, s 90(1), Sch 13, paras 36, 56(a).
Para 2: in sub-para (1) words 'chief executive' in square brackets substituted by the Access to Justice Act 1999, s 90(1), Sch 13, paras 36, 56(a).
Para 7: in sub-para (3)(a) words 'chief executive' in square brackets substituted by the Access to Justice Act 1999, s 90(1), Sch 13, paras 36, 56(b).
Para 8: in sub-para (a) words 'chief executive' in square brackets substituted by the Access to Justice Act 1999, s 90(1), Sch 13, paras 36, 56(b).

SCHEDULE 13 *(Repealed by the Finance Act 1967.)*

SCHEDULE 14 *(Not reproduced)*

SCHEDULE 15 *(Repealed by the Statute Law (Repeals) Act 1974.)*

Licensing (Special Hours Certificates) Rules 1982
SI 1982/1384

[A.140]

1 (1) These Rules may be cited as the Licensing (Special Hours Certificates) Rules 1982 and shall come into operation on 1st October 1982.

(2) The Licensing (Special Hours Certificates) Rules 1962 are hereby revoked.

[A.141]

2 In these Rules 'the Act' means the Licensing Act 1964.

[A.142]

3 (1) At least [twenty-one] days before applying to the licensing justices for a special hours certificate [under section 77 or 77A of the Licensing Act 1964] [or the variation of any limitation to which such a certificate is subject] the applicant shall give notice in writing to the chief officer of police for the area in which the premises to which the application relates are situated and to the [chief executive] to the licensing justices of his intention to make the application.

[(1A) Not more than twenty-eight days nor less than fourteen days before so applying the applicant shall display notice of his intention to make the application for a period of seven days in a place where it can conveniently be read by the public on or near the premises to which the application relates; and not more than twenty-eight days nor less than fourteen days before so applying (and, if the licensing justices so require, on some day or days outside that period but within such other period as they may require) he shall advertise notice of the proposed application in a newspaper circulating in the place where the premises to which the application relates are situated.]

(2) A notice under this Rule shall be signed by the applicant or his authorised agent and shall state the address of the licensed premises to which the application relates.

Amendment

Para (1): words 'twenty-one' in square brackets substituted by SI 1988/1338, r 2, Schedule, para 1; words 'under section 77 or 77A of the Licensing Act 1964' in square brackets inserted by SI 1996/978, r 2(2); words from 'or the variation' to 'certificate is subject' in square brackets inserted by SI 1988/1338, r 2, Schedule, para 1; words 'chief executive' in square brackets substituted by SI 2001/1096, r 2(c).

Para (1A): inserted by SI 1988/1338, r 2, Schedule, para 2.

[A.143]

[3A   A person intending to oppose an application for the grant of a special hours certificate under section 77 [or section 77A] of the Act or for the variation of any limitation to which such a certificate is subject under section 78A(4) of the Act shall give notice in writing of his intention to the applicant and to the [chief executive] to the licensing justices, specifying in general terms the grounds of the opposition, not later than seven days before the commencement of the licensing sessions at which the application is to be made, and unless notice has been so given the licensing justices shall not entertain the objection.]

Amendment

Inserted by SI 1988/1338, r 2, Schedule, para 3.

Words 'or section 77A' in square brackets inserted by SI 1996/978, r 2(3); words 'chief executive' in square brackets substituted by SI 2001/1096, r 2(c).

[A.144]

4   (1) At least seven days before applying to the licensing justices under subsections (2) or (4) of section 81 of the Act for the revocation of a special hours certificate, the chief officer of police shall give notice in writing to the holder of the justices' licence for the premises to which the certificate relates and to the [chief executive] to the licensing justices of his intention to apply for the revocation of the certificate.

(2) A notice under this Rule shall state the grounds on which the chief officer of police will rely in his application for the revocation of the special hours certificate.

Amendment

Para (1): words 'chief executive' in square brackets substituted by SI 2001/1096, r 2(c).

[A.145]

5   [(1) At least seven days before applying to the licensing justices under section 81A(3) [or section 81AA(1)] of the Act for the attachment to a special hours certificate of a limitation or for the variation of any limitation to which such a certificate is subject, the chief officer of police shall give notice in writing to the holder of the justices' licence for the premises to which the certificate relates and to the [chief executive] to the licensing

justices of his intention to apply for the attachment or variation of the limitation as the case may be.]

(2) A notice under this Rule shall state the grounds on which the chief officer of police will rely in his application for [the attachment or variation of the limitation].

Amendment
Para (1): substituted by SI 1988/1338, r 2, Schedule, para 4; words 'or section 81AA(1)' in square brackets inserted by SI 2001/921, r 2(1), (2); words 'chief executive' in square brackets substituted by SI 2001/1096, r 2(c).
Para (2): words 'the attachment or variation of the limitation' in square brackets inserted by SI 1988/1338, r 2, Schedule, para 5(2).

[A.146]

6   On the consideration of an application under subsections (2) or (4) of section 81[, section 81A(3) or section 81AA(1)] of the Act the procedure before the licensing justices shall be as nearly as may be the same as in the case of opposition to the renewal of a justices' licence and the provisions of the Act relating to procedure shall apply accordingly with any necessary modifications.

Amendment
Words ', section 81A(3) or section 81AA(1)' in square brackets substituted by SI 2001/921, r 2(1), (3).

[A.147]

7   Subject as aforesaid the procedure on any application to the licensing justices under section 77[, 77A [, 81 or 81AA]] of the Act shall be the procedure ordinarily adopted on the consideration of an application for the grant of a new justices' licence.

Amendment
Words in square brackets beginning with the reference ', 77A' substituted by SI 1996/978, r 2(4); words ', 81 or 81AA' in square brackets substituted by SI 2001/921, r 2(1), (4).

[A.148]

[**8**   (1) A special hours certificate shall be in one of the forms specified in Part I of the Schedule to these Rules, or in a form to the like effect.

(2) A declaration that a provisional special hours certificate is to be final shall be in the form specified in Part II of the Schedule to these Rules, or in a form to the like effect. A special hours certificate shall be in the form specified in the Schedule to these Rules, or in a form to the like effect.]

Amendment
Substituted by SI 1996/978, r 2(5).

[SCHEDULE

FORM OF SPECIAL HOURS CERTIFICATE]

Rule 8

[A.149]

[PART I

LICENSING ACT 1964

Special Hours Certificate

At the licensing sessions held at   on the   day of   19 , for the   Licensing District.

The licensing justices for the said licensing district, being satisfied as respects the licensed premises known as

(a)   that a music and dancing licence is in force as respects the premises; and

(b)   that (the premises are) (the following part of the premises, that is to say, is) structurally adapted and bona fide (used) (intended to be used) for the purpose of providing for persons resorting to the premises music and dancing and substantial refreshment to which the sale of intoxicating liquor is ancillary,

hereby grant under section 77 of the Licensing Act 1964, this special hours certificate as respects the said premises.

(By virtue of section (78A) (and) (80) of the Licensing Act 1964 this certificate shall be limited to (the following times of day, namely   ) (the following *days*, namely   ) (and the) (following part(s) of the year, namely   ) (where different limitations are imposed for different days, specify accordingly)).

Licensing justices

LICENSING ACT 1964

Provisional Special Hours Certificates

At the licensing sessions held at   on the   day of   19 , for the   Licensing District.

The licensing justices for the said licensing district, being satisfied as respects the premises known as

(a)   that a music and dancing licence, whether or not subject to a condition that it shall be of no effect until confirmed, is in force as respects the premises; and

(b)   that (the premises are) (the following part of the premises, that is to say,   is) intended to be used, and, if completed in accordance with plans deposited with the licensing justices, will be structurally adapted for the purpose of providing for persons resorting to the premises music and dancing and substantial refreshment to which the sale of intoxicating liquor is ancillary,

hereby grant under section 77A of the Licensing Act 1964 this special hours certificate as respects the said premises.

This certificate is (granted subject to the limitations endorsed hereon, and) shall not be valid until it has been declared final by the licensing justices.

Licensing justices]

Amendment
Substituted by SI 1996/978, r 3, Schedule.

[PART II

LICENSING ACT 1964

Declaration of special hours certificate to be final

At the licensing sessions held at   on the   day of   19 , for the   Licensing District.

The licensing justices hereby declare the foregoing special hours certificate granted under section 77A of the Licensing Act 1964 to be final, the certificate to have effect from the date hereof.

Licensing justices]

Amendment
Substituted by SI 1996/978, r 3, Schedule.

Draft Conditions

[A.150]

Justices are entitled to attach to a justices' on-licence (other than for wine alone) such conditions as they think proper in the interests of the public (s 4(1)). Care should be taken not to negate the licence created by statute (eg by creating a new form of licence excluding the sale of beer—see the case of *Sitki* at para **1.11**). It may be expedient for the notice of application to incorporate any proposed conditions, but this is not a legal requirement—see chapter 2. Possible combinations appear below, although it will rarely be necessary to attach more than a very limited selection in any individual case. In the case of off-licences, the justices are not empowered to attach conditions and may only seek undertakings or assurances.

Categories of premises	*Conditions or undertakings that might be considered*
Cafés/wine bars	1, 2, 3, 4 (part only), 5, 7, 8, 60, 71, 76, 110
Nightclubs	3, 5, 6, 9, 10, 11, 14, 15, 26, 27, 36, 44, 47, 52, 58, 69, 84, 88, 92
Leisure centres, community centres and sports clubs	3, 16, 18, 19, 23, 38, 83, 86, 87, 88, 91, 92, 93, 94, 108
Restaurant and/or residential	4* (restaurant), 61 (hotel), 101 (hotel), 102, 103* (hotel), 106
Proprietary clubs	16, 17, 18, 19, 20, 21, 22, 23, 24, 25, 27, 43, 48, 50, 51, 64, 71, 82, 89, 97, 98
Cinemas and theatres	3, 33, 34, 35, 72, 77, 90, 91, 92, 95, 96, 97, 107, 109
Casinos and bingo clubs	50, 89, 91, 92, 95 (casino), 96, 97, 98, 99
Universities and technical colleges	19, 29, 30, 31, 40, 41, 105
Offices, hospitals etc	2, 3, 4, 53, 77, 104

Off-licences	68, 73, 75, 81
Supermarkets/grocers/ department stores/ wholesale outlets	63†, 65 (wholesale), 66, 67, 68, 73, 74 (department stores), 75, 78, 79, 80, 81
Miscellaneous	12, 13, 23, 26, 28, 32, 37, 39, 42, 45, 46, 47, 49, 54, 55, 56, 57, 58, 59, 62, 70, 71, 77, 83, 85, 93, 100, 105

* Conditions required by statute.

† Given as assurances or undertakings.

CONDITIONS

1   That no more than [   ] beer(s) and [   ] lager(s) should be available on draught.

2   That all beers and lagers shall be served in half-pint measures only (or the nearest metric equivalent thereof).

3   Off sales shall be confined to the area delineated on the deposited plan.

4   In the area hatched [*colour*] on the deposited plan, intoxicating liquor shall not be sold or supplied [on the premises] otherwise than to persons taking table meals there and for consumption by such a person as an ancillary to meals served in the licensed premises.

5   Service in the [   ] and [   ] areas shall be by waiter/waitress only. [*Appropriate where supervision is restricted.*]

6   No persons under the age of 18 to be admitted to the premises after [   ] in the evening.

7   Substantial food and non-alcoholic beverages including drinking water to be available at all times the premises are open to the public.

8   No cooking on premises other than reheating by microwave oven.

9   A minimum of [   ] video surveillance cameras shall be installed inside and [   ] video cameras shall be installed outside the premises. [The latter will be sited so they have a view in both directions along the public footpath. All cameras (whether inside or outside the premises) will continually record and the tape will be retained for a period of seven days for evidential purposes.]

10   A doorman who shall be qualified under the [   ] scheme will be stationed at the door of the premises from [   ] pm on any trading night until all customers have left the premises.

11   There shall be a minimum admission charge after [   ] pm on [   ] night(s) of £[   ].

12   Application for final declaration to be made within [   ] months of the grant of this provisional licence.

13   On final declaration the existing [provisional] justices' licence for [*premises*] will be offered for surrender.

14   When the noise levels in the [*premises*] are [   ] decibels [and the
      spectrum shape accords with the values contained in the report of   ]
      [and dancing takes place in the said premises] then the background
      noise levels [contained in the said report] of [decibels] shall not
      be exceeded in the said premises.

15   The overall volume control in the [*premises*] should be clearly
      marked for the periods prior to 20.00 hrs, between 20.00 hrs and
      22.00 hrs and after 22.00 hrs so as to achieve sound levels in the
      [*premises*] of [   ] decibels, [   ] decibels and [   ] decibels
      respectively.

16   Intoxicating liquor may only be sold or supplied on the authority of
      this licence to the following:
      (a)   members of the [*club name*] social club who shall have been
            admitted to membership at least 48 hours prior to their
            admission to the licensed premises;
      (b)   bona fide guests of such members limited to [   ] per member
            [introduced in accordance with the club rules] [and entertained
            at the expense of the member introducing such guests];
      (c)   persons attending a bona fide private function;
      (d)   persons who have each paid an entrance fee of £[   ] for
            admission to the licensed premises;
      (e)   a member of a visiting sports team competing in matches at the
            club and their bona fide supporters;
      (f)   any person attending the premises as a participant or spectator
            at a special exhibition match sponsored or organised by the club
            or proprietor and open to the public on payment of a proper
            entrance charge;
      (g)   any employee of the club.

17   The communicating door within the bar servery and connecting the
      function room with the players' bar shall be closed at all times that
      this licence is being exercised.

18   There shall be no permitted hours before/on [*here insert the times
      and days when the applicant will require the premises for use by
      persons under the age of 14 years, see ss 60(7) and 168(1)*].

19   At all times that the licence is being exercised there shall be an
      attendant on the main door of the function room for the purpose of
      supervising admission to the room.

20   The premises shall be used as a proprietary club for the purposes of
      providing members with facilities for the playing of snooker and
      billiards together with restaurant and social facilities which are
      ancillary thereto.

21   Notwithstanding conditions [   ] intoxicating liquor may be sold or
      supplied to the following persons:

(a)   persons paying a minimum admission fee of £[   ] (not to be credited against liquor or consumables) for music, dancing or entertainment; or

(b)   persons who have paid a minimum annual admission fee of £[   ] payable in advance (and not to be credited against liquor or consumables) for music, dancing or entertainments; or

(c)   bona fide guests of the proprietor specially invited prior to admission (a list of whom shall be kept at reception); or

(d)   artistes or persons employed at the premises; or

(e)   persons attending a private function who enter the premises (a list of whom shall be kept at reception).

22   Members shall not be allowed to introduce more than three guests at any one time and no guests shall be introduced more than six times in any period of 12 months.

23   Persons under 18 years of age shall not be admitted to the bar.

24   A list of the names and addresses of duly elected members of the club shall at all times be maintained on the premises and be available for production to a police officer in uniform.

25   A copy of the rules of the club shall be deposited with the chief executive to the licensing justices and the chief constable. Notice of intention to make any alterations to the said rules shall be given in writing to the said chief executive to the licensing justices and the chief constable, not less than 14 days before such alterations are proposed to take effect.

26   There shall not be more than [*number*] persons on the premises at any one time.

27   The sale of intoxicating liquor shall take place only to members of the public who have paid for admission or who are otherwise entitled to be on the premises.

28   Intoxicating liquor may be sold only to persons who are attending the licensed premises at the invitation of the proprietors.

29   Alcohol to be served only in conjunction with the catering course.

30   Not to be used as a classroom when alcohol dispensed.

31   Drinks to be served only by a teacher.

32   After [   ] pm, intoxicating liquor shall not be sold or supplied to persons in or on the external areas to the front of the licensed premises.

33   Only ticket holders over the age of 18 to be allowed to purchase alcohol.

34   Whilst the bar in the lower ground-floor foyer area is being used for sale of intoxicating liquor children and persons under 18 years of age shall not be permitted to wait within that area.

35   Intoxicating liquor shall be supplied only to or on behalf of persons partaking of main meals or attending organised lunches, dinners,

suppers, dances, receptions, concerts, recitals, lectures, dramatic productions and entertainment of a like kind at the premises.

36   No sale of intoxicating liquor except to persons admitted by ticket to the premises and to those persons for whose admission payment has been made and to employees of [*name of company*].

37   Sale and consumption of intoxicating liquor to be confined to the bar areas within the licensed premises.

38   Intoxicating liquor shall not be sold or supplied other than to:
   (a)   members of the [*name*] yacht club;
   (b)   associates holding a [*name*] yacht club security pass; and
   (c)   persons attending pre-booked functions.

39   Not to sell wine other than that for use at Holy Communion.

40   In the area outlined in [*colour*] on the deposited plans, intoxicating liquor may be sold or supplied under authority of this licence only to the following persons:
   (a)   any persons attending any course of study held at the University of [*name*], or any persons in possession of a students union card or national students union card;
   (b)   bona fide guests of such persons;
   (c)   employees of the University of [*name*];
   (d)   persons attending bona fide functions, exhibitions, seminars or conferences;
   (e)   members of the public attending events limited to 12 per annum [provided that 24 hours' prior notice shall be given to the chief officer of police where it is anticipated that the event shall continue beyond normal permitted hours].

41   When organised athletic or sporting functions are held at [*name*] University, the sale of intoxicating liquor shall be restricted to members or students at and staff employed by any members of the club, association, team or group participating in any organised or athletic, sporting or social function at [*name*] University.

42   The number of persons permitted within the lounge/bar and terraced area at any one time should not exceed [   ].

43   Intoxicating liquor shall not be sold or supplied on the premises otherwise than to:
   (a)   members of the [*name*] club meeting at the within-mentioned premises for consumption by those members and their bona fide guests. No persons shall be admitted to membership of the said club without an interval of at least two days between nomination or application for membership and admission.
   The name and address of the persons so applying must be prominently displayed in the club premises, in a place frequented by the members, for at least two days before election;

(b)   persons attending and paying a minimum fee for admission to the premises for the purposes of music, dancing and entertainments. The fee is not to be credited against consumable items.

44   Not to play amplified music within the licensed premises or to play or allow to be played music within the said premises at a level which is audible in neighbouring residential premises.

45   All ventilation plant to the premises will be switched off every night at [   ] on [   ] day to [   ] day and at [   ] pm on all other days.

46   No tables to be placed outside in the evening after [   ] pm.

47   No striptease.

48   No gaming on the premises other than by machines authorised under Part III of the Gaming Act 1968.

49   No direct access to the street from any bar.

50   No payment to be made by or on behalf of the licensees for bringing customers or members to the premises.

51   Cards will be issued to all members, bearing their photograph.

52   No person under the age of 25 years will be admitted as a member. The application form for membership will ask for proof of age to be provided.

53   Intoxicating liquor shall be sold or supplied only to persons either employed by [*name of company*] or who have professional or other connections which concern any of the activities of the company or their bona fide guests or visitors.

54   Parking will be monitored and illegal parking prevented.

55   Intoxicating liquor for consumption on the premises shall be supplied only to persons taking table meals at the premises and for consumption by such person as ancillary to his or her meal, but this condition shall not prevent the sale or supply of intoxicating liquor to persons attending at the premises as members of a private party for a dinner and/or dance or other pre-booked function or occasion for which tickets or other rights of access are not on sale or available to the general public at or near to the premises immediately prior to the occasion of such dinner/dance or other function at which intoxicating liquor is to be sold or supplied.

56   The supply of intoxicating liquor is restricted to the parts of the premises defined on plans deposited with the chief executive to the licensing justices.

57   No members of the general public shall be allowed to be present in any part of the premises licensed for the sale of intoxicating liquor where any such private party, dinner, dance or other function is being held.

58   Notices will be displayed in the premises asking members to park properly and to leave quietly.

59 On a day when [　] FC is playing matches in the FA Cup, [　] Cup, or Football League, then the licensee shall observe the following rules between [　hours] (weekdays) and [　hours] (Saturdays):
  (a) admission to the premises to be strictly controlled;
  (b) the licensee to employ not less than [　] responsible door persons;
  (c) entry to the premises to be restricted to the doors at the rear of the premises, adjoining the car park;
  (d) pool table to be covered and all equipment secured away from the public;
  (e) windows and curtains to [　] to remain closed;
  (f) occupancy to be limited to [　] persons.

60 There shall be no dancing or discothèque at the licensed premises.

61 The licence shall not be exercised if there ceases to be an hotel at the premises.

62 Floodlights to be positioned above the rear entrance.

63 That there shall be no sale or supply of intoxicating liquor except to staff employed by [*name*] Wholesaling or registered customers of [*name*] Wholesaling.

64 The membership book and records shall be available for inspection by the police on request.

65 That no shop front will be constructed at the depot.

66 The off-licence department must be supervised at all times by a responsible assistant wearing a badge, indicating that he or she is concerned with beer, wines and spirits.

67 During non-permitted hours a screen, partition or grille will be maintained in front of the licensed department to make it clear that it is closed.

68 No person under the age of 18 years will be employed to sell intoxicating liquor.

69 There shall be no admission to the premises after [　] pm.

70 There shall be no permitted hours on Saturdays or Sundays.

71 The premises shall not be used as a discothèque and shall be used as a cabaret club and/or live music venue and during any opening period at least 50 per cent of the music played shall be live performance at the premises.

72 Intoxicating liquor may be sold or supplied under the authority of this licence only to the following persons:
  (a) persons attending at the said premises for the purpose of a play, concert or other musical entertainment;
  (b) persons attending at the said premises to take part in a performance and persons attending at the said premises to use the rehearsal/recording facilities;

    (c)   persons attending a bona fide conference, seminar or other private function at the premises which has been authorised by the owners.

73   The range of non-licensed commodities to be offered for sale in the shop may include the following but no others:

    (a)   confectionery, soft drinks, nuts, crisps and other goods normally regarded as ancillary to licensed goods;

    (b)   tobacco, cigarettes, matches and associated goods;

    [(c) general groceries of all kinds.]

74   Intoxicating liquor will be sold in the area outlined in [*colour*] continually throughout the year. The licensee undertakes to inform the chief executive to the licensing justices immediately in the event of a decision being made to abandon the said licensed area.

75   Intoxicating liquor will be sold only within the area outlined in [*colour*] on the plans deposited with the chief executive to the licensing justices.

76   In the area edged [*colour*] the sale and supply of intoxicating liquor shall be limited to the sale and supply of spirits, wine and bottled or canned beer or cider together with one brand of draught beer or cider and all sales of beer or cider will be dispensed for consumption in vessels of a capacity not exceeding half a pint or its metric equivalent.

77   No [advertising or any other] indication[s] that licensed facilities are available therein are to be [published or] displayed on the exterior of the premises (excepting the statutory notice).

78   Intoxicating liquor will be sold only by [*name of proprietor*] in specially designed pre-packed and pre-wrapped gift packs.

79   When the store is open outside permitted hours covers will be placed over the intoxicating liquor displays to make it clear that no sales may take place during those times.

80   That a prominent notice will be displayed on each fixture where intoxicating liquor is sold, indicating that it is an offence for persons under 18 years of age to buy or attempt to buy intoxicating liquor.

81   The shop will normally be open for business during the following times [*state times*].

82   No person shall be admitted as a guest on more than two occasions in any calendar month.

83   Suitable and effective speed ramps will be maintained on the main driveway.

84   The pay desk shall be manned at all times up until the last admission time for the premises.

85   If the primary use of the premises ceases to be for the purpose of [   ] this licence shall cease to have effect.

86   Competitors will not be permitted to drink alcohol either before or during a race meeting.

87 Intoxicating liquor shall not be consumed in the viewing area or track area outlined in [*colour*] on the deposited plan.

88 The maximum occupancy figure shall be:
    (a) singing and dancing – [   ];
    (b) functions where tables and chairs are set out around the perimeter wall – [   ].

89 The licence holder shall be relieved of the necessity to display a notice under s 183 of the Licensing Act 1964.

90 The bar will be opened only during evening licensing hours and shall be closed after the last evening intermission.

91 [Prior to the premises re-opening] the licensee will ensure that the opening of all emergency exits will cause an alarm to sound behind the bar within the premises.

92 Adjoining each emergency exit, notices shall be displayed prohibiting the use of those doorways other than in an emergency.

93 There shall be supervision of the outside areas at all times when those areas are in use for the sale or consumption of intoxicating liquor.

94 Intoxicating liquor shall not be sold otherwise than to:
    (a) persons who have paid the admission charge to the sports centre or on whose behalf such charge has been paid, or persons who have paid or on whose behalf have been paid such other charges the [City] Council may from time to time require a person to pay to participate in any of the sports or any other activities of the centre;
    (b) members of any club or other organisation and their guests or visitors authorised to use any of the facilities of the sports centre on terms from time to time approved by the [   ] Council;
    (c) members or employees of the [   ] Council authorised to enter the Sports Centre; or persons attending a bona fide function in respect of which 24 hours' prior notice has been given by the licensee.

95 No intoxicating liquor shall be sold, supplied or consumed in any gaming area [save the cardroom when 30 minutes shall elapse between change of use].

96 The sale, supply and consumption of intoxicating liquor shall be confined to those parts of the premises which are shown coloured [*colour*] on the deposited plan.

97 Intoxicating liquor may be sold or supplied only to members of the club meeting at the club premises, for consumption by those members.

98 No person shall be admitted to membership of the club without an interval of at least one day between nomination or application and admission to membership.

The names and addresses of persons so applying must be prominently displayed in the club premises in a part frequented by the members for at least one day before admission to membership.

99   Off-sales shall be confined to the provision of intoxicating liquor as prizes or gifts to members.

100   Intoxicating liquor shall be sold, supplied or consumed only on occasions when social functions are held at the station, or on occasions when visitors are on the station for official or social occasions. Intoxicating liquor shall be sold or supplied only to members of the social club, their guests or visitors.

101   There shall be afforded in the premises for the persons provided with board and lodgings for reward adequate sitting accommodation in a room not used or to be used for sleeping accommodation, for the service of substantial refreshment or for the supply and consumption of intoxicating liquor.

102   Permitted hours in the premises shall be restricted so as to exclude any time (before or after) the afternoon break.

103   Intoxicating liquor shall not be sold or supplied on the premises otherwise than to:
(a)   persons taking table meals there for consumption by such persons as ancillary to their meals;
(b)   persons residing there or their bona fide guests entertained by them at their own expense by such persons or their private friends so entertained by them either on the premises or with meals supplied but to be consumed off the premises.

104   Intoxicating liquor may be sold or supplied only to:
(a)   employees of the ABC Company [and its associated and subsidiary companies] and their bona fide guests;
(b)   persons attending meetings or functions to which admission is only by ticket or written invitation issued in advance of the day in question.

105   Alcohol only to be served in conjunction with a catering course.

106   There shall be no direct access from the street to any bar.

107   Intoxicating liquor shall not be sold, supplied or consumed except:
(a)   in the bars in the mezzanine floor foyer;
(b)   by waiter or waitress service in the auditorium to customers at tables;
(c)   at the customers' bar in the auditorium, as shown coloured [*colour*] on the deposited plan;
(d)   there should be no direct access from the street to any bar.

108   Intoxicating liquor may be sold or supplied only to:
(a)   persons who are members of the community centre or of an affiliated group;

    (b)   persons attending functions at the centre which have been authorised by the centre.

109 Intoxicating liquor may be sold or supplied only to persons admitted by ticket to or employed on the premises.

110 In the basement of the premises only intoxicating liquor of the description of wine may be sold or supplied.

Precedents

AMUSEMENT WITH PRIZES

Application for grant or renewal of permit under the Gaming Act 1968 for amusement machines

[A.151]

[Gaming Act 1968, s 34; Sch 9, para 5]

To [the licensing justices for the licensing district of   ] [the council
   of the [London borough of   ] [county district of   ]]

I, AB of   the [holder of the justices' on-licence in respect of the
   premises known as   at   ] [[proposed] occupier of the premises
   known as   at   ] hereby apply for the [grant] [renewal] of a
   permit [granted to me on   ] under section 34 of the Gaming Act
   1968 authorising the use on the said premises of   machines for
   amusement with prizes.

                              Dated the   day of   200[ ]
                                             (signed) AB

REGISTERED CLUBS

New application

Application for a registration certificate

[A.152]

[Licensing Act 1964, s 40; Sch 5; Sch 6]

To the magistrates' court for the   of   .

THE   CLUB
1   I, AB, of   , the [chairman] [secretary] of the above-named club,
    make application for the [issue] [renewal] [variation] of a registration
    certificate.

2　The objects of the club are

3　The address of the club is

4　A list of the names and addresses of the members is kept at the address given in paragraph 3 above.

5　Under the rules of the club persons may not be admitted to membership, or be admitted as candidates for membership to any of the privileges of membership, without an interval of at least two days between their nomination or application for membership and their admission, nor may persons becoming members without prior nomination or application be admitted to the privileges of membership without an interval of at least two days between their becoming members and their admission.

6　The club is established and conducted in good faith and has not less than twenty-five members.

7　Intoxicating liquor is not supplied, or intended to be supplied, to members on the premises otherwise than by or on behalf of the club.

8　The purchase for the club and the supply by the club of intoxicating liquor (so far as not managed by the club in general meeting or otherwise by the general body of members) is managed by an elective committee as defined in Schedule 7 to the Licensing Act 1964.

9　No arrangements are, or are intended to be, made:

(a)　for any person to receive at the expense of the club any commission, percentage or similar payment on or with reference to purchases of intoxicating liquor by the club; or

(b)　for any person directly or indirectly to derive any pecuniary benefit from the supply of intoxicating liquor by or on behalf of the club to members or guests, apart from any benefit accruing to the club as a whole [and apart also from the benefit derived by members indirectly by reason of the supply giving rise to or contributing to a general gain from the carrying on of the club].

10　The club is accordingly qualified to receive a registration certificate [or will be so qualified if, as regards the provisions of rule[s]　of the rules of the club, the court sees fit to give a direction under subsection (2) of section 42 of the Licensing Act 1964].

11　The names and addresses of the members of the committee having the general management of the affairs of the club [including the purchase for the club and the supply by the club of intoxicating liquor] are [as follows:] [set out in the document annexed hereto marked 'A'].

[The names and addresses of the members of the committee concerned with the purchase for the club or with the supply by the club of intoxicating liquor are [as follows:] [set out in the document annexed hereto, marked 'B'].]

The names and addresses of any officers of the club not included in the above-mentioned list or lists of members are as follows:

12 The [changes in the] rules of the club [since the last application for the issue or renewal of a certificate] are [as follows:] [set out in the document annexed hereto marked ' '] [There has been no change in the rules of the club since the last application for the issue or renewal of a certificate].

13 The premises for which the [issue] [renewal] [variation] of [a] [the] registration certificate is sought consist of   [and are [different from] [additional to] the premises to which the said certificate relates] [have been enlarged since the said certificate was [issued] [last renewed]]].

14 The said premises are [to be] occupied by and habitually used for the purposes of the club.

15 The said premises are [to be] open to members during the following times:

The hours fixed by or under the rules of the club as the permitted hours are as follows:

16 The interest held by or in trust for the club in the premises is   [and the name and address of the person to whom payment is [to be] made of [rent under the lease] [*or as the case may be*] are as follows:]

17 [Particulars of any property other than the premises referred to in paragraph 13 above which is [to be] used for the purposes of the club and not held by or in trust for the club absolutely, and the name and address of the person to whom payment is [to be] made for the use of that property are [as follows:] [set out in the document annexed hereto marked ' '].]

[There is no property other than the premises referred to in paragraph 13 above which is or is to be used for the purposes of the club and not held by or in trust for the club absolutely.]

18 [Particulars of any] [There is no] liability of the club in respect of the principal or interest of moneys borrowed by the club or charged on property held by or in trust for the club [and the name and address of the person to whom payment is [to be] made on account of that principal or interest are [as follows:] [set out in the document annexed hereto marked ' ']].

19 [Particulars of any] [There is no] liability of the club or of a trustee

for the club in respect of which any person has given any guarantee or provided any security [and particulars of such guarantee or security and the name and address of the person giving or providing it are [as follows:] [set out in the document annexed hereto marked ' ']].

[In the case of an application for renewal the paragraphs numbered 17–19 above may be deleted, the following paragraph substituted and the subsequent paragraphs numbered accordingly:]

[17   There have been no changes since the last application by the club for the issue or renewal of a registration certificate in the particulars required by paragraph 6 of Schedule 5 to the Licensing Act, 1964] [except as [follows:] [set out in the document annexed hereto marked ' ']].

20   [Particulars of any] [There are no] premises other than those referred to in paragraph 13 above which have within the past twelve months been occupied and habitually used for the purposes of the club [and the interest held by or in trust for the club in those premises [and the name and address of the person to whom payment was made of [rent under the lease] *[or as the case may be]]* are [as follows:] [set out in the document annexed hereto marked ' '].]

[21   *[In case any such rent was not paid by the club or the trustees for the club:]* The name and address of the person by whom the rent referred to in paragraph 16, 17 or 20 above was paid are as follows: .]

[22   The club is a registered society within the meaning of the Industrial and Provident Societies Act 1893, or the Friendly Societies Act 1896.]

Dated the   day of   200[ ].

[Signature of chairman or secretary]

Notice of application for the issue of a registration certificate (or the renewal of a certificate in respect of different, additional or enlarged premises)

[A.153]

[Licensing Act 1964, Sch 6, para 5]

To whom it may concern

LICENSING ACT 1964

THE   CLUB

NOTICE is hereby given that an application has been made to the magistrates' court for the   of   for the issue [renewal] [variation] of [a] [the] registration certificate for the premises of the above named club [in respect of [different] [additional] [enlarged] premises].

The premises are situated at   and consist of

Dated the   day of   200[ ].

Chairman [or secretary].

LICENSED PREMISES

New applications

Notice of application for a new justices' licence or the removal of a justices' licence

[A.154]

To the chief executive to the licensing justices for the licensing district of

To the [Commissioner of Police for the City of London] [Commissioner of Police of the Metropolis] [chief constable of   ].

[To the town clerk of the [City of London] [London Borough of   ].]

[To the proper officer of the   district council.]

[[*in a parish with a parish council*] To the proper officer of the   parish council.]

[[*in a parish without a parish council*] To the chairman of the parish meeting of the parish of   .]

[[*in a community with a community council*] To the proper officer   of the   community council.]

[[*in the case of a removal*] To EF (the holder of the licence) [*if not the applicant*] and to CD (the registered owner of the licensed premises).]

To   [*the authority discharging in the area where the premises are situated the functions of fire authority*].

I, AB, now residing at   [*except in the case of a removal of a licence held by the applicant*] having during the past six months carried on the trade or calling of   do hereby give notice that it is my intention to apply at the [general annual licensing meeting] [transfer sessions] for the said district to be held at   on the   day of   next for [the grant to me of] [an order sanctioning the [special] [ordinary] removal of] a justices' licence, authorising me to sell by retail intoxicating liquor of [all] [the following] description[s] [namely

,] for consumption [either on or] off the premises situate at   [and [to be] known by the sign of ‘   ’] [from such premises to premises situate at   and to be known as ‘   ’] of which premises CD of is the owner. [*If, in the case of an application for an on-licence, the applicant desires a six-day or early-closing licence, or a seasonal licence, or a restaurant, residential or residential and restaurant licence, he may add here so much of the following as may be appropriate:*] And it is my intention to apply to the justices to insert in such justices’ licence [a condition that on Sundays there shall be no permitted hours [*and/or*] that the permitted hours shall end one hour earlier in the evening than the general licensing hours for the district] [a condition that during the following part(s) of the year, that is to say   , there shall be no permitted hours in the premises] [the conditions required for it to be granted as a restaurant, residential or residential and restaurant licence [*as the case may require*]].

Given under my hand this   day of   200[ ].

AB

Suitability of premises

[A.155]

This form originally appeared as Appendix 7 to the Good Practice Guide. Applicants and practitioners are advised to establish with the office of the Chief Executive to the Justices whether its use has been adopted in the Petty Sessional Division in question.

This form should be completed and signed by the applicant in respect of applications for new justices’ licences, and for applications for Provisional Grants to be Declared Final.

Please complete and return the questionnaire to the Chief Executive to the Licensing Justices, Magistrates’ Court, (*insert court address and facsimile number*) before the date of the hearing.

Please complete:

DATE OF HEARING:	
COURTHOUSE:	

NAME OF APPLICANT:	SOLICITOR:
TELEPHONE NO:	TELEPHONE NO:
FACSIMILE NO:	FACSIMILE NO:

NAME OF CLUB TO WHICH APPLICATION RELATES:

ADDRESS OF CLUB:

OWNERS:

Please complete and delete where appropriate. All three sections must be completed.

1 LOCAL AUTHORITY ISSUES

Either

There are no outstanding issues to be resolved with the Local Authority relating to the use, or suitability, of the premises named above for the sale of intoxicating liquor.

Or

The following issues are still to be resolved. (**Give details and the likely date upon which decisions will be made*)

* I am prepared to give the committee an undertaking in respect of these matters in accordance with the note referred to at the end of this form.

2 FIRE SERVICE ISSUES

Either

There are no outstanding issues to be resolved with the Fire Service relating to the use, or suitability, of the premises for the sale of intoxicating liquor.

Or

The following issues are still to be resolved. (**Give details and the likely date upon which decisions will be made*)

* I am prepared to give the committee an undertaking in respect of these matters in accordance with the note referred to at the end of this form.

3 DISQUALIFICATION OF PREMISES

I do not know of any legal restriction on the proposed use of the premises for the sale of intoxicating liquor.

SIGNATURE OF APPLICANT (OR SOLICITOR ON BEHALF OF APPLICANT)

Note: If the Local Authority and/or Fire Service are not opposed to the grant of a justices' licence in principle the justices will normally be prepared to deal with the application for the grant of a new licence on receipt of a written undertaking by the applicant that the applicant will not commence trading following grant until such time as there is produced to the justices a written letter of confirmation from the Local Authority and/or Fire Service that there are no outstanding issues relating to the use of suitability of the premises for the sale of intoxicating liquor

Fitness of applicant

[A.156]

This form originally appeared as Appendix 4 to the Good Practice Guide.

This form should be completed and signed by the applicant in respect of applications for new justices' licences. Approval of Prospective Licensees, applications for Provisional Grant to be Declared Final, Protection Orders, Interim Authorities, Transfer and Removal of justices' licences. If there is more than one applicant a separate form should be completed by each applicant.

Please complete and return the questionnaire to the Chief Executive to the Licensing Justices, Magistrates' Court, (*address and facsimile number of court offices*) **before the date of the hearing.**

NAME OF PREMISES TO WHICH APPLICATION RELATES:

DATE OF HEARING:

COURTHOUSE:

FULL NAMES: DATE OF BIRTH:

TELEPHONE NO: FACSIMILE NO:

Any other name by which you have been known, ie Deed Poll, Maiden Name:

Please supply the names and dates of birth of any spouse, or partner who will be involved in or have an influence on the day-to-day running of the licensed premises:

1   Date of Birth:

2   Date of Birth:

Please supply the names and dates of birth of any person(s) other than the applicant(s) who will be managing the premises:

1   Date of Birth:

2   Date of Birth:

Name and address of owners of premises to which application relates:

Except for holidays and illness will the applicant be present at the licensed premises throughout the period when the premises are open to the public for trade? YES/NO

If NO, please give the reasons

What training has the applicant received which is relevant to the work carried on by the licensee?

Date	Training Course	Duration of Course	Subjects Covered

Please list details of any convictions (including spent convictions) in a criminal court, or cautions, which have been recorded against the applicant, his/her spouse or partner, together with the penalties or sentences imposed.

Has the applicant, his/her spose, or partner previously been reused a justices' licence, or had a licence revoked, by any licensing committee? If so, state which committee, when and briefly the reasons why.

Is the applicant, his/her spouse or partner disqualified for holding a justices' licence? YES/NO

Has the applicant, his/her spouse or partner at any time been invited to resign from, or been dismissed from, the position of licensee? YES/NO

If YES, state briefly the circumstances and the name and address of the brewery or company concerned.

Is the applicant a holder of other justices' licences? If YES, give details of the name, address and type of licence held.

Interim authorities

Has the applicant held a justices' licence at any time in the last 3 years?　YES/NO

If YES, supply details of all licences held and their duration.

Transfers only

What is the reason for the transfer of the justices' licence?

(*Please specify which of the provisions under Section 8 of the Licensing Act 1964 applies*)

Signed:　　　　　　　Dated:

Please note that the Licensing Justices have laid down general rules and have prescribed a policy in respect of applications for licences, a copy of which may be inspected at the offices of the Clerk to the Justices by appointment.

Magistrates reserve the right to ask questions direct of applicants concerning their fitness to hold a licence and that failure to provide satisfactory replies may lead to the application being postponed or dismissed.

Notice of application for provisional licence to be declared final

[A.157]

To the chief executive to the licensing justices for the licensing district of

I, AB, now residing at　　　being the holder of a provisional justices' licence for premises situated at　　　and [to be] known by the sign of '　　' granted to me [by way of removal] on the　　　day of 200[ ], [and affirmed on the　　day of　200[ ], hereby give notice that it is my intention to apply at the [general annual licensing meeting] [transfer sessions] for the said　　　to be held at　　　on the　　day of　　next for the said provisional grant to be declared final.

　　　　　　　　　　Dated the　　　day of　　200[ ].

　　　　　　　　　　　　　　　　　　　　AB

Certificate of service—application for licence

[A.158]

I the undersigned hereby certify that a copy of the within written notice of application for the grant of a new [provisional] justices' licence was sent by [*method of sending*] on the [*date application sent out*] to the following authorities:

To the chief executive to the licensing justices,   Petty Sessional Division, [*full address of court*]

To the chief officer of police,   Constabulary, c/o [*officer dealing*], [*full address of police station*]

To the proper officer,   [City] [Borough] [District] Council, [*full address of council*]

To the proper officer,   [Town] [Parish] [Community] Council [*full address of council*]

To the   County Council (as fire authority), [*address of council*]

To the chief fire officer, [*full address of fire station*]

[*Signature*]

[Secretary in the employ of   ]

Checklist for licence applications

[A.159]

Applicant/premises:

Court/hearing:

		Action	Date	Initial
1	Procedure—open file and:			
	(1) confirm licensing division for location			
	(2) obtain practice directions			
	(3) confirm licensing dates (*see item 5)			
	(4) advise clients and property department	Advise		
2	Notices—to be received by authorities 21 days clear before hearing (ie hearing *Wednesday* receipt *Tuesday* 3 weeks before; hearing *Monday* receipt *Friday* 3 weeks before)	*Dispatch by:		
3	Notices—check receipt by court	*Received		

4 (a) Store plans—serve with notice or as
     soon as possible   Sent:
   (b) Radius plans—instruct
     licensing surveyors to prepare   Instructed

5 Advertisements—to appear in local press
  14 *clear* days before hearing (NB check
  on opening file—some papers weekly) *Appear on

6 Advert—confirm receipt, date of insertion
  and circulation area of newspaper *Confirmed

7 Display of notice—to appear in suitable
  position 7 *clear* days before hearing (ie
  Monday if hearing on a Tuesday) Display by

8 Display—confirm receipt, date and manner
  of display with applicant. Ask for copy of
  newspaper to be kept for hearing. (NB if
  linked with purchase, advise of agents'
  telephone number for keys/access. Remind
  of need for notice to be *read* by public.) *Confirmed

9 New development—contact developers/
  agents—obtain plans and copy planning
  permission Obtained

10 Court—speak 7 days prior
  — papers OK?
  — inspection planned? *Court
  — practice directions: full compliance? OK

11 Documents—available for hearing:
  plans (6); brochure (6); certificate of
  service; newspaper; radius plans and proof;
  promotional literature (6)

12 Interest in premises—check with solicitors
  /conveyancing department Checked

[*Enter in diary*]

Requirement for plans

[A.160]

(*General—where no policy document or relevant provision*)

If the following guidelines are observed it will considerably assist the licensing process and ensure that the plans are acceptable to the majority of licensing committees.

1 Scale (floor layout) 1:50/1:100.

2 Layout to include bar servery/counter, seating areas, tables, gondolas, vision panels, storage areas, toilet accommodation, access/egress to/from exterior and details of all basement areas and upper floor area. Adjoining properties (ground floor) to be identified on either side of premises.

3 Merchandising (for shops): this is optional, but will assist any new application which is likely to be contentious.

4 Fire precautions: where the requirements of the fire officer can be anticipated, the appropriate details should be shown.

5 Colouring: Ideally the court should be asked to indicate its preference. Failing that the following codes might be adopted, save where the justices have a declared policy to the contrary: areas to which the public have access (save for the toilets), as well as the kitchen and cellar area, all to be outlined in red.

6 Block/layout plan—to be endorsed upon the main plan: scale 1:1250/2500. Details of draughtsmen/architect—an increasing number of courts are asking for the plans to be signed by the architect, who should give his name, business address and qualifications. The date of the plan should also be shown.

7 Freeholder of the property (if known).

8 Distribution of copies as follows: clerk to justices—4 copies; police—1 copy; fire officer—2 copies; building inspector—2 copies; local authority(ies)—1 copy each; applicant—1 copy; solicitors—3 copies.

Deadline: Plans to be received by solicitors 28 days before hearing.

Renewals

Application for the renewal of a justices' licence

[A.161]

To: The Clerk to the Licensing Justices

Justices' Clerk's Office

[*Address of Court Office*]

I hereby apply for the renewal of the Justices' licence for the premises named below and I enclose the fee of £30.00.

I confirm that the particulars given below are correct and the premises are still trading under the licence.

Signature of applicant licensee:
Date of birth:

Please print name:

Name/Sign under which premises currently trade:

Licensed premises: [insert full address]
Telephone No:

Owner of premises: [insert name and address]

PLEASE ENCLOSE A STAMPED ADDRESSED ENVELOPE FOR THE RETURN OF YOUR LICENCE.

Transfers and protection orders and interim authorities

Notice of intention to apply for transfer of a justices' licence

[A.162]

To the chief executive to the licensing justices for the Petty Sessional Division district of

To the [Commissioner of Police for the City of London] [Commissioner of Police of the Metropolis] [chief constable of   ].

[To the proper officer of the [City of London] [London Borough of   ].]

[To the proper officer of the   district council.]

[[*in a parish with a parish council*] To the proper officer of the   parish council.]

[[*in a parish without a parish council*] To the chairman of the parish meeting of the parish of   .]

[[*in a community with a community council*] To the proper officer of the community council.]

To AB of   [*the holder of the licence*].

I, CD of   having during the past six months carried on the trade or calling of   hereby give you notice that it is my intention to make application at the [transfer sessions] [general annual licensing meeting] to be held on   at   for the transfer to me of the [provisional] justices' licence for the sale of [intoxicating liquor] [*or as the case may be*] by retail for consumption [either on or] off the premises mentioned below [now] [lately] held by   in respect of [the] premises [about to be constructed] [in course of construction] [about to be altered or extended] [situate] at   [and [to be] known by the sign of   ].

Given under my hand this   day of   200[ ].

CD

Application for an interim authority

[A.163]

To the chief executive to the licensing justices for the Petty Sessional Division of [   ]

To the chief officer of police

Take notice that I, [*name of applicant*] of [*address of applicant*] having for the past six months carried on this trade or calling of [*occupation*] make application to the licensing justices for the said Petty Sessional Division of [   ], for the grant of an interim authority entitling me to sell such intoxicating liquor as is authorised to be sold by virtue of the justices' licensee in respect of the premises situate at [*address of premises*] and known as [*name of premises*] [with effect from the [   ] of [   ] 200[ ]].

And further take notice that the power of licensing justices to transfer the said justices' licence having become exercisable on the [   ] day of [   ] /200[ ] following the [*death*] [*incapacity or infirmity*] [*bankruptcy*] [*departure or intended departure*] or [*grant of a protection order under s 10(3) of this Act]*, an interim authority shall be deemed to have been granted in respect of the said premises for a period of 14 days beginning with the date of this application.

I *[have/have not]* held a justices' licence within the three years' immediately preceding this application.

I am not a person who is disqualified from holding a justices' licence.

Dated this . . . . day of . . . . 200[ ].

. . . .

[Applicant or his authorised agent]

[Address]

Notice of application for protection order

[A.164]

[Licensing Act 1964, s 10]

To the clerk to the justices for the Petty Sessional Division of [   ].

To the [Commissioner of Police for the City of London] [Commissioner of Police of the Metropolis] [chief constable of   ].

I, AB, of   , having during the past six months carried on the trade or calling of   , hereby give you notice that it is my intention to apply to the magistrates' court for the   of   to be held at   on the   day of   next for authority to sell on the licensed premises situated at   known by the sign of   such intoxicating liquors as are authorised to be sold by virtue of the justices' licence now held by   to sell by retail   to be consumed [either on or] off the said premises.

Dated the   day of   200[ ].

[Signature of applicant]

Consent of outgoing licensee

[A.165]

I the undersigned hereby consent to the protection order and transfer of the justices' licence attaching to the premises known as *[name of premises]* and situate at *[address of premises]* presently held in my name.

[Date]

[Signature of outgoing licensee]

[Full name of outgoing licensee]

Checklist for interim authority protection order/transfer/ prospective licensee applications

[A.166]

Premises:

Chief executive to the licensing justices*	Protection order
Address:	Date:
Tel:	Time:
Fax:	Place:
Proper officer (city/borough/district council)	Transfer
Address:	Date:
Tel:	Time:
Fax:	Place:
Clerk (town/parish council)	Outgoing licensees*
Address:	1
Tel:	2
Fax:	3
	4
Chief officer of police*	Ingoing licensees
Address:	1
Tel:	2
Fax:	3
	4
Chief fire officer†	
Address:	
Tel:	
Fax:	
Section 34 permit	Letter to head office
Yes No	Yes No
How many?	Who?

Additional information
       Protection order dates:
       Transfer session dates:

[**Protection orders and interim authorities—serve court, police and outgoing licensee(s)*]

[†*Prospective licensee—notices as for transfer and Fire Authority*]

Application for approval of a prospective licensee

[A.167]

To the chief executive to the licensing justices for the Petty Sessional Division of [   ]

To the chief officer of police

To the proper officer of [   ] city/borough/district council

To the clerk to [   ] town/parish/community council

To the county council (as fire authority) [address of council]

To the chief fire officer [full name of fire station]

And to all whom it may concern

Take notice that I [*name of applicant*] of [*applicant's address*] having for the past six months carried out the trade or calling of [*occupation*] intend to apply to the [*licensing justices for the said Petty Sessional [Division] [Area] sitting at [address of hearing]* at the transfer sessions to be held at [   ] o'clock in the forenoon on the [   ] day of [   ] 200[ ] for my approval as a prospective licensee for premises situate at [*address of licensed premises*] and known as [*name of premises*].

       Dated this . . . . day of . . . . 200[ ]

       [Signed by applicant/authorised agent] . . . .

Notice of election by prospective licensee

[A.168]

To the chief executive to the licensing justices for the Petty Sessional Division of [   ]

To the chief officer of police

Take notice that I, [*name of prospective licensee*], having been approved by the said licensing justices on the [   ] day of [   ] 200[ ] as a prospective licensee for premises situate at [   ] and known as [   ].

Do hereby give you notice of my election that the enactments relating to the sale of intoxicating liquor and to licensed premises shall apply as if the justices' licence were transferred to me from the date of this notice following the [*state which circumstances under s 8(1), relating to the existing licensee, apply – eg departure etc ...*] of the existing licensee.

Dated this . . . . day of . . . . 200[ ]

. . . .

Prospective licensee/his authorised agent

[*Address of signatory*]

Supper hour certificate

Notice of intention to apply for certificate under s 68 of the Licensing Act 1964

[A.169]

[*Licensing Rules 1961, r 3*]

To the [Commissioner of Police for the City of London] [Commissioner of Police of the Metropolis] [chief constable of   ] and to the chief executive to the licensing justices for the   of   .

I,   , of   , hereby give you notice that it is my intention to apply at the [general annual licensing meeting] [transfer sessions] to be held on the   day of   200[ ] at   for a certificate that the licensing justices for the said   are satisfied that the licensed premises known as   situated at   in the said   are structurally adapted and bona fide [intended to be] used for the purpose of habitually providing for the accommodation of persons frequenting the premises substantial refreshment to which the sale and supply of intoxicating liquor is ancillary.

[And further take notice that, if such certificate is granted [paragraph (a)] [paragraph (b)] [both paragraphs] of section 68 of the Licensing Act 1964 will apply to the said premises from the   day of   next.]

Dated the   day of   200[ ].

[*Signature of the applicant or his authorised agent*]

Extended hours order

Notice of application for an extended hours order

[A.170]

[*Licensing Act 1964, s 70; Licensing (Extended Hours Orders) Rules 1962*]

To the chief executive to the licensing justices for the licensing district of

To the [Commissioner of Police for the City of London] [Commissioner of Police of the Metropolis] [chief constable of   ].

[To the proper officer of the [City of London] [London Borough of   ].]

[To the proper officer of the   district council.]

[[*in a parish with a parish council*] To the proper officer of the   parish council.]

[[*in a parish without a parish council*] To the chairman of the parish meeting of the parish of   .]

[[*in a community with a community council*] To the proper officer of the community council.]

To   [*the authority discharging in the area where the premises are situated the functions of fire authority*].

I, AB, of   , having during the past six months carried on the trade or calling of   being a person [applying for] [holding] a justices' licence for premises to which section 68 of the Licensing Act 1964, applies, situated at   and known as   , which premises are structurally adapted and bona fide [intended to be] used for the purpose of habitually providing, for the accommodation of persons frequenting the premises, musical or other entertainment in addition to substantial refreshment as required by the said section (the sale and supply of intoxicating liquor being ancillary to that refreshment and entertainment), hereby give you notice that I intend to apply at the [general annual licensing meeting] [transfer sessions] for the said to be held at   on the   day of   next for an order that the permitted hours in the said premises shall be extended for the purposes of section 70 of the Licensing Act 1964, as provided in the Schedule to this notice.

Dated the   day of   200[ ].

[*Signature of applicant*]

Schedule

[*Where applicable*: The application relates to the [following] parts of the premises [indicated on the plan deposited with the chief executive to the licensing justices]:

Day	Time to which permitted hours extended
[*Specify the weekdays and if the order is to be limited to a particular period or periods of the year, specify the period(s).*]	

Special hours certificate

Notice of application for special hours certificate

[A.171]

[Licensing (Special Hours Certificates) Rules 1982, r 3]

To the [Commissioner of Police for the City of London] [Commissioner of Police of the Metropolis] [chief constable of   ].

To the chief executive to the licensing justices for the   of   .

[where application is made for Sundays – To the proper officer of [City][District][Borough] Council   ]

I, AB, of   , hereby give you notice that I intend to apply to the said licensing justices at the [general annual licensing meeting] [transfer sessions] to be held at   on the   day of   next for a special hours certificate under section 77 of the Licensing Act 1964, for [the part mentioned below of] the licensed premises situated at   and known as   [that is to say   ].

[And further take notice that if such a certificate is granted section 76 of the said Act will apply to the said [part of the] premises from the   day of   next.]

*[Any person intending to oppose the application shall give notice in writing of his intention to the applicant and to the chief executive to the licensing justices specifying in general terms the grounds of his opposition not later than 7 days before the commencement of the above sessions.]**

Dated the   day of   200[ ].

[Signature of the applicant or his authorised agent]

*This paragraph is optional, but check the relevant policy document.

Revocation

Notice of intention to apply for the revocation of a justices' licence

[A.172]

[Licensing Act 1964]

To [name of licensee] of   and to the chief executive to the licensing justices for the licensing district of   .

I   of   hereby give notice that I propose to apply [at the licensing sessions for the licensing district of   to be held at   on   at

[am] [pm]] for the revocation of the justices' licence under section [20A] of the Licensing Act 1964 in respect of the premises known as   on the grounds that

Dated   200[ ].

[Signature of [authorised agent on behalf of the] applicant]

Occasional licence

Application for the grant of occasional licence

[A.173]

I, AB, of   being the holder of a justices' on-licence hereby apply for an occasional licence authorising me to sell any intoxicating liquor to which my justices' licence extends at *[specify place]* on *[specify date or period]* between the hours of   on the occasion of *[specify nature of function or reason for licence]*.

Dated the   day of   200[ ].

AB

Miscellaneous

Particulars to be affixed to licensed premises under s 183 of the Licensing Act 1964

[A.174]

[Full name of licence-holder]

Licensed to sell by retail [all intoxicating liquor] [beer] [and] [cider] [and] [wine] for consumption [with meals on] [either on or] [off] the premises.

[Six-day] [and] [early-closing] licence.

Notice of intention to apply for a children's certificate under s 168A of the Licensing Act 1964

[A.175]

To the Chief Constable of the   Police and to the chief executive to the licensing justices for the licensing division of

I, AB, of   hereby give you notice that it is my intention to apply at the (General Annual Licensing Meeting) (Transfer Sessions) to be held on the   day of   199 at   am for a certificate that the licensing justices for the said division are satisfied that the [parts of the] licensed premises known as   situate at [location of premises] [as delineated on a plan lodged with the chief executive to the licensing justices] in the said licensing division constitute an environment in which it is suitable for persons under 14 to be present between the hours of   am/pm and   pm [on weekdays and   pm and   pm on Sundays]   and that meals and beverages other than intoxicating liquor will be available for sale and consumption in that area.

Dated the   day of   200[ ].

[*Signature of applicant*]

Children's certificates

[A.176]

'Typical' conditions

[*Committees may wish to note that the Government's stated intention during parliamentary debate was that there should be the least possible alteration to the bars concerned. Many committees impose no conditions.*]

1 Accompanying adults must be able to supervise the children with them at all times in areas covered by the children's certificate.

2 There shall be no smoking in the area to which the certificate attaches during the operational period of the certificate and notices to that effect shall be clearly displayed.

3 Unbreakable containers for drinks must be available for children.

4 The licence holder shall ensure that no danger is likely to be caused to any person by virtue of any wires, cables, leads, sockets or any other similar item. All fires and heating appliances shall be fitted with suitable guards.

5 Sufficient high chairs should be made available for very young children. The high chairs must allow stable seating of the child and have restraints to ensure that the child can be safely retained in the chair. Persons under the age of 14 years shall not eat or drink at the bar counter.

6 Suitable baby changing facilities shall be provided and maintained in a room separate from the ladies and gentlemen's toilets [where space is limited in the premises so that these facilities cannot be provided in a separate room and the premises comply with all other criteria then these facilities shall be provided within both the ladies and gentlemen's toilets].

7   There shall be no gaming machine present in the area during the operational period of the certificate [unless such machine is completely covered].

8   A notice shall be displayed prominently adjacent to the entrance to the premises identifying the area to which the children's certificate applies and the hours during which the certificate is operational.

9   A children's menu shall be available during the operational period of the certificate.

10 The licensing justices have visited and determined the bar area is a suitable environment for children: no alteration to that area shall be made without the consent of the licensing justices.

Notice stating the effect of s 168A of the Licensing Act 1964

[A.177]

Licensing Act 1964

Notice

Children's certificate

The provisions of s 168A of the Licensing Act 1964, apply to this bar, between the hours of   am/pm and   pm [on weekdays and between   pm and   pm on Sundays]. Children under 14 accompanied by a person aged 18 or over may remain in this bar during these times. They may remain for up to 30 minutes thereafter if they or their accompanying adult are consuming a meal purchased before the certificate ceases to be operational.

(*State the effect of any conditions attached to the certificate.*)

INDEX